The Pear Stories

Cognitive, Cultural, and Linguistic Aspects of Narrative Production

The Pear Stories
Cognitive, Cultural, and Linguistic Aspects of Narrative Production

WALLACE L. CHAFE, *Editor*

University of California, Berkeley

Volume III in the Series

ADVANCES IN DISCOURSE PROCESSES

Roy O. Freedle, *Editor*

ABLEX Publishing Corporation
Norwood, New Jersey 07648

Printed in the United States of America

ISBN 0-89391-032-5   ISSN   0164-0224

ABLEX Publishing Corporation
355 Chestnut Street
Norwood, New Jersey 07648

LK3.22

Contents

Preface to the Series

Roy Freedle
Series Editor

This series of volumes provides a forum for the cross-fertilization of ideas from a diverse number of disiplines, all of which share a common interest in discourse—be it prose comprehension and recall, dialogue analysis, text grammar construction, computer simulation of natural language, cross-cultural comparisons of communicative competence, or other related topics. The problems posed by multisentence contexts and the methods required to investigate them, while not always unique to discourse, are still sufficiently distinct as to benefit from the organized mode of scientific interaction made possible by this series.

Scholars working in the discourse area from the perspective of socio-linguistics, psycholinguistics, ethnomethodology and the sociology of language, educational psychology (e.g., teacher–student interaction), the philosophy of language, computational linguistics, and related subareas are invited to submit manuscripts of monograph or book length to the series editor. Edited collections of original papers resulting from conferences will also be considered.

Volumes in the Series

Preface to Volume III

In 1975 the editor of this book received a grant from the National Institute of Mental Health (MH25592) to conduct research on what was then titled "Language and Experience." He was unusually fortunate in enlisting the collaboration of the five other authors represented here. The main object of the project, as originally proposed, was to look for linguistic evidence that knowledge is stored in the mind in part analogically, and not only propositionally. What such evidence might be like is sketched in Chafe (1977a). As the project developed, however, a number of other hypotheses and findings regarding the relation between what people know and what they say began to emerge. This book presents some of the hypotheses and findings we think worth putting into print. They are highly varied, covering a wide range of cognitive, cultural, and linguistic topics, but they are unified in their relation to a single body of data. They are written from a linguistic point of view, since the authors are all linguists, trained in linguistic approaches and having linguistic biases. We hope, nevertheless, that psychologists, anthropologists, and others interested in the relations between cognition, culture, and language will find here something of value.

To begin with, we were interested in how people talk about things they have experienced and later recall (Chafe, 1977b). We assumed that much of human knowledge is stored nonverbally, as is evident, for example, by our often having difficulty putting thoughts into words, as well as by our seldom verbalizing the same thoughts in the same way on different occasions. Processes of verbalization must be applied in order to communicate knowledge, and probably even in order to think about it in certain modes of thinking.

We believed it would be useful to collect examples of different people talking about the same thing, as well as the same person talking about the same thing at different times, in order to see what similarities and differences emerged between different verbalizations of what was, at least to a large extent, the same knowledge. This research was to be in the tradition of Bartlett (1932), who among other things asked people to read a folktale and then write what they remembered of it. We wanted data that differed from Bartlett's in two ways: they would be based on an input that was initially nonverbal, and they would be verbalized orally rather than in writing. Since we were interested in the conversion of nonverbal into verbal material, it seemed important that what people first experienced not already be in verbal form. And we suspected that oral language provides valuable clues to verbalization processes that are missing in written language. We also wanted to collect data in a number of different languages in order to compare our findings cross-linguistically.

It was impossible to imagine how to present the same "real" experience to different people in different places at different times. Although we did manage to record some interesting narratives from witnesses of a fire, a parade, and the removal of a bees' nest, we wanted an experience that we could take to people around the world. Since people's mental processing of films appears in various ways to approach the processing of "reality" (we remember and often talk about the events in a film; films can make us laugh and cry), we decided that a useful compromise would be to present people with a film and later ask them to recall and talk about what happened in it. It would then be possible not only to show the film to people at different times and in different places; we could also control the content of the film in whatever ways we thought were desirable.

At first we hoped to find a segment of a commercially made film that would be satisfactory for this purpose, but we could not find anything close to our requirements and soon decided to produce a film of our own. We wanted something that would include a set of events, some in sequence and some simultaneous, some highly codable and some not, some trivial and some salient, with a set of people and objects that participated in the events in various ways, themselves varying in codability and salience. We wanted to allow for ambiguity of interpretation, but at the same time, we wanted the film to be easily interpretable in some way by people in a variety of different cultures. It was important not to have language in the film, but we did want a sound track that would provide an auditory as well as a visual experience.

In the beginning we thought of universal interpretability in terms of the same range of interpretations being available to members of different cultures. But that was obviously impossible. For example, we had to include a physical setting, characters, objects, and happenings that would have different significances or nonsignificances in different parts of the world. If the actors were American, people would be bound to attribute to them whatever characteristics they habitually attributed to Americans. And the film would necessarily seem more exotic to a resident of northern Malaysia than to a northern Californian. We decided not to worry about problems of this sort, but to accept such differences as potentially interesting aspects of the data we hoped to collect.

With the help of a professional filmmaker we planned and produced a 16mm color and sound film. We will refer to it as *the pear film,* for reasons which will become obvious. Although we tried to keep interpretive editing to a minimum, the film does, of course, introduce some interpretation through cuts, camera angles, distances, and so on. We cannot assess how much the nature of the film as a film influenced the perception, storage, recall, and verbalization processes of our narrators. But Carroll and Bever's (1976) data do suggest that a film cut alone, without a change in the action portrayed, does not have a significant cognitive affect. We hope that the future will bring more research on similarities and differences between cinematic and natural experience.

The film begins with a man picking pears on a ladder in a tree. He descends the ladder, kneels, and dumps the pears from the pocket of an apron he is wearing into one of three baskets below the tree. He removes a bandana from around his neck and wipes off one of the pears. Then he returns to the ladder and climbs back into the tree.

Toward the end of this sequence we hear the sound of a goat, and when the picker is back in the tree a man approaches with a goat on a leash. As they pass by the baskets of pears, the goat strains toward them, but is pulled past by the man and the two of them disappear in the distance.

We see another closeup of the picker at his work, and then we see a boy approaching on a bicycle. He coasts in toward the baskets, stops, gets off his bike, looks up at the picker, puts down his bike, walks toward the baskets, again looking at the picker, picks up a pear, puts it back down, looks once more at the picker, and lifts up a basket full of pears. He puts the basket down near his bike, lifts up the bike and straddles it, picks up the basket and places it on the rack in front of his handlebars, and rides off. We again see the man continuing to pick pears.

The boy is now riding down the road, and we see a pear fall from the basket on his bike. Then we see a girl on a bicycle approaching from the other direction. As they pass, the boy turns to look at the girl, his hat flies off, and the front wheel of his bike hits a rock. The bike falls over, the basket falls off, and the pears spill out onto the ground. The boy extricates himself from under the bike, and brushes off his leg.

In the meantime we hear what turns out to be the sound of a paddleball, and then we see three boys standing there, looking at the bike boy on the ground. The three pick up the scattered pears and put them back in the basket. The bike boy sets his bike upright, and two of the other boys lift the basket of pears back onto it. The bike boy begins walking his bike in the direction he was going, while the three other boys begin walking off in the other direction.

As they walk by the bike boy's hat on the road, the boy with the paddleball sees it, picks it up, turns around, and we hear a loud whistle as he signals to the bike boy. The bike boy stops, takes three pears out of the basket, and holds them out as the other boy approaches with the hat. They exchange the pears and the hat, and the bike boy keeps going while the boy with the paddleball runs back to his two companions, to each of whom he hands a pear. They continue on, eating their pears.

The scene now changes back to the tree, where we see the picker again descending the ladder. He looks at the two baskets, where earlier there were three, points at them, backs up against the ladder, shakes his head, and tips up his hat. The three boys are now seen approaching, eating their pears. The picker watches them pass by, and they walk off into the distance.

The film has been shown to more than 50 speakers of English in California, and to at least 20 speakers each of Chinese in Taipei, of Japanese in Tokyo, of Malay in northern Malaysia, of Thai in Bangkok, of Persian in Tehran, of Greek in Athens, of German in Berlin, of Creole in Haiti, and of Sacapultec, a Mayan language in Guatemala. For all these languages, we obtained narratives within a short period of time (5 to 25 minutes) after viewing; for some, we obtained repeated narratives by some of the same people approximately 6 weeks later, and second repeats after a year had passed. More recently similar sets of narratives have been obtained from first- and fourth-grade children in Berkeley. Independently of these spoken narratives, we obtained a number of written narratives (from other people) in English, Greek, and Japanese. Written narratives were also obtained from the same schoolchildren who provided the oral versions. Except for the children, 30 of the American adults, and a few people in some of the other languages, all the narrators were women, nearly all of them adults below the age of thirty. Our intent was to have relatively homogeneous and roughly comparable samples for each language. We suspected that in some parts of the world women might be less acculturated to Western patterns than men. For practical reasons, nonetheless, our samples from most of the languages have consisted of university students, well-educated and probably Westernized to a greater degree than would have been true for the population of these countries at large. The least educated narrators were those in Guatemala, and some in Malaysia and Haiti.

With some variation dictated by local circumstances, the film was usually shown to five persons at a time. Each person was then interviewed separately by someone of the same sex and approximately the same age and background, who said more or less the following: "We're studying how people talk about things they've experienced. In this case we're interested in how people who have seen a movie tell about it to people who haven't seen it. I actually haven't seen the movie which you just saw, and I'd be interested in having you tell me what happened in it." No one balked at this request, and although a few people expressed some uncertainty as to how much detail they should include, everyone produced a narrative which could be characterized as a spontaneous and reasonable description of what the film contained.

Our processing of these tape-recorded narratives began with transcribing them. It is interesting how much the Western scientific approach to data depends on putting them into visual form. One could imagine a more orally oriented tradition in which auditory data were worked with more directly, without the selection and distortion which a "reduction" to a visual format necessarily entails. True to our Western heritage, however, we took this as our first step.

Our transcriptions were painstaking, and the final product was the result of a large number of passes over the same material by several transcribers, working both independently and together. We were particularly concerned with recording all hesitation phenomena, including pauses, pause fillers ("uh," and the like), false starts, repetitions, stutterings, and lengthenings. We then obtained continuous acoustic displays for each narrative, showing the speech signal, an amplitude display (a rectified and integrated version of the signal), and an extracted fundamental frequency which gave us a picture of intonation contours whenever the fundamental was clear enough to provide one. These displays allowed us to measure pauses to an accuracy of about .05 seconds, and the measurements were entered into the transcriptions. We did not try to enter a detailed analysis of intonation contours, largely through ignorance of what distinctions were significant. Recording of intonation in the transcriptions was limited to the use of a period for sentence-final falling pitch, a question mark for sentence-final nonfalling pitch, and a comma for any of several clause-final but not sentence-final contours.

What we then did with these transcriptions will emerge from the chapters which follow, each of which depends to a certain extent on its own form of analysis. The chapter by Chafe looks at the production of a narrative from the point of view that the creating of speech through time parallels and expresses the movement of consciousness through time. Consciousness is seen as the selective activation of small amounts of available information. Each "focus" of consciousness appears to be expressed in a spurt of language, called here an *idea unit*. Larger units of speech, more or less those which are called *sentences*, reflect the manner in which the focus of consciousness is used to scan "centers of interest." Focuses of consciousness are limited by built-in information-processing capabilities, whereas centers of interest vary greatly in size and complexity and appear to be determined by judgments and learned schemas. There is evidence that peripheral consciousness requires various kinds of orienting information, which are typically provided at the beginnings of narratives. The movement of consciousness runs into difficulty when orienting information must be modified. The result is the spoken equivalent of a "paragraph" boundary. These principles are illustrated with numerous examples from the pear film narratives.

Tannen is concerned with cultural differences. Her essay compares the oral narrative strategies used by Greeks and Americans in telling about the pear film. There were two overall differences which seemed to grow out of differing definitions of the event and hence the narrative task. The Americans tended to discuss the film as a film and focus their critical attention on its cinematic technique, whereas the Greeks talked directly about the events in the film and focused their critical attention on the characters' actions and motives. In general, the Americans seemed to be performing a memory task, including as many details as possible as accurately as possible. In contrast, the Greeks tended to interpret the events in the film, making better stories. The chapter discusses numerous subtle and gross differences arising out of these differences in approach to the task. The narratives, then, furnish evidence for the hypothesis that ways of telling about events are culturally determined and conventionalized, and that such conventions in turn contribute to the impressions made by speakers on members of different cultures or subcultures.

Chapter 3 continues the comparative interest, switching from Greek to Japanese. There, Downing attempts to define and evaluate the relative importance of factors influencing lexical choice. Cognitive factors, such as the existence of a basic level of categorization, are of considerable importance, but they are sometimes overridden by textual and contextual considerations. Thus, the speaker's choice of a particular word may be determined by the identity of the addressee, the nature of the speech situation, the speaker's goals and perspective, the stylistic level of the text as a whole, or the word's position within the text. Examples from the English and Japanese narratives illustrate the ways speakers weight these various factors within the constraints imposed by the standarized lexical resources of their language.

Clancy (Chapter 4) continues within the English and Japanese framework, examining one of the many ongoing decisions which the narrators had to make: the selection of appropriate forms for referring to the characters in the film. In analyzing the referential choices made by the English and Japanese narrators, she focuses on the cognitive and discourse constraints which seem to be responsible for those choices. The cognitive constraints include limits on the number of clauses, sentences, and mentions of other characters which can occur between a pronominal or elliptical reference to a particular character and the prior mention of that character. Referential choice is also guided by a range of discourse factors, including the narrator's need to introduce new characters into the story and establish them as old information, to avoid ambiguity when switching subject reference, to mark important discourse boundaries, and to create a point of view for narration in scenes having more than one character. Although the cognitive constraints tend to influence referential choice in a similar manner in English and Japanese, both individual preferences and language-specific factors, such as differences in syntax and available referential options, also play a part in determining how speakers of each language refer to characters in the course of narration.

In Chapter 5, DuBois looks at how speakers first introduce people and objects into a narrative and then trace them through that narrative. Speakers indicate whether a referent is newly introduced or already identifiable by their choice of the definite or indefinite article (among other formal devices). But they also control certain choices which affect the way an object is presented. If an object is deemed salient in its own right, it will demand a careful tracing through the narrative. But if it serves only as a prop to shed light on some character in the plot, or to flesh out the expression of a general activity, the speaker may choose not to trace its continutity of identity back to an earlier mention. At any one point in a narrative, speakers seem to employ one of two distinct discourse modes. Characters are introduced and background information is supplied in the descriptive mode, whereas the story line is advanced in the narrative mode. The two modes are distinguished by differences in the use of articles, selection of verbs, and treatment of adjective modification, and probably represent different ways of viewing the experience to be verbalized. There is a right time and a wrong time to use each mode. An object is ordinarily introduced when it first appears in the story line, but if it is first mentioned after this critical introduction period has passed, its introduction will take a distinct form. Linguistic evidence suggests that consciousness may be focused on either the task of introducing or the task of narrating, but not on both at once.

Chapter 6 returns to the topic of consciousness and examines its relevance to the familiar linguistic problem of why a particular noun phrase in a clause is expressed as the subject of the clause. Bernardo hypothesizes that subjecthood depends on (1) the degree to which an individual is activated in the speaker's consciousness, (2) the salience of an individual as determined both by intrinsic properties, such as humanness, and by semantic roles, such as causation. He reports a task in which referential and contextual factors were manipulated, and judgments were made which supported the degree-of-activation hypothesis. He finds support in the pear film narratives as well. Another experiment involving "why" questions supports the hypothesis that the human and causal roles of individuals increase their likelihood of being subjects. He then shows how prior activation and salience also influence *subchunking*—the way larger chunks of conceptual material are broken down into smaller chunks. People try to select material so that individuals with low activation will be avoided as subjects, and individuals with high activation will be available for subjecthood.

We are aware of the limitations of the pear film data. The initial input, being cinematic, was different from ordinary experience, and we cannot be sure how much the viewers' interpretations were influenced by the filmmaker's devices. But more of a problem was the situation under which these narratives were told. To be shown a film and then be asked by a stranger to tell what happened in it certainly does not happen to a person every day. We might doubt that the speakers' motivations were those which usually govern their narration of experiences in normal conversations. Although they spoke naturally and spontaneously, their intentions must have been different than normal conversational intentions. But we do not believe that these artificialities of the situation distorted significantly the kinds of things that are discussed in this book. Preliminary, less detailed studies of narratives taken from natural conversations in fact suggest that the findings discussed here are generalizable to other, less artificial data. What is called for now is an effort to collect and explore such data in depth, and we see that as our assignment for the future.

REFERENCES

Bartlett, F. C. *Remembering. A study in experimental and social psychology.* Cambridge: Cambridge University Press, 1967.

Carroll, J. M., & Bever, T. G. Segmentation in cinema perception. *Science,* 1976, *191,* 1053–1055.

Chafe, W. L. Creativity in verbalization and its implications for the nature of stored knowledge. In R. O. Freedle, (Ed.), *Discourse production and comprehension.* Norwood, N.J.: Ablex Publishing Corporation, 1977(a).

Chafe, W. L. The recall and verbalization of past experience. In R. W. Cole (Ed.), *Current issues in linguistic theory.* Bloomington, Ind.: Indiana University Press, 1977(b).

Acknowledgments

We are grateful to a number of people who collected pear film narratives in various languages: Mary Erbaugh in Chinese, Masako Katoh in Japanese, Arfah Aziz in Malay, Kanita Roengpitya in Thai, Reza Bateni in Persian, Swantje Ehlers in German, and Francine Desmarais in Haitian Creole. Martha Kendall carried our film to Thailand and Iran and oversaw its use. Karen Carroll, Janice Schafer, and Sarah Michaels collected and transcribed narratives from schoolchildren in Berkeley. To all these people we are much indebted, as we are to others who did the interviewing in various countries, and to the several hundred people who sat through our film and then told about it. We regret that not all of these data are discussed in the present volume. We are also grateful to Susan Bowman for her help in making the acoustic displays in the Berkeley Phonology Laboratory, directed by John Ohala, to Jonathan Gifford for measuring pauses and typing the transcripts, and to Nancy Ickler for measuring pauses and participating in other constructive ways.

The Pear Stories

Cognitive, Cultural, and Linguistic
Aspects of Narrative Production

Introduction—
The Search for a Cultural Niche:
Showing the Pear Film
in a Mayan Community*

John W. Du Bois
University of California, Santa Barbara, Berkeley

There comes a time when the student of language wonders how a speaker of a Western language and a speaker of a language which differs radically from the Western type would express the same experience. For the purposes of our project, we decided to show a film to people who spoke very different languages—including American English and Quiché Maya of Guatemala—in order to shed light on this question. From the beginning we addressed the problem of making the film accessible to speakers of any language, and accordingly we excluded all dialogue from the film, among other measures. But in Guatemala the real problem turned out to be how to present the personal interaction itself—both watching the film and talking about it afterwards—in a way that could be interpreted within the indigenous culture. In the end it was found unfeasible, and undesirable as well, to impose on traditional Mayans the Western social context of "an experiment." Rather, a niche had to be found in the indigenous culture itself into which the film-viewing experience could fit. What follows is an account, necessarily from a personal point of view, of two failures and a success in the search for a cultural niche.

I arrived in the Quiché Maya village of Olintepeque in the summer of 1975 with a copy of the film we had just finished making, and with some months' prior experience working on the Quiché language. With invaluable help from Janet Shuster Trump, an American anthropologist who had lived among the Olintepeque Quiché for a year and who spoke the language fluently,

*The research described here was partially supported by a grant from the Survey of California and Other Indian Languages and by NIMH Grant MH25592.

preparations were begun. A local convent of Maryknoll nuns graciously supplied a projector and projectionist. About twenty-five Quiché speakers had been invited well in advance to come to see the film, in the hope that perhaps fifteen would actually come. Only six showed up. The others explained to the native assistants who had come for them that they were busy—presumably at activities that made more sense to them than this strange and uninterpretable interaction being orchestrated by a foreigner. The six who did show up were mostly young teen-age girls who apparently had nothing better to do. As they waited nervously to see what was going to happen, they were handed a pencil and a half-page questionnaire and asked to fill it out. When their ensuing embarrassment was understood—most were illiterate—our interviewer, a young Indian woman who was to become a schoolteacher, helped them. Even then, the questions which in the United States had seemed so innocent—"Occupation? Amount of education?"—had them terrorized. Their experience with filling out forms, if any, had of course taken place in the as yet unfamiliar world of official personages.

The next trouble came from an unforeseen source—the affable Irish-American priest who had lent us a room. We had taken pains to avoid an atmosphere in which people might worry about how to verbalize the film while they were watching it. The idea was that only after they had assimilated the film's content would they be informed that we wanted them to put the experience into words. But as the young girls sat there jittery, waiting for the film to begin, the priest came in and made one of his wry jokes: "You know you all have to pass an exam on the film afterwards, don't you?"

When the film began they all relaxed considerably—to the point of chatting among themselves about the film. We had wanted to avoid such conversation, for obvious reasons. When one viewer referred aloud to an object in the film as a *pera* ('pear') I naturally was disturbed: in saying this she no doubt influenced the way those who heard her would later code the referent. This kind of interaction had been easily avoided in the United States, where people seemed to know that the expected behavior in an experiment is silence.

After the film ended, one speaker at a time was led into a corridor, where she was seated at a table with the interviewer and the tape recorder. The inverviewer explained that she had not seen the film, and asked the girl to tell what happened. In my quest for "control" I had at first tried to get the interviewer to use an exact translation of the directions used in the United States, but this proved impossible. When the interviewer was not allowed to speak in her own words she sounded stilted, as though she were not asking a real question. It was best to let her explain things in her own way. Her exuberant manner was encouraging to her interviewees, which was good, but she did sometimes interrupt them. By the time the day's session was over, we had obtained just half a dozen Quiché narratives, recorded under somewhat confused circumstances. By now my time in Guatemala was running out, and I did not get another chance to show the film to Quiché speakers.

Nearly two years passed before I returned to Guatemala. This time I had come to the small village of Sacapulas, to study the Sacapultec language. Sacapultec is a little-known Mayan language, closely related to Quiché, which has only recently come to the attention of Western linguists and remains largely undocumented. After a period of preliminary linguistic investigation, I turned my attention to the pear film once more. Although I was still in the early stages of grammatical elicitation, I felt that having a number of texts that expressed similar content in slightly varying form would be a valuable resource in my on-going grammatical investigations, as well as in later inquiry into discourse functions.

I was very fortunate to have as my assistant a young Sacapultec fellow by the name of Jacinto Mutás Lopez. His fine sense of the Sacapultec and Spanish languages had already helped me to secure accurate judgments on grammar and meaning during my elicitation work with him. But as I was to discover, his strongest point was his natural talent for diplomacy. He knew how to make people feel comfortable and how to address them in their own terms. Beyond this, he was able to appreciate somewhat the purpose which a Western investigator brings to his study, since he had had more contact than most with the world of scholarship through his years in the Spanish-speaking school system. Later, after he had observed the workings of my project for a while, he was to offer some quite valuable suggestions on adapting the project to Sacapulas conditions.

The only movie projector for miles around was in the hands of the priest, a fiery and aggressive Basque from Spain. He grudgingly agreed to let us use it, along with the open air showing area in the church compound. But it soon became clear that we could not count on him for more than a couple of showings of the film, which meant we could not afford more than one mishap.

I asked Jacinto and my other language assistants to start inviting people to the showing. The assistants tended to invite their own relatives; Jacinto, who was a Protestant convert, in addition invited fellow Protestants. The invitation to watch a movie was problematic for the Protestants who received it, since the evangelical Protestant sects which are popular in Sacapulas have a rather restrictive code. They disapprove of drinking, dancing, nonreligious music, and—movies. The problem was aggravated by the fact that the film was to be shown in a Catholic-owned place, the church compound in which the priest showed the weekly *ranchero* shoot-em-up movie. Some Protestants were able to rationalize that our movie was not a *ranchero* movie but one of those good "educational" films. But, interestingly, one strong inducement for Protestants to abide by their religion's prohibitions is the vigilance of Catholics who do not share the Protestant prohibitions. Catholics know what things Protestants are not supposed to do, and will make pointed comments about a Protestant who is seen, for example, at a dance or a traditional celebration. Protestants sometimes cite these comments as one reason they dare not watch some ceremony or dance. One Protestant woman who had come intending to see our film told us that she left before the film started because she saw a lot of Catholics there. Apparently she did not wish to be bothered with questions as to what she, a Protestant, was doing watching a movie.

Our invitations for the first showing were made about a week in advance. For purposes of cross-linguistic comparison we had decided to use only women as our sample, so I had my assistants stress that it was women I was interested in. This gave rise to some jealous suspicions among several husbands, Jacinto informed me later—what did that gringo intend with all the women? This problem was easily corrected for a later showing by making it clear the husbands were welcome too.

The day of the first showing arrived and for a time it looked as though all would go well. My assistants went by the houses of our half-dozen guests to gather them for the showing, and within an hour or two after the scheduled time we were able to begin showing the seven-minute film. After the film was over, I was just ready to take the first speaker to a separate area where she could be interviewed when I noticed the anxiety, anger and distrust on the women's faces. Jacinto seemed to be trying to smooth out some problem, but without result. He soon explained the trouble. One of the women had said I was going to steal their voices with the tape recorder. Now the others were afraid to let themselves be recorded. After our weeks of preparation, only one recording was made that night.

Later I thought back to an unfortunate joke I had made in my first days in Sacapulas. Some women who were selling goods in the market asked me how I supported myself. Rather than explain the intricacies of research grants, I foolishly joked that I got my money out of a volcano. I was aware that in the highland area there were folktales of people getting their money magically from volcanoes, and I thought they would appreciate the joke. I had not reckoned on how seriously my words might be taken. Maybe the women to be interviewed believed that I was the sort who would make a deal with the underworld, and hence could not be trusted with their voices. It can perhaps be understood how, in the dimly lit corridors of the church compound, they must have puzzled at what my real intentions were. The situation in which they found themselves was so bizarre as to have no precedent or explanation in their experience of things. Although I had managed to arrange the film showing so that my goal of eliciting narratives could be fulfilled, I had failed to present the personal interaction involved as something that the Sacapultecs could interpret. The lack of a discernable motive for my actions must have given credence to the supernatural motive that was suggested.

Jacinto had now seen my entire operation from start to finish, and he had witnessed my considerable discouragement at the failure of our first effort. Now that he was clear about what I intended, he was able to offer some much-needed advice. His proposal was simple but ingenious: after the film I would invite the viewers to my home for bread and coffee. While they were having coffee they would be interviewed. The giving of bread and coffee is a hospitality that accompanies many familiar social occasions in Sacapulas. So our speakers, instead of troubling themselves over hidden motives, could be enjoying the uncommon (but interpretable) experience of receiving hospitality in the home of an American. What Jacinto's simple plan did was point out a cultural niche, a pattern for personal interaction that was already available in the indigenous culture. With some minor accommodations between the indigenous pattern and our own Western pattern, the project could go forward.

So we began preparations for the second showing. Probably my assistants could feel more confident in their inivitations, now that they knew what was involved. We decided to try to get all our interviews in just one more showing of the film, since the priest's patience with us was wearing thin. When the night of the showing came, word had somehow gotten around that there would be a free movie at the church compound. So instead of a private showing to the twenty-five invited guests, we also had half the kids in town, it seemed, bouncing in their chairs. Things calmed down during the film, but it was once again impossible to keep people from conversing. When the film was over, we repeated our invitation to come for bread and coffee. The invitation was delivered in Sacapultec by Ralph McCluggage, an American missionary friend who was helping with the project, in order to filter out the many uninvited Ladinos (Spanish-speakers) who were present.

So the group of guests slowly made its way over the short distance to my house. Indian women, some carrying babies on their backs, filed in with shy excitement. They filled the available seats, and still kept coming. Soon my living room held about thirty-five people, many of them comfortably arrayed on the tile floor. They were quiet and expectant at first—looking forward, it seemed, to whatever diversion was to come. Jacinto, Ralph and I began serving bread and coffee to each guest, and soon they were relaxed and talking among themselves. From what I could overhear, their talk was not much concerned with the film. I believe the rare opportunity to observe an American in his natural habitat provided a more interesting topic for conversation.

While the guests enjoyed their coffee, I would ask for one volunteer to step into the next room and have a talk with our interviewer, who was a native woman. This usually gave rise to a few humorous comments about why I was inviting one woman to join me in another room. But the brave who had gone first were soon putting the pressure on those who had not taken their turn, and in a short time all but a few of the women had been interviewed. While this was happening the few men present were being interviewed by a second interviewer, a native man. Soon the interviews were completed, and the bread and coffee were gone. But several people stayed a while longer. They expressed curiosity about this or that unfamiliar household item, and asked about the various people in my pictures from home. I was happy to let this evening linger.

So finally, after false starts and adjustments to unforeseen circumstances, we had achieved our goal of collecting the Sacapultec version of the pear film story. The transcripts will provide a fertile ground for a contrastive approach to discourse functions, among other things. But there remained a few loose ends. A secondary goal of the project was to see how one person talks about the same experience on two different occasions, so we needed to get the speakers to tell the pear story one more time. This second telling was to be made six to eight weeks after the first. Given the vagaries of appointments in Sacapulas, Jacinto and I decided to go to each speaker's home to make the recordings. Soon we found ourselves lugging a bag of recording equipment through the streets of Sacapulas, stopping in to visit our former guests. We brought with us a new interviewer, a native women who had neither seen the movie nor heard its plot, so that the interviewee would not be in the artificial position of saying the same thing twice to the same person. When we arrived at a house, our host would invite us in with some anticipation. After a suitable chat we came around to the actual reason for our coming: could our host please tell what happened in that movie once more? After much giggling and many protestations of forgetfulness, the speaker usually consented to retell the story. Jacinto and I tried to make ourselves scarce during this time to avoid influencing the speaker by our presence, and my Western experimental notions would have been better satisfied if the curious family members had also gone out of the room. But in Sacapulas one has little privacy from other family members even at the most intimate of times—newlyweds often sleep in the same room as the man's parents. Forcing the speaker to isolate herself from her family would probably have injected an alien tension into an otherwise relatively natural setting. What an American would appreciate as a provision of privacy, a Sacapultec would probably resent as a cutting off from company. And by this time I saw my function as fitting our elicitation unobtrusively into the pattern of everyday Sacapulas interactions, rather than training the Sacapultecs to act in accordance with Western protocol for participating in an experiment. So the speakers were allowed to tell the pear story in the accustomed circumstances, with family members looking on.

Another loose end was the need for background information on each speaker. Because of my earlier experience, I had rewritten the questionnaire to make it less intimidating. I had also added a useful question asking whether the speaker had ever seen a movie before, due to Francine Desmarais' advice that this was significant for Haitian Creole speakers. Most important, I asked Jacinto to elicit the information from each speaker only after the narratives were already taped, in order to avoid making the speakers tense before they spoke. This required Jacinto to go to people's houses for the information, and in this connection he made another useful proposal. He would give each interviewee a free calendar after they answered his questions. These advertising calendars are valued as wall decorations, and Sacapultecs are familiar with the idea that one may have to do something in order to get one, such as buying a sample of the advertised product. (In acquiring these calendars from the local pharmacy, we ended up with a rather large supply of unneeded aspirin.) In any case, the familiar incentive of a free calendar seemed to help things go smoothly.

The difficulties I have been describing need not automatically arise in all non-Western cultures. In Japan we found it much easier to work with the more sophisticated university students. Although the differences in language and culture between Japan and the United States are vast, the long familiarity of the university students with scholarly methods—and tape recorders—apparently made the viewing and taping experience interpretable to them, so that they were able to give a natural rendition of the pear film story. In Guatemala it would in fact have been possible to seek out more sophisticated and Westernized Sacapultec speakers from among those who have migrated to the cities in search of jobs or education. But since we had the opportunity to work with Mayans who continue to maintain a way of life so different from ours, it seemed more valuable to adapt our project to these people rather than seek others who would be more adaptable to our project. We did lose some of the control which is sought after by Western scientists, but this seemed preferable to imposing an alien way and receiving stilted and unnatural narratives in return. We were able to accomplish our investigation with a minimum of distortion by seeking out an indigenous cultural niche into which the film showing and taping could fit. Once we had redesigned the interaction so that speakers could make sense of it in their own terms—though of course it could never fall perfectly into previous categories of experience—the speakers were more willing to give us wholehearted cooperation, telling their story in an environment that was as familiar to them as we could make it.

1 The Deployment of Consciousness in the Production of a Narrative

Wallace L. Chafe
University of California, Berkeley

People are conscious at different times of different things. It seems that how people use language depends very much on what they are conscious of from one moment to the next—on the focus of their internal attention, coupled with a concern for what is going on in the consciousness of the listener. My aim in what follows is to give a partial justification of this statement and to begin to explore some of the ways in which an understanding of how consciousness works is essential to an understanding of how language works.

First, one should point out that consciousness is a notion which has not fared very well in twentieth-century psychology. On this issue, I can do no better than to quote from a recent article by Csikszentmihalyi (1978:335):

> The fate of "consciousness" as a scientific concept is one of the most ironic paradoxes in the history of psychology. Once the central issue, the very essence of what psychology was all about, it is nowadays a peripheral concern, an antiquated idea about as useful as ether and phlogiston are to physicists. [The author mentions] two currents of thought that have displaced consciousness from center stage: behaviorism on the one hand, and psychoanalytic depth psychology on the other.

Behaviorism found consciousness too subjective to be taken seriously:

> Psychology as the behaviorist views it is a purely objective experimental branch of natural science. Its theoretical goal is the prediction and control of behavior. Introspection forms no essential part of its methods, nor is the scientific value of

its data dependent upon the readiness with which they lend themselves to interpretation in terms of consciousness (Watson, 1913:158).

Psychoanalysis found it unimportant: "The most complicated achievements of thought are possible without the assistance of consciousness" (Freud 1900:632). The twentieth century has left consciousness largely to the phenomenologists (Gurwitsch, 1964, surveys those aspects of phenomenology relevant to the approach to be followed here).

Nevertheless, as another author has remarked, during the last few years "consciousness has again come under scientific scrutiny, with discussions of 'the problem' now appearing at entirely respectable locations in psychology's literature. . . . Participating in this discussion feels like conforming to a trend that promises to return consciousness to psychological center stage" (Natsoulas, 1978:907). But if consciousness is reentering the limelight, after almost a century in the backstage shadows, there is as yet a great deal of uncertainty about what should be done with it. Natsoulas' article is a discussion of seven meanings of the word *consciousness* taken from the Oxford English Dictionary. One would hardly need such a discussion in, for example, an article on perception.

A few years ago, in an article called "Language and Consciousness," I suggested that what linguists often call *old information* or *given information* is actually information which a speaker assumes is in the consciousness of the listener at the moment of speaking (Chafe, 1974; see also Chafe, 1976). Words whose referents have this property are pronounced with weak stress and low pitch; more often than not, they are pronouns rather than full nouns, or are ellipted altogether (as, for example, in Japanese; see Chapter 4). Thus, probably in all languages, the explanation of certain prosodic phenomena as well as of pronominalization and deletion depends ultimately on a recognition of the role of consciousness in language production. This idea has at least intuitive appeal. The notion of consciousness is, naturally enough, especially accessible to introspection; one might say that looking into one's consciousness is what introspection is all about. The connection between consciousness and "given information" has thus been apparent so far as investigators have been willing to introspect. But at the same time—and this, of course, has been the problem all along—consciousness has been frustratingly difficult to monitor externally. In spite of the difficulty, a combination of careful and consensual introspection with other kinds of data may be able to carry us rather far. My approach here will be to use the way people talk about what happened in a film as data relevant to the study of consciousness, and particularly, of the manner in which consciousness is deployed through time.

THREE COMPONENTS OF THINKING

We need at the outset a theoretical framework that will help us understand the role of consciousness in thinking, especially the thinking which underlies language. The following model is one I have found useful in explaining the various observations that will be introduced. It is, I hope, intuitively plausible, and I ask the reader's patience with the lack of what might be considered "hard" supporting evidence. Some evidence, especially from language, will be supplied as we proceed, and much of what is presented will be suggestive of further possibilities for research.

Suppose we regard thinking as involving three major components: I will call them *information,* the *self,* and *consciousness.* To begin with information, at any given time a person has available a large fund of knowledge from several sources. One source is perception of the world around us, another is memory, a third is affect—the emotions, feelings, and attitudes associated with what we perceive and remember. It is enough for our purposes to lump these sources together and agree simply that a person has a large amount of information which s/he can make use of.

The second component of thinking I will call the self. I do not have much to say about this component, except that it is essential to the model I am describing. It is enough to recognize that there is some sort of "executive" who provides the central control over what is happening. This executive has a variety of needs, a variety of goals associated with the fulfillment of those needs, and a variety of interests in things which are associated with the goals and their attainment. Presumably the needs are in some way directed toward the maintenance of homeostasis in each human organism. But human needs are complicated, without a doubt, and also produce interests in such things as excitement and beauty. The topic has vast ramifications. All we need to assume here is the existence of a self, with complicated goals and interests.

The third component is consciousness, which I take to refer to the activation of some available information in the service of the self. Most of the information available to an individual is quiescent at any given time, only a small selection of it being activated in such a way that we would say we are paying attention to it, aware of it, or conscious of it. The picture I have in mind is shown in Figure 1. Consciousness is, then, the mechanism by which the self makes use of information.

Consciousness has four properties which fit naturally into this model. First, it has a limited capacity. Whereas the total amount of information available is enormous, the amount that can be activated at any one moment is very small in comparison. Second, it has a limited duration. It rests only briefly in any one place in the available information. "Thought is in constant

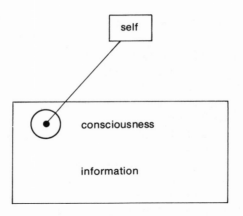

FIG. 1.

change... Now we are seeing, now hearing; now reasoning, now willing; now recollecting, now expecting; now loving, now hating; and in a hundred other ways we know our minds to be alternately engaged" (James, 1950:229–230). Third, consciousness moves in jerks; it does not flow continuously across the information available, but "like a bird's life, it seems to be made of an alternation of flights and perchings" (ibid. 243). Thought is less like the running through of a movie film than like examining a series of snapshots. Finally, consciousness has a central focus and a periphery; that is, at any moment, an especially small amount of information is maximally activated, while there is also a larger amount of other information of which a person is to some extent conscious, but which is not being "focused" on. It is quite possible that there are several distinct degrees of peripheral awareness, but I will not make use of that possibility here (cf. Chafe, 1973).

In summary, the self has available to it a mechanism, consciousness, which can be regarded as the activation of restricted pieces from the vast array of available information. Consciousness is highly limited in capacity. It is also highly limited in the time it can dwell on one piece of information. It is jerky; that is, it rests on one thing and then another and does not scan information continuously. And it has a focus and a periphery; that is, there is a maximum degree of activation and lesser degrees. The self deploys this mechanism over centers of interest which are related to its needs and goals. In this deployment, it presumably follows paths which are determined by associations between one focus and the next, and by schemas—already known paths which have been established for the same or similar areas of information in the thinker's past experience.

Before we move on to language more specifically, we can note that eye movements may provide some independent evidence for these properties of consciousness. The eye can take in only a small portion of available information at one time; its fixations are limited in duration; it moves jerkily rather than smoothly; and it is organized into a central area, the fovea, which processes information with maximum acuity, and a peripheral area where acuity is diminished. It is tempting to suppose that both vision and consciousness reflect the same basic strategy for information processing. And in fact this is likely to be more than a coincidence. Just and Carpenter (1976:441–442) put it in these terms:

> The primary proposal is that the eye fixates the referent of the symbol currently being processed if the referent is in view. That is, the fixation may reflect what is at the "top of the stack." If several symbols are processed in a particular sequence, then their referents should be fixated in the same sequence, and the duration of fixation on each referent may be related to the duration that the corresponding symbol is operated on.

I take it that "top of the stack" is a way of referring to the focus of consciousness, and that there is a close relation between visual processing through time and the movement of consciousness.

FOCUSES OF CONSCIOUSNESS
AND SPURTS OF LANGUAGE

A property of spontaneous speech readily apparent to anyone who examines it closely is that it is produced, not in a flowing stream, but in a series of brief spurts. In listening to speech we apparently iron out its intermittent quality, retaining an impression of integrated smoothness that was not actually present in what the speaker transmitted. But it is necessary only to listen with this property in mind to notice how intermittent speech actually is. Halliday (1967) called attention to these spurts of language some time ago, giving them the name "information units." More recently Grimes (1975) has called them "information blocks." The "tone-unit" of Crystal (1975:15–22) is essentially the same. Kroll (1977:89–91) uses the term "idea unit," which I adopt here. Syder and Pawley (in preparation) note that "in truly spontaneous speech, the lexical content of discourse is composed in stages, each stage corresponding to a single simple clause or part of a simple clause." Their "stages" are evidently these same idea units. The pear film narratives confirm these observations. The following sequence of idea units is typical (Speaker 11):

(1) (a) .. So he takes the whole basket,
    (b) .. and puts it near his bike,
    (c) .. lifts up the bike,
    (d) .. puts the basket on .. the front part of his bicycle,
    (e) [.5] and rides off.

In the pear film narratives the mean length of these idea units is about 2 seconds (including pauses), or about 6 words. Three obvious criteria aid in identifying idea units. One is intonation. Most idea units end with an intonation contour that might appropriately be called *clause-final:* usually either a rise in pitch, such as we are marking here with a comma, or a fall, such as we are marking with a period. A second factor is pausing. Idea units are typically separated by at least a brief pause, often only the slight break in tempo marked here with two dots, but often also a longer, measurable pause as at the beginning of example 1(e). Syntactically there is a tendency for idea units to consist of a single clause: one verb, with whatever accompanying noun phrases are associated with it. Furthermore, many idea units begin with the word "and," or less often with another conjunction, such as "but" or "so."

Although idea units have a tendency to be set off by all three of these factors—intonational, hesitational, and syntactic—all three are not always present, nor does the presence of any one of them necessarily signal the boundary of an idea unit. There is no reason to expect, and it would be surprising to find, that any cognitive entity is consistently manifested in some overt linguistic phenomenon, let alone a conjunction of three such phenomena. What is going on in the mind may in fact usually be manifested in a conjunction of certain overt signals, but it is unlikely to be always so represented.

It seems to be the case that clause-final rising or falling pitch is the single most consistent signal of what we would intuitively like to call an idea unit. Possessing the syntactic structure of a clause is a less necessary criterion, which is sometimes violated by information units which are less than clauses, like the following examples from various narratives (Speakers 10, 10, 19, and 10):

(2) (a) sunny day,
   (b) dirt roads,
   (c) on a ladder,
   (d) in the movie

and sometimes by idea units that contain an embedded relative or complement clause (Speakers 10 and 11)

(3) (a) he has an apron that he puts them in,
   (b) and then he decides he wants the whole basket,

Not all idea units are separated by hesitations, and when there are hesitations they may vary greatly in length—from the unmeasurable break in timing illustrated between most of the idea units in example (1), to pauses of several seconds. Furthermore, pauses frequently occur within idea units as well as between them. In other words, although the intonational and syntactic criteria associated with idea units are more often than not accompanied by at least a brief pause, the mere presence of a pause is not a sufficient indicator of an idea unit boundary. Although the idea units in a narrative cannot always be identified through some mechanical reliance on intonational, syntactic, and hestitational criteria, in most cases the identification of idea units is not a difficult task, and problematic cases are relatively few in number.

I would like now to make a hypothetical leap and suggest that these idea units, these spurts of language, are linguistic expressions of focuses of consciousness. I wish there were clear nonintrospective evidence to support this hypothesized connection. Unfortunately there is not, but there is a line of research which might establish a relation between idea units and eye movements. Many years ago Buswell (1935:142) identified "two general patterns of perception" when people look at pictures:

> One of these consists of a general survey in which the eye moves with a series of relatively short pauses over the main portions of the picture. A second type of pattern was observed in which series of fixations, usually longer in duration, are concentrated over small areas of the picture, evidencing detailed examination of those sections. While many exceptions occur, it is apparent that the survey type of perception generally characterizes the early part of an examination of a picture, whereas the more detailed study, when it occurs, usually appears later.

In a study recently performed at Berkeley, Charlotte Baker showed a woman various pictures and monitored her eye movements as she looked at them. Each picture was then removed and the woman was asked to describe it from memory. One picture was of a statue of the founder of Gallaudet College with a young student standing beside him, holding a book and looking up at him. The two patterns described by Buswell are clearly identifiable in the eye movements of Baker's subject over this picture. She began with two fixations on the vertical axis of the statue, then swept across the background with brief fixations on some trees, some buildings, and again the trees, where there was a cluster of fixations near the tops of the trees before she moved on to a detailed examination of the faces of the two figures and the book being held by the girl. Her verbal description of the picture from memory corresponded remarkably well to these eye movement patterns:

(4) (a) This time I saw a statue,
    (b) [.1] it looked like it was in a park,
    (c) [.3] and there were some [.3] apartment houses behind it,
    (d) [.6] it looked like it could have been in wintertime,
    (e) [.1] cause there weren't any leaves on the trees.
    (f) [.8] The statue was of an old man,

> (g) and a little girl holding a book.
> (h) [.5] The little girl looked like she was [.8] going to ask the old man to read the book,
> (i) .. or something like that.

The first 10 eye fixations, corresponding to the initial pattern described by Buswell, appear to have established in the speaker's mind the information later expressed in idea units a–e. The remaining 17 fixations are reflected in idea units f–i. It is noteworthy that the longest pause in the description (.8 seconds) came at the boundary between these two patterns. Within the first pattern the order of fixations, from statue to trees to buildings and back to a closer examination of the upper parts of the trees, evidently established a series of focuses in the subject's mind that were then verbalized in just that order. The inference regarding wintertime in (d) seems likely to have been made during the three fixations lasting a total of 1.4 seconds where the subject scanned the treetops. Similarly, in the second major pattern the subject looked first at the man, then at the girl and the book, then back and forth between the two. The order of idea units in her description again reflects the general order in which the information was acquired.

The hypothesis is, then, that similar principles are involved in the way information is acquired from the environment (for example, through eye movements), in the way it is scanned by consciousness during recall, and in the way it is verbalized. All three processes may be guided by a single executive mechanism which determines what is focused on, for how long, and in what sequence. A systematic program of data collection is needed to confirm these correspondences.

Types of Focuses

I will from now on assume that idea units do express focuses of consciousness. We ought then to be able to learn, from examining the content of idea units, the kinds of things that the self is interested in. From the vast amount of information available either from the environment or from memory, what is it that the self uses consciousness to pick out? The answers are potentially important to an understanding of humanness. Csikszentmihalyi (1978:356) suggests that "personal development and the development of sociocultural systems both depend on the economy of attention. How much attention is paid, to what, and under what conditions—i.e., voluntarily or under constraint—determine the characteristics of persons and social systems." The content of idea units may thus give us crucial insights into the nature of both individuals and societies.

Here I will mention and exemplify some of the typical types of focuses which emerge from the pear film narratives. It is possible to classify focuses according to various criteria, and the following typology is not the only one that might be invented. I believe, however, that it is one which sheds useful light on the processes of narrative construction. For each idea unit the question is asked, "In what way does the focus of consciousness which this idea unit expresses contribute to the development of knowledge which, focus by focus, the speaker is constructing?" In other words, the typology is based on the functions of focuses as parts of the total picture which is being communicated, piece by piece.

One can divide such functions into those which have to do with (1) personal interaction between the speaker and his or her audience, (2) processes of recall as such, (3) the recall of the narrative as a series of introductions of characters and their engagement in states and events, (4) evaluative comments (cf. Labov, 1972). In the class of personal interactions, for example, are indications by the pear film narrators of their acquiescence in the interviewer's request that they "tell what happened in the movie" (Speakers 1, 20, 12, and 7):

(5) (a) OK.
   (b) Sure.
   (c) Certainly.
   (d) I'll try.

Many narratives were framed at either end by focusing on the act of recall itself (Speakers 2 and 6):

(6) (a) Well,
   (b) Let me see,

and the conclusion of the recall of this particular memory (Speakers 6, 8, 9):

(7) (a) And that's it.
   (b) And that's where the movie ends.
   (c) And that's the end of the story.

Occasionally a speaker will focus on memory processes in the middle of a narrative (Speakers 7 and 16):

(8) (a) And there's one sequence right there that I've forgotten.
   (b) But I don't remember who it was.

Personal interaction and memory processes may be combined in one focus (Speaker 16):

(9) You should have caught me ten minutes ago when I remembered.

As for the recall of the narrative itself, it is well known that many narratives begin with the establishment of a setting (Speakers 5, 11, 14, 17):

(10) (a) the setting looks like it's a place maybe in California,
     (b) the landscape is like a sort of peasant landscape
     (c) it was in the country,
     (d) the landscape is sort of an agricultural area,

Temporal orientation was conveyed with focuses like (Speakers 10, 12, 19):

(11) (a) And it opens up probably around noon,
     (b) so it didn't look like morning,
     (c) it seems to be morning.

References to weather may also be included (Speaker 19):

(12) it's bright and sunny,

But the majority of focuses in a typical narrative have to do with people, their characteristics, and their actions. It is people and their involvements that we, as people ourselves, are most interested in. The backbone of a narrative consists of the introduction of people, their description, and especially their engagement in activities which are worth telling about. The following types of focuses involving people appear frequently in our data:

Introducing a person (Speakers 5, 7, 7):

(13) (a) There's a farm laborer,
     (b) Along comes a young boy,
     (c) And there are three other boys standing there,

Characterizing a person (Speakers 9, 17, 17):

(14) (a) He lookes like a Chicano American,
     (b) And he's dressed in sort of faded red clothing,
     (c) With long braids,

Locating a person, or an object (Speakers 19, 4, 19):

(15) (a) In the trees,
     (b) Standing on a ladder in a pear tree,
     (c) In deep pockets,

Engaging a person in a durative background activity (Speakers 20, 11, 14):

(16) (a) And he was picking pears,
    (b) He's riding a bike,
    (c) One's playing with this pongo,

Engaging a person in a punctual event (Speakers 15, 1, 14):

(17) (a) And he went down the ladder,
    (b) he puts it on his bicycle,
    (c) So they picked up his hat,

Reintroducing a person (Speakers 14 and 9):

(18) (a) And then you switch back to the man,
    (b) But then it goes back to the farmer,

Sometimes more than one narrative focus type is combined into a single focus, as in the following example which combines the introduction of a person with his engagement in a durative event (Speaker 19):

(19) And a boy comes by riding a bicycle,

Usually, however, a focus is restricted to one type.

As for evaluative focuses, although subcategories can undoubtedly be established, I list here only some instances of this major type; that is, of focuses having to do with the speaker's judgment or attitude toward elements of the narrative or its context (Speakers 11, 17, 18, 7):

(20) (a) [cough] so it's kind of funny,
    (b) but he's very brazen,
    (c) and he'd never make it as a fruit picker,
    (d) the colors were just very strange,

An interesting question for future investigation is the correlation of focus types with grammatical (syntactic and morphological) patterns. For example, there appears to be a high correlation in English between the introduction of a person and the locution, "There's a . . . who . . ." One might say that this rather special construction in English functions specifically to express this kind of focus. One finds, of course, a strong tendency for locational focuses to be expressed with "progressive" verb forms, for punctual events to be expressed with simple past or present tenses, and so on. Many if not all focus types seem to have their own characteristic grammar which is usually, although of course not always, adhered to.

WHY DOES LANGUAGE HAVE SENTENCES?

There is a property of most spontaneous speech which is as overtly conspicuous, when one listens for it, as its production in the spurts I have been calling idea units. Even in listening to an unfamiliar language one can hear that every so often an idea unit ends with that distinctive falling intonation contour which we naturally associate with "the end of a sentence." To us English speakers, certainly, and probably to the speakers of most or all languages, this sentence-final intonation communicates an impression of completeness: the impression that the speaker has come to the end of something which has some kind of significant closure. This impression contrasts with the impression of incompleteness given by the intonation contours at the end of other idea units, marked in our transcripts with commas. From intonation alone, then, language sounds as if a series of nonfinal information units is punctuated every so often by some kind of finality.

This sentence-final intonation contour often, though certainly not always, coincides with syntactic closure. That is, the sequence of information units which ends with this intonation often constitutes what grammarians would identify as a complete sentence. The following excerpt illustrates this sort of organization. The intermediate idea units are marked with comma intonations, the sentence-final ones with periods. Each grouping of idea units which ends with a period (that is, a–b, c–i, j–n, o–s, and t–v) is syntactically a sentence (Speaker 16):

(21) (a) [4.7] Someone came along before the kid on the bicycle,
  (b) but I don't remember who it was.
  (c) [.45] Then a kid came along on a bicycle,
  (d) and parked the bicycle,
  (e) [.85] a--nd checked the tree to make sure the man wasn't looking,
  (f) and he was about to steal . . a pea--r,
  (g) . . but he t he . . he . . picked up a basket, [.2] instea--d,
  (h) [.9] a--nd [.3] went riding along [.45] the road,
  (i) . . on a bicycle.
  (j) [.6] A--nd he passed [1.3] a . . little girl on a bicycle,
  (k) . . and [.35] turned his head,
  (l) . . and hit a rock,
  (m) [.65] and fell over,
  (n) and spilled the pears all over the [.7] road.
  (o) In the meantime,
  (p) . . some other little kids came along,
  (q) . . a--nd helped him pick up the pears,

(r) .. a--nd brushed him off,
(s) [.9] a--nd that sort of thing.
(t) [.65] A--nd [.45] he went on walking,
(u) and one of them stopped him,
(v) [.85] cause he had forgotten his hat.

If we assume that sentence-final intonation and syntactic sentencehood indicate closure on something, the question remains as to what that something might be. Sometimes we find that the unit involved is a single focus of consciousness. Thus we sometimes find in narratives a sentence-final intonation after nothing more than one idea unit. This phenomenon is common when the speaker of one of our pear film narratives expresses acquiescence in the interviewer's request that she tell what happened in the movie, as illustrated in example (5) (Speakers 4, 20, 7):

(22) (a) OK.
     (b) Sure.
     (c) I'll try.

or when she brings her story to a close (Speakers 7, 9, and 11):

(23) (a) [1.1] And [.75] I think that was it.
     (b) [.35] And that's the end of the .. story.
     (c) .. And it ends.

But sentence-finality for a single idea unit may also be expressed occasionally within a narrative (Speakers 13, 15, and 11):

(24) (a) [.25] And then it .. it .. pans into this man.
     (b) [.25] The man was picking pears.
     (c) [.85] He's a little [.45] bewildered.

It was comparatively rare for an adult speaker to signal closure after a single focus, except at the beginning and end of a narrative. With young children, on the other hand, it is possible that single idea units with closure may be more common, as in the following example from a first grader:

(25) (a) And then, ... the ... he tripped over a rock.
     (b) ... When he wen ... when he .. drove off.
     (c) ... Went off that is.
     (d) ... And then ... he tripped over a rock,
     (e) because he ... he saw ... this--s girl.

    (f) And then...um these three boys...um...came and helped
       him up.
    (g) ...And then,...the boy drove off again.
    (h) ...With the peaches.

At the opposite extreme is the case where the only (or almost the only) sentence-final intonation comes at the very end of a narrative. In such a case, closure is given only to the entire *memory,* as I have been calling the totality of information which is sequentially activated to produce a story (Chafe, 1979). It is interesting that children also produce narratives of this type. In the following example from another first grader, the only intermediate closure (in m) comes at a point of climax:

    (26) (a) It was about...this man,
        (b) he was um...um
        (c) ...takes some um..peach--...some pears off the tree,
        (d) and then this little boy came along,
        (e) ..and he took a box a..s--ome of em
        (f) and put em on the..front of his bike,
        (g) ...and then he dro--ve off with em,
        (h) and then,...his father was in the tree,
        (i) ...and then..he met this girl,
        (j) he was lookin back at
        (k) ..and he wasn't seein where he's goin',
        (l) and he had bumped into a rock,
      (m) ..and...and he cra--shed.
        (n) ..And the peaches fell out on the groun
        (o) and..he had a wreck on his bike,
        (p) and these boys came
        (q) ..and put em back in it,
        (r) ..and he game em some,
        (s) ..and he started back on where he was goin'
        (t) ..and this man blowed a whi..um uh..he blowed
        (u) ..and then...the..the boy had blowed his whistle
        (v) and then...he had...then...gave him his hat
        (w) and then..he had gave em some pear
        (x) ..and when that..when he passed..by that man
        (y) t...the man..the man came out the tree,
        (z) ..saw the pear was go--ne,
      (aa) and then..he didn't knew who had got em
      (bb) ..cause his son
      (cc) (Interviewer: Huh?
      (dd) Cause his what?

(ee) Say that again.
(ff) He didn't know who had got em.)
(gg) Uh uh... cause y--ou know when his son
(hh) this.. when they.. when them boys.. passed who... eatin em
(ii) and the--n.. he didn't know it w--as his son that gave em to em
(jj) cause he always give away stuff.

Although in one sense example (25) and (26) are opposite ways of treating focuses of consciousness (the first giving closure to each focus, the second to the entire memory), there is another sense in which these two narratives are alike. Neither makes much of any use of closure at an intermediate level, between the focus and the whole memory. The insertion of intermediate closure is evidently something to be learned. All our evidence suggests that learning to exploit intermediate closure effectively in speaking is a slow process, and in fact that adults never fully learn it either. Effective division of a narrative into sentences remains a problem at all ages.

There are, in fact, occasions when adults produce long sequences of idea units or even a whole narrative like example (26). A German speaker provided the following narrative, in which almost the only sentence-final intonation comes at the very end:

(27) (a) *Ein Bauer ist bei der [.15] Birnenernte,*
　　　(b) *[1.05] er hat.. zwei Körb volle Körbe schon geerntet,*
　　　(c) *[1.5] u--nd [1.5] es kommen Passanten vorbei,*
　　　(d) *ein Junge auf 'm Fahrrad,*
　　　(e) *[.55] sieht die Birnen,*
　　　(f) *[1.35] möchte sich erst eine nehmen,*
　　　(g) *[.45] kommt dann auf die Idee sich den ganzen Korb auf sein Fahrrad zu laden,*
　　　(h) *[1.3] fährt [1.0] mit dem [1.05] Korb und dem Fahrrad weg,*
　　　(i) *... äh... [3.0] trifft auf eine andere Fahrrad [1.0] Fahr [.1] auf ein anderes Fahrrad fahrendes Mädchen,*
　　　(j) *[.8] und verliert seinen Hut,*
　　　(k) *guckt sich um,*
　　　(l) *wo der geblieben ist,*
　　　(m) *dabei [.1] stösst er an einen Stein mit seinem Fahrrad,*
　　　(n) *... äh--.. [2.45] und fällt um,*
　　　(o) *[.85] sämmtliche Birnen sind aus dem Korb.*
　　　(p) *ausgeschüttet dadurch,*
　　　(q) *[1.0] und wie er noch [.4] überan überlegen ist wie er am schnellsten die Birnen wieder einsammeln kann,*

(r) .. *kommen da drei.. andere Jungen vorbei,*
(s) *die helfen ihm die* [.5] *die Birnen einsammeln,*
(t) *helfen ihm auf,*
(u) [.1] *und* [.6] *halten auch das* [.1] *Fahrrad* [.1] *hoch,*
(v) [1.05] *äh* [.2] *er fährt dann weiter,*
(w) .. *und die Jungen kommen dann an seinem* [.15] *Hut vorbei,*
(x) .. *den er.. beim Zusammenstoss mit dem Mädchen auch* [.1] *verloren hatte,*
(y) [1.0] *pfeifen,*
(z) .. *und bringen* [.2] *ihm den Hut* [.1] *zurück,*
(aa) [2.0] *er bedankt* [.15] *sich,*
(bb) [.55] *indem er den Jungen drei* [.1] *Birnen* [.1] *schenkt,*
(cc) [.25] *und fährt weiter*
(dd) [.7] *die Jungen gehn weiter*
(ee) *in Richtung.. äh.. [2.0] des-- [.5] erntenden Bauern,*
(ff) [.65] *der kommt.. äh* [.3] *in der Zwischenzeit runter,*
(gg) *sieht dass also ein* [.3] *Korb* [.2] *fehlt,*
(hh) [1.0] *wundert* [.15] *sich,*
(ii) [.85] *wo der geblieben sein könnte,*
(jj) [.1] *in dem Moment kommen die drei Jungen* [.55] *vorbei*
(kk) .. *und essen.. die Birnen*
(ll) *und da* [.3] *e--r.. kann sich überhaupt nicht erklären*
(mm) .. *wo die drei Jungen halt die Birnen* [.55] *herhaben*
(nn) [1.0] *das* [.1] *wars.* [*Lachen*]

(27') (a) A farmer is harvesting pears,
(b) he's already harvested two full baskets,
(c) and people come by,
(d) a boy on a bicycle,
(e) sees the pears,
(f) wants first to take one,
(g) then gets the idea of putting the whole basket on his bicycle,
(h) rides off with the basket and the bicycle,
(i) meets a girl riding another bicycle,
(j) and loses his hat,
(k) looks around,
(l) where it went,
(m) in doing so hits a rock with his bicycle,
(n) and falls over,
(o) all the pears come out of the basket.
(p) Dumped out by it,
(q) and as he thinks about how he can pick up the pears most quickly,

  (r) three other boys come by,
  (s) they help him pick up the pears,
  (t) help him up,
  (u) and hold up the bicycle,
  (v) then he rides on,
  (w) and the boys find his hat,
  (x) that he had also lost in the collision with the girl,
  (y) whistle,
  (z) and bring the hat back to him,
  (aa) he thanks them,
  (bb) by giving the boys three pears,
  (cc) and rides on
  (dd) the boys go on
  (ee) in the direction of the farmer who is harvesting,
  (ff) in the meantime he comes down,
  (gg) sees that a basket is missing,
  (hh) wonders,
  (ii) where it could have gone,
  (jj) at that moment the three boys come by
  (kk) and eat the pears
  (ll) and he can't at all explain
(mm) where the three boys got the pears
  (nn) that was it. (laugh)

When an adult speaks in this way, I would not interpret it as a sign of childishness, but rather as an indication that she has decided that the entire memory is at the moment the one and only unit she is concerned with. The speaker of (27) seems to have interpreted her task as the expression of an undifferentiated series of focuses of consciousness, with no closure to be shown until that was accomplished. She erred in this course only momentarily when she came to the narrative's climax in (o), which was powerful enough to cause her to introduce a momentary intonational closure, but she quickly supplemented it in (p) and continued with her list of focuses.

Although the English narratives contain nothing as extreme, the following excerpt is similar as far as it goes (Speaker 12):

(28) (a) [.6] Uh [.35] the opening scene,
    (b) .. was .. uh .. a-- [1.8] kind of middle-aged round,
    (c) [1.0] possibly,
    (d) he looked like he was made up [.25] to be [.2] a Mexican,
    (e) [.25] or th [.95] that [.45] kind of person,
    (f) [1.0] picking .. pears from a tree,
    (g) and he had three baskets beneath the tree,

     (h) there was w--
      (i) one was full,
      (j) one was halfway full,
     (k) and one was empty,
      (l) [.6] and he had a ladder up .. to the tree,
   (m) and it was
     (n) [.75] the rooster crowed in the beginning,
     (o) so [.35] it didn't look like morning,
     (p) [.45] and it looked like [.15] it was filmed in California,
     (q) those dusty kind of hills that they have out here by Stockton
        and all,
      (ı) [.9] so .. it's very funny to make this telling.

This speaker seems to have started out in the same fashion as Speaker 27, but later to have shifted to a more typical pattern.

But what does a more typical pattern consist of? Within the framework so far discussed, both a single focus of consciousness and a total memory have the status of cognitive "units." We are in some sense able to remember stories as wholes, and we are able to focus our consciousness on small pieces of information within such memories. It therefore makes sense that we should sometimes find speakers giving closure to an entire memory, and sometimes to a single focus. But are there other kinds of cognitive units, intermediate between single focuses and entire memories, to which closure can also be given? That intonational sentences in the pear film narratives have a mean length of about three idea units suggests that there are such units. If so, what is their nature?

First, a speculation of the functional adequacy of focuses of consciousness. It seems likely that what can be embraced within a single focus is often too little to serve adequately the needs of the human organism. We might suppose that the basic adaptive function of a focus of consciousness is to alert the organism to some piece of information that is potentially useful to it. It may well be that the amount of information which will serve the organism best is often of an amount that overflows the very limited capacity of one focus. In such a case, it is necessary to allow several focuses to scan such information, in order that all of it can be comprehended and acted on. Such, I am suggesting, is the nature of what I will call a *center of interest* (a term taken from Buswell (1935:chap. 2). Too great to be taken in at once with a single focus, it can be used and acted on only by allowing a series of focuses to play across it. It is the conclusion of this scanning of a center of interest, I would speculate, that is typically signaled with sentence-final intonation and syntactic closure.

If this explanation has merit, it would seem that the information-processing capabilities of the human organism lag behind its needs. When we were fish or simpler mammals, it may have been enough for us to be aware of only as much information as a single focus of consciousness would provide.

The simple presence of food, a predator, shelter, or a mate was all we needed to be aware of, and such a presence could be sufficiently established one focus at a time. Our cognitive devices may still reflect the days of more limited cognitive needs and interests. If our information-processing mechanisms were wholly adapted to our current needs, they would enable us to process more information in a single larger focus. As it is, we must sequentially deploy the more limited focus—which is all that is available to us—over pieces of information too large to be comprehended at once. The combining of focuses into the centers of interest which are expressed in speech with intonational and syntactic closure appears to result from this kind of sequential deployment.

If we provisionally accept this general explanation, it will be useful now to look at some examples of how a speaker organizes focuses of consciousness into the expression of centers of interest. Earlier we saw that one type of focus has at its content the setting against which people are subsequently introduced. In the adult pear film narratives it is always the case that the setting is too large and complex a piece of information to be taken in with a single focus. A typical kind of playing over different aspects of the setting is the following (Speaker 16):

(29) (a) The movie opened up on this [.3] nice scene,
    (b) [.35] it was in the country,
    (c) .. it was oaks,
    (d) .. it was seemed like West Coast.

Such sequences, it may be noted, convey a single mental image about which several things are simultaneously true, and the speaker has focused on each of these things in turn, completing the sequence with a sentence-final intonation. The example suggests that the notion "center of interest" is relatable to the notion "image," and although I will not pursue that possibility in detail here, it does seem plausible enough to merit further study. The general idea would be that sentence-final intonations occur when a speaker judges that he or she has achieved adequate communication of an image.

At a similarly early point in these narratives, every speaker introduces the pear picker. A single focus on the presence of this man is not, however, usually judged enough to convey the image of him which the speaker has in mind. Again she will play over a center of interest by introducing the man, perhaps characterizing him, and then perhaps focusing on the durative activity in which he is engaged (Speaker 9):

(30) (a) [1.55] tsk [.35] There's [.65] a farmer,
    (b) [.15] he looks like a uh .. Chicano American,
    (c) [.5] he is picking pears.

Such a center of interest is almost always initiated with a focus on the man himself; yet subsequent focuses seem relatively free, from narrative to narrative, in what may be chosen and the order in which the focuses may occur. In the following example, the introduction is followed by a characterization, a location, and another characterization (Speaker 14):

> (31) (a) [.4] There .. is [.2] a uh [.5] there's a man,
> (b) [.6] who-- looks of Latin descent,
> (c) [.75] a--nd [.25] he-- i--s on a ladder
> (d) he's rather large.

Besides settings and introductions of people, another common type of center of interest is one in which a series of punctual events are followed to some kind of conclusion. For example, a sequence which begins with the picking and ends with putting the pears in a basket sometimes constitutes a center of interest (Speaker 26):

> (32) (a) [25] A--nd um-- [3.35] he's just picking them,
> (b) he comes off of the ladder,
> (c) [.35] a--nd he-- uh-- [.3] puts his pear into the basket.

Whether this center of interest can be identified with a single mental image is an interesting question, since it includes movement and change of location. Quite possibly the notion of "image" should allow for movement and change, so that the unity of a sequence like (32) could also be attributed to imaginal unity, as with the preceding examples. In any case, it is easy to see why the speaker brought the center of interest to a close with (32c): that focus represents a goal of the preceding events. The achievement of the goal of some actions is what typically brings closure to an event sequence. Similar centers of interest may conclude with the boy's decision to take a whole basket of pears (Speaker 8):

> (33) (a) [1.15] A--nd [.1] then a boy comes by,
> (b) [.1] on a bicycle,
> (c) the man is in the tree,
> (d) [.9] and the boy gets off the bicycle,
> (e) and .. looks at the man,
> (f) and then [.9] uh looks at the bushels,
> (g) and he .. starts to just take a few,
> (h) and then he decides to take the whole bushel.

Or a center of interest may end with the helpful actions of three other boys after the first boy has fallen and strewn his pears on the road (Speaker 12):

(34) (a) [1.15] So he's f--a .. the pears have fallen off,
    (b) [.45] a--nd [3.7] uh-- [2.4] and they help him pick up the pears,
    (c) and they kind of toss them back into the [.5] basket,
    (d) where .. he-- has had them,
    (e) [1.1] a--nd he [.3] gets up,
    (f) [.7] uprights his bike,
    (g) they put the basket .. on,
    (h) and .. send him on his way.

Another similar kind of center of interest, which usually includes a projection of thoughts onto the pear picker, is likely to occur toward the end of the narrative, when the three boys pass by the picker, eating their pears (Speaker 7):

(35) (a) [1.3] A--nd [.35] these three boys [.9] go walking by,
    (b) and they each have a pear in their hands,
    (c) so he's .. kind of looking at them,
    (d) trying to make a connection
    (e) wondering [.35] how they got the pears,
    (f) .. and .. if they were his pears,
    (g) .. you see how this is just all what [.6] what you're projecting on the man.

Spontaneous spoken language, then, suggests the existence of some sort of cognitive entity which I am calling a center of interest, and which corresponds roughly to what is expressed in a linguistic sentence. It bears a resemblance to a mental image, but often includes a set of events leading to a goal. We need now to look more closely at how a center of interest is verbalized.

DISCREPANCIES BETWEEN INTONATIONAL AND SYNTACTIC CLOSURE

The careful reader may have noticed a curious fact about most of the foregoing examples. Earlier in this section I spoke as if the intonational and syntactic criteria for sentencehood supported each other—as if sentence-final intonation coincided with syntactic closure. But in these recent examples there have been many instances of syntactic closure occurring within an intonationally defined sentence, cases where syntactically independent sentences have not been given sentence-final intonation. In the immediately preceding example, there is syntactic closure at the end of (35 f), with (35 g) a separate syntactic sentence, but the falling pitch intonation does not appear until the end of (35 g). In 31 there is an example of syntactic closure in (31 c), occurring before the intonational closure in (31 d). More extreme examples are (29) and (30), where each of the idea units is an independent sentence syntactically, although sentence-final intonation occurs only after three or four of them have been uttered.

Although we might like to suppose that intonational and syntactic sentencehood coincide, empirically we find in spontaneous speech a very frequent mismatch. Why should that be? If intonational sentences signal closure to the scanning of a center of interest, perhaps something more needs to be said regarding syntactic sentences.

Syder and Pawley (in preparation) distinguish among three strategies available to speakers in constructing connected discourse: an "adjoining" strategy, a "coordinating" strategy, and a "subordinating" strategy. In our terms the adjoining strategy is to treat each idea unit syntactically as an independent sentence, as in (29) and (30). The coordinating strategy is to link idea units together with coordinating conjunctions: usually "and," less often "then," "but," or "so." This kind of linkage is characteristic of the pear film narratives; for example (Speaker 2):

(36) (a) [1.15] I don't know,
(b) I thought [.15] here was this bad little boy just stole the pears
(c) and these other little boys come
(d) and they're helping him,
(e) and they're very helpful,
(f) [.5] and they [.95] put all the pears in the basket,
(g) [.55] a--nd um-- [.75] you know this little .. other little boy just has to go on.

"In the subordinating strategy," say Syder and Pawley, "sentences are complex, and a variety of subordinating devices are exploited, ranging from the nesting of one clause inside another, discontinuous clause to the chaining of continuous, relatively complete clauses which are linked by a subordinating conjunction such as if, while, because, or although." They find a "strong statistical preference . . . for a coordinating, or chaining style of syntax, over a subordinating or integrating style." They suggest that speakers formulate speech "one clause at a time"—in our terms one idea unit at a time—and that "most times a speaker commits himself to a multiclause sentence beginning with a novel clause he takes a gamble. Having composed only a fragment in the first encoding stage, he gambles on being able to formulate in mid-sentence an acceptable continuation and completion." It is easy to string idea units together with "ands," but trying to do something more complex in spontaneous speech typically leads to awkwardness (Speaker 9):

(37) (a) [1.05] The boy who has the pears',
     (b) [.3.] hat,
     (c) .. is way back on the road,
     (d) so when the .. boys are
     (e) the--.. three boys .. are walking down the road,
     (f) [.25] after they're helped him,
     (g) and .. the other one's on his way,
     (h) [.7] one of them .. whistles back to the guy on the bicycle,
     (i) "Here's your hat."

Syder and Pawley also mention "structural crutches"—various syntactic structures that are memorized independently of lexical content, and that "reduce the risk of commitment to an unfinishable sentence." In the following example, the formula "there's a . . . who . . . " ties together the second and third idea units syntactically. The speaker has not, however, by that time finished her scanning of the center of interest, and she completes this task by adding two more syntactically independent clauses (Speaker 11):

(38) (a) [.9] A--nd [2.9] the next people .. who come by,
     (b) [.9] and there's a little boy on a bicycle,
     (c) .. who comes by from the other direction,
     (d) .. he's riding a bike,
     (e) .. it's a little too big for him.

If it is the intonation which is the primary indication that a speaker has achieved closure for a center of interest, the information units which express the separate focuses within such a sequence may be expressed syntactically with varying degrees of independence or integration. At the extreme of maximum independence is the expression of the focus as a complete syntactic sentence, as with all the focuses in (29) and (30), as well as (31 d) and (38 d,e). Slightly more integrated into the sequence are idea units beginning with "and," like (31 c), or more than half of the idea units in (21). A little more integrated are information units beginning with "but" or "so," like (21 b) and (28 o). Perhaps a still greater degree of integration is shown by the use of a relative pronoun, such as the "who" in (31 b). In other kinds of focuses the distinction between expressing or not expressing a subject would fall somewhere on this scale [cf. (21 d)]:

(39) (a) and he parked the bicycle
     (b) and parked the bicycle

as would the inclusion or omission of both subject and copula with prepositional phrases [cf. (21 i)]

(40) (a) he was on a bicycle
     (b) on a bicycle

Greater degrees of integration than these appear to be relatively rare in spontaneous speech, being more often found in written language. A separate study could investigate the circumstances under which these various degrees of integration of idea units are employed. Such a study would try to explain, for example, why the speaker in (31 b) chose the third of the following possibilities rather than any of the others:

(41) (a) he looks of Latin descent,
     (b) and he looks of Latin descent,
     (c) who looks of Latin descent
     (d) apparently of Latin descent,

Such distinctions are subtle, and I will not try to explain them further here.

The following conclusions seem warranted from all of this: sentence-final intonation serves to express a speaker's judgment that he or she has completed the scanning and communication of a center of interest. There exist at the same time a number of syntactic devices by which the idea units within a sentence may be integrated into a coherent whole and which express the different kinds of relations these idea units may bear to each other within that whole. A speaker's use of these devices may range from ignoring them (the adjoining strategy), through employing them in a way that still allows him or her to attend to the verbalization of one focus of consciousness at a time (the coordinating strategy), to the employment of more difficult and complex expressions of integration (the subordinating strategy). In spontaneous speech, the third course requires a greater and more lasting focusing of consciousness on the verbalization process itself than speakers can easily afford. Hence the results described by Syder and Pawley, and confirmed in the pear film narratives: speakers tend to avoid such integration, or to use only its simpler varieties, and when they attempt something more elaborate they are prone to get into trouble. The trouble, I suggest, is caused by an overtaxing of the focus of consciousness, which, with its limited capacity and duration, cannot easily handle syntactic devices that call for too much commitment of its resources to verbalization processes over too long a period of time.

PERTURBATIONS IN THE EXPRESSION
OF CENTERS OF INTEREST

Speakers do not achieve the expression of a series of centers of interest without some trouble; natural speech exhibits a variety of perturbations in this process. Among the major types of perturbations evident in the pear film narratives are the following:

(42) (a) Abandonment of a plan for the expression of a center of interest
    (b) Postponement of the expression of a center of interest
    (c) Pursuit of a side interest, with subsequent return to the main track
    (d) Insertion of a center of interest on a different level of interest
    (e) Supplementation of a center of interest after preliminary closure has been reached.

Abandonment relates to the class of phenomena often called "false starts" or "corrections" (Linde, forthcoming; Polanyi, 1978). Speakers often begin to express a center of interest in a certain way, only to abandon that way of doing it and switch to another. The abandonment is typically in the middle of an idea unit (Speaker 2):

(43) (a) He just has the
    (b) [1.0] I don't know,
    (c) I wonder how the hell he's going to carry this basket.

or even in the middle of a word (Speaker 6):

(44) (a) [.8] In the ba
    (b) .. and .. you see a guy leading a goat,
    (c) .. past the tree where he's picking the pears.

Whereas in the examples above the initial verbalization was abandoned, there are many cases in which a speaker starts off with a particular sequence of focuses in mind, then realizes that something else should be verbalized first, and finally returns to repeat the initial focus. I am calling these cases postponements. For example (Speaker 17):

(45) (a) [.4] And the he picks up
    (b) [.4] Uh the li .. the three little boys sort of go in the opposite direction,
    (c) down the road,

(d) [.45] a--nd one of the little boys,
(e) [.55] sees his hat.
(f) [.25] And he picks it up.

Postponements may also occur in the middle of a word (Speaker 15):

(46) (a) [.6] And he disco
(b) .. and he's dumping the pears that he has in his apron,
(c) [.4] into the basket.
(d) [.8]And .. they discover [1.75] and he discovers that his basket is gone.

The pursuit of a side interest is similar, except that the initial interest is not interrupted but leads naturally into a side track which is concluded, at which point the speaker returns to the main track. For example (Speaker 19):

(47) (a) And he comes down,
(b) .. from the ladder,
(c) [1.1] and he's wearing an apron,
(d) that holds the pears,
(e) in deep pockets.
(f) And he dumps them [.45] into some baskets .. that he has.

As she follows the pear picker, in her imagery, down the ladder, the speaker's attention is captured by his apron, which we intentionally included in the film as an unusual prop. She devotes to it the three focuses of consciousness expressed in idea units c–e. In e she comes to the end of this center of interest, and signals the achievement of this goal with sentence-final intonation. The apron has, however, been a side track which led momentarily away from the main line of the center of interest which she began in a–b, and to which she returns in f. Another example (Speaker 13):

(48) (a) [.5] And then he whistles at the boy at the bicycle,
(b) and .. the boy on the bicycle s [.45] stops,
(c) [.75] um-- [.8] he was walking it at that time,
(d) .. he didn't [.55] he didn't ride it.
(e) [.7] A--nd the--n um-- [.2] he whistles out at him,
(f) .. and takes the hat .. back,
(g) [.25] to him,
(h) [.2] and in exchange,
(i) .. the boy gives him three pears.

Within the center of interest whose primary basis is the exchange of the hat and the pears, the focus on the boy in (b) leads to the side track which has to

do with his walking and not riding his bicycle. That track is concluded in (d).
The speaker then returns to the main track in (e), where she reverbalizes the
focus she began in (a), before continuing with the further events which are
concluded in (i).

Sometimes the sequence of focuses which leads toward the conclusion of a
center of interest is interrupted by one or more focuses from a different realm
of interest, in effect a parenthetical aside (Speaker 1):

(49) (a) [.69] A--nd and you look at them,
    (b) and and they see him,
    (c) and they come up,
    (d) [.95] a—nd without saying anything,
    (e) there's no speech in the whole movie.
    (f) [.6] Without saying anything,
    (g) [.6] they.. um--.. help him.. put the pears back in the
        basket.

The focus in (e) is clearly related to that in (d), but does not smoothly follow
out of it as in examples (47) and (48). Rather, (e) represents a switch to
another realm: a general commentary on the entire film in the midst of focuses
which follow a sequence of events within the film. A parallel but more
complex example is the following (Speaker 5):

(50) (a) And they see,
    (b) [.7] him on the ground,
    (c) with all these [.5] pears strewn out all over the road,
    (d) .. and so they decide
    (e) [.65] like.. there's no spoken.. communication at all.
    (f) .. Going on.
    (g) .. Throughout the whole movie,
    (h) and they just [.6] pick up his basket.

Both the form and the content of (50 e) is like that of (49 e), except that (50 e) is
supplemented by (f) and (g); the latter fails to be separated intonationally
from the main sequence which is returned to, and concluded in (h).

This last example serves as an introduction to supplementation, the
phenomenon which, more than any other in the pear film narratives, disturbs
the positing of a one-to-one relation between centers of interest and
intonationally defined sentences. It happens over and over again that a
speaker will indicate with sentence-final intonation that she has achieved the
goal of communicating a center of interest, only to double back and rescan the
same center of interest for one or more additional pieces of information. As
one example we can look at the way the excerpt given in example (29)
continues (Speaker 14):

(51) (a) The movie opened up on this [.3] nice scene,
  (b) [.35] it was in the country,
  (c) .. it was oaks,
  (d) .. it was seemed like West Coast.
  (e) .. Maybe it wasn't.
  (f) [.25] But it was hills and dry grass,
  (g) [1.1] um [1.15] and scrub.

Whereas earlier we identified closure of the center of interest at the end of (d), expressed by the falling pitch intonation, we see now that the closure was not a final one. Example (51) can hardly be said to consist of three centers of interest, as the three sentence-final intonations might suggest. Rather, if we regard what is being talked about in (51) as a coherent mental image, the number of centers of interest expressed here is really only one. The speaker makes an initial pass at scanning it and verbalizing it in the four focuses concluded in (d), and expresses closure with her intonation. But she cannot leave things there. First, she realizes that what she said in (d) may not have communicated accurately what she had in mind, so she adds the hedge in (e). But then she judges it desirable to add more about the vegetation, which she accomplishes in the two focuses (f–g). The initial scanning in (a–d) is followed by the expression of supplemental focuses in (e–g). The total sequence of initial and supplemental focuses is finally expressed in what may be called an *extended sentence*. Thus the unity of (a–g) is only haltingly expressed by the three sentence-final intonations. It is even less straightforwardly expressed by the six points of syntactic closure in (51 a, b, c, d, e, and g). Sentences per se, whether intonationally or syntactically defined, are less expressive of cognitive interests than are extended sentences.

The deployment of focuses of consciousness illustrated in (51) is not at all usual, but is on the contrary quite typical. We can examine a more complex example (Speaker 19):

(52) (a) All right,
  (b) [.35] it [.8] starts,
  (c) [.15] it seems to be morning.

In this initial pass at expressing her first ideas about the film, the speaker moves through three separate "worlds": in (a), the world of the interview in which she is currently a participant; in (b), the world of the recently completed film viewing experience; and in (c), the fictional world inside the film, the world in which she will largely remain for the rest of her narrative. She introduces closure in (c) presumably because she has now succeeded in arriving at the setting inside the film world, and not from any final judgment that she has successfully verbalized that setting. For now she goes on to add another focus within the same center of interest:

> (d) [.8] In the countryside.

momentarily treating it too as conclusive with her intonation. But immediately she proceeds to add a series of other supplemental focuses:

> (e) In rolling hills,
> (f) [1.7] it's bright and sunny,
> (g) [1.2] and you hear roosters [.2] crowing.

Although she has temporarily reached another point of closure, what she had said so far leads to another association:

> (h) .. So it's a very pastoral setting.

But she is not yet finished. Her conception of the center of interest itself has been changing and developing, and now it has become clear that she wants to communicate that aspect of the setting which is most relevant to the action which follows:

> (i) [.35] There's some trees.

But still the trees must be further characterized:

> (j) .. An orchard.

And now at last the setting has been crystalized and adequately scanned. Her separate focuses and many premature attempts at closure have finally produced a background against which she can go on to introduce a main protagonist. She moves to a new center of interest:

> (k) [.6] And a ma--n,
> (l) [.5] is [.75] picking pears.

But this man needs to be related to the scene already established, so that this initial scanning, too, requires a supplement:

> (m) [1.6] In the trees.

And there is another salient aspect of this image:

> (n) [.55] On a ladder.

The most common pattern followed by our pear film narrators is well illustrated by this example. The typical strategy was to close off an initial scanning with sentence-final intonation, only to decide that the closure was premature—that further aspects of the center of interest must be attended to. The final result is not a linguistic sentence (where are the sentences in this example?), but a repeatedly extended sentence, cognitively unified, but intonationally and syntactically a very mixed bag.

THE VARIABLE CONTENT OF CENTERS OF INTEREST

Centers of interest, as expressed in extended sentences, show significantly greater variation in the amount of information they contain than do focuses of consciousness, as expressed in idea units. I assume that a roughly satisfactory way to measure amounts of information in centers of interest and focuses of consciousness is by counting the number of words in their verbalizations. The mean number of words per idea unit in our pear film narratives was 6.01, with a standard deviation of 3.27. The mean number of words per extended sentence was 25.64, with a proportionally much greater standard deviation of 21.52. The number of words in extended sentences ranged from 1 to 153. I take this as evidence for an important hypothesis: *that centers of interest are not governed by capacity and duration limitations of the sort that restrict the content and duration of focuses of consciousness.*

One also finds that the organization of content into centers of interest shows considerable variation across speakers, and even for the same speaker at different times. The following excerpt (Speaker 5) contains two centers of interest that differ greatly in length. The first is expressed in (a–k), the second in (1). The first is eleven idea units long, the second only one.

(53) (a) [.75] And [.25] on his way,
    (b) riding,
    (c) he comes across another [.3] bicyclist, [.25] bicyclist,
    (d) it's a young woman,
    (e) [.5] and [1.15] for some reason she catches his attention,
    (f) and he's [.4] turning his head,
    (g) .. behind him,
    (h) looking at her,
    (i) and [.2] there's a rock in the r road,
    (j) and he [.25] hits it with his bike,
    (k) and falls.
    (l) [.3] A--nd then [.7] his um [1.15] pears go all over the road.

With this may be compared the following (Speaker 11), which covers the same segment of the film, but which treats it in terms of five expanded focuses:

(54) (a) .. And then [5.2] tsk so– .. then we switch to the boy riding on the bicycle,
   (b) and he's riding down the gravel.. path.
   (c) [1.4] (clears throat) A--nd [1.0] we see it,
   (d) .. the gravel path,
   (e) from his point of view,
   (f) [.8] and then we see.. a girl riding a bike,
   (g) coming the opposite direction.
   (h) [.9] And then.. the camera's backed up
   (i) and you see them going like this.
   (j) .. And then you see it from his point of view again.
   (k) .. And [.3] his hat blows off,
   (l) [.55] when they cross,
   (m) [.25] and [.65] his bike hits into a rock,
   (n) .. and he falls down,
   (o) the bike falls down,
   (p) and all the pears scatter.

Clearly (53) and (54) show quite different ways of dividing the "same" objective information in terms of centers of interest. But it is also of interest that the speaker of (54) came back six weeks later and reverbalized the same portion in still another way, as follows:

(55) (a) [.8] And [.8] tsk [.65] ri--des down the path.
   (b) [2.9] And a camera follows him,
   (c) and um [2.95] tsk sudden there's a [.15] girl riding a bicycle,
   (d) coming the opposite direction,
   (e) [.5] and as they cross each [.25] each other,
   (f) [1.25] they boy's cap [.35] flies off his head.
   (g) [.85] A--nd [.5] he-- [.2] hits something,
   (h) [.8] hits something on the [.25] r path,
   (i) and [.4] loses his balance,
   (j) the bike falls over,
   (k) he falls over,
   (l) [.55] pears [.8] go all over the ground.

From (53) and (54) we learn that a particular span of experience does not necessarily dictate a particular division into centers of interest. From (54) and (55) we learn that even the same speaker may make different divisions at different times. The latter fact, especially, suggests that a center of interest is not a unit of information processing—not a unit of perception, storage, or recall. Rather, it appears to result from variable intellectual judgments—the kind of judgments that may be made on the spot during the ongoing process of verbalization. A focus of consciousness, in contrast, does appear to be a unit constrained by processing limitations. In this sense, there is a fundamental qualitative difference between the cognitive and linguistic units we have been discussing. Idea units express focuses of consciousness, which have well-defined properties determined by built-in information processing limitations. Sentences (or extended sentences) are not determined by such mechanisms, but rather by the intellectual judgments speakers make about centers of interest within the information available to them

That is, of course, far from the whole story with respect to centers of interest. We cannot conclude our investigation by saying that extended sentences result from judgments made by speakers as they are talking, and that such judgments vary from speaker to speaker as well as for the same speaker at different times. That is less a conclusion than an invitation to further research. Unless we are willing to believe that such judgments are random, sooner or later we will need to identify the factors on which they are based, factors likely to be complex and interesting. Potentially rewarding, but not to be pursued here, is the contribution of past experience and learned schemas to the establishment of centers of interest. Here I will explore something else, something which may also contribute significantly to our understanding of consciousness as it is reflected in language.

BACKGROUND ORIENTATION AND THE TRANSITION FROM ONE CENTER OF INTEREST TO THE NEXT

A property of consciousness mentioned early in this chapter was its division into a focus and periphery. It seemed intuitively plausible that consciousness has a focus, a maximal activation of information, surrounded by a lesser degree of activation embracing information of which we are in some sense aware, but with a lesser degree of acuity. It is not surprising that there should be a parallelism between consciousness and vision in this respect as in others. The division into focal and peripheral processing may well have evolved in eye and brain together as a way of dealing with both perceived and remembered information. The well-known properties of the eye are thus likely to be a manifestation of a more general division of information-processing functions into a focal component with high acuity and a peripheral component with lesser acuity which serves to provide a context for the focus, and to guide the focus to possible next resting places. "The very edge of the human retina does not even give a sensation when stimulated by movement; it merely initiates a reflex to direct the eyes to the source of movement, so that we can see it with our developed foveal eye" (Gregory, 1966:48). Just so, it is likely that peripheral consciousness functions to direct our consciousness to its next perch. Consciousness is thus able to move in some orderly way from one focus to the next. If other focuses are potentially available in the periphery, then there can be some rationale to the moves. The next perch need not be randomly chosen, but can be a focus of which the thinker/speaker has already been peripherally aware. This possibility helps to explain how consciousness is able to deal with centers of interest, since it allows such centers to be "kept in mind" as wholes, while the focus of consciousness scans various pieces of information within them.

Beyond that, however, there is reason to suppose that there are different kinds of information which peripheral consciousness "requires," without which the self, as the user of consciousness, is uncomfortable and disoriented. Included in this category may be information regarding the thinker's location in space and time, the social context in which the thinker finds himself or herself, salient characteristics of the people who make up that context, and any ongoing activity in which such people may be engaged. The need for information of these kinds follows plausibly from the need of the self to operate in a world in which it has expectations that enable it to function effectively. *Disorientation* is the name for the state which results from the absence of such expectations.

For example, it is a requirement of the self that it know where it is located in space. Folklore has it that a person who has been knocked unconscious, upon regaining consciousness, asks before anything else, "Where am I?" An awareness of time is another requirement. The victim's next question might be, "What time (or what day) is it?" These two requirements together explain the stereotyped beginnings of fairy tales: "Once upon a time, in a kingdom far away," and the kind of scene-setting which is indicated in plays: "It is after dinner in January 1906, in the library in Lady Britomart Undershaft's house in Wilton Crescent" (Shaw, Major Barbara).

Furthermore, for everyone except perhaps the hermit who has come to terms with solitude, there is also a need to know in what social context one finds oneself: with what people one is dealing. Our accident victim might ask, "Who are you?" Our fairy tale is likely to add people as soon as time and place have been established: "When good King Arthur reigned, there lived near the land's End of England, in the county of Cornwall, a farmer who had one only son called Jack." And when a person is introduced, the self appreciates knowing something of his or her salient characteristics: "He was brisk and of a ready lively wit, so that nobody or nothing could worst him" (Jack the Giant-Killer).

Furthermore, people are characteristically engaged in doing routine kinds of things, and the self finds it good to have some knowledge of background activity in peripheral consciousness. Our accident victim might ask, "What's going on?" Our tale may involve the initial protagonist in a background activity: "Once upon a time in the middle of winter, when the snowflakes were falling like feathers from the sky, a queen sat at her window working, and her embroidery frame was of ebony" (Snow-White and the Seven Dwarfs). This last example shows too that weather may be another relevant part of orientation, as may some physical object or prop which the protagonist is using. We can imagine our accident victim asking, "What's it like out?" with respect to the weather, and "What have you got there?" with respect to a prop.

In summary, the self evidently has a general need to be informed about at least the following aspects of its environment: place, time, people, their salient characteristics, background activity, and perhaps the weather and relevant props. If such information is not in some way inferrable, it needs to be placed at the beginning of a narrative in an appropriate sequence of focuses of consciousness. Once established in that manner, it can be retained in peripheral consciousness as background orientation for the particular, localized events which may then be focused on. Furthermore, the teller of a narrative takes account of the needs of the listener's self when tales are begun in the traditional way, or when a pear film narrative begins (Speaker 17):

(56) (a) Well,
    (b) first thing you see,
    (c) is-- .. uh--
    (d) .. the landscape i--s .. um-- [.9]sort of an agricultural .. area,
    (e) it's quite green,
    (f) [.35] and a lot of trees around.
    (g) [.5] A--nd you see a middle-aged [.2] um-- Chicano man,
    (h) [.55] who's wearing .. a-- .. navy blue shirt,
    (i) [.5] and a bright red [.2] kerchief around his neck,
    (j) [.4] and a white apron.
    (k) [.6] A--nd [.3] he-- climbs a ladder,
    (l) and is
    (m) [.15] all right,
    (n) ei either that or he's on a ladder,
    (o) already,
    (p) and he's picking [1.0] pears,
    (q) off a tree,
    (r) and they look to be-- [.4] not quite ripe yet.
    (s) They're still quite gree--n,
    (t) .. and they look [.35] still hard.
    (u) [.7] A--nd [.65] he's
    (v) [.15] it .. the .. camera spends a lot of time watching him [.55] pick these pears,
    (w) [.45] putting them in his apron,
    (x) [.35] and the--n .. um-- going .. down off the ladder,
    (y) and putting them into these bu .. bushel baskets.

(z) [1.15] tsk um-- [.85] So that's [.25] part of the activity of the [.25] the first [.5] portion of the film.

The amount of hesitating between idea units varies considerably, from none at all to 10 seconds or so of pausing and stumbling. Generally speaking, hesitating is less when the thinker/speaker is moving around within a center of interest than when he or she is moving from one center of interest to the next. That is, roughly, there is less hesitating between the idea units within a sentence than between the idea units across a sentence boundary (Chafe, 1979). Hesitating is even greater between the "extended sentences" discussed earlier. The amount of hesitating across sentence (or extended-sentence) boundaries shows much variability, however. The following is typical (Speaker 7):

(57) (a) [.85] A--nd [.15] he [.35] sees this three three pear [.2] these three baskets of pears,
  (b) and then sees this man up in the [.5] tree,
  (c) and decides [.45] that he'd like some pears.
  (d) And at first looks like he's going to take one or two.
  (e) [.6] Then decides that he'd much rather take a whole basket,
  (f) [.55] puts the basket on the bike,
  (g) [.9] tsk a--nd .. kind of struggles
  (h) cause it's much too big for him.
  (i) And the bike is much too big for him.
  (j) [.8] A--nd .. gets on the bike,
  (k) and [.2] rides off.
  (l) [1.85] The--n [.2] he's riding .. across this .. great [.25] expanse,
  (m) and [1.15] a girl comes,
  (n) [.4] riding a bike in the opposite direction,
  (o) [.55] and [.4] you can see them riding [.65] towards each other,
  (p) and you wonder if there's going to be a collision.

Between the sentence which ends in (c) and that which begins in (d) there is no hesitating. At the beginning of (e) and (j) there is a moderate amount, but still less than 1 second, whereas at the beginning of (l) there is significantly more: 2.7 seconds elapse before the idea unit begins in earnest with "he's riding," but even then there is considerable hesitancy which carries over into the 1.15 second pause in (m). The following excerpt, from a corresponding point in another speaker's narrative, is more extreme, with a total of 6.1 seconds of hesitation before the words "then we switch" (Speaker 11):

(58) (a) .. And then [5.2] tsk so-- then we switch to the boy riding on
the bicycle,
(b) and he's riding down the gravel .. path.

Thus, although a speaker can often move from one center of interest to the
next with less than a second of hesitating, in other cases the transition takes
much longer. These are the places in a narrative where, if the narrative were
written, we would expect to find a paragraph boundary. How do we explain
these more time-consuming transitions?

From an examination of the kinds of transitions in content which occur at
sentence and extended-sentence boundaries, and from attempts to correlate
these content changes with amounts of hesitating, the following hypothesis
emerges: the amount of difficulty in moving from one center of interest to the
next increases with the amount of reorientation that is necessary—with the
amount of change in background information. In other words, it is hard for a
thinker/speaker to find a new center of interest in a new area where a new
orientation in terms of space, time, people, and background activity is
necessary. It is harder to find a new perch when the background for the perch
must first be established.

In recalling and telling about the pear film, the greatest reorientation that is
necessary occurs midway in the film: after the boy has stolen the pears and
before he meets the girl on the road and has the accident in which the pears are
spilled. At this point there is a major spatial reorientation, since the scene
changes from the pear tree to the road. The film also enters a new temporal
sequence, within which events will follow each other tightly, whereas the
amount of time which passes between the theft and the accident is transitional
and of uncertain duration. As far as people are concerned, the boy provides a
link between the two scenes, but we are now leaving the pear picker (the chief
background protagonist) and are about to meet the girl. Before long we will
meet the three other boys; perhaps they are already entering peripheral
consciousness. We are also leaving the background activity of pear picking
and entering that of bicycle riding. All these factors combine to produce a
heavy reorientation burden on the thinker/speaker, which generally results in
longer hesitations at this point than at most other points in the narratives. In
addition to what can be seen in (57) and (58), the following is a conspicuous
example (Speaker 6):

(59) (a) [.45] And .. as he's holding on to the handlebars
(b) he t takes off with them.
(c) [1.1] Um-- [.7] then [.4] uh-- [2.1] a .. girl on a bicycle,
(d) [1.15] comes riding toward him,
(e) .. in the opposite direction.

Here there is a total of 6.35 seconds of hesitating from the beginning of (c) to the words "a .. girl." Another speaker goes to some effort to verbalize the new orientation (Speaker 15):

(60) (a) but then he decides he's gonna [.15] he's gonna take the whole basket.
     (b) [1.4] Um-- [1.45] then he drives a [.5] he-- rides away on his bicycle.
     (c) [1.1] A--nd [1.9] oh goodness.
     (d) [.6] And he's as he's riding through an open field,
     (e) [1.0] um hills in the background,
     (f) and .. stuff like that,
     (g) [.9] he-- um [1.45] a girl [.3] with long pigtails,
     (h) [.16] happens by,
     (i) going the other way,
     (j) [1.1] on a bicycle,
     (k) and there's a long shot,
     (l) [.35] you see both of them,
     (m) .. converging,
     (n) and you see him.

There are totals of 3.5 seconds of hesitating at the beginnings of both (b) and (c)—including the "um" and "and"—and the exclamation "oh goodness" seems to express overtly the speaker's difficulty with resetting the orientation.

Change of orientation is not something which is simply present or absent at certain points in a narrative. It is present to varying degrees at different points. Two reasons suggest themselves for why change in orientation may be a matter of degree. First, we have identified various components of an orientation, not just one, and one or two or all of these components may be present at any particular point of transition. Changes of space, time, people, etc., tend to cluster, but they need not all be present at the same point. Beyond that, the components themselves are scalar: there may be more or less of a change in location, more or less of a shift to a new time frame, more or less of a change in protagonists, more or less of a shift in background activity. For example, after we have seen the man picking pears and putting them in a basket, the boy arrives on his bicycle. There is a small shift in location as our attention is directed to the area near the tree where the boy first appears. There seems to be no major break in timing, but we expect a new sequence of events to take place against the background pear picking. The strongest reorientation at this point is to the new and potentially major protagonist. The bicycle riding is a new background activity, superimposed on the pear picking. Speaker 6 hesitates significantly at this point, but not as long or as conspicuously as in (59):

(61) (a) .. and you see a guy leading a goat,
     (b) .. past the tree where he's picking the pears.
     (c) [.95] Then um-- [1.5] a little boy on a bicycle,
     (d) [1.15] comes riding past the tree,
     (e) [.75] a--nd [.2] sort of goes past the pears [.3] the [.2] pears in
          the basket
     (f) and then stops,

Initial orientation to something not yet brought into consciousness in the
course of a telling seems much more difficult a process than the reactivation of
an orientation that was earlier in consciousness, though temporarily dropped.
Prior activation facilitates reactivation. Thus, for example, the return to the
man in the pear tree late in the film, after the events on the road, results in less
time-consuming reorientation. What we do find, just after the return to this
earlier scene, is a significant amount of difficulty caused by the need to deal
with a temporal overlap: to say something about what the pear picker was
doing while the events in a different location were going on. Speaker 6's
narrative is typical at this point also, with no unusual hesitating as the tree and
the picker are reintroduced, but subsequent difficulty—a total of 3.05 seconds
of hesitating at the beginning of (e)—as the temporal overlap is dealt with:

(62) (a) [1.0] Um [.15] and they start eating them.
     (b) [.15] And then they walk past the [.35] the tree,
     (c) where the picker,
     (d) .. was picking the pears,
     (e) [.9] a--nd uh-- [.9] he has already come down from the
          ladder,
     (f) [.65] to deposit his [.4] more of the pears that he picked up in
          the basket
     (g) and then he notices that there are only two baskets instead of
          three.

Thus, as a narrative proceeds there are varying degrees of orientation and
reorientation which the speaker must accomplish in his or her own
consciousness. In the verbal output the results are varying degrees of
hesitating. It is interesting to note that the largest amount of reorienting we
find evidence for in these narratives is actually not the change of space, time,
characters, and background activity that takes place as boy is about to meet
girl, but rather the various instances in which the speaker shifts from one
"world" into another. During these interviews our speakers were peripherally
conscious, certainly, of at least two quite disparate worlds: that in which they
found themselves sitting across from an interviewer who had just asked them
to do something a little strange, and the world inside the film which they were

rescanning with their consciousness, a world with pear picking and stealing, a boy on a bicycle who fell and was helped by three other boys, and so on.

The narratives dealt with the world inside the film most of the time. But occasionally, and more often for some speakers than for others, there was an emergence into the interview world. A shift of worlds is the most radical kind of reorientation one can make, involving as it does not only spatio-temporal and social differences, but a fundamental difference in expectation. Thus it is not surprising to find maximum hesitating and stumbling when the world is being shifted. The following speaker takes a total of 4.45 seconds to get into a comment on the colors—from the beginning of (a) to the word *Something* in (b)—and 2.25 seconds to get back into the world inside the film—(from the beginning of (g) to the word *was*—(Speaker 7):

(63) (a) [.9] A--nd [2.5] I don't know.
    (b) Something I noticed about the movie particularly unique was that the colors.. were [.35] just [.5] very strange.
    (c) [.2] Like [.3] the green was a [.2]. inordinately bright green,
    (d) [.55] for the pears,
    (e) [.4] and [.25] these colors just seemed a little [.5] kind of bold,
    (f) almost to the point of [1.15] being artificial.
    (g) [.6] Tsk [.1] a--nd [.75] he-- [.35] was going up and down the ladder,
    (h) [.9] tsk.. picking the pears,
    (i) [.25] and [.25] depositing them in [.35] three baskets,
    (j) [.7] that were down below.

We have noted that once an orientation has been activated in a narrative, it is not so difficult to return to it later. It seems to remain in a state of peripheral semi-activation which facilitates subsequent use. The same appears to be true for the major kind of orientation shift involving different worlds. Speaker 11 required a total of 7.05 seconds to shift to a comment on the sound track of the film:

(64) (a) [2.55] Um [4.05] the thing I noticed all the way through is that.. there's [.5] there's no--.. dialogue in the film,
    (b) but there.. is [1.0] a lot of sound effects.
    (c) [1.1] Which are not [.55] totally um-- [1.45] consistent.

But later she was able to shift into this world again with a minimum of difficulty:

(65) (a) And all this time the guy's up in the [.6] tree,
    (b) .. and he doesn't notice it.
    (c) [.9] However the sounds are extremely loud.
    (d) (cough) [1.3] So.. it's kind of funny.

SUMMARY

In this chapter I have tried to use spontaneous spoken language as a clue to the nature of consciousness and the ways it is deployed through time as a speaker speaks. I began with a basic model in which the self, having various goals and interests, makes use of consciousness as a mechanism by which available, potentially relevant information is activated. I described several intuitively plausible properties of consciousness which are related to its deployment through time during thinking and speaking. These properties include its highly limited capacity, its limited duration with respect to any particular piece of information, its jerky rather than continuous movement, and its division into a focus and periphery. I pointed out that vision shows the same properties. I then turned to language itself and noted that spontaneous speech has the property of being produced in spurts, which I called *idea units*. I described some of the syntactic and content characteristics of these idea units, and suggested that they are linguistic expressions of focuses of consciousness.

I then called attention to another easily observable property of spoken language: that it is punctuated every so often by a sentence-final intonation contour. I suggested that this contour signals the completion of the scanning of a *center of interest*. I contrasted focuses of consciousness, whose properties apparently belong to our built-in information-processing capabilities, with centers of interest, which apparently are based on learned schemas, intellect, and judgment. I suggested that in thinking and speaking we deploy the limited mechanism of the focus of consciousness to scan these centers of interest, which are typically too large to be taken in with a single focus.

I speculated that cognitive evolution in human beings has created a kind of mismatch between the amount of information which can be focused on at one time and the amount in which we are interested. But I noted that peripheral consciousness is helpful in this situation, since it permits us to be aware to some degree of more than just the small amount of information on which we are focusing and helps to guide us from one focus to the next. I noted that centers of interest often coincide with "mental images." I then showed various ways in which centers of interest fail to be expressed in intonationally or syntactically defined sentences in any clear-cut, one-to-one fashion. I introduced the notion of the *extended sentence* as something closer to the expression of a center of interest. And I showed how the composition of centers of interest varies, not only for different speakers, but even for the same speaker at different times, suggesting that judgments about centers of interest are not necessarily stored in memory, but may change from one telling to another.

I then turned to the apparent need of the self for orientation with respect to space, time, people, their salient characteristics, background activity, weather, and relevant props, some or all of which are typically focused on, if they cannot be inferred, before a speaker proceeds to focus on a series of events. I pointed out that speakers exhibit marked differences in the ease with which they move from one center of interest to another at different points in a narrative, sometimes making smooth and effortless transitions, sometimes hesitating and stumbling, producing in the latter case the spoken equivalents of paragraph boundaries. I suggested that the amount of difficulty in this process increases with the amount of reorientation the speaker must undergo in his or her own consciousness and must transfer to the consciousness of the listener. I noted that orientation as to space, time, people, background activity, and so on, may change in different combinations and to different degrees, producing different degrees of hesitating. And I noted that the highest degree of orientation shift is involved in a change of worlds, as occurs especially often in our narratives in the form of comments on the film.

The investigation of consciousness through careful observation of the properties of spontaneous speech is a line of research with almost no tradition behind it. It should not be surprising, therefore, that this chapter has been speculative and suggestive rather than conclusive. I hope that at the very least it has conveyed something of the fascination which the study of spontaneous oral language can hold for one who is interested in the stream of human thought. I hope also that it has provided some useful leads for further research into the intriguing interplay between consciousness and language.

ACKNOWLEDGMENTS

This chapter would have been totally impossible to write without this assistance of my collaborators on the pear film project—Robert Bernardo, Patricia Clancy, Pamela Downing, John DuBois, and Deborah Tannen. I am extremely grateful to them, as I am to Karen Carroll and Sarah Michaels, who collected and transcribed the children's narratives quoted in examples (25) and (26), and Swantje Ehlers, who collected and transcribed the German narrative in example (27).

REFERENCES

Buswell, G. T. *How people look at pictures. A study of the psychology of perception in art.* Chicago: The University of Chicago Press, 1935.
Chafe, W. L. Language and memory. *Language,* 1973, *49,* 261–281.
Chafe, W. L. Language and consciousness. *Language,* 1974, *50,* 111–133.
Chafe, W. L. Givenness, contrastiveness, definiteness, subject, topic, and point of view. In C. Li (Ed.), *Speaker and topic.* New York: Academic Press, 1976.

Chafe, W. L. The flow of thought and the flow of language. In T. Givón (Ed.), *Discourse and syntax.* New York: Academic Press, 1979.

Crystal, D. *The English tone of voice.* London: St. Martin, 1975.

Csikszentmihalyi, M. Attention and the holistic approach to behavior. In K. S. Pope & J. L. Singer (Eds.), *The stream of consciousness. Scientific investigations into the flow of human experience.* New York: Plenum Press, 1978.

Freud, S. *The interpretation of dreams.* New York: Avon Books, 1965.

Gregory, R. L. *Eye and brain. The psychology of seeing.* New York: McGraw-Hill, 1966.

Grimes, J. E. *The thread of discourse.* The Hague: Mouton, 1975.

Gurwitsch, A. *The field of consciousness.* Pittsburgh, Pa.: Duquesne University Press, 1964.

Halliday, M. A. K. Notes on transitivity and theme in English. Part 2. *Journal of Linguistics,* 1967, *3,* 199–244.

James, W. *The principles of psychology* (vol. 1). New York: Dover Publications, 1950.

Just, M. A., & Carpenter, P. A. Eye fixations and cognitive processes. *Cognitive Psychology,* 1976, *8,* 441–480.

Kroll, B. Combining ideas in written and spoken English: a look at subordination and coordination. In E. O. Keenan & T. L. Bennett (Eds.), Discourse across time and space. *Southern California Occasional Papers in Linguistics* No. 5. Department of Linguistics, University of Southern California. Los Angeles: 1977.

Labov, W. The transformation of experience in narrative syntax. In *Language in the inner city.* (Chap. 9). Philadelphia: University of Pennsylvania Press, 1972.

Linde, C. Speech errors, error correction, and the construction of discourse. (Forthcoming.)

Natsoulas, T. Consciousness. *American Psychologist,* 1978, *33,* 906–914.

Polanyi, L. False starts can be true. *Berkeley Linguistics Society,* 1978, *4,* 628–639.

Syder, F., & Pawley, A. *English conversational structures.* (In preparation.)

Watson, J. Psychology as the behaviorist views it. *Psychological Reivew,* 1913, *20,* 158–177.

2

A Comparative Analysis of Oral Narrative Strategies: Athenian Greek and American English

Deborah Tannen
Georgetown University

As continuing interest in the Sapir-Whorf hypothesis attests, linguists, along with psychologists and anthropologists, have tried to understand the relationship between language and cognition and to determine the influence of culture on thought. Scholars and laypeople alike are intrigued by apparent differences in the perceptions and behavior of members of different cultures. As Friedrich and Redfield (1978) point out, linguistic phenomena which continue to fascinate laypeople are particularly appropriate for scientific study, first, to apply the specialists' expertise to aspects of language whose obviousness to the nonspecialist is evidence not that they are insignificant but that they are "basic" and "true," and second, to reimbue the science of linguistics with the layperson's "visceral fascination."*

Recent research documenting cultural differences has spanned a broad range of fields, including cognitive style (Cole and Scribner, 1974); nonverbal behavior (Hall, 1959; Erickson, 1976); and facial expressions (Ekman, 1973). In linguistics, work in discourse analysis has begun to shed light on text-building principles and mechanisms in written and oral language. Among the

---

*I shall always be grateful to Wallace Chafe for untiring encouragement and guidance. I want to thank, as well, the University of California for a travel grant which contributed to my air fare to Greece; the Danforth Foundation for continuing support; Bruce Houston for making available to me the facilities of the Hellenic American Union in Athens; Cleo Helidonis for her able assistance in gathering and transcribing the Greek narratives; Evsevia Tziraki for her help in checking the transcriptions; and Charles Fillmore, John Gumperz, Paul Kay, and Bambi Schieffelin for helpful comments on earlier drafts. An earlier and significantly shorter version of this study was presented at the Fourth Annual Meeting of the Berkeley Linguistics Society, February 1978, and appears in the Proceedings of that meeting.

most important research in the area of narrative text-building is Becker's (1979) on Javanese, demonstrating that basic text-building constraints are cultural conventions. Whereas Western texts hinge on temporal unity and linear causality, Javanese shadow theater plots hinge on coincidence and are constrained with regard to place rather than time. For example, events in a Javanese shadow play must begin and end in a certain place and pass through a certain other place midway.

In a study of written expository texts, Kaplan (1966) examined 700 essays written by foreign students in English and compared them to essays published in those students' native languages. Kaplan concludes that each of the language groups he studied favors a unique, conventionalized rhetorical structure. In Arabic (and other Semitic languages) "paragraph development is based on a complex series of parallel constructions" (p. 6); Chinese and Korean writing "is marked by what may be called an approach by indirection" (p. 10); and "much greater freedom to digress or to introduce extraneous material is available in French, or in Spanish, than in English (p. 12). All these rhetorical strategies contrast with the favored American English structure which Kaplan characterizes as a straight line, to illustrate the notion of "coming right to the point."

Other research has illuminated various ways in which use of language in conversation is culturally influenced. Robin Lakoff (1979) demonstrates that style differences may grow out of differing notions of politeness which give rise to communicative strategies differing with respect to degree of involvement among interlocutors and between speakers and their subject matter. The work of cognitive anthropologists and ethnographers of speaking have made available insight into culture-specific definitions of speech events (Gumperz and Hymes, 1972; Bauman and Sherzer, 1974; Sanches and Blount, 1975). The recent work of John Gumperz (1977) identifies and analyzes the paralinguistic and prosodic mechanisms by which speech events (in his terms, "speech activities") are recognized and carried out.

Continuing in this fruitful tradition of discourse analysis, research done in connection with the present project afforded a unique opportunity for systematic analysis of how the same events are transformed into narrative by members of different cultures. The present paper compares the narratives told in English by students at the University of California, Berkeley, with those told in Greek by students at the Hellenic-American Union in Athens.[1]

---

[1]The Hellenic American Union is a binational center in Athens, Greece. Participants in this study were women attending evening classes in the English language. Two were university graduates; seven were university students; four were employed high school graduates; and six were high school students. They ranged in age from sixteen to twenty-six, with a median of nineteen. American women participating, students at the University of California, Berkeley, were slightly older, ranging in age from eighteen to thirty, with a median of twenty-three. No attempt was made to choose speakers of "comparable" socioeconomic status, since our goal was simply to

To say that the events which inspired the narratives were the same—that is, the same film—is not to say that the movie-viewing event had the same significance for members of the two groups; it is highly unlikely that this would be so. The ways in which speakers defined the event surely played a key role in shaping their verbalizations. Similarly, it is not assumed that the content of the narratives is the same. Quite the contrary, the question of how the content of the film is transformed into narrative content is at the heart of our investigation. As suggested by previous work such as Becker's, and as supported by data from the present study, there can be no "identical content," since content itself is mediated by cultural and personal differences. Polanyi (1979) reminds us that "what stories can be about is, to a very significant extent, culturally constrained: stories, whether fictional or non-fictional, formal and oft-told, or spontaneously generated, can have as their *point* only culturally salient material generally agreed upon by members of the producer's culture to be self-evidently important and true."

Polanyi's observation about the point of a story is related to C. Wright Mills' (1940) notion of "vocabularies of motives." Mills' hypothesis is that speakers learn to express motivations or explanations of their own and others' actions in terms of justifications which they know will be regarded as reasonable by other members of their culture. Just as there are agreed-upon vocabularies of motives, so are there conventionalized ways of choosing particular elements of the action and setting experienced or seen for inclusion in verbalization (and indeed in memory), and of organizing those events into narratives.

The ensuing discussion compares narratives told by Greek and American young women in response to the question, "What happened in the movie?" It cannot be assumed that the narratives thus elicited represent "universal" narrative styles in the cultures involved. This is not to say that the narratives are not "natural." As Nessa Wolfson (1976) wisely argues, "natural" speech is simply speech appropriate to an occasion. An interview with a stranger in the presence of a tape recorder is a special sort of occasion; the present study demonstrates that the Greek and American women who participated did indeed "define" the task differently. How their approaches differed is the question to be answered by a comparison of the two sets of narratives which were naturally produced by members of two different cultures under comparable external circumstances.

---

discover different rhetorical systems. It turned out, however that the occupations of the fathers of the Greek and American subjects were roughly comparable, including such traditional middle-class occupations as businessmen and civil servants. Almost all the American women had been raised in cities, and most of the Greeks had been born and raised in Athens, except for one from Istanbul and four from Greek towns. It should be noted, however, that a typical Athenian has closer ties with rural life than do American city-dwellers, as Athenians often make "excursions" to the villages, and many have relatives living in the countryside whom they visit regularly.

DIFFERENCES IN NARRATIVE STRATEGIES

There were two striking overall differences between the Greek and American oral narratives about the pear film. First, the Americans[2] tended to discuss the film as a film, whereas the Greeks tended to recount the events depicted without saying that they had occurred in a film.

The Americans used cinematic jargon to comment upon and criticize technical aspects of the film's production, noting, for example, that the soundtrack was out of proportion, the costumes were unrealistic, or the colors were unnatural. In fact, the film's sound effects formed the main point, or "coherence principle,"[3] for four American narratives, including one which will be presented. Still another American structured her narrative around repeated contrasts between what she expected to happen as the film progressed and what actually happened. Thus the coherence principle of her narrative was the re-creation of her experience as a film-viewer. Moreover, the film-viewer perspective was generally maintained throughout the American narratives, by direct reference as well as allusion to the fact that the events discussed occurred in a film.

In contrast, the Greeks tended to talk directly about the events depicted without noting that they were in a film. If they did make overt reference to the film as a film, they did so at the beginning or the end of their narratives, by way of introduction or conclusion, rather than maintaining the perspective of a film-viewer in the course of narration. Furthermore, if the Greek speakers made judgments about the film, they largely commented on its message rather than the technique of its production.

The second major difference between the two sets of narratives is related to the first. The Americans in our study seemed to be reporting events as objectively as they could, often describing actions in detail, worrying over temporal sequence, and so on. In general, they appeared to be performing a memory task. The Greeks, on the other hand, tended to "interpret" the events. They ascribed social roles and motives to the characters, and they offered explanations as well as judgments of the action. In general, they appeared to be telling a story. Whereas the Americans seemed to be trying to include as many elements from the film as they could remember, the Greeks tended to

---

[2]Throughout this chapter, the words *Greeks* and *Americans* refer to those Greeks and Americans who participated in our study. There is no implication that there exists a homogeneous "Greek" or "American" culture, nor that those in this sample are "typical Americans" or "typical Greeks." This chapter demonstrates that the Athenian women and Berkeley women who participated are members of groups that may be distinguished from each other by the ways in which they perform the narrative task at hand. Members of the two groups evidence such differences despite the fact that there are, no doubt, subcultural differences among members of each group.

[3]I have borrowed this term from Charlotte Linde who attributes it to Alton Becker.

omit details that did not contribute to the theme they were developing, with the result that the Greek narratives were significantly shorter. (The average number of "idea units"[4] for the American narratives is 125, as opposed to an average of 84 for the Greek. The American narratives range in length from a total of 61 idea units to a total of 256; the Greek range from 26 to 150).

These two striking differences: (1) the tendency to talk about the film as a film vs. talking directly about the depicted events, (2) the tendency to "report" in detail vs. "interpreting" events, may both be related to the apparently different definitions of the narrative acts being performed. Whereas the Americans in our study focused their critical acumen on the skill of the film makers and seemed to define the event as a test of memory, the Greeks brought their critical acumen to bear on the events and characters in the film and seemed to approach the task more as they would a narrative in conversation. In short, insofar as any verbal performance is an exercise in presentation-of-self (Goffman, 1959), it seems that the Americans were concerned with presenting themselves as sophisticated movie viewers and able recallers, while the Greeks were concerned with presenting themselves as acute judges of human behavior and good storytellers.

SAMPLE NARRATIVES

Before we proceed with a more detailed presentation and analysis of these broad and other finer differences, it will be useful to see sample American and Greek narratives. First, an American example:[5]

> E14 The movie opened up on this...nice scene,...it was in the country,...it was oaks,..it /was/ seemed like West Coast... Maybe it wasn't. ...But it was hills and dry grass,...um...and scrub. ...But there was pear trees in it,..and that was odd. ...And there was this man with a moustache and a hat, picking...unripe pears, ...um and he was in this...he went up the ladder,...in the tree,...cause the tree was high, it wasn't pruned,...like..they usually are,...to keep them prostrate,... but it was...it had a large...uh...tall trunk,...and he's [tense ambiguous] picking unripe...unripe pears. ...And what I noticed...first off,..was that all the noises in the movie,...were

---

[4]See Chapter 1 for a discussion of "idea units."

[5]"E14" refers to the fourteenth narrative told in English. Narratives told in Greek will be denoted by "G" plus number. Thus "E14" also refers to American Speaker 14; "G10" is Greek Speaker 10. Pauses are uniformly represented by three dots rather than precise timing (which is available), since the present analysis does not make use of pause measurements.

u--m...out of proportion...Like you could hear the..the creaking...of the...ladder,...and the picking of the pears, and then from a long way off..they zoomed in on a.../on a/...a...child on a bicycle, and you could hear the...the gears on the bicycle going around, more than...it was...way out of proportion of everything else....And u--m...this man came by,...walked by, and he's leading a goat,..that didn't want to go with him,.../ah/...and this first...Okay,...let me see.... ...The man climbed down out of the tree,..and put the pears in the basket, and it looked like he was...giving birth....It did!..He was just kind of..[creaky voice]...rolling them out of his pouch, in his...in his apron,...and u--m...then this-- he came /back/ down,...and put the pears in the basket,...and he went back up the ladder, and you could hear the creaking,..and then you could hear the goat...a long way off,..and it was braying....But it was...a very..like..a lo--ng drawn-out bray, like the movie...the sound track had been slowed down, so it was "buhhh" [creaky voice]....um...And he went...and he went by, and there was two baskets of..pears there, and one empty one,...and then this little kid came by,...and you could hear the gears in the...on the bicycle,...and you could hear the crickets,..and the..grass-hoppers,...and the little kid came by, and he si...and he...hesitated, but then he stole,..one of the baskets of pears,..and put it on his...bicycle and rode off....And as he was...riding down the r...this...this uh..dirt road,.../it/ was full of rocks,..you could hear the..the rocks creak under-neath,...u--m...this other little girl in pigtails,..black pigtails,...rode by,...and he tipped his hat to her,...and as he did that,...lost his hat,..and ran into a b--ig rock, and the...pears spilled all over....Out of nowhere,...he looks up, and out of nowhere,...everyone else,...even the viewers are s...there's...three other little boys, one's playing with this...pongo?...A little...paddle?..And a ball with it on /the/ end of the elastic?...And you could hear this paddle-ball going,...a--nd uh--...and they help him pick up the...pears, and put them back on his bicycle, and dust him off,...a--nd u--m...then he goes off, and..nobody ever smiles in the movie, there isn't any emotion on any /of/ body's faces....A--nd then they nowt..they were walking along down the road, they notice his bicycle was there,...I mean his hat was there,...so they picked up his hat, and whistled to him....and they ran back, and you could hear the running...And it was just so much out of proportion, it was...easy to notice....u--m...And they gave him his hat,..and

the ... the little .. boy that fell off the bicycle gives him ... gives
them three--.. pears, ... and they went back, ... a--nd .. then you
switch back to the ma--n, that's .. climbing down out of the tree,
again with another .. pouchful of .. of pears. ... And he kneels
down to put the pears in the .. third empty basket, ... and he
s ... scratches his head, and ... u--m ... he goes .. one two
three, ... and but there isn't a third one there, and he scratches his
head some more, and looks, and these little .. three little boys go
by, ... just walking, not paying any attention, .. no--t paying any
attention to the man, /and/ ... eating these pears. ... And that's
the end of the movie.

Following is an example of a Greek narrative. (An English translation follows
the Greek.)

G10 eh ... *Itan ena--s .. uh erghatis, .. enas choriatis, ... foruse mia
aspri podhia ke ena kokino mandili, ... mazeve kati achladhia. ... I
skala olo ligho etreme, ... /iche fovo/ na pesi ... eh-- ta evale se ena*
[laughter----------]
*kalathi, ... tria prepi na itane, ... tsk ... to ena to yemize, ... ke--
pernas perase ena pitsiriki, ... forondas ke afto mandili pali, ... ena
podhilato, ... stin archi pighe na pari-- dhio tria .. ala tu arese olo
to kalathi to pire olo. ... Ala eh ... pighenondas .. sinandise ali mia
kopela, ... mia mikri stin ilikia tu, ke-- kitazondas to anapo-
dhoyirise. ... tsk Tu epesan kato ta achladhia, ... vrethikan kati ali-
sinomiliki tu, ... ke-- to mazepsan. ... Aftos omos dhe--... tus
efcharistise as pume, ... ke* [clears throat] *... tsk ke .. fevghondas i
fili tu ferane to kapelo pu tu iche pesi .. kathos tsughrise me tin
kopela, ... ke tu to edhosan ke tote tus efcharistise. ... Fevghondas
afti per perasan ap ton anthropo, ... ke idhan oti--... idhe o
anthropos oti troghane--... ta achladhia. Ke paraxeneftike. ...
Yiati--elipan ta tria kalathia. ... /m/ Afto. ... Dhen echi alo.*

eh ... (There) was a--.. uh worker, .. a villager, ... (he) was wearing
a white apron and a red scarf, ... (he) was gathering some
pears. ... The ladder kept shaking a bit, ... /(he) was afraid/ of
[laughter------------
falling, ... eh-- (he) put them in a basket, ... three (there) must have
--------]
been, ... tsk ... (he) was filling one, ... a--nd passes passed a
kiddie, ... wearing a scarf too, ... a bicycle, ... in the beginning (he)
went to take-- two or three .. but he liked the whole basket (he) took
it all. [laugh] ... But eh ... going .. (he) met another girl, ... one

young in age, a--nd looking (he) overturned it. . . . tsk The pears fell down, . . . there were some other-- contemporaries of his, . . . a—nd they gathered it. . . . He however didn't--. . . thank them let's say, . . . and [clears throat] . . . tsk and . . leaving the friends brought the hat which had fallen . . as (he) crashed with the girl, . . . and they gave it to him and then (he) thanked them. . . . (As) they (were) leaving (they) pa passed by the man, . . . and (they) saw tha--t . . . the man saw that (they) were eating--. . . the pears. And (he) was surprised. . . . Becau--se the three baskets were missing. . . . / m / That('s it). . . (It) doesn't have (any) more.

Let us look more closely at some differences between these narratives, and between the two sets of narratives from which they come.

MAINTENANCE OF FILM PERSPECTIVE

The ways in which these two sample narratives begin are typical. E14 (the American) begins with an overt reference to the film:

E14 The movie opened up on this . . . nice scene,

She uses the word *movie* and emphasizes it by increasing her pitch and loudness on the word. Furthermore, she uses movie-specific jargon ("opened up," "scene") as well as a conventionalized rhetorical structure associated with telling about a movie (beginning with a description of the scene). In contrast, G10 (the Greek) talks directly about the film's contents:

G10 eh . . . (There) was a--. . uh worker,

In fact, fifteen Greeks (as opposed to four Americans) never mention the word *movie* or *film* (Greek *tenia* or *film*) at all. Furthermore, not only do more Americans refer directly to the film, but those Americans who do use the words *movie* or *film* do so more often than the Greeks who do. (See Table 1.) Of the five Greeks who use the (cognate) word *film* or *tenia* ("film"), four use it only once; of these, two use it in their first sentences and two in their last sentences. The one Greek who refers directly to the film twice, does so in her first and last sentences. Thus the references to the film serve as opening and

---

[6]Transliteration is designed to reflect pronunciation as closely as possible. *ch* is the Greek χ, a voiceless velar fricative. *gh* is the Greek γ, a voiced velar fricative. *x* is the Greek ξ, pronounced like the English "x." *dh* is the Greek δ, a voiced interdental fricative, pronounced like "th" in "then."

TABLE 1
Occurrence of Nouns *movie* or *film* (Greek *tenia* or *film*)

Number of speakers	Number of mentions per narrative:						
	0	1	2	3	4	5	6
American	4	8	2	1	2	1	2
Greek	15	4	1	0	0	0	0

closing devices, rather like a cinematic zoom-in and zoom-out technique. No Greek speaker refers directly to the film more than twice. In sharp contrast, six Americans use the word *film* or *movie* three or more times in their narratives. Of the eight who directly mention the film once, only half do so at the very beginning or very end of their narratives. The other four do so somewhere in the middle, indicating that the film-viewer perspective intrudes in the course of their narratives rather than functioning simply as an introductory or concluding device. E14, for example, uses the word *movie* five times:

(a) The movie opened up on this... nice scene,
(b) And what I noticed... first off,.. was that all the noises in the movie,... were um--... out of proportion.
(c) like the movie... the.. sound track had been slowed down,
(d) and.. nobody ever smiles in the movie,
(e) ..and that's the end of the movie.

By repeatedly referring to the movie, E14 maintains the "film frame," that is, the perspective of a viewer observing and recounting events in a film. (See Tannen, 1979b for explanation of use of the term "frame.") This may be considered a recontextualizing device. Each time she refers to the film, she is reminding the listener of the context of her story.

Although direct mention of the world *film* is the most obvious evidence that a film-viewer perspective is being maintained, the same function is served by indirect reference to the film as a film. Indirect references, or "allusions," to the film frame include the use of cinema-associated jargon or expressions, such as "the camera pans," "protagonist," "soundtrack," and so on. In the Greek narratives, allusions include use of the verb *edhichne* or *dhichni* ("[it] showed," "[it] shows"), in which the deleted subject "it" refers to the film. Allusions also can take the form of such expressions as "then we saw" or "you could see," since they presuppose an audience and, by implication, a film, as contrasted with direct statements, such as "then the boy got on his bicycle." For example, the following expressions in E14's narrative alluded to the fact that what is being told about is a movie:

(a) this . . . nice scene,
(b) they zoomed in
(c) the . . sound track had been slowed down,
(d) the viewers
(e) you switch back to

Her reference to herself as a viewer also activates the film-viewer perspective:

(a) I noticed . . .
(b) you could hear [repeated eight times]

All these references serve to remind the listener that what is being talked about is a film. This is not to imply that any speaker or listener might forget that the events described occurred in a film. The difference is simply in narrative point of view established by what is selected for verbalization.

Table 2 shows the number of times Americans and Greeks allude to the film as a film or the film-viewer perspective.

TABLE 2
Number of Allusions to Film
as Film or Film-Viewer Perspective

Number of speakers	Number of allusions:		
	0	1–8	10–15
American	1	14	5
Greek	5	15	0

Three-fourths of both groups have from one to eight such allusions in their narratives, but one-fourth of the Greeks have none at all (i.e., they never make overt reference to the fact that they are telling about a film); one-fourth of the Americans have between ten and fifteen allusions (they persistently maintain the film-watcher point of view).

Tallies of direct mentions of, and allusions to, the film as a film are a concrete indication of the point of view maintained in the narratives which can be seen on examination of the narrative content. For example, nine Americans and only one Greek mentioned that the film had no dialogue. In addition, a number of Americans also indicated their expectation that a character introduced into a film should play a significant role in the film's action, as seen in the following comments:

E7 They don't seem to have too much to do, . . . with . . what's going . . on.

E12 ...That was all that..you saw of her in the movie.

E2   ...a--nd uh--...you wonder how she's going to figure in on this.

No similar comments appear in the Greek narratives.

DESCRIPTIONS OF ACTION

The difference between the "direct" point of view established by the Greek speakers and the "film-viewer" point of view preferred by the American speakers can also be seen in their descriptions. For example, a number of speakers in both groups describe how the man in the film picks pears. First of all, more Greeks than Americans choose to describe the man's pear-picking action. Most Americans (seventeen of twenty) report that he was picking pears without commenting about the way he did it. Of the three Americans who do describe his actions, only one comments on his movements:

E12 ...And-- uh--...tsk he was picking pears. ...Just rather slowly, and he did it.../ $\overset{so}{that}$ / you could hear the sound of the pears being... torn from the... tree, and he put them in an apron /that he had/,.../the whole idea/ he picked pears came down the ladder,...put them...one by one..into this basket. ...He...y you got...the feeling that he pretty much liked his pears,.. because he was so..gentle with them /??/.

In commenting on the man's actions, E12 preserves the perspective of herself as a film-viewer, for she repeats "you could hear" and "you got the feeling...." This latter choice of phrase is particularly interesting, for E12 began by saying "...He... " but then aborted that beginning and switched to "y you got...the feeling." It seems that her first impulse was to report directly what the man felt, but that she then self-corrected to reflect her awareness that she was telling about her reaction, not what was shown in the film. This is in sharp contrast to the Greek renditions, which will be seen presently.

The two other Americans who describe the man's actions in picking pears make their comments about the film, not the man.

E17 ...A--nd...he's...it..the camera spends a lot of time watching him...pick these pears,

Here again can be seen the initial impulse to report directly ("he's... "). That is aborted, and E17 says instead "it" and then makes overt the referent of "it" with another self-correction ("the camera"). Thus we see an elegant example of the process of overt contextualization in action, as E17 formulates a statement about how the film was made rather than what the man did.

The third and last American who describes the pearpicker's actions begins
by talking directly about the man but then comes up with a reminder of the
film-viewer perspective.

> E18 He's very deliberately... plucking the.. the um... the pears off the
> tree, and... you know you hear this... s-- sharp little crunch
> as.. as he pulls each one off, and he's doing it.. very slowly, and
> putting them in [breath] his apron. [breath]... tsk And
> then.. climbing very carefully.. down the... the ladder, and
> placing them in baskets, and he'd never make it as a
> fruitpicker. ... [laugh] He would starve.

The last comment suddenly reimposes the film perspective, referring to the
man as an actor, not a pearpicker. Once again, there is an implied criticism of
the filmmaker: the film failed to be realistic in its portrayal.

In sharp contrast, seven Greek speakers interpret the man's behavior in
picking pears without indicating that he was in a film. In a few cases, the way
in which this scene is described sets the tone for the entire narrative. This is
how G11 describes the man's motions:

> G11 *Evlepe to.. eh me mia evla--via xeris t'achladhi. Poli evlavika.*
> (He) regarded the.. eh with a piety you know the pear. Very
> piously.
> [He looked at the pear with, you know, great piety. Very piously.]

As she says this, G11's voice takes on a soothing quality which is most
pronounced in the onomatopoetic lengthening of the vowel on *evla--via* ("pi--
ety"). Her voice communicates great earnestness, with rises and falls in pitch
which are generally more characteristic of Greek women's speech than of
American women's, but which are particularly pronounced in this narrative.
The fact that G11 is talking about a film is implicit in the very beginning of this
passage, in the deleted subject of "(it) insisted," although even here one might
argue that the deleted subject is "he" in underlying structure, referring to the
man. After that, however, G11 goes on to talk about the man and his feelings
directly, with no reference to herself as a film-viewer.

G11's description of the pear-picking action is part of her romantic
interpretation of all the events in the film. G12 creates a similar effect:

> G12 ... *Ke-- m tsk epemene oti-- afto pu ekane to zuse. ... To n--
> dhiladhi-- m--... to oti-- kalierghuse ti ghi--, oti mazev'afta--... to
> sighomidhi, ... itane yi'afton kati to idhietero. ... Axize kati--
> ...... tsk to zuse afto pu ekane, tu arese.*

A--nd mm tsk (it) insisted tha--t that which (he) did (he) lived. ...That n-- in other words-- m--...the fact tha--t (he) was cultivating the ea--rth, that (he) was gathering the--se...the harvest,...was for him something special. ...(It) was worth somethi--ng...tsk (he) lived that which (he) did, he liked (it).

G12 also speaks these lines in a way that communicates earnestness through voice quality, marked shifts in pitch, intonation, and elongation of vowels. Another Greek speaker interprets the pearpicker's motions differently:

G16 ...tsk Ke-- ta mazevi-- etsi me--...me poli--...eh-- sa na ta theli dhika tu. Me poli etsi-- /s/ idhioktisia dh dhichni mesa.

...tsk A--nd (he) gathers-- them like with--...with a lo--t...eh-- as if (he) wants them (to be) his own. With a lot (of) li--ke /s/ proprietariness (he) sh shows inside.

Still another Greek interprets the man's movements negatively:

G15 ...I kinisis tu vasika-- mazev...mazevondas ta fruta dhen dhichni anthropo...pu ta aghapai poli ta travai para poli..dhen xero. ...Dhen mu arese ghenika o tropos pu ta travaye.

...His movements basically-- gath...gathering the fruits don't show (a) person...who loves them very much (he) pulls them very..(I) don't know. ...I didn't like generally the way (he) was pulling them.

The striking aspect of these descriptions is that the Greek speakers relate their interpretations of the man's feelings and their own feelings about the man's actions without noting that they are talking about a film which was intentionally made. Again, this is not to say that they have forgotten that they are talking about a film, but rather that they do not choose to focus on that element of the events, and that they consider it appropriate to attribute motivations and attitudes to the man as well as to verbalize their own.

The Greek speakers in our study did not maintain the film-viewer perspective throughout their narratives, yet they were evidencing a culturally agreed-upon film-viewer stance just the same. That is, they seemed to consider it appropriate to view a film for its "message" rather than its technique. G6 indicates as assumption that one is supposed to interpret the messages of a film when she says, at the end of her narrative,

G6 ...Alo an /dhini/ tora--...o kathenas ales erminies.

...(it's something) else now if each person /gives/ other interpretations.

This indicates that her interpretation of the film was the focus, or the coherence principle, of her narrative. A negative statement at the end of another Greek narrative reveals a similar expectation about interpretation of the film's "meaning":

G9 ... *Tora to topio vevea itan ore--o.* ... *Ala dhen xero na to exighiso.*

... Now the landscape certainly was lo--vely. ... But (I) don't know (how) to explain it.

After saying a few more sentences about the landscape, she repeats, "but I don't know how to-- explain it." Her repetition of the negative statement indicates that she feels uncomfortable about not being able to explain the film's message. She seems to dwell on the landscape as a convenient substitute conclusion, given her inability to end with what she considers appropriate: a summary of the film's meaning.

Another way that the film-viewer perspective surfaces in verbalization is in the speakers' choice of verb tenses. The Americans exhibited a strong tendency to tell their narratives in the present tense, whereas the Greeks preferred the past. Table 3 shows the tenses used by speakers in our study. Thirteen Americans as opposed to three Greeks used only the present tense throughout their narratives. Eight Greeks as opposed to two Americans used only the past. In a pattern which is part of a general pattern of greater stylistic variation in the Greek narratives, eight Greeks and only one American switched back and forth between past and present tenses (shown in Table 3 as "mixed"). Of these eight Greeks, however, six used mostly the past tense (the percentages of idea units in the past tense for these six were: 56, 65, 71, 77, 81, 85). Thus a total of fourteen Greeks showed marked preference for the past tense. Furthermore, the number of Americans who preferred the present tense increases to seventeen when it includes the four who began by telling their narratives in the past but then switched to the present and stuck with it.

TABLE 3
Verb Tenses Used in Narratives

Number of speakers	present	past	mixed	past → present
Americans	13	2	1	4
Greeks	3	8	8	1

Surely it is necessary to study the use of verb tenses in other contexts by both Greeks and Americans; it may be that the differences found here reflect habitual conventionalized choices.[7] It is unclear, for example, whether the Americans were using a "historical present" associated with telling about works of art, such as films, which are presumed to exist permanently, or, as seems more likely, the present tense of vivid personal experience narration. Nevertheless, the past tense of the Greek narratives is consistent with the perspective of recounting events which occurred once and are done, that is, events directly experienced rather than viewed in a permanent work such as a film.

INTERPRETATION OF EVENTS

The tendency of Greeks to talk about events directly as opposed to talking about the film as a film can be seen in the ways in which both bring to bear the faculty I have called *interpretation*. I use this term to refer to cognitive leaps made by a speaker, resulting in her reporting information which was not actually depicted in the film, and which therefore represents the imposition of her own knowledge, experience, and expectations on what she saw. Interpretation, in this sense, takes many forms, ranging, for example, from (1) reporting as repeated events what appeared in the film as a single event (e.g., saying that the man went up and down the tree repeatedly, whereas the film showed him ascend and descend just once), thus altering the precise details of the film but not violating its intentions (it is often the case in a film, or in life, that an action seen to occur once may be safely assumed to occur repeatedly); to (2) inferring characters' emotions, thoughts, and intentions—that is, supplying information where the film gave none but not distorting events as they appeared; to (3) making value judgments about characters' behavior.

My notion of interpretation is closely related to what Labov (1972) calls *evaluative elements* in oral narrative. (See Chapter 1 for related discussion of interpretation as well). Labov defines evaluative elements as "the means used by the narrator to indicate the point of a narrative," or to answer in advance the question "So what?" Including such phenomena as subjective statements (e.g., "Here's the best part ..."), negative statements, expressive phonology, and use of adjectives, such elements contribute to the "coherence principle"

---

[7]We cannot assume that tenses conventionally named *past* and *present* in English necessarily function the same way as tenses with similar names in Greek, nor that they divide up time in the same way. Nevertheless, the preferences which were evidenced in this study do seem to reflect more general story telling conventions. Kostas Kazazis (personal communication), who lived in Greece until the age of eighteen, notes that for a long time the American habit of telling jokes in the present tense ("There's this guy ...") struck him as "strange" and "illogical." This suggests that the past tense is the conventionalized choice in Greek.

motivating the story. They are among the linguistic devices I have elsewhere discussed under the heading "evidence of expectations" (Tannen, 1979b), for they simultaneously create and grow out of speakers' cultural constructs. Such elements, then, furnish ready-made lenses for inspection of cultural differences.

For example, there are significant differences in the way G10 and E14 (the Greek and American speakers whose narratives were quoted in full) presented the incident in the film in which the boy gives pears to the three boys who have helped him after his fall from his bicycle. The American (E14) is typical of our American speakers:

> E14   and the ... the little .. boy that fell off the bicycle gives him ... gives them three-- .. pears,

The Greek (G10) reports the event this way:

> G10   and then (he) thanked them.

E14 described the events she saw in the film; G10 substituted an interpretation which she believed captured the significance of the events. Moreover, G10 had earlier commented, after reporting that the three boys helped the fallen boy,

> G10 ... he however didn't-- ... thank them let's say,

Labov (1972) notes, as others have observed as well, that a negative statement expresses the defeat of an expectation that its affirmative would have been the case. In the example above, the negative statement represents G10's expectation that the boy would have thanked his helpers, and furthermore it constitutes a kind of moral censure, indicating G10's judgment that the little boy did not behave well, that he should have thanked the other boys (i.e., given them pears) as soon as they helped him up, rather than waiting until they had left and returned with his hat.

The preferred strategy of the American speakers was, like E14's, to report the exchange of pears without commenting on its significance, that is, without interpreting the actions in their narratives. The general tendency of the Greek speakers was to make explicit, like G10, that they regarded the exchange as a gesture of thanks. Two Americans and seven Greeks said that the boy gave the pears in order to thank the threesome. Two other Americans commented that the boy should have given the pears earlier, indicating indirectly that they considered the exchange a gesture of thanks. Two more Greeks indicated this interpretation by saying, respectively, that the boy gave the pears "as a gift" and that the scene in which the exchange took place was "a lovely scene." A total then of nine Greeks and four Americans made overt their interpretations of the pear exchange. It seems safe to assume that any of the speakers, if asked, would have said that the boy gave pears to the three other boys in order to thank them for their help. The narratives show, however, that the Greeks more often chose to verbalize that interpretation. What we are concerned with is not the cognitive act of interpretation but its linguistic realization, that is, what speakers deem appropriate for verbalization in their narratives.

A strikingly overt form of interpretation is a moral judgment, a narrative act which is often accompanied by linguistic evidence of emotional involvement, such as, for example, hestitation, false starts, repetitions, and so on. Note the tremendous amount of such verbal fussing that G16 goes through in getting out the idea that the boy should have thanked his helpers sooner:

> G16 ... ke-- tote to pedhi, .. katalaveni stin a eno eprepe kanonika-- otan to voithisan na dhos na-- ton voithisan na ta-- dhos ta achladhia pa na ta vali sti thesi tus, eprepe kanonika ... na dhosi na prosferi eh-- na-- ... se ol se osa pedhia itane na prosferi-- ligha achladhia, ke dhen prosfere. ... Ala otan idhe na t'tu xanapighan ton fonaxan yia na-- tu pane to kapelo ... tote sa na katalave oti-- eprepe na prosferi stin archi, ... ke prosfere meta ap' afti ti chironomia pu to xanafonaxan yia to-- ... na tu dhosun to kapelo tu.

> ... a--nd then the child, ... realizes in the beg while (he) should have ordinarily-- when (they) helped him to give to-- (they) helped him to give them-- the pears (he) goes to put them in their place, (he) should have ordinarily ... given offered o--ne-- ... to al to as many children as there were to offer-- a few pears, and (he) didn't offer. ... But when (he) saw them giving him back they called him in order to-- give him the hat, ... then as if (he) realized tha--t (he) should have offered in the beginning, ... and (he) offered after this gesture of calling him back in order to-- ... to give him his hat.

This passage is riddled with false starts, hesitations, lengthening of sounds, rewordings, and repetitions, indicating that the content is of emotional significance to the speaker and is perhaps disturbing to her. Such evidence of emotional involvement with the events of the film and of the narrative is not seen in American narratives in our sample.

The tendency of Greek speakers in our study to "interpret" more than Americans can be seen very clearly in the following complete narrative told by G12. Although this is an extreme case, it exhibits a tendency which appears to some extent in most of the Greek narratives about the film.

G12 eh *Ap oti katalava--,... ita--n......ena episodhio,.. eyine-- sto*
Mexiko. ... Ipotheto,.. mu fanikane Mexikani-- i anthropi,... ke--
mm edhichne ti--n... pos mazeve enas anthropos ta achladhia,... ke--
mm tsk *epemene oti-- afto pu ekane to zuse. ... To n-- dhiladhi--*
m--... to oti-- kalierghuse ti ghi--, oti mazev'afta--... ti
sighomidhi,... itane yi'afton kati to idhietero. .. Axize kati--... tsk
to zuse afto pu ekane, tu arese. eh-- *mm Ke edhichne mia skini--*
.. /m/ prepi na itane malon i-- mm.. i aghrotiki zoi--, tis periochis
ekinis,.. enas pu perase me mia katsi--ka--,... ena-- pedhaki--
.. ena pedhaki me podhilato,.. pu idhe to kalathi, me ta achladhia,
ke to pi--re, [slight laugh]... *ke meta-- kathos pernaghe,..*
sinandise mesa ston aghro-- pa--li,.. ali mia kopela me
podhilato,... ke opos tin kitaghe dhen prosexe ligho,... ke tu
epese to-- tu epese to kalathi me ta achladhia,... ke eki pali itane--
mm ali tris fili tu,... pu-- amesos to voi--thisa--n... ke afto itane
pandos kati pu edhichne poso ta pedhia-- metaxi tus aghapionde,..
. echun alilegii,... to voithisan na ta mazepsi,... ke-- m--... ke
opos xechase ke to kapelo tu, itane mia orea skini pu tus edhose ta
achladhia... ke yirise pali piso. ... Dhiladhi--... yenika nomizo
oti itane mia skini--,... tsk ... tis aghrotikis zois tis periochis ekinis
pu edhichne....... Afta.

eh From what (I) undertoo–d,... (it) was......an episode,.. (it)
happened-- in Mexico. .. (I) suppose,... the people seemed (like)
Mexicans to me,... a--nd mm (it) showed the--... tsk how a person
gathered the pears,... a--nd mm tsk (it) insisted tha--t that which he
did (he) lived. ... The n-- in other words-- m--... the (fact) that (he)
was cultivating the ea--rth, that (he) was gathering the--se ... the
harvest,... was for him something special. ... (It) was worth
somethi--ng ... tsk (he) lived that which (he) did, he liked
(it). ... Eh--, and (it) showed a sce–ne.. /m/ (it) must have been
probably the-- mm tsk the agricultural li--fe, of that region,.. one
who passed with a goa--t,... a-- littlechi--ld ... a littlechild with a
bicycle,.. who saw the basket, with the pears, and too--k it, [slight
laugh]... and then-- as (he) was passing,.. (he) met in the fie–ld
a--lso,.. another girl with (a) bicycle,... and as (he) looked at her (he)
didn't pay attention a little,... and fell the-- fell the basket with the
pears,... and there too were-- mm three other friends of
his,... who--... immediately he--lped him ... and this was
moreover something which showed how much children-- love each
other,... (they) have solidarity,... (they) helped him to gather
them,... a--nd m--.. and as (he) forgot his hat too, (there) was a
lovely scene where (he) gave them the pears ... and returned back
again. ... In other words--,... generally (I) think that (it) was a

sce--ne, ... tsk ... of the agricultural life of that region which (it) showed. ...... These. [i.e., "That's it."]

A vast array of interpretive devices operate here to support G12's coherence principle: an idealized view of agricultural life which she takes to be the film's message. First of all, her intonation creates this effect; she draws out many of her vowels, creating a "soothing" effect, and she strings her clauses together with a combination of lengthened vowels and steady clause-final pitch, giving the entire narrative the sound of a list: a recital of matter-of-fact circumstances rather than novel events. The effect of this intonation is particularly apparent when she tells that the boy took the pears. Nothing in her intonation communicates that anything special is happening, so the taking of the pears, in her narrative, is not interpreted as a theft at all; it is just one more everyday rural event.

G12 discusses the pearpicker's attitude toward his work as if it were known to her, and she concerns herself continually with the "message": for example, when she notes that the helping scene serves the purpose of showing that "children love each other." Similarly, her use of the adjective "lovely" to describe the scene in which the boy gives the others pears constitutes an interpretation of its meaning. She "plays down" elements that do not contribute to her interpretation and "plays up" those that do.

INTERPRETIVE NAMING

Narratives exhibit interpretation not only in their explicit statements about the actions and characters but in more subtle ways as well. The intonation has an interpretive effect, as has been seen. So does lexical choice. For example, G12 called the pears "the harvest" (*ti sighomidhi*), after rejecting the less marked categorization, "these..." (*afta*), presumably the beginning of "these fruits" or "these pears."

> G12 *oti mazev' afta-- ... ti sighomidhi.*
> that (he) gathered the--se ... the harvest.

The choice word of the *harvest* grows out of the interpretation of the man as an independent farmer and contributes to a romantic notion of his relationship to the fruit he is picking. Another speaker calls the pears "his yield" or "his production" (*tin paraghoghi tu*), to similar effect, setting the tone for her similarly romantic description of his disposition:

> G2 ... *Eh-- ... ola itane-- orea yi'afton--, efcharista pernuse--,*
> ... Eh-- ... everything wa--s lovely for hi--m, (he) was passing (his time) pleasantly,

Similarly, G12 called the threesome the boy's "friends;"

G12 ...*ke eki pali itane-- mm ali tris fili tu,*
...and there too were-- mm three others friends of his,

There is no indication in the film that the boys knew each other. Harry C. Triandis points out (personal communication) that in Greece helping behavior is expected only in the ingroup; hence the fact that the boys helped the bicycle boy makes them friends. G10, whose narrative was quoted at the outset, also used this categorization. In keeping with Triandis's analysis, G10 calls the threesome the boy's "contemporaries" (*sinomiliki tu*) when they first appear, but the next time she mentions them, they have become "his friends" (*ifili tu*). In all, three Greeks and no-Americans called the threesome the boy's "friends."

Interpretive naming is a very effective narrative device, because lexical choice has an air of inevitability about it; it takes much more sophistication to deduce that an interpretation is being made by the choice of a word than it does to recognize an overtly stated interpretation.[8] As a narrative device, categorization (i.e., choice of a word) can function to create an interpretation by triggering a series of associations (a familiar frame, script, or schema).

For example, G10, in the narrative quoted at the beginning, started by saying,

G10 (There) was a--..uh worker,..a villager,

This categorization represents a complex interpretation of the action of the man picking pears; it implies a great deal of information about the man, his way of life, and the motivations of his actions—certainly far more than is actually shown in the film. In our study, far more Greeks than Americans commit themselves to an interpretation of the pearpicker's occupation through the noun they choose to refer to him by. This can be seen in Table 4, which shows the names used for the man and how many speakers used them.

The noninterpretive nouns used are *man* and *guy* in English, "person" (*anthropos*) and "gentleman" (*kirios*, rather like "mister" or "sir") in Greek. At least one of these unmarked categorizations is used by all speakers at some point in their narratives. There is also a set of nouns used for the man in English which are particular but still not interpretive. Two Americans call him the *pearpicker* and the *protagonist*. These nouns give more information about the man than do the unmarked nouns *man* and *guy*, but not more information than is presented in the film.

---

[8]The ability to recognize lexical choice as an interpretive device is one of the basic skills of critical reading and writing which are taught in Freshman English and Academic Skills classes.

TABLE 4
Words Used for Pearpicker

English	Number of Speakers	Greek	Number of Speakers
Noninterpretive		*Noninterpretive*	
man	16	*anthropos* ("person")	12
guy	4	*kirios* ("gentleman")	8
total	20	total	20
Particular			
pearpicker	1		
protagonist	1		
total	2		
Interpretive		*Interpretive*	
Chicano man	1	*mesilix* ("middleaged one")	1
farm laborer	1	*erghatis* ("worker")	3
farm worker	1	*yeorghos* ("farmer")	3
farmer	1	*aghrotis* ("farmer")	3
total	4	*farmer* ("farmer")	1
		idhioktitis tu ktimatos ("proprietor of the land")	1
		choriatis ("villager")	1
		total	13

71

The name *Chicano man* used by one American is interpretive of the man's identity, just as the Greek word for "middleaged one" (*mesilix*) represents a judgment based on the man's appearance. Therefore these words are considered "interpretive." Yet they are not so in the same sense as the others in that category. Judgments about the man's ethnic identity and age do not represent broad assumptions about his way of life as do the words *farmer* and *worker*.

It is not surprising that no Greeks chose a categorization for the man which reflects an interpretation of his ethnic identity, given the practical irrelevance of Chicano identity in Greece. Although only one American used "Chicano man" as the noun phrase with which to refer to the pearpicker, fully half of the American speakers gave some verbal indication of similar interpretations. They commented that the man was, for example, "sort of Spanish looking" or "of Spanish or Mexican descent." The high frequency of this interpretation likely comes from the ethnic heterogeneity of American society and the consequent salience of ethnic identity for members of that culture.

In contrast, only one Greek commented on the man's ethnic identity; this was G12, whose narrative has already been presented.

G12 (it) happened in Mexico. . . (I) suppose, . . . the people seemed (like) Mexicans to me,

G12 did not differentiate the pearpicker from the other characters when she assigned ethnic identity. Rather, she identified all the characters as Mexican and therefore decided that the film took place in Mexico.[9] In other words, the ethnic identity of the pearpicker in particular did not have significance for her.[10]

More Greek than American speakers attributed to the man an occupation motivating his activities. Three Americans decided that he was a farmer, or a farm laborer or worker. In contrast, eleven Greeks—more than half—made an interpretation of the man's occupation. Three called him a worker; eight decided he was a farmer.[11] A twelfth called him a "villager," which is not a

---

[9]This is another instance of the phenomenon I have dubbed *generalization* (Tannen 1979b); that is, an element which was seen is recalled as having occurred more often or in greater number.

[10]An even more striking contrast was found by John Dubois, in narratives told by Guatemalan villagers who had seen the pear film. The Guatemalans often described the ethnicity of the boys ("gringos") but never that of the man.

[11]The categorization "farmer" took three different lexical forms in Greek, as a result of the diglossic Greek langauge situation (see Ferguson 1972). *Yeorghos* is the term in *katharevusa* ("puristic" or "learned"; Ferguson's "high register"). *Aghrotis* is the term in demotic, the commonly spoken idiom (Ferguson's "low register"). *Farmer* is the loan word from English. All three forms are common in Greek conversation. Furthermore, the designation "proprietor of the land" seems to presuppose that the man is a farmer.

profession but does indicate assumptions about his way of life. That the Greeks were more likely to characterize the man as a farmer is easy to attribute to the preponderance in Greece of small owner-operated farms. What is interesting for our purposes is that the Greeks were more inclined to make that interpretation overt.

INTERPRETIVE OMISSION

It has been seen that G12 "played down" parts of the film which did not contribute to her interpretation. She also omitted parts of the film which would have detracted from her rosy picture of the film's world. For example, she omitted to mention that the boy fell off his bicycle. She also omitted the entire last scene in which the three boys pass by the tree where the man has discovered that his pears are missing.

G12's narrative is extreme in this sense but indicative of a pattern which is widespread in the data. As shown by their being shorter on the average, the Greek narratives are less likely to include information which does not contribute to their themes. This can be seen clearly in the ways in which the Greeks and Americans told about the scene where the boy falls off the bicycle. The events depicted in the film are as follows:

1. The boy is riding his bicycle.
2. A girl is riding her bicycle.
3. The boy and girl pass each other on their bikes.
4. The boy's hat flies off his head.
5. The boy turns his head backwards.
6. A bicycle wheel hits a rock.
7. The boy is on the ground under his fallen bike.

Although causality is not clearly discernible in the film, most speakers in both groups speculate about or impute causality in their stories. However, Americans tended to mention all the elements in this sequence of events, whether or not they included them in an interpretation of causality, whereas the Greeks tended to mention only those elements which they used in their explanations of why the boy fell. Table 5 shows who and what got mentioned in the narratives.

Regardless of how they explained the reason for the fall, most Americans (thirteen) mentioned all three possible causes in their stories (the girl, the rock, and the hat). Only four Greeks did this. The rest of the Americans (seven) mentioned two elements of that scene (the girl and the rock). No American mentioned only one. Nearly half the Greeks, however, did just that: mentioned only one element (only the girl or only the rock). In most cases, the

TABLE 5
Objects Mentioned in Fall Scene

Speakers Mentioning	English	Greek
Girl only	0	7
Rock only	0	2
Girl and hat	0	1
Girl, rock, hat	13	4
Girl and rock	7	6

one element mentioned was that to which they attributed causality. The overall pattern, in other words, is, once again, for the Americans to include details simply because they were there, whereas the Greeks tend to include details only if they contribute to the story line being developed.

ATTRIBUTION OF CAUSALITY

The line between interpretation and incorrect statement is often thin. For example, the narrative by G10 quoted at the beginning of this chapter includes the statement that the boy lost his hat "as he crashed with the girl." The film shows no collision between the two bikes; the collision is a reconstruction based on the speaker's expectations about what might happen when two bikes are shown heading for each other in a film. But G10 is not alone in this error. She is one of four Greek speakers who make such a statement. Although no Americans in our study actually state that the two bikes collide, yet they clearly have the same expectations, as shown in the comments of the following two:

E2 and you think "UH." You know "Are they going to collide,"
E7 and you wonder if there's going to be a collision. ... But .. instead they just .. kind of .. brush .. by each other

Again we see a pattern in which Greeks and Americans have similar expectations, but for the Greeks the expectations form the basis for development of an interesting story line, whereas the Americans take account of the expectation in their recall of detail and their report of their experience as movieviewers.

Although none of them attributes the fall to a collision, the Americans nonetheless explain the fall in some way. Any explanation of causality is in effect an interpretation; a film cannot "show" *why* something happened. Therefore, there are variations in speakers' accounts of why the boy fell off his bike. For the Americans, however, the range of explanations given is strikingly narrow. As seen in Table 6, three-fourths of the Americans (fifteen of them) explain that the boy fell because he turned and his bicycle hit a rock;

TABLE 6
Explanations of Cause of Fall

Cause	Number of Speakers Giving Cause	
	American	Greek
Turning and hitting rock	15	8
Tripping on rock	4	4
Looking at girl	0	2
Meeting with girl	0	1
Collision with girl	0	4
Rushing (and maybe also girl)	0	1
Tipping hat	1	0

four more give the compatible but more succinct explanation that he hit a rock. The largest number of Greek speakers (eight) also say that the boy turned and hit a rock, another four say only that he hit the rock. But eight other Greeks give one of four other explanations: the boy collided with, met, or looked at the girl, or he was rushing.

Besides the four Greeks who said that the bicycles collided, another said that the boy fell during his "meeting" (*sinandisi*) with the girl, thus implying, though not stating, that the bicycles made contact. In general, the Greeks made more of the role played by the girl in this series of events. No American attributed the boy's fall to the girl's presence, but nine (nearly half) of the Greeks considered the girl to be involved in the causality. (It is impossible not to speculate that this may reflect a greater tendency among the Greeks to interpret along lines of cultural clichés such as boy-meets-girl.) All but one of the Americans limited themselves to talking about the events which were depicted in the film: the bicycle wheel hit the rock, and the boy turned his head. Again, the Greeks showed greater variety in their accounts. One noticeable exception is the American who erroneously recalled that the boy had tipped his hat: a gesture associated with a boy-meets-girls script.

PHILOSOPHIZING AND PERSONALIZING

A number of Greek speakers interpreted events to the point of philosophizing. For example, G16 continued to comment on the film after she had finished telling what happened in it. She showed herself to be a very perceptive film analyst in a literary criticism tradition by focusing on the existence of conflicts in the film. Following is her commentary. (The passage is rendered in English without pauses and false starts to facilitate reading.)

G16 *Pandos echi-- stichia etsi-- fisika ke to-- ke o nearos pu pire to kofini. . . egho to krino as pume oti-- kanonika dhen eprepe na to pari. . to pire. . stin archi. . . ala meta me tis me tin praxi ton nearon*

pu to xanafonaxan eno dhe zitisan . . tus-- e--dhose meta achladhia.
Ke--. . . ke stin archi etsi o-- kirios pu ta mazeve t'achladhia /???/
poli ta proseche ta--. . afto . . . dhichni etsi anthropo pu--
. . . dhiladhi iche poles andithesis mesa to ergho. . . Eno stin archi--
prodhiath prodhiatithes oti--. . . tha dhosi-- achladhia as pume to
pedhi xero 'gho . . sikonete ke fevghi. . . . Ala meta-- tin ora pu tu
dhinun to kapelo metanioni ke xanadhini. Ke o kirios pu mazeve
stin archi ke nomizes oti--. . . ta mazeve yia ton eafto tu ke dhichni
enan anthropo alo ti stighmi pu-- vlepi ta pedhia pu
xanafevghune . . . ke-- /ena/ kathenas kratai to achladhi ke vlepi
ot'ine dhika tu dhe-- ke dhen tus fonazi . . erchese se sighrusi ke les
kitaxe dhen itan etsi /pu icha sto nu./ . . . Echi poles sighrusis mesa
ke--

It has such elements as, of course, and the young man who took the
basket, I believe that he shouldn't have taken it, he took it at first,
but then with the young men's deed who called to him and didn't
ask, he gave them pears. And in the beginning the gentleman who
was gathering pears took great care of them, this shows the man to
be, that is, there are many contrasts in the film. Although in the
beginning you believe that the child will give them pears, he goes
away. But then after they give him the hat he changed his mind and
gives them also. And the gentleman who was harvesting in the
beginning and you thought that he was collecting them for himself
and it shows a different man when he sees the children going away
each holding a pear and sees that they are his and doesn't call them
you see a conflict and you think it wasn't as I thought. It has many
conflicts in it and--

Whereas G16 focused on the theme of repeated conflicts in the film, G11 saw
coherence in the many "falls" in it and related this to her own philosophy and
emotions:

G11 *Mono pu-- egho tha'legha oti . . . oles ekines i ptosis pu mas*
edhichne to dhendro apo ti ghi-- uh opos epefte . . to dhendro . . . sti
ghi uh to to fruto tu dhendru sti ghi . . . ithele na dhixi oti ola ta
praghmata archizun ap ti ghi ke katalighun pali sti ghi yiat' iche
poles ptosis. Dhe xero dhen-- ala . . . egho tha'thela kati para pano
y'afto. Afto ipa oti kati mu lipi. Ne. Ine poli oreo . . eh ala-- su ipa . .
tha ithela na edhichne ke kati alo. Emena mu fanike lighaki lipso.
Isos yiati to /pira/ ap tin archi . . mm afti ti skepsi epidhi . . prosexa
poli tin ptosi tu achladhiu apo to dhendro. Isos mu 'mine afto ke
ime lighaki pesimistria . . . pistevo oti ola proerchond'ap to
skotadhi ke xanapighenun sto skotadhi. Kitaxe na to paris ke--

mm . . tsk . . . ke epistimonika pes . . choris fandasia . . . oli . .
silamvanometha sti mitra mias ghinekos mesa s'ena skotadhi . . . ke
xanapighenune ston tafo . . pali se skotadhi. Ime pesimistria dhen
echo dhi pote kalo sti zoi mu ute-- xero an tha dho . . . dhen me
endhiaferi an tha dho . . y'afto to idha kapos milo mirolatri/s/
/???/ . . . ke isos epidhi echo ke prosopika provlimata afti tin
epochi . . . im' epireazmeni dhen skeftomun pote-- dhiaforetika
dhiladhi dhen ipirxa pote esiodhoxi . . . dhe nomizo oti
ipirxa. . . . Tipot' alo. Efchom' omos na iparxi mia stighmi pu tha'ne
kali yia mena. Ke yia sena. Dhen xero. Ine pola praghmata pu
/???/ . . . xeris . . . otan pistevis poli se kati . . ke xafnika su--
. . . vlepis oti ine-- chalkino ot'ine-- tipotenio . . . /?????/ ine fovero--
xeris . . . ke egho'cho klonisti afto to xero . . yiati me parakoluthuse
/?????????/ afto leme xeris efchome na mi perasi para na
apodhichti oti-- tsk . . . oti . . eh-- dhen ine chalkino ot'ine chriso ke
oti tha lampsi. Afto thelo.

G11 Only I would say that all those falls that it showed us . . . the tree
from the earth-- uh as it was falling the tree to the earth uh the the
fruit of the tree to the earth (it) wanted to show that all things begin
from the earth and end up in the earth because (it) had a lot of falls.
I don't know I don't-- but I would have wanted something more for
this (reason). That's what I said that something was missing for me.
Yes it's very nice eh-- but-- I told you I would have wanted it to have
shown something else too. To me it seemed a little lacking. Maybe
because I took it from the beginning this thought because I paid a
lot of attention to the fall of the pear from the tree. Maybe this
stayed with me. And I am a bit of a pessimist I believe that
everything originates from darkness and goes again into darkness.
Look! Take it even-- mm tsk even scientifically say without
imagination everything is conceived in the womb of a woman inside
a darkness and we go again to the grave again to the darkness. I am
a pessimist I have never seen good in my life neither do I know if I
ever will I don't care if I do that's why I saw it somehow
fatalistically . . . and perhaps because I also have problems at this
time . . . I am influenced I never thought differently because I was
never optimistic. I don't think I was. Anything else. I hope however
that there will be a time that it will be good for me. And for you. I
don't know. There are many things that /?????/ you know when you
believe very much in something and suddenly you . . . you see that it
is-- copper that it is-- nothing. It is terrible. You know and I have
been shaken this I know because /?????/ followed me that's what we
say. I hope that it's not passing but that it is gold and that it will
shine. That's what I want.

This is an extreme example. The Greek interviewer found G11's monologue somewhat amusing. But it seems likely that if an American speaker had gone on in this way, the American interviewer would not have simply been amused but would have begun eying the door, fearing she might be closed in with an unbalanced person. These results support my impression, based on several years' residence in Greece, that philosophizing is more common in casual Greek conversation than it is among middle-class Americans. These results correlate, as well, with findings in another study (Tannen, 1979a) in which speakers from these two groups were asked to interpret and comment on a sample conversation. In that study, Greeks turned out to be more likely to personalize their answers.

STYLISTIC VARIATION

The Greek pear narratives give the impression of greater stylistic variation than the American. This results from greater variation on many levels. The tendency to interpret, which has been demonstrated in detail, contributes to this effect. In addition, the choice of lexical items and intonation show greater stylistic range in the Greek pear stories.

The terms used for characters and objects show greater regularity in the American pear narratives than in the Greek. For example, there are twice as many different terms used for the three boys in the Greek than in the American narratives (see Table 7). In all, seven different terms are used to refer to the threesome in the American narratives, and fourteen different terms in the Greek. The American speakers show a marked preference for one term, *boys,* used by sixteen speakers in all and by ten speakers as first mentions. Two other terms, *little boys* and *kids,* are used by six and seven speakers respectively; the word *guys* is used by three. Thus four terms are used by more than one speaker; three other terms (*little kids, buddies, people*) are used by only one speaker each. In other words, only three speakers use distinctive terms, that is, terms they alone employ. The Greek narratives also exhibit marked preference for one term: *pedhia* ("children"), used by fifteen speakers in all and by ten speakers as first mentions. However, there is greater variety in the other terms used. Five other terms are used by more than one speaker; eight terms are so distinctive that each is used by only one speaker.[12]

---

[12]Each of the Greek terms has its own connotations and associations, as is the case with all stylistic variables. English equivalents are necessarily rough approximations. Figure 7 shows four different but related forms, for example, based on the same root, each of which has a slightly different meaning. *Pitsirikádhes* is the plural of *pitsirikás* (necessarily male, and somewhat stylized); *pitsiríki* is the plural of *pitsiríkos* (necessarily male, and less stylized); *pitsiríkia* is the plural of *pitsiríki* (used for male or female children); *pitsiriká* is an aberrant form (neither I nor any of my native informants could report having heard it before. *Pitsiríka,* with penultimate stress, is used for a female child, but the speaker uttered the word with final stress.)

TABLE 7
Terms Used for the Threesome

| Term | American | | |
	Number of Mentions	Number of Speakers Mentioning	Number of Speakers Using for First Mention
boys	44	16	10
little boys	21	6	6
kids	14	7	3
guys	6	3	0
little kids	1	1	1
buddies	1	1	0
people	1	1	0
	Greek		
pedhia ("children")	37	15	10
neari ("young men")	5	3	1
pedhakia ("little children")	4	3	2
aghoria ("boys")	3	3	1
aghorakia ("little boys")	3	1	1
fili tu ("his friends")	2	2	1
pitsirikadhes ("kids")	2	2	0
pitsiriki ("kids")	4	1	0
bobires ("runts")	2	1	1
pitsirikia ("kids")	1	1	0
pitsirika ("kids")	1	1	1
mikri ("little ones")	1	1	0
mikra pedhia ("little children")	1	1	1
sinomiliki tu ("ones of the same age")	1	1	1

79

Stylistic variation is seen (or, rather, is heard) in the intonation characteristic of the Greek narratives. Most of the Greek stories give the impression of sharply rising and dropping intonation patterns, with striking contrasts between the peaks and falls. The acoustic displays which resulted from processing the narratives in a pitch extractor clearly show the difference between the Greek and American styles (see Figure 1). Each section shown is typical of the displays resulting from the respective set of narratives. The entire set of displays for the American speakers looked more or less like the section shown in Figure 1(a); the entire set of displays for the Greek speakers looked more or less like the section shown in Figure 1(b). Comparison of the top lines, which are the amplitude displays, shows that the Greek speaker used more dramatic shifts in loudness. The lower lines, the pitch displays, dramatize the sharp rises and falls in pitch which yielded the striking intonational variation of the Greek stories, in contrast with the relatively flat intonation of the American speakers.

Stylistic variation on all these levels contributes to the overriding effect of the Greek narratives as "good stories," in keeping with the emerging goal of the Greek speakers. This phenomenon yields concrete evidence which may explain, in part, why American speakers often sound "monotonous" and "dull" to Greek listeners, whereas Greek speakers often strike American listeners as "colorful" and "dynamic."

CONVENTIONS OF MOVIE COMMENTARY

In asking why the Greek and American narratives based on the pearpicking film differed in the ways discussed, we must consider a range of possible influencing factors. To begin with, the question—"What happened in the movie?"—though translated from English to Greek, cannot be considered identical in the two languages; the pragmatic effect of these "comparable" words might be very different when used in the different cultures. Moreover, the situation in which the stories were elicited must have had different social significance for members of the two cultures. Being the subject of an experiment is an identifiable and expectable activity for undergraduates at the University of California, Berkeley; it is not so for students at the Hellenic American Union in Athens. Psychology, as conceived in American social science, does not exist as a discipline even at the Greek university. Differing definitions of the task at hand must necessarily trigger different verbal strategies, especially in an interview situation in which the speaker is trying to satisfy what she perceives as the requirements of the questioner.

Telling about a movie, however, is a practice that many modern city dwellers engage in under a variety of social circumstances. Expectations about how this speech activity is done must have influenced the narratives in

Pitch Extractor Displays

(a) Section of display of an American speaker's narrative

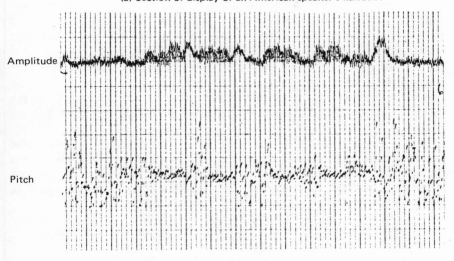

(b) Section of display of a Greek speaker's narrative

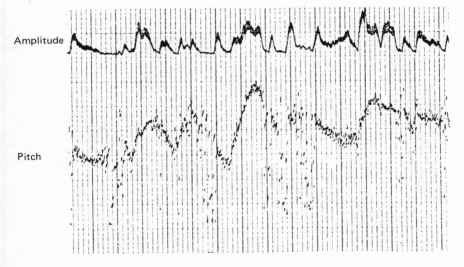

FIG. 1.

81

the present study. As the popular culture critic Michael Arlen (1974) points out, Americans are media-wise and pride themselves on "an assertively cynical savviness" about behind-the-scenes machinations of movies and TV. This was seen in the American speakers' preoccupation with the film's soundtrack, camera angles, costumes, and so on. There is no evidence that such media-sophistication is valued in Greek society.

To gain some insight into conventional modes of talking about movies, I turned to movie reviews in Greek and American newspapers. It is clear, of course, that movie reviews are part of a written rhetoric, whereas the pear narratives were spoken. But striking similarities between the approaches found in the published reviews and the spoken narratives suggest that the strategies used in the two forms are conventionalized and related to each other.

Following are excerpts taken from reviews published in newspapers of comparable standing in San Francisco and Athens. The reviews are both of Russian director Eisenstein's *Ten Days That Shook the World.* The two accounts begin similarly, but they develop rather differently. The American reviewer comments on Eisenstein's contribution to cinema:

> From his first film "The Strike," he developed new principles for building up dramatic action, enhanced the cinema language, and pioneered expressive potentials in sharp cutting and foreshortening. Nowhere is the force of his images felt as remarkably as in his "Ten Days That Shook the World."
>
> —Norman K. Dorn, *San Francisco Sunday Examiner and Chronicle,* Mar. 2, 1969, p. 4.

Now the Greek review, which also harks back to Eisenstein's first film and addresses his contributions to cinema:

> *Stin proti kiolas tenia tu o Sergei Michailovits Aizenstain edhixe tin pliri orimotita tis technis tu, pu ine sinchronos politiki praxi ke piima. ... Omos simera ... vlepume pali me thavmasmo tis ikones tu Aizenstain dhiavghis, sklires san dhiamandi n'anditithende ke na organononde rithmika s'ena ekriktiko optiko piima, to piima tu prodhomenu lau, pu telika tha nikisi.*
>
> Even in his first film, Sergei Michelovitch Eisenstein shows the full maturity of his art, which is at the same time political act and poetry. ... Today ... we see again with admiration Eisenstein's images, clear and hard as diamonds, juxtaposed and organized rhythmically in a bursting optical poem, the poem of the betrayed people who will triumph in the end.
>
> —G. Bakoyiannopoulos, *Kathimerini,* April 8, 1975, p. 2.

Both reviewers draw attention to Eisenstein's visual images, but the American reviewer uses cinematic jargon ("sharp cutting and foreshortening") and discusses the director's technical accomplishments ("developed new principles...”). In contrast, the Greek reviewer uses nonspecific poetic language ("bursting optical poem," "hard as diamonds"), makes broad statements of praise ("full maturity of his art"), and focuses, finally, on the film's message ("the betrayed people who will triumph") rather than its technique.

Another pair of reviews concerns Swedish director Sjoman's *I Am Curious Yellow*. An American reviewer, Vincent Canby, begins by saying the film is "a good, serious movie about a society in transition, told in terms of recording devices—pads and pencils, posters, cinema verité interviews, tape recordings and the fiction film." Near the end of the review he writes:

> Sjoman is a former assistant to Ingmar Bergman and has great fun playing with the movie medium. At one point he cuts to the Stockholm Board of Film Censors as the gentlemen register their surprise at Lena's behavior. There is an extended sequence depicting the imaginary implementation of a national policy of nonviolence. In a moment of complete frustration, Lena fantasizes on her general war with males and her specific victory over Borje as she cstrates him. All of this makes for a distant, cold and tricky movie.
>
> —*New York Times*, Mar. 11, 1969, p. 42.

The following is the final section of an Athenian review of the same film.

> *I tenia, lipon, telika ine ochi mono mia oxia kritiki tu suidhiku prototipu, ala ke tis sexualikis eleftherias. Kato apo ton epithetiko anarchismo tu o Sgheman afini na provalun ta ichni tu sindiritismu ke tu puritanismu tu. Sighchronos dhen fenete na sinidhitopii oti me ton tropo pu dhichni ton eafto tu ke to sinerghio ghenai ena neo epipedho fandasias. Pios pezi "rolo" pios zi ti zoi tu? Pu ine i alithia ke pu i techni?*
>
> The film, then, ultimately is not only an acute critique of the Swedish prototype but also of sexual freedom. Beneath his offensive anarchism, Sjoman allows the traces of his conservatism and puritanism to emerge. At the same time he doesn't seem to be aware that with the way in which he reveals himself and his studio, a new level of fantasy is born. Who is playing a "role"? Who is living his life? Where is truth and where is art?
>
> —G. Bakoyiannopoulos, *Kathimerini*, April 8, 1975, p. 2.

Again, the American review uses cinematic jargon ("cuts," "extended sequences"), whereas the Greek review uses language of broader artistic application ("critique," "truth," "art"). Both reviewers comment upon the intrusion of the director into his film. Canby is interested in the cinematic impact of the technique ("playing with the movie medium," "a distant, cold and tricky movie"). In contrast, Bakoyiannopoulos is concerned with the emerging artistic vision and its message ("Who is playing a 'role'?" "Where is truth and where art?").

At the same time that published commentators, such as movie reviewers, much reflect the values of their culture, expressing ideas in a way that is expected, they also create expectations: repeated exposure to such standardized forms of rhetoric must influence members of a culture over time.

CONCLUSION: CONTRASTING RHETORICS

In an attempt to understand the bases of the contrasting rhetorical conventions which surfaced in the Greek and American narratives, I turned to recent research on the contrasting rhetorical strategies associated with oral and literate tradition (Cook-Gumperz and Gumperz, 1980). Basil Bernstein (1972) suggested that working-class speakers of British English employ a "restricted code" which does not make contextualization overt; middle- and upper-class British speakers employ an "elaborated code" in which they explicitly contextualize, that is, fill in pronoun referents, background information, underlying assumptions, and so on. Bernstein's hypothesis has been misinterpreted to imply linguistic deficit in lower-class speakers and egregiously misapplied, but he was among the first to observe that groups of speakers differ in their choices of linguistic content.

Bernstein's dichotomy is similar to that which underlies the excellent work of Goody and Watt (1962), Goody (1977), and Olson (1977) on the contrast between oral and literate strategies. According to these scholars, the verbal strategies associated with oral tradition differ from those associated with literate tradition. Literate culture does not replace oral culture in any society but rather is superimposed on it. As Goody (1977) points out, literate culture becomes associated with formal education, "for schools inevitably place an emphasis on the 'unnatural,' 'unoral,' 'decontextualized' processes of repetition, copying, verbatim memory" (p. 22). There exists then a "gap between the public literate tradition of the school, and the very different and indeed often directly contradictory private oral tradition of the family and peer group" (Goody and Watt, p. 342). I would postulate that the Greeks in this study, as a result of their cultural and historical development, were employing conventionalized forms and strategies associated with the oral tradition of the family and peer group, and the Americans were employing strategies associated with the literate tradition of schools. Cook-Gumperz and Gumperz (1980) point out that American and perhaps other Western European societies have conventionalized literate rhetorical strategies for oral use in many public situations.

Thus, as was seen, Greeks did not use direct mention of, or allusion to, the film as a film. They knew that the hearer knew that they were talking about a film; they did not need to make that shared background knowledge and context overt. Furthermore, by building a story which includes characters' thoughts and emotions as well as judgments of their actions and which omits irrelevant details and focuses on events significant for the theme, the Greeks were telling stories designed to interest their listeners—also strategies associated not with school but with social or peer interaction. Hence, for example, to say that the two bicycles collided makes a better story than to say that they might have collided but did not. In contrast, to the extent that Americans were preoccupied with accuracy of detail and correct recall, they were adhering to strategies associated with the literate culture of schools.

In these senses, the code used by Greek speakers may be considered *restricted*—that is, less detail is made overt. The American narratives then may be considered examples of an *elaborated code,* insofar as they were longer and more full of detail. These differences, however, only reflect strategies associated with the specific task at hand: telling about a movie in answer to an interview question. In the study of conversational style associated with in-group talk (Tannen, 1979a), I found that in commenting on the expression of preferences in a conversation between a married couple, Greek respondents expected far more elaboration then Americans. In that setting, the code preferred by Greeks turned out to be elaborated, whereas the Americans showed preference for a restricted code.

I would postulate, then, not differences in underlying cognitive processes but in conventionalization of appropriate rhetorical forms. This hypothesis is in keeping with Bruner's (1978) analysis, explained in a review of a recently released study conducted in 1932 by Russian psychologist Alexander Luria. Examining differences in cognitive style between illiterate and educated peasants, Luria indicated that his illiterate subjects employed functional and concrete reasoning rather than abstract reasoning. Bruner notes, however, after examining Luria's data, that the peasants' reasoning, though different, is "abstract" in its own way. He observes:

> Most of what has emerged from studies of Africans, Eskimos, Aborigines, and other groups shows that the *same* basic mental functions are present in adults of any culture. What differs is the deployment of these functions: what is considered an appropriate strategy suited to the situation and the task (p. 88).

This is substantially the conclusion of Cole and Scribner (1974), who assert, "We are unlikely to find cultural differences in basic component cognitive processes" (p. 193) but rather in *"functional cognitive systems,* which may vary with cultural variations" (p. 194). In yet another realm, Ekman (1973) concludes that people from different cultures exhibit the same facial expressions in association with specific emotions; they differ with respect to "display rules"-- that is, when they deem it fitting to allow others to witness those facial expressions of emotion.

The cultural differences which have emerged in the present study constitute real differences in habitual ways of talking which operate in actual interaction and create impressions on listeners—the intended impression, very likely, on listeners from the same culture, but possibly confused or misguided impressions on listeners from other cultures. It is easy to see how stereotypes may be created and reinforced. Considering the differences in oral narrative strategies found in the pear narratives, it is not surprising that Americans might develop the impression that Greeks are romantic and irrational, and Greeks might conclude that Americans are cold and lacking in human feelings. In fact, Vassiliou, Triandis, Vassiliou, and McGuire (1972) documented the existence of just such mutual stereotypes.

As John Gumperz (1977) points out in his work on other ethnic groups, conversation with a particular member of a different cultural group, forms the basis for conclusions about the other's personality, abilities, and intentions. In a culturally heterogeneous society like the United States, such conclusions in turn form the basis of decisions not only of a personal nature, such as whether to pursue a friendship, but also in professional matters, such as public service, educational, and employment situations-- where the results of misinterpretations can be tragic. By locating the sources of such judgments in ways of talking, that is, in conventionalized rhetorical strategies, we may hope to contribute to improved understanding of communication between members of different cultural or subcultural groups.

REFERENCES

Arlen, M. *The view from Highway One*. New York: Ballantine, 1974.

Bauman, R., & Sherzer, J. *Explorations in the ethnography of speaking*. London: Cambridge University Press, 1974.

Becker, A. L. Text-building, epistemology and aesthetics in Javanese shadow theatre. In A. L. Becker and A. A. Yengoyan (Eds.). *The imagination of reality*. Norwood, N.J.: Ablex, 1979.

Bernstein, B. Social class, language and socialization. In P. P. Giglioli (Ed.), *Language and social context*. London: Penguin, 1972.

Bruner, J. Review of Alexander Luria, *Cognitive development: its cultural and social foundations. Human Nature*, (January 1978).

Cole, M., & Scribner, S. *Culture and thought: A psychological introduction*. New York: Wiley, 1974.

Cook-Gumperz, J., & Gumperz, J. From oral to written culture: the transition to literacy. In M. F. Whiteman (Ed.), *Variation in writing*. New York: Lawrence Erlbaum, 1980.

Ekman, P. *Darwin and facial expression: a century of research in review*. New York: Academic Press, 1973.

Erikson, F. One Function of Proxemic Shifts in Face to Face Interaction. In A. Kendon, R. Harris, & H. R. Key (Eds.), *The organization of behavior in face to face interaction*. The Hague/Chicago: Mouton, Aldine, 1976.

Ferguson, C. Diglossia. In P. P. Giglioli (Ed.), *Language and social context*. London: Penguin, 1972.

Friedrich, P., & Redfield, J. Speech as a personality symbol: the case of Achilles, *Language, 54* (June 1978).

Goffman, E. *The presentation of self in everyday life.* New York: Doubleday Anchor, 1959.

Goody, J. R. Memory and learning in oral and literate culture: The reproduction of the Bagre. (Ms., 1977.) Department of Social Anthropology, University of Cambridge.

Goody, J. R., & Watt, I. The consequences of literacy. In P.P. Giglioli (Ed.), *Language and social context.* London: Penguin, 1972.

Gumperz, J. Sociocultural knowledge in conversational inference. In M. Saville-Troike (Ed.), *28th annual roundtable: monograph series on languages and linguistics.* Washington, D. C.: Georgetown University, 1977.

Gumperz, J., & Hymes, D. *Directions in sociolinguistics: the ethnography of communication.* New York: Holt, Rinehart & Winston, 1972.

Hall, E. *The silent language.* New York: Doubleday, 1959.

Kaplan, R. Cultural thought patterns in inter-cultural education. *Language learning,* 1966, *16.*

Lakoff, R. T. Stylistic strategies within a grammar of style. *The annals of the new york academy of science,* 1979.

Mills, C. W. Situated actions and vocabularies of motive. In Manis and Meltzer (Eds.), *Symbolic Interaction: a reader in social psychology.* Boston: Allyn & Bacon, 1967.

Olson, D. From utterance to text: the bias of language in speech and writing. *Harvard Educational Review, 47* (August 1977).

Polanyi, L. 1979. So what's the point? *Semiotica, 25*:3/4.

Sanches, M. & Blount, B. *Sociocultural dimensions of language use.* New York: Academic Press, 1975.

Tannen, D. Ethnicity as conversational style. *Sociolinguistic working paper #55.* Austin, Texas: Southwest Regional Development Laboratory, 1979 (a).

Tannen, D. What's in a frame? Surface evidence for underlying expectations. In R. Freedle (Ed.), *New directions in discourse processing.* Norwood, N.J.: Ablex, 1979 (b).

Vassiliou, V., Triandis, H., Vassiliou, G. & McGuire, H. Interpersonal contact and stereotyping. In H. Triandis (Ed.), *The analysis of subjective culture.* New York: Wiley, 1972.

Wolfson, N. Speech events and natural speech: some implications for sociolinguistic methodology, *Language in Society,* 1976, *5,* 189–209.

3 Factors Influencing Lexical Choice in Narrative

Pamela Downing
University of California, Berkeley

The speaker who decides to tell a story must decide much more than *what* to tell. The decisions he makes as to *how* to tell it, the way he (literally) puts it into words, will be important in determining not only whether his addressees follow the story, but also whether they correctly perceive and go along with the point of the story, how they evaluate the speaker's personality and skill as a narrator, and how they assess the relationship between speaker and hearer. Certain principles of lexical choice remain constant from situation to situation, from speaker to speaker, from language A to language B. Others are highly language- or context-dependent. Thus, though the speaker may tell "the same story" to his grandmother and his friends at the local bar, the *way* in which he tells it is likely to differ considerably on the two occasions.

With an eye toward ferreting out some of these principles of lexical choice, I have considered the usage of content words (as opposed to function words) in the twenty English and twenty Japanese narratives collected in response to our film, evaluating in detail all nominal references to concrete entities (1363 in the English narratives, 786 in the Japanese).[1] The results of this analysis suggest that speakers of both languages make extensive use of a body of referentially "basic" lexemes, but that any of a number of cognitive, stylistic, and textual constraints may cause the speaker to abandon these basic terms in

---

[1]The striking discrepancy between the number of nouns used by English and Japanese speakers occurs in part because the Japanese narratives were, on the whole, much shorter than the English ones. In addition, the Japanese speakers often exercised their option of dispensing with nominal references to entities assumed to be in the focus of the addressee's consciousness at that point in the narrative.

categorizing a given object at a given point in her discourse. In this paper I try to characterize the interaction of these principles and constraints, using illustrative examples drawn from our English and Japanese film narratives.

As a starting point, let us assume that, before she begins speaking, our would-be narrator has a rough idea of what it is that she wants to talk about. That is, she has in mind certain states and events, as well as participants in those states and events, which she wishes to describe in intelligible fashion to her listeners. This situation can be contrasted with one in which the speaker initially has in mind certain words which she wants to use and manages to come up with a linguistic context into which she can embed them. Although speakers may occasionally use this second technique, it was probably not a dominant factor in the way our subjects constructed their narratives, which were spontaneous and based on a topic determined by the addressee.

Suppose, for example, that the speaker wishes to describe the episode in our film in which a man picks pears, periodically climbing down the ladder on which he is standing to deposit his fruit in some baskets on the ground. First of all, she must make some decisions about how detailed her description will be; will she characterize the entire episode in one sentence or draw it out into a sequence of clauses? These decisions will of course have important consequences in terms of the matter of lexical choice; if the description is to be brief, words of broad referential scope are likely to be chosen, since by their use the speaker is able to capture and convey the entire scene she has in mind. Or one significant subevent, and the lexeme denoting it, may be chosen to represent the larger episode as a whole. If the speaker opts for a more detailed description, more lexemes of narrower referential scope are likely to appear.

Different speakers choose different strategies. Compare, for example, the following descriptions of the pear-picking episode produced by two of our American subjects:

(1) (a) Subject A: Um--... A man was picking pears in ... what seemed to be his orchard,
   (b) Subject B: Um--... the s- the scene opens up ... with .. um ... you see a tree k kay? And there's .. a ladder coming out .. o of the tree, and there's a man at the top of the ladder, you can't see him yet.... And--... then it shifts, and you see him, plucking a pear from the tree.... And you watch him pluck a few pears and he'd drop them into his ... thing, .. he's wearing like an apron with huge pockets.... but I don't think you see the apron at first. (...) ... And--uh--... and then he gets down out of the tree, and he ... dumps all his pears into the basket, and the basket's full, and one of the pears drops down to the floor, and he ... picks it up, and he takes his kerchief off, and he ... wipes it off, and ... places it in in the basket which is ... very full.... That's why it fell off in the

first place.... And--um--then he climbs back up the ladder,...and he...starts picking pears again.... And then while he's up in the ladder,..let's see is it while he's up in the ladder? or...or before.... um--...anyway a guy comes by leading a goat. (...) Then they walk by--...the man who was picking the pears.... who looks like a Mexican-American if that's important?...um-- ...And he's ge he's getting down out of the tree, and fucking with the ladder,...and--...he sees..and and there's one...full basket of pears there, and and an empty basket.

Subject B has chosen to break the event down and describe it in much greater detail than Subject A. Thus, when we consider the vocabulary used in the two instances, we find that subject B has used a great variety of specific verbs to describe the actions that Subject A handles with a single verb, *pick*, which, in this case, expands to encompass the entire series of activities which includes the actual picking of the pears as its most salient component:

(2)		*Subject A*	*Subject B*
	General action:	pick	pick
	Specific actions:	—	pluck, pick
			drop
			get down
			dump
			drop down, fall
			pick up
			take off
			wipe off
			place
			climb up
			fuck with

Subject B also mentions explicitly many of the participants in the scene: the tree, the ladder, the man, individual pears, the apron, the apron pockets, an individual basket, and the man's kerchief; Subject A confines herself to the mention of the man, the pears, and the orchard.

Although the narratives of these two subjects represent the extremes of our sample, the discrepancy between them illustrates nicely how the decisions the speaker makes with respect to *what* she will talk about, in what degree of detail, have an important effect on the matter of lexical choice. The speaker who chooses to describe an episode in only the sketchiest terms typically uses more general lexemes which can refer to entire events containing many subevents, e.g., *pick* as opposed to *pluck,* and mentions high-level participants composed of many potentially mentionable subparts, e.g., *tree* as opposed to *trunk, leaves,* etc. Those speakers who choose to produce a more fine-grained description usually make use of a number of specific terms in their narratives, although the general terms are crucial in introducing and summing up the episode as a whole. Thus, all 20 American subjects used the verb *pick* to refer to the actions of the pearpicker in general, but no single subevent was mentioned by every subject, and no subjects mentioned subevents, such as going up and down the ladder, dumping the pears, etc., without embedding them in a description of the episode as a whole.

The same trend is evident in the choices our subjects made about which entities to mention as participants in the events they described. Just as it was possible to break the pearpicking episode down into any number of subevents, it was possible to mention the participants in the episode as wholes or as parts of wholes. Thus, one subject might choose to mention the pearpicker, his ladder, and the pears he was picking; another subject might choose to mention the pearpicker's hands and face, individual pears, the rungs of the ladder. As Table 1 (pp. 94–95) illustrates, however, subjects generally preferred to mention the whole as opposed to its constituent parts, and subjects who mentioned the parts almost always referred to the whole first. (This table does not include a tabulation of references to the considerable number of entities mentioned *only* as wholes.)

In some instances our speakers chose to refer, not to individual wholes or parts of those wholes, but to apply a single label to a *collection* of individuals, as in (3).

> (3) you got the feeling of spring or summer anyway, at least I did because it was very...the sky was blue, and it seemed...seemed warm....from the activities of *the people.*

This strategy was confined to mentions of a small set of referents in the English narratives and was even less common in the Japanese narratives. Collective mentions are tabulated in Table 2. (This table does not include a tabulation of references to entities which were *never* referred to collectively by any speaker.)

Overall, tabulating the mentions of *all* wholes, collections of wholes, parts, and collections of parts, we have the distribution shown in Table 3, where the preference for mentioning wholes emerges clearly.

A similar pattern emerges with respect to mentions of articles of clothing, which occur only 118/61 times (English/Japanese), compared to the 1435/394 mentions of the persons who wear them. Although clothes cannot strictly be considered parts of human wholes, they generally appear accompanied by people who wear clothes nearly as predictably as they possess heads, arms, and legs. In general, only articles of clothing which are unusual—e.g., the pearpicker's apron—or which are not consistently worn in the traditional manner—e.g., a hat which flies off—are mentioned in our narratives.

It is also interesting to note that mentions of all these parts of wholes (including proper parts and temporary parts, such as articles of clothing) are often preceded in our English narratives by possessive or definite articles, even on initial mentions, which might be expected to be indefinite. These parts are seen as affiliated to their wholes, and this affiliation is expressed by the use of possessives, which occur before 85 percent of the mentions of body parts, for example, and by the use of definite articles which can be appropriately used only because the whole has already been mentioned, setting up the expectation that the part also exists. Thus, in (4) below, the leaves can immediately be referred to as *the* leaves because they have already been introduced indirectly through mention of the tree which bears them.

(4) It opens with um–...I guess a farm worker,...picking pears,...in a tree...And--um–...you see him taking...picking the pears out of *the leaves* and putting them in a...white apron

When our subjects did choose to mention parts, their choice was in general traceable to one of several apparent causes:

(a) the parts belonged to a highly salient, significant, and codable[2] whole, e.g., human body parts
(b) the part mentioned was a clearly delineated element of the whole and was directly involved in the action being described, e.g., ladder rungs, bike rack, apron pockets.
(c) the whole was uncodable and could best be described as a sum of its parts, e.g., paddleball ball, paddle, and string

94 percent of the mentions of (proper) parts in our narratives can be characterized in one of these three ways.

Given the preference for wholes over parts, why, we might ask, did our subjects also prefer to mention *individual* wholes as opposed to *collections* of wholes? In many parts of the film which the subjects were describing, there were collections of individuals which acted, for greater or lesser periods of time, as unitary participants in the events depicted, e.g., a man and a goat and a rope, a boy and his bicycle, each human character and the clothes he or she

---

[2]In using the term *codability* I refer to the ease with which a speaker of a given language can refer to a given entity, as determined by the existence or nonexistence of an appropriate standardized label for it in the lexicon of the language in question. Thus, an entity with a well-known standardized label will be highly codable. For a discussion of various measures of codability, see Brown and Lenneberg (1954), Lantz and Stefflre (1964).

TABLE 1

Nominal and Pronominal Mentions of Concrete Entities: References to Wholes vs. References to Parts

Entity	Wholes		Parts	
	Number mentions in all 20 narratives	Number subjects who mention whole, not parts	Number mentions in all 20 narratives	Number subjects who mention parts, not whole
English:				
Human beings	1435	5	Head 11	0
			Hair 4	0
			Legs 3	0
			Moustache 2	0
			Neck 2	0
			Face 2	0
			Knee 2	0
			Hand 1	0
			Feet 1	0
			Fingers 1	0
	1435		29	
Goat	56	17	Face 1	0
			Neck 1	0
			Stripe 1	0
			Eyes 1	0
	56			
Bicycle	147	8	Rack 4	0
			Handlebars 13	0
			Wheels 2	0
			Front wheel 1	0
			Gears 2	0
	147			

Object			Part		
Ladder	43		Rungs	14	1	0
Apron	19		Pockets	9	4	0
Tree	70		Leaves	15	1	0
			Branch		1	0
			Trunk		1	0
	70				3	
Paddleball	33		Paddle	5	11	3
			Ball		10	3
			String		5	1
	33				26	
	1803				89	

Japanese:

Object			Part		
Human beings	394		Legs	11	4	0
			Head		4	0
			Hands		2	0
			Moustache		2	0
			Hair		2	0
			Face		2	0
			Eyes		2	0
			Neck		1	0
			Chest		1	0
	394				20	
Bicycle	78		Rack	11	6	0
Apron	7		Pockets	2	8	1
Paddleball	5		Ball	2	1	0
			String		2	0
	484				27	

TABLE 2

Nominal and Pronominal Mentions of Concrete Entities: References to
Individuals vs. References to Collections of Individuals

Entity	Individuated Mentions	Collective Mentions
	(Number mentions in all 20 Narratives)	
English:		
Human beings	1058	377
Pears	36	317
Baskets	118	51
Clothing	110	2
Trees	66	8
Rocks	28	2
Roosters	4	1
Wheels	1	1
Braids	—	3
Leaves	—	1
Hands	—	1
Eyes	—	1
Fingers	—	1
Feet	—	1
Pockets	2	2
	1423	769
Japanese:		
Human beings	296	98
Pears	148	31
Baskets	69	15
	513	144

TABLE 3

Nominal and Pronominal Mentions of Concrete Entities

	Indiv. Wholes		Coll. Wholes		Indiv. Parts		Coll. Parts	
English	1723	(67%)	758	(29%)	75	(3%)	11	(0%)
Japanese	660	(78%)	144	(17%)	37	(4%)	—	

wore, the pears in a basket. Yet rarely were these collocations referred to with a single all-inclusive noun phrase. In some cases, the members of the group were mentioned individually, but in most instances the group was implicitly referred to by means of the mention of its most salient part(s). Thus, in lieu of saying "The boy and his hat and his shirt and his pants and his belt and shoes and socks and his bicycle moved off down the road," our narrators were typically content with such sentences as "The boy went off on his merry way."

Because the existence of a temporary collocation consisting of the boy and his bicycle and his clothes had been previously established by means of explicit mention or by failure to note any striking departure from our standard expectations regarding appropriate attire, etc., it would be redundant for the speaker to mention repeatedly all the participants in the temporary entourage. Reference to a single token representative will suffice, at least until the composition of the collocation changes.

Another limiting factor can be found in the dearth of lexicalized labels for temporary collections of individuals. This situation presumably derives from the fact that it is the business of a language to provide lexical options with which speakers may refer to referents which are important to the community as a whole. Since an individual speaker of the language encounters, in the course of this lifetime, innumerable temporary collocations of individuals, it would obviously be uneconomical (not to mention impossible) for the language to provide specialized labels for each such grouping.[3]

The speaker might, of course refer to temporary groupings by using extremely general labels such as *thing, entity, stuff,* etc., but, as we shall see, words such as these are very rarely used. Turning back to Table 2, we can see that, in all cases where collections of individuals were referred to by means of a single noun phrase, they were always of the "same type," where *type* is defined at a fairly high level of specificity. That is, the groupings were composed of pears or baskets or boys, not "animals" or "things."

Recent work by Cecil Brown (Brown, 1976) and other investigators of body part terminology in various languages suggests the existence of a similar lack of lexicalized labels for *parts* of wholes. Brown reports, for example, that in all the body part partonomies he has investigated,[4] the whole, as well as certain parts, e.g., arm, finger, fingernail, are always labeled, but that the partonomy never exceeds five levels of depth. That is, certain parts are not labeled, although the whole always is.[5]

---

[3]The unaccepatbility of compound words composed of constituents which refer to entities which bear only a temporary relationship to each other has been noted by Denny (1976) with respect to frozen classifier-noun forms in Bantu and by Downing (1977) with respect to English compound nouns. Thus, for example, a compound noun, such as *water-fence* may be used to refer to a fence used (habitually) under water or a fence (permanently) composed of water, but it is unlikely to be applied to a fence that has merely been rained on recently.

[4]Brown defines *partonomies* as "hierarchical systems of one or more labeled parta, each of which is either immediately or nonimmediately possessed by an entity which is not a parton of the partonomy, i.e., The Whole" (1976, p. 401).

[5]Brown (1976) speculates as to the nature of possible developmental schemes for partonomic nomenclature (similar to those described for color and botanical nomenclature by Berlin and Kay, 1969; Berlin, 1972), but notes the difficulty that "probably all languages have developed extensive lexicons for human body parts, and all should therefore be regarded as advanced in this respect" (1976, p. 411). It seems likely that the difference in codability of the whole versus the component parts would jump considerably in the case of objects which are less familiar, less significant.

The extent to which the lack of a standardized label influences a speaker's choice of a referent is of course difficult to decide on the basis of the data at hand. Clearly, speakers are not incapable of referring to groups of entities or parts of entities which possess no lexicalized label. Descriptive devices are always available even when a perfectly appropriate name is not.

Setting aside the issue of the degree and directionality of the influence that low codability and infrequent reference exert on each other, it seems likely that they are both manifestations of the same phenomenon: the greater salience of wholes over parts, which is owing (at least in part) to the fact that wholes *act* as such. The disposition of parts is typically predictable, given the disposition of the whole, but the reverse is not true.

Thus, reference to wholes seems to be preferred, most importantly, because it allows the speaker to avoid hazards attendant on the mention of either collections or parts of wholes: underspecification, redundancy, overspecification. The same principle is relevant, of course, in the speaker's choice of what events to describe. A newspaper article entitled "Business went as usual" would very likely be just as uninformative (and consequently, uninteresting) as a story about "people" or "dogs." A speaker who sketched his referents or described events in such general terms would undoubtedly have difficulty fending off the "So what?" response of his listeners.

On the other hand, a speaker who insisted on filling in his narrative about a shopping trip with details like "I closed the car door and put on my seat belt. Then, with my left foot, I pushed in the clutch, while with my right hand I inserted the key into the ignition switch and turned it to the right..." would very soon lose the interest of his listeners, if not the listeners themselves. This is because the actions of the narrator's hands, feet, eyes, etc., are sufficiently predictable, given the much more general information conveyed by a sentence like "I drove to the store." Not every change is perceived as an event, and not every relevant part of a participant in an event is perceived as a participant in its own right.[6]

When we consider *how* the speaker refers to an entity, once she has decided to talk about it, a wide range of cognitive and contextual influences on her choice of a label must be taken into account:

---

[6]These generalizations are, of course, subject to constraints imposed by the nature of the referent in question, e.g., grains of sand vs. trees vs. human beings, as well as by the textual context in which the mention is embedded, e.g., an account of the effects of a major disaster, such as an earthquake vs. a detailed description of a procedure, such as knitting a sweater or repairing a carburetor.

COGNITIVE FACTORS IN LEXICAL CHOICE

Codability

It is not only in the choice of *what* to talk about, how finely to segment the content of her narrative, that the speaker must contend with the codability of a given entity. Once the decision has been made to mention a particular referent, the freedom which the speaker enjoys with respect to how to mention it varies considerably, depending on the number of lexicalized labels available and the speaker's familiarity with them. For some entities, there is one standardized label which is sufficient for the purposes of most speakers in most situations. In such cases, a single speaker will consistently use the same label for successive references to the entity in question, and the same label will be used by most speakers. Consider, for example, the entities listed in Table 4, which were highly codable, on the basis of this criterion, for speakers of at least one language. (Only entities mentioned more than once by one speaker, or by more than one speaker, have been included in this table.) Other entities seemed to present codability problems for some or all speakers of one language or the other, as is reflected in the figures in Table 5: when speakers mentioned these entities, their choice of a particular lexeme sometimes seemed to represent an attempt to avoid the use of an inappropriate label, rather than a clear preference for the label which was in fact chosen. One of our Japanese subjects, for example, appeared to have difficulty in deciding whether or not the fruit involved in the film were apples. As can be seen from the sentences in (5), she attempted to stick with the noncommital form

TABLE 4
Consistently Labeled Entities

Entity	Number of Different Labels Used by English Speakers	Number of Different Labels Used by Japanese Speakers
Ladder	1	1
Ladder rungs	1	—
Bicycle wheels	1	—
Bicycle handlebars	1	—
Moustache	1	1
Face	1	1
Neck	1	—
Leg	1	1
Knee	1	—
Hand	—	1
Eyes	—	1
Paddleball ball	1	—

TABLE 5
Inconsistently Labled Entities

Entity	Number of Different Labels Used by English Speakers	Number of Different Labels Used by Japanese Speakers
Apron	3	1
Paddleball	11	3
Paddleball paddle	3	—
Bicycle rack	5	4
Pears	4	8
Goat	1	2
Baskets	6	4

kudamono ("fruit"), but occasionally slipped up and came out with *ringo* ("apple") instead.

(5) Mention 1: Et.. *Nanika kudamono* o totte iru hito ga ita deshoo?
"There was somebody picking some kind of fruit."
Mention 2: *Kudamono* o totte iru hito ga ite sa.
"There's this person picking fruit."
Mention 3:.. A! *Ano ringo* mottecchau n da na to omotta n da kedo ne,
"I thought they would take those apples, but...'
Mention 4: *Ringo* o mittsu o ne,... ageta wake.
"He gave them three apples."
Mentions 5 and 6:... A,... *ringo* to ieba, *kudamono* o totte iru tokoro e itte,
"Oh! Getting back to the apples, they get to the place where he is picking the fruit,"
Mention 7: Sono... sannin no otoko no ko ga, *ringo* tabenagara, *kudamono* o tabenagara, kite,
"The three boys come by, eating the apples, eating the pears,"

An American speaker describing a paddleball that one of the boys in the film was playing with demonstrates a similar insecurity, but instead of vacillating between general and specifc terms, her references, after an initial attempt at explanation, degenerate considerably in specificity:

(6) Mention 1:... and then one of them is.. playing like with... I don't remember, I used to play with it when I was a kid, but... it's like a... wooden paddle... that.. there's an elastic string attached to and there's a ball,... you know that that kind of thing that

you...you...I..don't remember the name of them,...but I played with them for hours.

Mention 2:...Um--...and he's..paddling...playing around with *this*

Mention3:...And the one kid is still hitting..playing with *the...the thing,*

Mention 4:...And the one kid, I think it was the kid who was playing with..*the* uh...*with..the whatever it was,*...stops and picks it up and whistles.

Mentions of these objects were typically characterized not only by the choice of different names by different subjects and name switching on successive mentions by a single subject—in many cases they were accompanied by lengthy pauses and false starts, as well as a higher than average number of modifiers, all indicators of low codability. And in some cases the names chosen for these entities were downright inappropriate, as when one English speaker referred to the apron the pearpicker was wearing as a "cape."

Some of these codability difficulties were confined to only a few speakers, which points up the fact that the codability of an entity for a speaker does not depend solely on whether there exists an appropriate name for it in her language. In some cases, the individual speaker may be unaware of the existence of the name which renders the entity highly codable for other speakers, or the context of the speech act may make it inappropriate to use a familiar name. What is highly codable when you are speaking to other adults, for example, may be difficult to explain to a child, whose vocabulary and conceptual universe are assumed to be limited. The codability of a given entity, then, is dependent not only on whether there exists an appropriate label for it in the language of the speaker, but also whether the speaker is aware of the label and willing to use it in a particular speech context.

Mentions of another set of objects in the film illustrate how the measurement of codability can be complicated by the existence of a number of lexical alternatives, any of which might appropriately be used in referring to a given referent. Consider, for example, the figures in Table 6: for each of these entities, speakers of the language(s) for which a figure is listed chose to use more than one label, but this was not necessarily because they found the entity uncodable. Mentions were not accompanied by the other trappings of low codability just discussed. The variability in naming seems rather to be related to the fact that there are a number of appropriate labels for these entities. This is strikingly the case with the lexical choices available to refer to human beings. Thus, our English speaking subjects used a total of 31 different head nouns to refer to the seven characters mentioned in our narratives, a mean of 4.4 categorizations per character across all the narratives,

TABLE 6
Labeling of Entities with Several Appropriate Labels

Entity	Number of Different Labels Used by English Speakers	Number of Different Labels Used by Japanese Speakers
Human beings	31	23
Hat	3	2
Pants	3	
Bandana	2	
Hair	3	2
Shirt	2	
Tree	2	4
Paddleball string	3	
Rooster	2	
Bicycle	2	
Baskets	6	4

considerably higher than the mean, 2.7, for all concrete entities mentioned in the narratives (including humans). These characters were referred to on the basis of their age, profession, sex, ethnic identity, role in the plot of the film, interpersonal relationships, location, and companions. This flexibility in naming was, of course, possible because of the density of the lexical field associated with human beings in both English and Japanese, as compared, for example, to the lexical choices available to refer to ladders, aprons, goats, etc. Similar lexical arrays were available for use in mentions of the other entities listed in Table 6, e.g., *basket—bushel basket—wicker basket; ki* ("tree")— *kudamono no ki* ("fruit tree") *nashi no ki* ("pear tree")—*seiyoonashi no ki* ("Western pear tree"), but the choices, even in these cases, were considerably more restricted than those available in choosing a name for a human referent.

Now, in cases like these, where the language provides a number of lexical options for referring to a given entity, what factors come into play in determining which word a speaker will use on a given occasion?

Basic Level Lexemes

One tendency of interest in our narratives is the preference of both English and Japanese speakers for referring to entities by using words of an intermediate degree of abstractness, when a choice is available. Thus, for example, most subjects used the term *bicycle/jitensha* rather than the more abstract term *vehicle/norimono* or more specific terms, such as *ten-speed/juudanhensoku* or *two-wheeler/nirinsha*.

This tendency has been remarked upon by other researchers. Roger Brown (1958) has argued, for example, that although most real-world entities possess a number of names, e.g., *dime, coin, money,* certain of these names are used more frequently and are considered to be the objects' "real" names. These names are often (but not always) shorter and are also those first taught to children. They are crucially characterized by the fact that they represent the object at its "usual level of utility."

Brown's ideas have been expanded by a number of researchers in various disciplines. D. A. Cruse (1977), for example, describes certain lexical items as possessing the property of "inherently neutral specificity." Berlin, Breedlove, and Raven (1973) have proposed that folk biological taxonomies typically possess a "generic" level of intermediate specificity which is of special psychological relevance to speakers. Folk taxonomies typically possess more named taxa at this level (as opposed to higher and lower levels in the taxonomy), and it is these names that are the most frequently used in speech and are the first learned by children. Thus, for example, the English generic term *horse* would be learned before and used more frequently than its subordinate *Appaloosa* or its superordinate *animal*.

Eleanor Rosch has made similar claims, based on her work with American English speakers. She proposes that "of the many levels of abstraction at which any given thing can be classified, there is one basic level of abstraction at which the organism can obtain the most information with the least cognitive effort" (Rosch, *et al.,* 1976). Thus, for example, *chair* is the basic level category in a hierarchy of abstraction which also includes *furniture* as a superordinate, and subordinates such as *kitchen chair, armchair,* etc. By defining *basic level* in this way, Rosch is providing a cognitive explanation for the apparent tendency for languages to develop elaborate name systems for categories at this level of abstraction, as well as for speakers' tendency to learn these names earlier and use them more frequently than names for superordinate and subordinate categories. The cognitive mechanism is thus reflected linguistically both in terms of *langue* (the structure of the standardized lexicon) and *parole* (actual usage).

On the basis of a series of experiments using city-dwelling American English speakers as subjects, Rosch has established the basic levels for nine categories of concrete objects: fruit, tools, clothing, vehicles, trees, birds, musical instruments, furniture, and fish. These basic level categories, Rosch argues, are established at the most abstract level at which the category members share a significant number of physical and functional attributes, elicit a consistent motor pattern from humans interacting with them, and exhibit a similar, easily recognizable shape.[7]

Thus, subjects can better recognize the shape of an average *chair* and can give more consistent and detailed accounts of what a *chair* is and how one

---

[7]This multifaceted characterization is clearly related to Brown's notion of "usual level of utility."

interacts with a *chair* than they can when asked to perform similar tasks with respect to the superordinate category *furniture*. Responses for subordinate categories, such as *kitchen chair, armchair,* etc. are somewhat more detailed than those for basic level categories on some tasks, but not all. And in no instance is the discrepancy between basic and subordinate level responses significant, whereas the basic-superordinate level differences consistently are.

On the basis of these results, Rosch predicts that, "universally, basic categories should be the basic classifications made during perception, the first learned and first named by children and the most codable, most coded, and most necessary in the language of any people" (1975, p. 435). These claims are similar to those made by Berlin, Breedlove, and Raven (1973), and Rosch presents several kinds of evidence in support. Citing the protocols from Roger Brown's Sarah, she reports that diary studies of child language acquisition show that, at least for the nine taxonomies of concrete objects she had investigated, the basic level names were learned and used before either superordinate or subordinate names.[8] In support of the notion that the lexical resources of a language will be most developed at the basic level, she reports that for the American sign language of the deaf (ASL), it is basic level categories which are most often represented by single signs, whereas signs for super- and subordinate categories are often missing.

It is, of course, the claim that these categories will be "the most coded," that is, the most frequently used in speech, that is relevant to our research here. In support of this contention Rosch has reported the results of an experiment in which subjects were asked to provide names for a number of concrete objects depicted in a series of drawings (Rosch *et al.,* 1976). They responded almost invariably with the basic level names (as determined by Rosch), even though they knew the correct super- and subordinate names for the entities in question. These results were obtained, however, within a context quite different from those in which linguistic categorizations are typically used. Rosch's subjects were simply producing names in response to sets of experimental stimuli.

---

[8]Anglin (1977) reports similar results in a series of experiments using groups of two- through five-year-old American children as subjects. That these names are the first acquired does not, however, indicate that the semantic material the child associates with them, or the perceptions to which they correspond, are equivalent to those of adult speakers who use the same names. Thus, for example, the diary literature contains many examples of apparent semantic overextensions in the use of words by young children, and experimental studies have provided similar findings. Nelson (1974) reports, for example, that five-year-olds sometimes listed items, such as soup and pizza when asked to name kinds of vegetables, although these entities would clearly not fall within the referential domain of the term *vegetable* as used by adults. The issue is also complicated by the fact that the child's lexical acquisition is conditioned by the lexical resources provided by the adults around him (see Brown, 1958). It is thus difficult to know exactly what the child is referring to when he uses a given term if its taxonomic super- and subordinates are absent at that point from his lexicon. Of course, that adults tend to use basic level names in speaking to children might be construed as another type of evidence for the priority of these names.

Turning to our data, however, we find that the usage of concrete nouns in our English and Japanese film narratives is in striking agreement with Rosch's hypothesis that her basic level names are most frequently used in actual discourse.[9] In Table 7, all nominal mentions of all concrete entities except people are classified as superordinate, basic, or subordinate, as defined by Rosch.[10] Basic level names clearly outnumber super- and subordinate names, constituting 93 percent of the nominal mentions in the English narratives and 83 percent in the Japanese narratives.

---

[9]In citing these distributions I do not wish to imply that the use in our narratives of basic terms as determined by Rosch (1975) necessarily corresponds to *perception* of their referents at this level. As will be discussed, lexical choice is sometimes conditioned by discourse rather than purely perceptual factors. And it is also impossible for us to know the exact nature of the referent each individual speaker associates with the usage of a lexical item unless we are aware of the overall structure of his personal lexicon. Because every individual has different areas of interest and expertise, his idiosyncratic lexical resources will not mirror exactly either those of the language as a whole or those of an "average" group of speakers, such as those used as subjects by Rosch. Thus, as Rosch herself suggests, although *airplane* may be a basic level term for English speakers in general, it is probably a superordinate for, say, airplane mechanics. But in the tabulation presented here I am neglecting these individual differences.

Like the lexicon of an individual speaker, the lexicon of the language as a whole may differ from that of an average group of speakers at a given point in time. This must be taken into account in considering the preponderance of conventionalized lexical items at a given level as evidence for the perceptual-semantic priority of that level for actual speakers of the language. Indeed, a mismatch between the lexicalized basic level and the semantic basic level for speakers of the language was encountered by Rosch in her research. Although the forms of such English labels for biological taxa as *oak, jay,* and *trout* would appear to conform to Berlin, Breedlove, and Raven's (1973) criteria for generic names in terms of the language as a whole, the basic level established by Rosch for her (city-dweller) subjects for these categories was one level higher, i.e., *tree, bird, fish.*

All this suggests that the question of basic levels can be considered from several perspectives— the resources of the language as a whole, the lexical competence of a group of speakers of the language at a given point in time, the personal lexicon of an individual speaker, and usage by a particular speaker in a particular discourse context. We need not expect all these basic levels to fall at an identical level of abstraction. Each is defined within its own system, which is not identical to any of the others, though all of them come into play any time an individual uses language.

We must therefore be cautious in interpreting evidence from one domain as support for our claims about another, although the apparent existence of basic levels within each of these domains, and the similarity among them, are striking indeed, suggesting that similar perceptual-cognitive factors may well be at work in each case.

[10]In the case of categories not specifically investigated by Rosch (1975) mentions were classified as basic, superordinate, and subordinate on the basis of parallelism with established norms for similar categories previously considered by Rosch. Although there were a small number of difficult cases, this was in general a fairly unproblematic task. Thus, for example, for mentions of members of the category *container,* it is easier to imagine the shape and physical and functional attributes of a *basket* (established as basic here) than it is to do the same for a *container.* The basic levels for Japanese were arbitrarily set at the level of the Japanese counterparts of the basic level terms in English, since no work like Rosch's has been done with Japanese subjects.

TABLE 7
Superordinate-Basic-Subordinate Level Distribution of Nouns Referring to All Concrete Entities Except Humans

Category	Superordinate		Basic		Subordinate	
	English	*Japanese*	*English*	*Japanese*	*English*	*Japanese*
Fruit	2	33	272	63	—	26
Tools	4	—	43	11	—	—
Clothing	—	—	110	58	4	3
Vehicles	—	—	141	77	12	5
Trees	—	—	62	31	5	1
Birds	—	—	—	—	12	1
Containers	—	1	109	64	2	—
Animals	—	—	43	18	3	—
Toys	8	2	8	1	2	—
Other Vegetation	—	—	1	—	—	—
Other natural objects	—	—	28	23	—	—
Other synthetic objects	6	4	41	12	6	—
Body parts	—	—	30	18	4	2
	20	40	888	376	50	38
	(2%)	(9%)	(93%)	(83%)	(5%)	(8%)

Mentions of people were excluded from these tabulations because of the difficulty involved in determining just which mentions would be considered "basic" in a sense comparable to that defined by Rosch. This difficulty was due in large part to our subjects' using an extremely wide range of different terms in referring to the human characters in the film they were describing. Since these terms denoted the characters on the basis of a number of classificatory parameters, such as age, profession, activity, nationality, sex, etc., it was impossible to arrange them into any neat taxonomy, where terms falling at given levels could be designated as superordinate, basic, and subordinate. It seems likely that if Rosch were to apply her experimental techniques to this lexical domain, the results would be equally problematic, since some of the parameters used by Rosch in her investigation of other categories, i.e., physical shape, associated motor movements, etc., may not be relevant to the way we classify human beings.

Among these terms, however, several stand out on the basis of their greater overall frequency, frequency on initial mentions of characters, and frequency as the sole categorization used for a given character by a given subject. These are the terms *man, boy, girl, kid,* and *guy/hito* ("person"), *otoko no hito* ("man"), *ko* ("child"), *kodomo* ("child"), *otoko no ko* ("boy"), and *onna no ko* ("girl"). Their predominance as indicated by these various measures can be seen in Table 8.

The similarity between the inventories of favored terms in the two languages is striking. They cannot be characterized as falling at a single "basic" taxonomic level, since, for example, among these terms, *hito* ("person") is superordinate to *ko* ("child"),[11] which is superordinate to *otoko no ko* ("boy"). They do, however, correspond to taxa in a taxonomy of humans based on the properties of age and sex.[12] The frequency distributions cited here do not, of course, constitute incontrovertible evidence that the perception and representation of human beings in terms of these categories

---

[11]P. Clancy points out that *ko* is also used among adults to refer to intimates who are clearly no longer children. There were no instances of this type of usage in our narratives, however.

[12]One possible representation of this taxonomy is as follows, with the relevant semantic parameters appearing in capital letters, the corresponding favored labels in small letters:

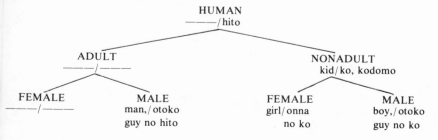

TABLE 8
Frequency Distribution of Favored Terms for Human Beings

	Total no. mentions		No. uses as first men. of a character		No. uses as sole cat. of a character		No. uses as most frequent cat. of a character	
	Eng /	*Jp*	*Eng /*	*Jp*	*Eng /*	*Jp*	*Eng /*	*Jp*
Favored	354 (87%)	294 (89%)	105 (81%)	91 (89%)	83 (87%)	47 (94%)	95 (100%)	77 (94%)
Other	51 (13%)	38 (11%)	24 (19%)	11 (11%)	12 (13%)	3 (6%)	0 (0%)	5 (6%)

are basic. But the frequent use of these terms suggests that information about a person's identity in terms of the parameters of age and sex may be important to English and Japanese speakers' understanding of what a person *is*, since it reveals much in a general way about how he or she looks; what his or her actions and concerns are likely to be; how others will interact with him or her. This information is not necessarily derivable from other appellations equally appropriate in an absolute sense, but which focus on different aspects of the individual's identity, e.g., *companion/nakama, farm worker/noofu-san.* Thus, these terms may denote human referents at their "usual level of utility" in the same way that the "basic" terms, as determined by Rosch's methodology, denote nonhuman entities at a level which is both sufficiently informative and cognitively manipulable.

Since both our American and Japanese subjects demonstrated such a significant preference for the use of basic terms, it is of some interest to consider the cases in which they deviated from the pattern and used super- or subordinate terms instead. In many instances, the deviation seems to have been conditioned by stylistic and textual constraints deriving from the fact that the word chosen was embedded in an ongoing narrative being told to a particular addressee. Some apparent effects of these considerations will be noted separately. In other cases the choice seems to have been dictated by cognitive considerations and by the imperfect match between the lexical needs of the speaker and the standardized lexical resources provided by the language she was speaking.

The use of superordinates, for example, frequently occurs when subjects refer to objects which are of poor basic level codability, for one of two reasons:

(a) The speaker is unaware of the existence of a conventionalized basic level label for the conceptually well-defined category in question.

(b) The specific referent at issue fits poorly into the conventionalized basic level category with which it is most closely associated. That is, it is a nonprototypical member of the category.

Our subjects often used superordinates in referring to the paddleball, which is depicted in Figure 1, for the benefit of those readers who have difficulty reconstructing it on the basis of descriptions given by our subjects. Some subjects were aware of the names *paddleball* and, in one case, *pongo*, but other were not. Some subjects assigned the object to related basic level categories bearing conventional and well-known names, e.g., *bat and ball;* others chose to use more-clearly appropriate subordinate labels such as *toy, thing/mono* ("thing"), and *doogu* ("instrument").

7 (a) ...and this one's.. playing with one of those... those wooden things that you hit with a ball.

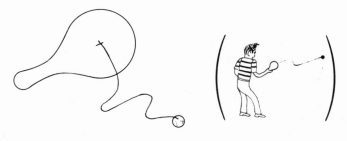

FIG. 1.

(b) ...Ano--...sono ko no hitori ga ne,...nan to yuu no ka koo,...koo...koko ni,...tenisu ja nai ya,...takkyuu no raketto mitai no o motteru n desu ne? Sore sore ni himo...himo ga tsuite te, gomu ga tsuite te,...booru ga tsuite te, ko pi pi pi pi pin tte yaru ga ano..Amerika atari de,...A...Nippon de wa mikakenai n desu kedo,...soo yuu doogu o motte te.

"...Um--...One of the kids is holding...what should I say?...not a tennis racket,...something like a ping-pong paddle. There is a string, a string attached to it, an elastic string attached to it,..a ball attached to it, Uh he's making it go pi pi pi pi pin. Um..in America...in Japan you don't see them but,...he had one of those instruments,"

In some cases, however, the fact that the referent was deemed a poor examplar of the basic level category in question motivated the speaker to use a subordinate rather than a superordinate term. Although *bird* has been established by Rosch, for example, as the basic level category, all American and Japanese subjects who referred to the only bird involved in the film referred to it by means of a subordinate level label: *rooster, cock/niwatori* ("chicken"). This is presumably because roosters are a well-known and well defined subset of birds which, in addition, are not particularly good exemplars of the bird category as a whole. This example suggests that there may be some members of basic level categories which are not perceived primarily in terms of their basic level identity, but in terms of their lower-level category membership. This may be because they lack the typical attributes of members of the basic level category, or because they are especially salient, familiar, or important members of the category as a whole. Other researchers have noted that such category members often merit special linguistic treatment.[13]

---

[13]See, for example, G. Lakoff (1972), Berlin (1972).

TABLE 9
Distributions for First vs. Repeat Narratives

	Superordinate		Basic		Subordinate	
First narratives	20	(2%)	888	(93%)	50	(5%)
Repeat narratives	22	(11%)	176	(85%)	8	(4%)

Repeat English narratives collected six weeks after the original narratives also suggest that the use of superordinates may be greater on occasions where speakers are referring to entities whose identities have been stored away in long-term memory for a significant period. These effects can be seen when the narratives recorded immediately after the subjects had seen the film are compared with the repeat narratives. As Table 9 illustrates, the frequency of use of superordinate terms is only 2 percent in the first narratives but jumps to 11 percent in the repeat narratives. (Human referents have once again been excluded from the tabulation.) This trend is exemplified by use of the superordinate term *fruit* nearly one-third of the time in the repeat narratives, whereas the basic level terms *pear* and *apple* were used in all but one instance in the first narratives. This effect appears to be part of a larger tendency, for the repeat narratives are on the whole less detailed than the earlier ones and contain mentions of fewer concrete objects (37 mentioned overall, as compared to 66 in the first narratives).

In these cases where a superordinate level noun is used, however, it is often accompanied by modifiers which serve to narrow down the referent class in question and create what can be viewed as an *ad hoc* basic level characterization. Thus, in example (7a), the speaker was not content to refer to the object in question as simply *one of those things*, but rather, she narrowed down the referent class she had in mind by specifying its physical composition (*wooden*) and a characteristic action associated with it (*that you hit with a ball*). The superordinate level nouns used by our subjects were modified in this way much more frequently than basic or subordinate level nouns were.

It is of course, not true that all modifiers serve to narrow down the referent *class* denoted by the noun they modify. As in example (8), some modifiers are used, rather, to enable the hearer to pick out a specific referent that the speaker has in mind or to convey additional information about this referent without consigning it to a *class* of, for example, boys who have fallen off bicycles or fruit that has fallen out of baskets.[14]

---

[14]Cf. Bolinger's (1967) distinction between referent and reference modification.

(8) (a) ... and the ... the little boy *that fell off the bicycle* gives him three--
.. pears

(b) *taorete korogatta ano ko nusunda kita kudamono o ... ano .. yoseatsumete kurete*
"they pick up for him the fruit which had tumbled out, which he had stolen."

It is not always possible to decide, in a given instance, whether a modifier is being used in a referent or a referent class-modifying function, but in some cases, as when the modifier denotes temporary states or actions of the referent, it is clearly the referent-modifying function which is involved.

Excluding cases of this type, intances of (referent class-) modifier-noun pairs can be seen as representing concepts more specific than those represented by the head nouns alone. Thus a (referent class-) modifier plus a superordinate level noun serves to denote the referent at a level of specificity comparable to that denoted by an unmodified basic level noun; a (referent class-) modified basic level noun refers at a level of specificity comparable to that denoted by an unmodified subordinate level noun.

Thus, if we consider the level of the characterization as a whole, including referent-class modifiers, rather than considering simply the level of the head noun, the distribution shown in Table 10 emerges. In this table, the superordinate heading subsumes only mentions consisting of unmodified superordinate level nouns. Mentions composed of modified superordinates are included under the basic heading, along with those composed of unmodified basic level nouns. Modified basic level nouns are similarly combined with mentions consisting of (modified or unmodified) subordinate level nouns under the subordinate heading.

Although the predominance of basic level characterizations defined in these terms is not so overwhelming as when only the level of the head nouns themselves is considered (cf. Table 7), in both cases it is clearly the basic level as established by Rosch which is favored.

This preference for basic level terms can be related to the observance of Grice's (1967) maxims of conversational quantity and manner (be as

TABLE 10
Distribution of Complete References, Including Referent-Class Modifiers

	Superordinate	Basic	Subordinate
English	1%	90%	9%
Japanese	7%	78%	15%

informative but not more informative than necessary; be clear), as well as to the special cognitive status attributed to basic level categories by Rosch and others. That is, it is typically basic level names which carry information sufficient for the addressee to be able to identify the category or individual being referred to by the speaker.

Intentional violation of Grice's maxims by the use of contextually redundant subordinate level names or insufficiently informative superordinate level names may thus serve as the source of conversational implicatures. As Cruse (1977) suggests, the professor who reminds his advisee that "all attractive blonde first-year students," as opposed to "all students," should meet with their advisor once a month might be accused of having more than his professorial duties in mind.

It is, of course, not always true that basic level lexemes, as determined by Rosch, constitute the contextually neutral level of lexical choice. Thus, a Blue Book that referred only to *cars,* or a medical textbook that mentioned only *muscles* or *nerves,* in preference to particular muscles or nerves, could be accused of violating not only the maxims of quantity and manner, but the cooperative principle as well. That is, special groups of language users or particular linguistic contexts may produce situations in which basic level lexical items, as defined on a context-free, society-wide scale, are *not* at the level of lexical specificity required for the speaker to communicate in accordance with the Gricean maxims.[15]

CONTEXTUAL FACTORS IN LEXICAL CHOICE

In considering the influence of a particular speech context on the lexical choices made by a speaker, it is necessary to take into account a number of factors: the sex, age, social status, educational, psychological and geographic background of both speaker and hearer, the intimacy of the relationship between them, the speaker's goals,[16] the geographic and temporal setting of the speech act, etc.

---

[15]I have not considered what the limits might be on how abstract or specific (in absolute terms) a contextually defined basic level may be. Nor is it clear to me how best to characterize the set of base-level-shifting contexts without degenerating to a description along the lines of "any context within which a superordinate or subordinate level term can be used without violating any conversational maxims." The difficulty here arises because, as our narratives reveal, any speaker reaches points in her discourse where the use of superordinate or subordinate terms becomes appropriate, if not necessary, although the level of lexical specificity she has in general adhered to throughout her narrative conforms to the societally defined, context-free basic level.

[16]For discussion of this point, see Labov (1972) and Bowditch (1977).

Observers of both English and Japanese linguistic usage have noted for example, that women command a body of lexical items seldom used by male speakers, and that women's speech is in general "more polite."[17]

Our subjects, however, were all females of roughly the same age, and the narratives of speakers of each language were all produced in the same physical setting, in response to one of two female interviewers. On the basis of this narrow sample, it is difficult to draw any striking conclusions about sociological determinants of lexical choice. And our data shed little light on such questions as the importance of vocabulary fads or the use of "private" vocabulary among intimates, since investigation of issues such as these requires a broader diachronic perspective than our narratives provide. It is clear, however, that recognizing the tendency for speakers to choose basic level terms does not fill in the whole picture.

Quite obvious in its dependency on contextual factors, for example, is the use of deictically based terms, whose appropriateness in a given situation cannot be decided without taking into consideration the identity of the speaker. Thus, for example, a woman who might be referred to as *my mother* by her children could not be denoted in this way by her neighbors.

Because our subjects were not personally involved in the incidents which formed the subject matter of their narratives, our transcripts in general provide few examples of the use of deictically based terms. The use of the donatory verbs *ageru* and *kureru* in our Japanese narratives, however, does provide an interesting illustration. The choice between these two verbs, which both mean "to give," depend on the relationship between the speaker and the recipient in the act of giving being described. If the speaker is herself the recipient, or if she feels close to the recipient, compared with how she feels with respect to the giver, she will use *kureru*. If the speaker is herself the giver, or if she feels no special attachment to the recipient, *ageru* will be used instead.

When we look for instances of the use of these two verbs in our narratives, we find that many of our subjects used *ageru* to describe all instances of giving, thereby taking no particular personal stance with respect to either the giver or the receiver. Other subjects, however, chose to use *kureru* when the recipient was the boy on the bicycle, *ageru* when the recipients were the three boys who helped him out. One subject, for example, described the exchange of a hat for three pears in the following way:

---

[17]Jespersen went so far as to suggest, that "it seems to be characteristic of the two sexes in their relation to language that women move in narrower circles of the vocabulary, in which they attain to perfect mastery so that the flow of words is natural, and, above all, never needs to stop, while men know more words and always want to be more precise in choosing the exact word with which to render their idea, the consequence being often less fluency and more hesitation" (1938, pp. 16–17).

(9) *Sorede, ... furimuite, ... de booshi todokete kureta no, sono hitori no otoko no ko ga. Dakara, ... sono yoonashi mitai na no o, mittsu agete,*

"Then, he turns around, and brings the hat back for him, one of those boys. So, he gives them three of those Western pear-like things."

thereby indicating rather explicitly that she as the speaker was taking the point of view of the boy on the bicycle, who had been, up to that point, the hero of the story.

In other cases there are a number of words available which are of the same level of referential specificity, but which differ from one another in terms of the level of formality associated with them and in terms of the subjective connotations which they carry, e.g., I am resolute, you are stubborn, he is pigheaded. The speaker's choice among these terms will, of course, depend on her social position with respect to both her referents and her interlocutors, as well as her general communicative goals. When Pope John Paul II, the first non-Italian Pope in 456 years, made his first public speech, for example, he referred to his new role as that of "Bishop of Rome," in an apparent bid for the favor of his Italian flock, although he had many other titles among which to choose: Vicar of Jesus Christ, Successor to the Prince of the Apostles, Supreme Pontiff of the Universal Church, Patriarch of the West, Primate of Italy, Archbishop and Metropolitan of the Province of Rome, Sovereign of the Vatican State.[18]

And in some instances a single term may have different effects when it is used in speaking to different addressees. As Maisie Maidan complains in *The Good Soldier* (Ford, 1927),

I heard Edward call me a poor rat to the American lady. He always called me a little rat in private, and I do not mind. But if he called me it to her, I think he does not love me any more. (p. 74)

In general, the use of Latinate words by the American speaker, Sino-Japanese words by the Japanese speaker, can lend a more refined, polite tone to the narrative,[19,20] as can the use of uncontracted forms, complex sentence

---

[18]As reported in *Time,* Oct. 30, 1978.

[19]The *politeness* I refer to here is that which derives from the speaker's not imposing on her addressee (Rule 1 in Lakoff's taxonomy), as opposed to that which derives from the speaker's attempt to seem friendly, to establish a sense of camaraderie with her addressee (Lakoff's Rule 3).

[20]The results of a survey of Japanese speakers investigating which linguistic devices they felt to be polite are presented in Kokuritsu Kokugo Kenkyuujo (1957) and are recapitulated for the English reader in Martin (1964).

structures, and in Japanese, the use of the polite verb ending, -*masu*. The Japanese speaker (especially the typically more polite female Japanese speaker) has available in addition a rich verbal system of both lexicalized and productively derived humble and honorific forms which allow the speaker to demean herself and members of her group and to indicate respect for others, as well as a pair of honorific prefixes *o/go*, which may be added to nouns in order to indicate respect for the addressee or referent.

In our Japanese narratives, however, there was virtually no use of these honorific verbs and prefixes. The subjects were talking with a female interviewer close to their own age, and the subject matter of their narratives did not include information about any individuals to whom linguistic deference was due. There was some variation in the subjects' choice of speaking style—two subjects used polite verb forms (with the -*masu* ending) exclusively, six used only plain verb forms, but the majority used a mixture of the two styles. The use of polite verb forms seemed to correlate to some extent with the use of more refined, deferential nominal choices (the use of *kata* instead of *hito*, both "person," for example), but in some cases subjects using polite verb forms chose surprisingly straightforward, pejorative labels for some of the characters in the film, e.g., *kozoo* ("brat").

Stylistic consistency was not a hallmark of the English narratives, either. Although most subjects adopted at the outset a rather casual style which they carried through to the end, the lexical choices in some cases represented rather surprising stylistic vacillations:

(10) Uh--...the movie is basically about uh..um--...a number of...individuals,...Uh a guy who's picking pears,...Um--...and a kid on a bicycle. Basically those are the two...protagonists in this. (...)...And he rips off..one of the...baskets of..of pears that he has.

These narratives were of course not planned in advance, but were produced on the spot, in response to a request from an unknown person of difficult-to-discern social status. It was thus not the speaker's primary goal to promote or maintain any particular interpersonal relationship with her addressee. These circumstances may have allowed the subjects the luxury of concentrating on simply getting the story out, as accurately as possible, without undue concern for proprieties of linguistic or social style.

This, of course, raises the question of whether, in addition to a basic taxonomic level, there exists a basic stylistic level which is used in the absence of any particular contextual constraints. Descriptions of Japanese have often used such terms as *neutral* to refer to verbal forms which are neither honorific nor humble, and the term *plain* to refer to those which do not carry the polite verbal suffix -*masu* and which have wider privileges of occurrence than the corresponding polite forms.[21] Both these terms imply that the use of neutral, plain forms constitutes the unmarked case in Japanese. Because stylistic variation is less rigidly marked in English, a neutral level corresponding to that proposed for Japanese is perhaps more difficult to define, although various suggestions have been made. Searle (1975), for example, proposes that speaking "idiomatically" is such an important part of ensuring communication that it should be added to the list of conversational maxims proposed by Grice, [22,23]

The problem, of course, lies in supporting the designation of any particular stylistic level as *basic*. If we define it as the level used by the speaker in "neutral" situations, where the speaker-addressee relationship is irrelevant or where, indeed, it has not yet developed, then we are in danger of producing a concept inapplicable to real linguistic encounters. The neutral levels suggested by written language or speech addressed to large groups of addressees, where individual speaker-hearer relationships are neutralized, may lead us to recognize an extremely formal style as basic. Complications are also provided by the fact that individual texts, even individual sentences, may contain considerable stylistic variation:

"Dear daughter shut your lousy yap." (Donleavy; *The Ginger Man*)

---

[21]Plain forms, for example, appear in relative clauses, polite forms generally do not.

[22]As Searle puts it, "In general, if one speaks unidiomatically, hearers assume that there must be a special reason for it, and in consequence, various assumptions of normal speech are suspended. Thus, if I say, archaically, *Knowest thou him who calleth himself Richard Nixon?* you are not likely to respond as you would to an utterance of *Do you know Richard Nixon?* Besides the Maxims proposed by Grice, there seems to be an additional maxim of conversation that could be expressed as follows: *Speak idiomatically unless there is some special reason not to* (!975, pp. 76–77).

[23]The humor in the following dialogue (from Donleavy's *The Ginger Man*) hinges on a violation of the maxim proposed by Searle (my specification of the participants):

Osgood: Dot has told me a great deal about New York, Mr. Dangerfield, it sounds a most amazing place. Must be frightening living in such tall buildings.
Dot: O nothing. Mommie and Daddy's apartment is right on the very top of one and it's just wonderful. Looks right over the river and I just loving throwing rose petals down.
Dangerfield: Miss Cabot, or rather Dot, did you know that in New York one is not allowed to throw dead animals in public waters, or to seive, agitate or expose ashes, coal, dry sand, hair, feathers, or other substances likely to be blown about by the wind or to transport manure or like substance through the streets, unless covered to prevent spilling, or to throw garbage, butcher's offal, blood refuse or stinking animal into the street, or to permit any human being to use a water closet as a sleeping place. Guilty of a misdemeanor.
Dot: Gee, I didn't know that. I never thought about that.
Osgood: I say, are you trying to be funny, Mr. Dangerfield?

Needless to say, Mr. Dangerfield has also violated every other conversational maxim in the book.

Because of these difficulties, I hesitate to propose that lexical choice is influenced by the existence of a basic stylistic level, as well as a basic taxonomic level, although the surprising stylistic similarity among our narratives does lend such a notion a certain intuitive appeal.

TEXTUAL FACTORS IN LEXICAL CHOICE

Contextual influences on the choice of a particular lexeme are of course not limited to extralinguistic factors. The preference for basic level terms is also subject to modification in keeping with the requirements imposed by the developing text in which the lexeme is embedded. The speaker's choice of words consonant with a particular stylistic level can be viewed, for example, as the result of an effort to produce a coherent text as well as to maintain a particular position with respect to the addressee.

In considering the influence of the developing text on lexical choice, it is especially instructive to look at the cases in our narratives where subjects deviated from the basic level lexical items which constituted the vast majority of the terms used, as well as the instances in which they abandoned the term they had been using to refer to a given entity and chose another.

Although avoidance of the repeated use of the same term is generally considered stylistically felicitous, our subjects obstinately stayed with the terms they had originally chosen in referring to most of the entities in the film. As Table 13 illustrates, instances in which subjects changed from one noun to another in denoting a single referent were quite rare, except in the case of human referents. The more frequent switching among terms denoting human reference can probably be traced, at least in part, to the fact that there exist in the lexicon significantly more terms denoting humans among which to switch.

When we consider the possible causes for term switching, it is clear that many factors other than a rather ill-defined desire to avoid the retention of a single term come into play. As I mentioned earlier, subjects often switch from one name to another in referring to objects of poor codability. In other cases, subjects alternate between two morphologically related labels for a single referent which differ from each other in some stylistic way too subtle to preclude their co-occurring in a single text. This was the case, for example, with our American speakers' use of the forms *bicycle* and *bike*. A similar nonchalance often seemed to characterize the frequent switches between the unmarked labels for human referents, for example, *guy* and *man* in English, *ko* and *kodomo* (both "child") in Japanese.

In addition to these more or less context-free determinants of lexical switching, there are a number of motivating factors which are based on the word's position in the ongoing narrative. Thus, certain lexical strategies seem to be favored at the beginning of a narrative, at changes of location or

TABLE 11
Instances of a Switch in Name between Two Successive Mentions of the Same Referent

Category	American Subjects		Japanese Subjects	
	Number switches	Number non-switches	Number switches	Number non-switches
Fruit	9	244	28	73
Tools	—	28	—	6
Clothing	7	62	4	28
Vehicles	31	74	—	51
Trees	9	45	6	17
Birds	—	—	—	—
Containers	3	98	3	46
Animals	—	25	1	4
Toys	7	3	—	—
Other vegetation	1	—	—	—
Other natural objects	—	6	—	6
Other synthetic objects	—	4	—	7
Body parts	—	2	—	2
Subtotal	67 (10%)	591 (90%)	42 (15%)	240 (85%)
Humans	63 (23%)	213 (77%)	98 (58%)	70 (42%)
Total	130 (14%)	804 (86%)	140 (31%)	310 (69%)

character, in descriptive passages. In other cases, the lexical choice is determined by the speaker's desire to ensure the continuity of the narrative by using certain words as connecting links between one portion and the next or by the need to avoid ambiguity at a particular point in the narrative.

A speaker will often use different labels in introducing referents into her narrative than she will use subsequently once their identity has been specified. Several distinct strategies are used in this fashion. One is to introduce the referent by means of a superordinate level lexeme, later switching to reference by means of the appropriate basic level term. The transition between the two terms is often mediated by a description of the referent that serves to make the appropriateness of the more specific basic level term apparent to the hearer as in (11) below:

> (11) Mention 1: ... Ano ... *Nan deshita ka,* ano *kudamono desu ne?* ano
> *s seiyoonashi mitai na no.*
> "What were they? Um Fruit. Um That looked like Western pears."
> Mention 2: ... *Mo .. ano ... moratta ... nashi desu kara*
> "because they were the pears that they had gotten"

In this example, the superordinate term seems to have been used to give the speaker time to think to avoid overcommitting herself until she had recalled the identity of the fruit she was talking about. In other cases, as in (12), the use of superordinate terms on initial mentions seems to soften somewhat the introduction of the new participant, giving the listener a moment to recognize that a change in the cast of characters has occurred without being forced to assimilate at the same time the full identity of the entrant.

> (12) Mention 1: Et .. *Nanika kudamono o totte iru hito ga ita deshoo?*
> "There was somebody picking some kind of fruit."
> Mention 2: *Kudamono o totte iru hito ga ite sa,*
> "There's this person picking fruit,"

After these two initial mentions, the second of which is a recapitulation of the first after a brief digression, the speaker (12) went on to denote this character with the more specific labels *ojisan mitai na hito* ("sort of a middle-aged man") and *ojisan* ("middle-aged man") for the remainder of her narrative. Unless the referent is of low codability, as in (11), this technique is typically not used to introduce unimportant props, but is reserved for the presentation of humans and props whose presence is crucial to the listener's understanding of what is to follow.

In other cases, the referent may be introduced by means of basic level labels and descriptions which clarify for the hearer the appropriateness of an otherwise incomprehensible subordinate level label which is used subsequently. In many cases, use of the subordinate level label (in preference to the basic level label) helps the listener avoid confusing two referents bearing the same basic level name. In addition, these labels often refer to characteristics or activities of the referent which are relevant to the progress of the "plot" of the narrative. By using them, the speaker provides for her listener constant reminders as to who is who in terms of the story line. Thus, for example, one American subject referred to a single character in the film by a series of labels *boy → thief boy → bicycle boy → bicycle thief,* names whose successive appropriateness was based on the character's participation in the series of incidents constituting the plot of the narrative.

In many instances, the superordinate or basic level introduction is left out, and the new entity is immediately introduced by the use of a description or a subordinate level term. Once the listener has been adequately acquainted, in this way, with the new referent, the speaker typically abandons the subordinate level label, using the basic level label (enriched by its predecessor with additional implicit information) instead. Our narratives, both English and Japanese, are filled with examples of this technique:

(13) Mention 1: and she brushed off *this little straw hat that he has on.*
Mention 2: . . . and so *his hat* . . comes off--,
Mention 3: . . . And then-- . . . one of the boys . . . uh-- . . finds *the hat,* . . lying on the road.
Mention 4: And-- then-- um-- . . he whistles out at him, . . and takes *the hat* . . back, . . . to him.

(14) Mention 1: Ano *ne--, saisho ni sugoi midori no ne, ... ano nashi no ki ga atta no.*
"Um, at first there was a really green uh pear tree."
Mention 2: *Sono . . otoko no hito ga . . . ki ni nobotte iru otoko no hito no ne.*
"That man, the one who was up in the tree"
Mention 3: *Sono ki ni nobotteta hito ga orite kuru wake yo.*
"The guy up in the tree comes down."

The use of the general term after the introduction of the character in more specific terms sometimes produces an effect tantamount to that of pronominalization, where the general noun serves to do little more than refer back to an individual already clearly established in the minds of both speaker and hearer.[24] Our Japanese narratives contain a number of examples, like (15) below, of this kind of usage.

---

[24]Halliday and Hasan (1976, especially chap. 6) comment on the grammatical (as opposed to lexical) nature of the usage of such general nouns as *thing, stuff,* etc., in sentences like "The poor little thing cried her heart out when she heard the news."

(15) *Onna no ko ga kite, ... soshite, sono hito ni mitorechatta wake.*
"A girl comes by, and he is fascinated by this person (her)."

Although the technique of switching from introductory subordinate level terms to more general terms is quite common in our narratives, once the switch has been made to the basic level term, the speaker does not always stay with it to the end. The narrative contains many internal boundaries, and a switch may be required at these points, in accordance with a change in character or locale.

Sometimes, for example, the speaker will switch to the use of a label which represents the viewpoint of one of the characters in the narrative, often that of a character who has just come in contact with the referent in question. One Japanese speaker, for example, consistently referred to the pearpicker in the film with the term *otoko no hito* ("man") until the appearance on the scene of a small boy who observed the man before deciding to make off with one of his baskets of pears. At this point in her narrative, she switched to the term *ojisan,* which is used to refer to middle-aged men, or to men a generation older than the speaker.

Another subject denoted the tree in the film as *ki* ("tree") throughout her narrative, until the final scene, when three boys, eating pears given to them by the boy who had stolen them from beneath the tree, return to the scene of the crime. The tree at this point is denoted as *nashi no ki* ("pear tree"). The switch of label here serves to ensure that the listener will recognize the scene as the one left behind much earlier in the narrative, and it serves as well to highlight the importance of the pears to the ongoing plot, since the meeting of the pearpicker and the boys eating his pears constitutes the climax of the film.

This last example also illustrates how the choice of a word may be conditioned by the actual words preceding it within the narrative, as well as by its position within the narrative as a whole. In the immediately preceding portion of the narrative, the speaker had been concerned with describing the transfer and eating of three of the stolen pears, *nashi.* Thus, the attention of both speaker and hearer was in part focused on the pears. For this reason it was natural that the tree should be specified in terms of its relationship to the pears, that is, as a pear tree. Cases of this type can be described as instances of lexical assimilation.

The effect of preceding lexemes on subsequent ones can also be discerned in cases where speakers use set phrases, e.g., *go on his merry way,* within which the lexemes at the end are predetermined by the choice of the earlier lexemes, which have restricted privileges of occurrence; i.e., they occur only in combination with the rest of the phrase. Although many phrases of this type were used by our subjects, lexical conditioning of this sort at no point reached the supreme importance that it acquires in some literary works, where the choice of a lexeme is virtually unpredictable except in the context of preceding ones:

> He taught that there is no such thing as the Aschan School or the Cache Cache School or the Cancan School. (Nabokov, *Pnin*)

This is due in part to the fact that our narratives in general had an unusual degree of thematic unity, since our subjects were simply answering with their narratives a single question, "What happened?" Thus, the coherency of topic as much as the influence of preceding lexemes conditioned the choice of a lexeme congruent with what had come before. For this reason, it is very difficult to distinguish between the assimilation of subsequent lexemes to preceding ones and the effect of the underlying referential unity, except in cases where the two diverge—at narrative boundaries, for example.

The influence of preceding lexemes can also be discerned in cases where speakers change the label associated with a given referent because it has become ambiguous in context. This was clearly the determining factor in a number of switches like the one made by one of our American subjects in the passage in (16).

> (16) ...and the.. boy with the bicycle who's now walking the bicycle, not riding it, turns around,...and sees that he's forgotten his hat.... A--nd ... the boy with the pingpong paddle brings the hat to *the bicycle boy*,... who gives him... three pears.

Instances such as these are then cases of lexical *dis*similation.

In citing all these cases where the speaker has changed her lexical categorization of an entity in the course of her narrative, I hope to have illustrated how tenuous is the link between the speaker's conception of an entity and her lexical representation of it. The words we use are not an automatic reflex of the world we perceive, since in using them we seek to convey information of a broader scope, to hint at if not overtly express our emotions and beliefs and cultural assumptions, to maintain and enhance our personal relationships with our interlocutors. Although cognitive factors, such as the existence of a basic level of taxonomic depth, do apparently play an important role in determining how a speaker will refer to an entity, other considerations are of equal importance:

1. The speaker's decisions with respect to how finely to break down her experience in describing it, which will influence how specific in referential scope the words she uses may be.

2. The speaker's perception of her addressee and her relationship with her addressee, which will affect the choice between polite and impolite, straightforward and euphemistic, familiar and formal, easy and difficult forms.

3. The speaker's attitude toward the referent, which will determine, in combination with her attitude toward her addressee, the choice among laudatory, neutral, and pejorative terms.

4. The number of lexical alternatives the speaker's language provides for referring to the entity in question. If the speaker is unaware of the existence of any lexeme which seems really appropriate, she may choose extremely general terms which would normally be discarded in favor of basic level terms, or she may switch from one term or description to another on successive mentions. If a number of appropriate terms is available, she may switch from one to another in order to avoid monotony, to avoid ambiguity, or to provide continuity within the text.

5. The speaker's goal in producing the text, which will affect the choice of stylistic level, the objectiveness of the descriptions, the degree of detail employed.

6. The speaker's perspective on the entity, which determines the choice among various deictically based terms.

7. The point in the text at which the lexeme appears, since the wording of introductory mentions and mentions occurring at narrative boundaries may be subject to different constraints than those governing mentions internal to these narrative units.

8. The history of references to the entity within the text, which may favor the consistent use of a single term or enable a more general term to serve as the entity's standard representative, bearing implicitly information introduced by more specific terms used earlier in the text.

9. The words surrounding a given lexeme within the text, from which it may be dissimilated, to avoid monotony or ambiguity; to which it may be assimilated, to provide textual cohesion.

In some cases, of course, many of these factors may not come into play. Once the speaker has decided how finely to structure her narrative, for example, she may find that there is one and only one perfectly appropriate basic level label available for the entity she wishes to refer to. In such cases she is not faced with the issue of deciding among completing descriptions, terms of different degrees of abstractness or stylistic refinement.

The fact that the decisions involved in deciding upon a particular lexical alternative may vary considerably from one case to another points up the difficulties that would undoubtedly be involved in any attempt to construct an algorithm for lexical choice based on the contributory factors suggested in this paper: the choices are so highly context-bound and the alternative strategies so numerous that it is only *post hoc* that the determinants of any particular choice can be dimly perceived. And in some cases the justification is difficult even then, for we have left the realm of linguistics and entered another, governed by the rules of aesthetics:

Finally, after interminable searching and measuring, he bent down near the piece of wood and there deposited the hollow metallic cylinder tapered at the front end, which had lodged a lead kernel until someone with a curved forefinger had exerted just enough pressure to evict the lead projectile and start it on its death-dealing change of habitat.

—Günter Grass, *The Tin Drum*

REFERENCES

Anglin, J. *Word, object, and conceptual development.* New York: W. W. Norton and Co., 1977.
Berlin, B. Speculations on the growth of ethnobotanical nomenclature, *Language in Society,* 1972, *1,* 51:86.
Berlin, B., Breedlove, D. E., & Raven P. H. General principles of classification and nomenclature in folk biology. *Ameircan Anthropologist,* 1973, *75,* 214–242.
Berlin, B., & Kay, P. *Basic color terms: their universality and evolution.* Berkeley: University of California Press, 1969.
Bolinger, D. (1967) Adjectives in English: attribution and predication. *Lingua* 1967, *18,* 1–34.
Bowditch, L. P. Why the whats are when: mutually contextualizing realms of discourse. In Thompson, H. *et al.,* Eds., Proceedings of the Second Annual Meeting of the Berkeley Linguistic Society. Berkeley: BLS, 1977.
Brown, C. General principles of human anatomical partonomy and speculations of the growth of partonomic nomenclature. *American Ethnologist* 1976, *3:*400–424.
Brown, R. W. How shall a thing be called? *Psychology Review* 1959, *65:*14–21.
Brown, R. W., & Lenneberg, D. H. A study in language and cognition. *Journal of Abnormal and Social Psychology,* 1954, *49:* 454–462.
Cruse, D. A. The pragmatics of lexical specificity. *Journal of Linguistics,* 1977, *13:*153–164.
Denny, J. P. What are noun classifiers good for? *Proceedings of the 12th Regional Meeting of the Chicago Linguistic Society.* Chicago: Chicago Linguistic Society, 1976.
Donleavy, J. P. *The ginger man.* Harmondsworth, Middlesex: Penguin, 1968.
Downing, P. A. On the creation and use of English compound nouns. *Language* 1977, *53:*810–842.
Ford, F. M. *The good soldier.* New York: Vintage, 1967.
Grass, G. *The tin drum.* New York: Random, 1971.
Grice, H. P. Logic and conversation. In Cole P. & Morgan, L. (Eds.), *Syntax and semantics* (Vol. 3). New York: Academic Press, 1975.
Halliday, M. A. K., & Hansan, Ruqaiya. *Cohesion in English.* London: Longman, 1976.
Jespersen, O. *Growth and structure of the English language* (9th ed.). Oxford: Blackwell, 1938.
Kokuritsu Kokugo Kenkyuujo. *Keigo to Keigo Ishiki.* Tokyo, 1957.
Labov, W. *Language in the inner city: studies in the Black English vernacular.* Philadelphia: University of Pennsylvania Press, 1972.
Lakoff, G. Hedges: a study in meaning criteria and a study of fuzzy concepts. *Proceedings of the Eighth Regional meeting of the Chicago Linguistic Society.* Chicago: Chicago Linguistic Society, 1972.

126 DOWNING

Lakoff, R. (1973) The Logic of politeness: or, minding your p's and q's, *Proceedings of the Ninth Regional Meeting of the Chicago Linguistic Society.* Chicago: Chicago Linguistic Society, 1973.

Lantz, DeLee, & Stefflre, V. Language and cognition revisited. *Journal of Abnormal and Social Psychology,* 1964, *69,* 472–481.

Martin, S. Speech levels in Japan and Korea. In D. Hymes (Ed.), *Language in Culture and society: A reader in linguistics and anthropology.* New York: Harper, 1964.

Nabokov, V. *Pnin,* New York: Avon, 1973.

Nelson, K. Variations in children's concepts by age and category. *Child Development,* 1975, *45,* 577–584.

Rosch, E. Human categorization. In N. Warren (Ed.), *Advances in cross-cultural psychology* (Vol. 1). London: Academic Press, 1975.

Rosch, E., Mervis, C., Gray, W., Johnson, D., Boyes-Braem, P. Basic objects in natural categories *Cognitive Pychology,* 1976, *8,* 382–439.

Searle, J. Indirect speech acts. In P. Cole & J. L. Morgan (Eds.) *Syntax and semantics* (Vol. 3). New York: Academic Press, 1975.

4 Referential Choice in English and Japanese Narrative Discourse

Patricia M. Clancy
University of California, Berkeley

The current popularity of discourse analysis has brought about a renewed interest in the study of reference and of the discourse factors influencing referential choice. For example, Hinds (1977), pointing out that the choice between nominal and pronominal reference in English is not entirely optional, gives an explanation in terms of paragraph structure. The recent volume *Papers on Discourse* (Grimes, 1978) contains several articles which examine referential strategies within the context of narrative structure. In this paper I shall explore in detail the relationship between discourse structure and choice of referential forms in the 20 English and 20 Japanese pear film narratives.*

In presenting a narrative involving a number of different characters, one of the many on-going decisions which a speaker must make is whether to refer to a particular character with a full noun phrase or some less explicit form of reference. What is the basis of this decision? Chafe (1976) has discussed the speaker's choice between pronominal and nominal reference in terms of the distinction between "given" and "new" information. "Given information," he states, "is that knowledge which the speaker assumes to be in the consciousness of the addressee at the time of the utterance." New information, in contrast, is information which the speaker assumes he is presently "activating" or "re-activating" in the hearer's consciousness.

*I am grateful to Janet Akaike-Toste, Jean Keller, and Yukiko Kurihata for their painstaking labor in transcribing the Japanese tapes, and to Masayoshi Hirose and Yukiko Kurihata for their help in interpreting and translating the narratives. I am especially grateful to Haruo Aoki for the many hours he spent explaining and discussing the Japanese data and to John Hinds for much interesting discussion of reference in Japanese.

Givenness can be established by the extralinguistic or the linguistic context; in narratives such as the present ones, it is the prior linguistic context which is important. The principal linguistic effect of the given/new distinction, Chafe suggests, is that in English, and perhaps all languages, "given information is conveyed in a weaker and more attenuated manner than new information." Thus in English given or "old" information is weakly stressed and subject to pronominalization, although speakers will tend to avoid the use of pronouns when ambiguity would result.

Once a referent has been introduced into the listener's consciousness, how long will that referent continue to be treated as given information? Clearly the speaker's treatment of an item as given should cease when he has reason to believe that the item has left his addressee's consciousness. Chafe suggests some factors which might underlie such a judgment, including the number of sentences which have elapsed without mention of a particular referent, or the effects of discourse boundaries, such as a change of scene, which brings a whole new set of items into the consciousness of the addressee, presumably pushing out old ones. Certain particularly salient items, such as the main character in a story, may have a stronger hold on givenness than other referents. One way of answering questions about givenness is to examine in depth the use of nominal vs. more attenuated forms of reference; such an investigation should give insight into the process by which new referents become established as given information, and into the factors influencing the loss or retention of that status throughout a discourse.

The task of the narrator, as just outlined, is "listener-oriented". From the speaker's point of view, he knows, before making reference to any particular character, whom he has in mind. In this paper, I avoid the question of the nature of referential forms in any underlying linguistic structure, and simply assume that what the speaker has in mind is the idea, and perhaps also mental image, of a particular referent.[1] Since at the moment of utterance the speaker himself needs no further specification of a referent beyond his own idea of that character, we can assume that explicit forms of reference would be unnecessary if, for example, the speaker were merely telling the story to himself. This suggestion finds some support in studies of children's "egocentric" speech as well as adults' "inner speech," cases in which the speaker is not concerned with the needs of a listener. Piaget (1955) has found extensive use of pronouns, even when they are entirely ambiguous, in the narratives and explanations of children, and Vygotsky (1962) claims that in his experiments on inner speech the omission of arguments of the predicate, in

---

[1] Given the findings of Downing (Chapter 3) on the wide variety of nominal terms used by a speaker in referring to a single character in these narratives, it would be impossible to state with any certainty what fuller linguistic form underlies any particular pronominal reference.

particular subjects, constituted the "basic syntactic form of inner speech." In normal discourse, it seems appropriate to conceptualize the referential choices of the speaker recounting a narrative as being based upon his assessment of the hearer's state of knowledge at any moment with respect to a particular referent, as Chafe has suggested. If it becomes difficult to decipher the identity of the referents mentioned by a speaker, as in the cases of ambiguity which occurred in these narratives, we can view the speaker as having failed, to some small degree at least, in performing the listener-oriented task of reference successfully.

Described in this way, the use of nominal vs. pronominal reference seems to be an appropriate area for psycholinguistic investigation, from the standpoint of cognitive abilities and constraints. If, for example, the human mind is capable of dealing with only a limited number of explicit and/or inexplicit references at a time, then this limitation will surely play a part in determining the nature of the "rules" for reference in any language. So far as adult speakers successfully empathize with their addressees' needs, the trends observable in speech samples such as these narratives should reveal the range of referential forms which a listener can process. Two possible cognitive constraints on this ability are the amount of time that has passed since the last mention of a referent and the number of other referents mentioned in that interval. In psychological studies, these factors of time and interference have often been proposed as parameters along which the capacity of short-term memory can be measured, although the nature of the dimensions, their exact roles, and possible interaction are still disputed (Norman, 1969). An examination of the possible effects of these factors on referential choice seems to be a useful starting point for a psycholinguistic investigation of reference. Therefore, the first section of this paper will examine the effects of time and interference on referential choice in quantitative terms, both in English and in Japanese, in an attempt to outline the range within which explicit and inexplicit forms of reference are normally used.

Although it seems likely that, in both languages, there should be general limitations on referential choice which reflect universal cognitive constraints, given the nature of discourse and the likelihood of individual differences as well, cognitive constraints alone will probably not be able to account for all the on-going referential choices which a speaker must make. In fact, research in this area points to a rather wide range within which a speaker's choice between nominal and attenuated forms of reference seems to be a matter of individual preference. Hinds (1977), for example, has examined the use of pronouns in written discourse, and points out the different referential options which are available in English to a newspaper reporter in the same context. The choice between nominal and pronominal reference, Hinds suggests, is one way in which a writer can organize information in order to convey differing degrees of prominence, with nominal reference indicating "semantically prominent" information.[2] Li and Thompson (1979) have found that in Mandarin the choice between pronominal and elliptical reference also has a discourse basis. Native speakers of Mandarin tended to insert pronouns into written narrative texts after certain adverbial expressions, such as time phrases and contrastive morphemes like "however," and at shifts between foreground and background information. Thus, at least in English and Mandarin there appears to be a range within which different forms of reference would be entirely correct, but the choice of one or the other has subtle implications regarding the structure of the discourse being presented.

The investigations of narrative structure based on the pear film stories which have been performed so far suggest that various discourse units have important psychological and linguistic implications. In recounting a narrative, speakers organize the information being presented into units of various sizes, from the episode to the sentence to the clause or case frame. These units have been shown to exhibit specific semantic, syntactic, and intonational properties. Thus episodes tend to begin with hesitations of longer than two seconds and are unified in terms of character configurations, spatial location, and coherent temporal and event sequences. Sentences tend to exhibit syntactic closure, often begin with heightened amplitude and/or pitch, usually end with falling intonation, and are separated by hesitations of about one second (Chafe, 1979). In semantic terms, sentences tend to be cohesive units which express "centers of interest" for the speaker, such as the setting of the story, introductions of characters or event sequences (Chafe, Chapter 1). The presence of such units in narrative discourse provides some indication of the organization of remembered material in the speaker's mind and also seems to have important effects on the listener's comprehension and memory (Bernardo, 1976). Apparently, the overt markers of these units, such as hesitations, serve as reflections of the speaker's cognitive processes in retrieving and organizing the material and also function as boundary demarcations for the listener to use in assimilating and storing the information. A speaker's choice of referential forms within these units may similarly be one more manifestation of the cognitive significance of such units and serve as an additional marker of these units for the hearer.

In summary, it seems clear that a speaker's choice of referential form at any particular point in his narrative will depend on a variety of factors, including his implicit awareness of the cognitive constraints on the listener's ability to decipher reference, the need to construct and mark discourse units of different

---

[2]In the present English data, however, there was no evidence of the tendency to use nominal reference at semantic "peaks" within a paragraph, as Hinds found. Perhaps this is a result of differences in referential strategies between journalistic style, which is highly conscious and edited, and more unplanned spoken discourse.

sizes, and the problems of clarity and viewpoint in recounting complex material.

In this paper I examine the 20 English and 20 Japanese narratives based on the pear movie in order to elucidate the nature of the relationship between discourse structure and referential choice. The first section of this paper provides a general comparative picture of the distribution of referential choices in English and Japanese and of the cognitive constraints which seem to be responsible for this distribution. Section 2 considers the ways in which new characters are introduced into discourse and become established as old information; the relationship between these introductions and sentential units will also be examined. In Section 3 the role of switch reference in guiding speakers' choice of nominal vs. attenuated forms of reference will be considered, including the relationship between referential choice, switch reference, and the establishment of sentence boundaries. Section 4 will focus in detail on the effects of episode boundaries on referential choice. The final section presents examples of the different referential strategies used by different speakers in describing the same scene, in particular, how they manipulate the referential possibilities of their language to avoid ambiguity and to create a point of view for their narration. By analyzing these problems of reference in both English and Japanese, it should be possible to gain some insight into which aspects of the usual range of referential choices in each language are the result of general cognitive constraints, which are based on language-specific exigencies such as the nature of the referential forms available, and which are entirely the choice of the individual speaker.

A QUANTITATIVE ANALYSIS OF THE DISTRIBUTION OF REFERENTIAL OPTIONS IN ENGLISH AND JAPANESE

In attempting a comparative analysis of reference in English and Japanese, an obvious starting point is establishing the frequency with which the available referential options were used in the speakers' narratives. In this paper I limit the analysis to third person human referents, although during their narratives, speakers did sometimes refer to themselves or address the interviewer and often mentioned inanimate objects. In English, the references to be considered include noun phrases, the various forms of the third person pronouns "he," "she," and "they," and ellipted subjects. In Japanese, the only two referential options which speakers used with any frequency were noun phrases and ellipsis. There were no occurrences in the 20 Japanese narratives of the so-called third person pronouns *kare* ("he"), *kanojo* ("she"), or *karera* ("they"), which suggests that these forms have a special status not corresponding to the role of pronouns in English. As Hinds (1978b) has suggested, these forms carry presuppositions, such as the existence of a personal relationship between the referent and the speaker, which make them inappropriate for use in these narratives. Rather, it is ellipsis which functions as the ordinary form of attenuated reference in the Japanese narratives. Ellipsis was common in English as well, but unlike its occurrence in Japanese, was limited to subject position and rather special semantic and syntactic circumstances. Since the speakers of both languages were telling the same story, they were dealing with essentially the same referential tasks in the course of their narratives. However, the inexplicit forms of reference commonly used by speakers of each langauge incorporate differing amounts of information about their referent: in English, number and gender, in Japanese, no information at all.

Table 1 presents a summary of the frequency of noun phrases, English pronouns, and ellipsis in referring to characters already introduced into discourse.[3] In English 32 percent and in Japanese 29 percent of all noun phrases were used to introduce new referents. Excluding these cases, which presumably allow speakers no freedom of choice and which account for very similar percentages of the total number of nominal references in each language, it is clear from Table 1 that in both English and Japanese, inexplicit or "old information" forms accounted for the majority of referential choices. The striking difference between the two languages is that Japanese speakers used noun phrases somewhat more than 10 percent as often as English speakers. Apparently Japanese speakers, who have available for use in such narratives only the "extremes" of full noun phrases or total ellipsis, rely more heavily on nominal forms for coreference than English speakers do.

Having established the frequency of coreferential devices in each language, we can proceed to investigate the distribution of these devices within the narratives. If cognitive constraints play a role in guiding the speaker's selection of referential form, then we might expect to find the factors of time and interference differentiating the distribution of explicit vs. attenuated forms of reference in each language. The dimension of *time* will be used to refer to the interval which has elapsed between two successive mentions of the same character within a narrative. In seeking a unit of temporal measurement, given the nature of discourse and the practical problems involved in making the measurement, it seems reasonable to use some unit of linguistic structure rather than a rigid temporal criterion such as the number of milliseconds which have passed. After all, from the standpoint of the listener, hearing a narrative does not involve simply the passage of time but rather the continuous cognitive task of processing the incoming information. From the

---

[3]The noun phrases considered in this paper include only those which were referential; the total numbers are therefore different from those in Downing's paper, since she included nonreferential noun phrases in her analysis.

TABLE 1
The Frequency of Forms Used for Coreference in
English and Japanese

	English		Japanese	
	%	No.	%	No.
Noun phrase	15.7	260	26.8	248
Pronoun	63.8	1056		
Ellipsis	20.5	339	73.2	677
		1655		925

speaker's point of view, the references which he makes to any particular character occur within discourse units of varying sizes at different points within the entire narrative and not just at certain temporal intervals. Therefore, the passage of time will be measured in terms of two linguistic units: the clause (or case frame) and the sentence. The psychological importance of the clause as a unit of linguistic processing during comprehension has been demonstrated in a number of experiments by Bever and his colleagues (Fodor et al., 1974). The cognitive significance of the sentence is also supported by experimental findings (Jarvella, 1971), Bernardo, 1976).

Of course, what is being measured in counting the clauses and sentences separating two mentions of a referent is actually a type of interference rather than merely the passing of time. And since the passage of certain clauses and sentences, such as those at episode boundaries, may have greater significance than others for the listener's processing, this measure must be regarded as providing merely a very rough general indication of the amount of cognitive activity which has been performed in the interval between two references to a particular character. As a measure of interference, the number of references to other characters which occur between two mentions of a referent has been used. Since various psychological studies have shown that to result in interference, the intervening material must be maximally similar to the original stimulus (Norman, 1969), only human referents have been counted as potential sources of interference in the interpretation of references to the characters in the narratives.

Thus the distribution of coreferential forms was described in terms of three measurements: the number of clauses separating two mentions of the same referent, the number of sentences separating the two mentions, and the number of other referents intervening between the two references. The first two of these measures were taken by counting clause and sentence boundaries; thus, if a particular referent was mentioned in one clause and then again in the immediately following clause, this was counted as "1" clause boundary). In English genitive pronouns constituted the greater majority of

"0" clause cases; there were no cases of more than one nominal reference to the same character within the same clause. Reflexive pronouns have not been included in the analysis owing to the difficulty of categorizing the Japanese form *jibun* ("self") in terms of a tripartite noun phrase/pronoun/ellipsis distinction and also because of the extremely small number of reflexives which occured. In Japanese, the "0" clause cases were all nominal references in which the speaker repeated, sometimes modifying, a noun phrase before completing the clause. (These cases will be discussed in more detail in the section on introducing referents into discourse.) Sentence boundaries were counted in the same way, with "0" indicating a reference occurring within the same sentence as the preceding mention of the same referent and "1" indicating that a sentence boundary separates the two mentions of the referent. Interference was measured by simply counting the number of other referents mentioned between any two references to the same character, disregarding the number of times the intervening referent was mentioned.

In English, taking the three measurements was relatively straightforward. Ellipted subjects were counted as occurring in preverbal position. It was sometimes difficult to make these tabulations in Japanese in such a way as to achieve "equivalent" figures, particularly because of the extensive use of ellipsis and the many syntactic differences between English and Japanese. (Footnote 4 presents a detailed discussion of how these problems were tackled.)

---

[4]Word order differences between English and Japanese raised problems requiring special treatment. In Japanese postposed subjects were counted as part of the clause and sentence containing their predicate, although in such cases a form of sentence-final falling intonation often occurs before the postposed subject is verbalized. In counting the number of clauses separating two mentions of a referent, relative clauses, which in Japanese precede their head noun, were not counted as clauses intervening between the mention of a referent in one clause and its occurrence as head noun of a relative clause in the following main clause. That is, the head nouns of relative clauses were treated as being "shared" by the preceding relative clause and the main clause in which the head noun functions as an argument of the verb. Thus if the referent of such a head noun had been mentioned in the preceding main clause, only one clause boundary would be counted despite the presence of the relative clause.

Various problems occurred in tabulating interference in Japanese due to ellipsis, since in many cases the number of interventions to be counted depends upon where in a clause one assumes the ellipsis of a referent to have occurred. Since the referents of missing arguments of a verb are primarily recoverable on the basis of the information in the verb, all omitted arguments were counted as if they occurred simultaneously with the verb. Thus in the following example

(a) *itta n da kedomo,*
    ...sono tochuu de,
    ano--...onna no ko ga tootta no ne?
    sono..onna no ko o..mite,

(he) went on but,
... on the way,
uh-- ... a girl passed.
(He) looked .. at that .. girl,

the bicycle boy is the subject of the first and last lines. Since in Japanese objects usually precede the verb, as does the direct object *onna no ko* in line 4, the ellipted subject in line 4 is counted as having occurred at the verb *mite* ("looked at"), and therefore is not counted as intervening between the two mentions of the girl. (Note that although the girl is mentioned twice, this is counted as only one intervening referent between two elliptical references to the bicycle boy.)

Another problem in Japanese arises in attempting to decide which verbs actually require nonsubject arguments. It is simple enough to assume that each verb takes a subject, but it becomes much more difficult to decide when nonsubject arguments are actually being ellipted. In making the tabulations, the general procedure followed was to be as strict as possible in counting ellipted nonsubjects; the only verbs counted were those which express actions that seem impossible to comprehend or form a mental image of without the presence of a human referent other than that of the subject. Thus, for example, the verb *ageru* ("give") was always assumed to involve both a subject and an indirect object. The number of these verbs was extremely small, also including *watasu* ("hand over"), *surechigau* ("pass"), *mitoreru* ("be fascinated by"), and a few others. The decisions were ultimately based upon the intuitions of a native speaker about the possibility of visualizing the event in question. Even verbs such as *miru* ("see") and *tooru* ("pass") were not counted as having ellipted nonsubject human arguments, since in the sentences in which they occurred, ambiguity was possible between a reading in which it was another character who was seen or passed and an interpretation in which it was an event or sequence of events that was seen or a place that was passed. Therefore, the number of ellipted nonsubjects counted as intervening referents probably represents a minimal, but reliable amount.

Using the same criterion, it was decided to count all actions embedded in verbs of giving and receiving as having human indirect objects. In Japanese actions performed by one person for the benefit of another are typically embedded in verbs such as *ageru* ("give"), *yaru* ("give"), *kureru* ("give") and *morau* ("receive"). These verbs therefore appeared very frequently in speakers' descriptions of the scenes in which the bicycle boy was helped by the threesome and then gave them three pears in exchange for his hat. However, the beneficiary of the actions in the case of the various verbs of giving and the agent in the case of *morau* were almost invariably omitted from explicit mention. In a sense, these verbs tend to function rather like inflectional transitivity, suggesting or implying that there was a beneficiary or agent in the action described. Since it is syntactically possible for the beneficiary or agent to be expressed, and since such verbs cannot be used unless there is a beneficiary or agent on the scene and therefore in any mental image of the event, all cases of events embedded in these verbs were counted as having ellipted beneficiaries or agents. Thus in the following example a reference to the bicycle boy is counted as an ellipted indirect object occurring at the verb *agete* ("gave"):

(b) ... *De otoko no ko ga sannin choodo toorikakarimashite,*
    ... *sore o* ... *ano hirotte agete,*

    ... And three boys just then passed by,
    ... and (they) ... uh picked it up (for him),

A truly perplexing problem is how to deal with cases in which both subject and nonsubject are ellipted in the same clause, as in the last line of the example above. If both referents, the bicycle boy and the threesome, are counted as occurring simultaneously with the verb, should each be counted as having an intervening mention of the other referent? Furthermore, in the cases of events embedded in verbs of giving and receiving, where should an ellipted subject referent be counted: with the first verb, the second, or both? It does not seem likely that there are two ellipted references to the subject in cases such as *hirotte agete* above; one piece of evidence is that in fast, colloquial speech the two verbs are often elided, as in *hirottagete,* so that the verbs of giving and receiving are treated rather like transitivity markers on the main verb. As for the ellipted beneficiary, since comprehension of constructions like *hirotte agete* seems to call to mind both actor and beneficiary, it seems intuitively correct to assume that at the utterance of such "double" verbs, a listener will call to mind both referents in much the same way as he does when understanding the verb *ageru* with two ellipted referents. Therefore, although there is no strong psychological evidence supporting this decision, all such cases were counted as having two ellipted referents, subject and indirect object, each of which intervenes between the current elliptical mention of that referent and the prior mention. Thus as a result of the last line in the example cited, an intervening mention of the bicycle boy will be counted as having occurred between the mention of the threesome in line 1 and the ellipted reference to the threesome at *hirotte agete.*

One final problem with ellipsis calls for comment, i.e., the treatment of genitive referents. Possessor noun phrases were, of course, counted, but it is extremely difficult to determine in Japanese when it would be appropriate to assume that a genitive has been ellipted. In these narratives the items which frequently occurred with possessor noun phrases and pronouns in English included body parts and a variety of "alienable" possessions, such as the bicycle boy's hat and bicycle and the pear man's apron, baskets, and pears. These objects, however, were also frequently preceded by definite and indefinite articles rather than genitives. In the Japanese narratives, these same items were sometimes preceded by possessor noun phrases and the genitive particle *no,* but most commonly the nouns occurred with no such modification. One set of candidates for possible ellipted genitives were those objects having a possessor who is crucially relevant to the narrative, such as the bicycle boy's hat, but are mentioned with no modifying phrase for the first time in mid-narration. Other likely candidates would seem to be objects whose possessor is ambiguous at the point of mention, such as *jitensha* ("bicycle") in the accident episode, where the boy and girl are both on bicycles. In Japanese the possessor in such cases was often the subject referent of the prior clause, as in the following example:

(c) *Un... kawaii onna no ko ga,*
    jitensha ni notte,
    mukoo kara kite,
    surechigatta no ne?
 5 *De,*
    mitoreta hyooshi ni,
    kaze de booshi o tobasarechatte,
    omake ni ookii ishi ga atta n de,
    soko ni,
    jitensha ga butsukatte,
    .. taorechatta n.

Uh... a cute girl,
riding on a bicycle,
came from the other side,
and passed (him), you know?
And,
when (he) was fascinated (by her),
(his) hat was blown off by the wind,

Figures 1a–c and 2a–c present a summary of the distribution of nominal, pronominal, and elliptical reference in English and Japanese with respect to the selected measures of "time" and "interference." The percentages on the ordinate indicate, for a particular type of reference in each language, what percentage of the total occurrences of that form fell within the limit specified by the numbers on the abscissa. Thus in English, for example, we can see in Figure 1 (a) that 24 percent of all noun phrases occurred in the clause immediately following the last mention of the referent in question, and 33 percent after 2–4 clauses had elapsed. Similarly, Figure 1 (b) shows that 21 percent of all noun phrases occurred within the same sentence as the prior mention, 39 percent following one sentence boundary. In Figure 1 (c), we find that of all nominal references in English 23 percent occurred with no intervening mention of any other character, 54 percent following the mention of one character. (Complete charts of the data on which Figures 1–3 (a–c) are based are in Appendix I.)

It is clear from Figures 1–2 (a–c) that within each language the distributions of the available referential choices are strongly differentiated from each other in terms of these parameters. In Figure 1 (a–c) the percentage of noun phrases in English which occur within the immediately following clause or same sentence as the last mention of the referent or with no intervening referents is extremely small compared to the percentages of pronouns and ellipsis, illustrating the comparatively greater constraints exercised by the forces of time and interference upon the inexplicit referential choices. Figure 2 (a–c) shows that similar distributional differences exist in Japanese, too. The great majority of elliptical references occur within the immediately following clause

---

and also there was a big rock,
and there
(his) bicycle ran into (it),
..and fell.

In this example the subject referent switches from the girl to the bicycle boy in line 6, and then both the hat and the bicycle are assumed to be his. The hat was being mentioned here for the first time, and would probably have been called "his hat" in English. Until much further research has been done on this topic in Japanese, it seems premature to assume that there must be an ellipted possessor in such cases. As Hinds (1978a) has pointed out, questions such as "whose hat" in these examples may not even be relevant to Japanese; the lack of specified possessors in these Japanese narratives never seemed to cause any serious problems or ambiguity that was not immediately resolved by the story line. Furthermore, since no attempt was made to isolate in the English narratives those cases of noun phrases, such as "the hat" or "the bicycle," which were used for items which were, in fact, ambiguous or insufficiently introduced, it would not be fair to assume ellipted possessors for all such cases in Japanese. Therefore, although possessor noun phrases have been counted, no ellipted genitives were included in the Japanese tabulations of ellipsis.

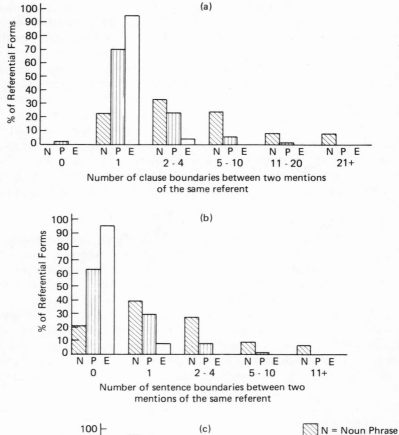

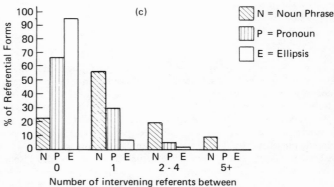

FIG. 1(a-c). Distribution of Coreferential Forms in English with respect to Time and Interference

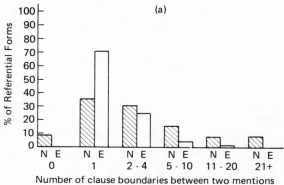

Number of clause boundaries between two mentions
of the same referent

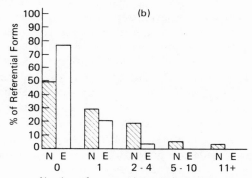

Number of sentence boundaries between two
mentions of the same referent

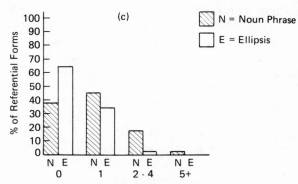

Number of intervening referents between
two mentions of the same referent

FIG. 2(a-c). Distribution of Coreferential Forms in Japanese with respect to
Time and Interference

or same sentence as the last mention of a particular referent or with no other referents intervening; this is true of less than half of nominal references.

If time and interference represent general cognitive constraints on the ability to decipher inexplicit references, then we might expect to find that these forces exert a stronger influence on the distribution of inexplicit as compared to explicit referential forms in any language. Comparing Figure 1 (a–c) with Figure 2 (a–c), it is apparent that the distributions of English pronouns and Japanese ellipsis are more similar than those of nominal references. With respect to the number of clauses elapsed since the last mention of a referent—(compare Figures 1(a) and 2(a))—the distributions of pronouns and ellipses are quite similar. In English 71 percent of pronouns and in Japanese 72 percent of ellipses occur within the same or immediately following clause as the last mention of a referent. (Genitive pronouns in English provided a tiny group, 1.2 percent, of same-clause inexplicit references which had no counterpart in Japanese.) Japanese speakers did use a noticeably greater proportion of ellipsis within a single sentence than was the case for English pronouns; however, a number of the Japanese speakers used considerably longer sentences than the English speakers. With respect to interference, the distributions of English pronouns and Japanese ellipsis are almost identical.[5] The slightly greater proportion of ellipsis after one intervention in Japanese as compared to English may occur because ellipted subjects in Japanese were counted as having one intervention if an oblique argument was also omitted from the case frame. In English, of course, since pronominal subjects precede pronominal oblique arguments, the status of the latter had no effect on the way the subject was counted. Whatever the inadequacies of the scoring techniques may have been, the overwhelming finding is that the distributions of inexplicit reference forms are basically the same in both languages. Apparently, the lack of information in Japanese ellipsis compared with English pronouns did not result in a more restricted use of ellipsis with respect to time or interference. Perhaps in order to be useful the ordinary inexplicit forms of reference in a language must be able to function at least within the range observed in Figures 1–2 (a–c); following one clause in which the referent has not been mentioned and following mention of one other referent. Since the forms of inexplicit reference in different languages convey different amounts of information about their referents, some languages will simply be more difficult to follow than others in deciphering reference. It would be interesting to compare the distribution of ellipsis in Japanese with another language which makes extensive use of ellipsis in order to discover whether the distribution of these forms in Figures

---

[5]Note that since the movie involved mostly male characters, the possibility of ambiguity with the pronoun "he" was perhaps greater than usual, making the English and Japanese distributions more similar than they might otherwise have been.

1-2 (a-c) represents an upper limit on the amount of work a language can force its hearers to perform in deciphering reference.

If we imagine the speaker as having his own inner "dial" set on an inexplicit form of reference, we can conceptualize his use of noun phrase reference as a response to various listener-oriented constraints. Since the distribution of forms of reference in both English and Japanese is clearly responsive to the effects of time and interference, we can use the percentage of nominal reference as an index of speakers' response to listeners' needs in a particular environment. Figure 3(a-c) summarizes the effects of time and interference in terms of this index, the frequency of nominal reference. Figure 3(a-c) provides a simple means of comparing English and Japanese speakers in their reaction to the effects of time and interference when deciding whether a noun phrase is necessary.

As Figure 3(a-b) reveals, in both languages as the distance from the last mention of a referent increases, speakers increasingly tend to select a noun phrase. Similarly, in Figure 3(c) we see that, as the number of intervening characters mentioned increases, speakers become less and less likely to treat a formerly mentioned referent as old information. Comparing the two languages we find that Japanese speakers are more likely to use nominal reference in the immediately following clause, within the same sentence and despite a lack of intervening referents, than English speakers. If these parameters can be taken as representing cognitive constraints, then it seems that Japanese speakers are much more likely to use nominal reference when there is no cognitive reason to do so. (The 100 percent rate of nominal reference within the same clause represents the cases of nominal introductions which were repeated before finishing the clause, and which will be discussed further. It was impossible to determine whether there were any cases of two elliptical mentions of the same referent within a single clause in Japanese).

In both English and Japanese, the passage of individual clauses apparently has a weaker effect in eliciting nominal reference than the occurrence of sentence boundaries or intervening referents. Comparing the two languages we see that both show more gradual increases in the frequency of noun phrases in Figure 3(a) than in 3(b-c); in the case of sentence boundaries or interference the percentage of nominal reference quickly rises above 50 percent. In Japanese by the time more than 10 clauses had elapsed, speakers used nominal reference in 12 of the 13 cases, whereas in English the percentage was noticeably smaller. One possible explanation for this is that the Japanese narratives were in general shorter than the English ones and therefore the passage of 10 clauses covers a larger portion of the whole narrative than the same number of clauses in English. As a variety of evidence will indicate, the crossing of an episode boundary tends to cause speakers to shift to nominal reference, and Japanese speakers necessarily crossed more episode boundaries within fewer clauses.

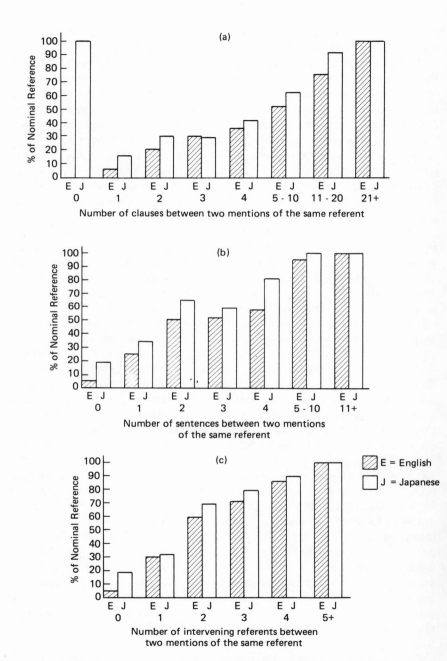

FIG. 3(a-c). The Frequency of Nominal Reference in English and Japanese

As we see in Figure 3(b), in both languages the occurrence of a sentence boundary, which represents the passage of a longer time and the completion of a more complex cognitive unit, elicited a higher frequency of noun phrases. In English the first two sentence boundaries are accompanied by major increases in the frequency of nominal reference. At the point of five sentence boundaries a single pronominal reference occurred; after this point all references were noun phrases. In Japanese the effects of sentence boundaries are rather difficult to evaluate, since speakers showed striking individual differences in sentence structure. Some speakers seemed to place sentence boundaries in much the same manner as English speakers; others used extremely long sentences, occasionally even recounting the entire narrative in from one to three long sentences. Thus for certain Japanese speakers the ordinary size of discourse units was reversed and sentences, which in English constitute a kind of intermediate unit between the case frame and the episode, incorporated several different episodes. This probably accounts for the comparatively greater increases in nominal reference with passing sentence boundaries in Japanese.

In both English and Japanese, interference generally played the strongest role in eliciting nominal references. In English the intervention of a single referent was accompanied by a 25 percent increase in nominal reference; the intervention of a second referent resulted in an additional 28 percent increase. In Japanese, given the higher base rate of nominal reference, the effect of a single intervention is smaller; it is interesting to note, however, that the frequency of nominal reference after one intervening referent is almost the same in both languages, 30 percent in English and 33 percent in Japanese. In contrast, the response of Japanese speakers to the intervention of two referents is somewhat greater than that of English speakers, producing a 35 percent increase. We might speculate that since the common alternative to nominal reference in Japanese is complete ellipsis, the dangers of ambiguity tend to be even greater than in English where pronouns convey information about number and gender.

In summary, speakers of both English and Japanese preferred inexplicit forms of reference for characters who had already been introduced into their narratives. In English speakers apparently feel that inexplicit reference is still comprehensible after the passage of two clauses, (with 84 percent of all pronouns falling within this range) or of one sentence (93 percent); Japanese speakers agree, with 86 percent of all cases of ellipsis occurring after two or fewer clauses and 97 percent after no more than one sentence boundary. In both languages at least 97 percent of all inexplicit references were made when no more than one other character had been mentioned. Yet as the exceptions to these trends reveal, time and interference cannot account for all referential choices. Therefore, in the following sections of this paper the content of the narratives will be examined in order to clarify how discourse structure may have influenced referential choice, particularly at the points when time and interference apparently did not dictate speakers' choices.

INTRODUCING NEW REFERENTS
INTO DISCOURSE

In the preceding section we saw that although Japanese and English speakers' choice of referential forms has much in common, Japanese speakers do tend to use a larger number of nominal references, even where cognitive constraints do not seem to be operating against the use of ellipsis. This suggests that perhaps language-specific discourse constraints are responsible for some of speakers' referential choices. One way to investigate this hypothesis is to examine those places in the Japanese and English narratives where nominal reference occurred, in order to establish whether anything about the nature of the discourse at these points might be responsible for the differences in form of reference in the two languages. An obvious starting point is examining the places in the narratives where new characters were introduced into the story line. As noted in the previous section, such introductions of new referents were responsible for 32 percent of all the nominal references in the English narratives and 29 percent of those in Japanese.

The introduction of a new character in the narrative seems to be one point in the discourse where the speaker has no options in his choice of referential form. It is clear that a prerequisite for treating a referent as old information in the context of the speakers' task in this experiment would be at least one prior mention of the referent in question. A basic question is whether introductions of new referents were always accomplished through the use of nominal reference in both languages. If this was not the case, what special conditions might be responsible for the use of inexplicit forms of reference in introducing new referents into discourse? Once a speaker has introduced a new character into the narrative, what does it take to establish that referent as old information? Is a single nominal mention sufficient to allow the speaker to assume that he may now use pronominal or elliptical reference? Since prior research has suggested that the introduction of a new referent is one of the major reasons for episode boundaries, an additional point for investigation is how introductions are accomplished with respect to discourse units. Here I shall be concerned only with the sentence. If a sentence represents a "chunk" of material which the speaker finds coherent enough to establish as a single unit, what might be the role of introductions of new referents in establishing these units?

Considering the first question, whether or not referents were introduced into discourse with noun phrases, we find that, surprisingly, although speakers usually used nominal reference in their first mention of a new character, this was not invariably true. In fact, two of the introductions in English were made with a pronoun, and three in Japanese with ellipsis. Since all these cases occurred at the introduction of the pear man, it appears that if speakers experienced difficulty in introducing a referent, it was primarily at the very beginning of their narrative.

Examining these cases in detail, there were a variety of reasons for the use of pronouns or ellipsis in introducing a new referent. In one of the English cases, it seems that the speaker merely became sidetracked in the middle of her introduction, and might have used a noun phrase if she had not decided to shift to the topic of the pear man's nationality. The momentary distraction or confusion of making this shift seems to have caused her to forget briefly about the needs of the listener.

(1) Uh...The opening scene..was..uh..ay--..kind of middle aged round,
...possibly he looked like he was made up..to be...a Mexican ...or th...that...kind of person,
picking..pears from a tree.

Two of the Japanese introductions using ellipsis seemed to be based on the speaker's presupposition that the listener was familiar with the character in question. In fact, this was a reasonable assumption since the speakers were aware that the interviewer had heard the narrative a number of times before their own telling. Thus part of the problem may have been that these speakers did not really approach the task in the same spirit as the others. In one case, the speaker gave an extremely abbreviated version of the plot, which would be incomprehensible to someone who was not already quite familiar with it. Thus the unusual introduction of the pear man was only part of the larger problem of performing the task of narration in this particular situation. After a description of the setting, this speaker simply plunged into the narrative without actually introducing the pear man.

(2) ...De koo...heiwa na sugoi nanka,
nani goto mo nai yoo na kanji no--...mura ka machi de,
...maa,
...nashi o...totte te,

...And uh...extremely peaceful uh,
in a village or town...where it seems like nothing is happening,
...well,
...(he) is picking...pears,

The other Japanese speaker who introduced the pear man using ellipsis was also approaching the entire task in a somewhat different manner from other speakers. She assumed from the beginning that the characters and basic plot of the story were familiar to the interviewer, and instead of recounting the plot as the new information, she presupposed the basic elements of the story as old information, and concerned herself primarily with presenting her own attitudes and on-going reactions when watching the film.

(3) *E--to ne,*
    . . . eto des . . mieta mono . . nanka,
    . . . ningen no . . . zai ga iroiro soo yuu no ga miete,
    . . . sos . . . nanka-- . . saisho--,
    . . . saisho ne?
    nanka . . . yagi o . . . tsureta
    . . . hito ga . . . kita toki ni wa,
    *. . . nanka yappari tanin no koto wa zenzen ki ni shinai no ka na tte
        omotte,*
    tsu . . tsugi no kodomo no toki ni wa,
    . . . nanka . . . motte itchatta ne?

    Well,
    . . . Well . . what (I) saw . . let's see,
    . . . (I) saw various sorts of human . . . failings,
    . . . and then . . . let's see . . . at first,
    . . . at first you know?
    uh . . . when a man
    leading . . . a goat came,
    . . . (I) thought that (he) isn't paying any attention to other people's
        business,
    and in the next scene with the child,
    . . . (he) carried something off, you know?

The above example raises the issue of the perspective or point of view from which speakers recounted the story. As Chafe has pointed out (1979), the speakers had been exposed to two distinct "worlds" of experience: the "real" world with the movie and the interviewer, and the world of the film, in which a man was picking pears, etc. The "real" world can be taken as including all references to the fact that the story had been seen as a movie, to the interviewer and the act of storytelling, and also to the interpretations and emotional responses experienced by the speaker. Although speakers generally presented the story in terms of the film world, as if describing events which had actually occurred, they often digressed into the real world, commenting on the quality of the movie or its message. Tannen (Chapter 2) discusses these differences in terms of a "direct" vs. a "film-viewer" perspective. The distinction between these two perspectives, or between the two "worlds" of experience had important effects on speakers' use of referential forms. In the preceding example, the speaker presented her narrative almost entirely from the "film-viewer" perspective and thus in the "real" world, and therefore felt free to let her referential choices reflect the interviewer's familiarity with the story.

One interesting result of this "double world" situation facing the speakers was that sometimes the first mention of a character would be made in the "real" world, but if the speaker then switched to the "story" world, she would introduce the character again.

> (4) Okay,
> well...it starts out
> ...it's...the setting looks like it's a place...maybe--...in
> California, the Santa Barbara area, ... or something like that.
> 5 ...uh-- there was ...this orchard's around him.
> ...I guess what he's picking is pears.
> ...There's a..uh...farm laborer,
> a Mexican farm laborer picking pears

This speaker began her narrative from the "film-viewer" perspective, and her first pronominal references to the pear man reflect the assumption, which is appropriate in the "real" world, that the interviewer knows which character she is referring to. At line 7 she abruptly shifts to the "story" world, leaving her own comments and reflections, and introduces the pear man with a noun phrase, as if he had not yet been mentioned. A very similar case was the remaining Japanese elliptical introduction:

> (5) ...eto ano..nanka...chotto..nanijin...ka..wakannakatta
> n dakedo, kurabu...A!
> kurabu ja nai.
> ...ano...nan tte yuu n kashira,
> 5 kudamono o nanka shuukaku shite te ne?
> Sorede,
> ...ano otoko no hito ga shuukaku shite,
>
> > ...Well uh..let's see...uh...I couldn't figure out what
> > nationality (he) was
> > but kurabu...Oh!
> > it's not kurabu.
> > ...uh...what do you call it,
> > 5 (I) guess (he) was harvesting fruit, you know?
> > Then,
> > ...uh a man was harvesting,

148 CLANCY

Here again the speaker begins her narrative in the "real" world, in which she is trying to think of the right word to describe the pear man's nationality, and almost seems to be talking to herself. At line 7 she abandons any further reflections on the pear man and enters the "story" world by introducing the pear man as if this was the first mention of that character.

Similar examples can be found in the English speakers' use of "the" in introducing new referents. Thus a speaker will sometimes make her first mention of a character in the "real" world, using "the" since she knows the interviewer will be able to identify the referent in question. Upon turning to the "story" world, however, the same character will be reintroduced using "a."

>   (6) ... A man was picking pears in ... what seemed to be his orchard,
>   ... and-- ... came along first,
>   .. / someone/ came along first.
>   ... Someone came along before the kid on the bicycle
>   but I don't remember
>   who it was.
>   ... Then a kid came along on a bicycle,

In this case the speaker began in the "story" world, introducing the pear man, but then had to switch back to the "real" world to explain to the interviewer that she could not remember the next character who appeared. In doing so, she makes her first mention of the bicycle boy using "the," correctly assuming that the interviewer will know who she means. However, upon returning to her narration, she reintroduces him as "a kid."[6]

These examples raise the question of what it takes to establish a referent as old information in a narrative. If the extralinguistic context allows speakers to assume that the listener is aware of the referent they have in mind, as was the case in the "real" world of the experimental situation, pronouns and ellipsis can be used even when no prior mention of the character has been made, as in examples (1–3). As examples (4–6) reveal, however, such a mention is often not felt to be sufficient to establish a referent as old information in the "story" world, and a nominal reference will be used to do so. Thus it appears that the "prior mention" condition on the use of attenuated forms of reference should in some cases be modified to "prior mention in the same world." Some of the most striking examples of such

---

[6]A more subtle shift in the narrator's orientation than such "world" changes, but which also affects forms of reference in introductions, involves changes in "mode" from narration to description, as DuBois (Chapter 5) describes. In example (6) the speaker's inability to recall the appropriate information for an adequate descriptive introduction of the goat man has apparently triggered the change in "world" in line 4. The shift from narrative to descriptive mode occasionally, but by no means always, coincides with a shift from "story" to "real" world.

reintroductions occurred when the speaker's shift of "worlds" involved real digressions from the story line, as in example (7) below, or sudden time shifts such as the flashback in example (8).

(7) ...and then...definitely when he's up there,
...a kid comes by on a bicycle.
...from the direction where the goat man left, okay?
...And--...uh...the bicycle's way too big for the kid.
...I'm giving you all these details.
I don't know if you want them.
...um...the...the reason I've giving you the details is cause I don't know what the point of the movie was.
...Okay?
So maybe you can see something that I didn't.
...Okay?
um--...g a kid comes by on a bicycle,

(8) ...and then he..starts going back...up his ladder,
and-- um--...Oh!
...The film starts off..with just...sort of a scene...of the country..and a path.
...And you hear..a rooster crowing.
...And then it..it..pans into this man.

It is important to note that not all speakers made such a distinction between worlds during their introductions of characters; in fact, the most common tendency was to pronominalize a newly introduced referent immediately after the first mention in English, despite any shifts in worlds that may have occurred. The following example is typical:

(9) ...And then um--...he's...fixing himself up,
and...then all of a sudden you see these three little boys who've...saw this whole thing.
...And they come down,

In this example the speaker shifts from a "direct" perspective to a "film-viewer" point of view in line 2 with the words "you see..." and then shifts back to the story in line 4 without reintroducing the threesome in the "story" world. Therefore, it seems that this phenomena may be most appropriately described by saying that there are certain points in a discourse where the speaker has the option of using nominal reference, although a pronoun would usually be expected. Apparently one such "vulnerable" position in a narrative is during the introduction of referents, who may be introduced separately into different worlds of discourse. In Japanese, where the narratives tended to be shorter, such digressions during introductions did not occur. With the exception of example (5), there were no cases in which a character introduced in one world was reintroduced with a noun phrase in another world. As in English, the distinction between worlds was usually ignored as far as referential choice was concerned, as the following example illustrates:

(10) *tsu... tsugi no kodomo no toki ni wa,*
... nanka... motte itchatta ne?
... Sorede,
.. nan tte yuu ko daroo to omotte,

and in the next scene with the child,
... (he) carried something off, you know?
... Then,
... (I) thought, "what an awful kid,"

The data in the preceding section have shown that the use of nominal reference is more common in Japanese than in English, and that this is apparently not the result of cognitive constraints alone. In particular, Japanese speakers used a large number of noun phrases within the same or immediately following clause as the preceding mention of a referent, when no other referents had been mentioned. Many of these cases result from the way in which new characters were introduced into the Japanese narratives. In English there were 17 cases in which a referent was mentioned with a noun phrase following introduction even though no other referents had intervened. The major reason for such cases, accounting for 13 instances, was a shift of worlds during the introduction of a referent into discourse, as described earlier. However, in Japanese there were 39 cases in which newly introduced referents were not immediately treated as old information following their first mention, only one of which could be attributed to a world shift. Examining the Japanese introductions in detail should help clarify this use of nominal reference.

In Japanese there were two major reasons for the use of noun phrases to refer to newly introduced characters after their first mention. One-third of these cases involved the repetition of the noun phrase, usually with the addition of some descriptive modifiers, immediately following the first mention and before continuing the rest of the sentence. Sometimes the speaker seemed to be dissatisfied with the taxonomic level at which he first categorized the character being introduced. In these cases the speaker would often give a more specific categorization of a character first mentioned in more general terms as in examples (11) and (12). (cf. Downing, Chapter 3, for more detailed discussion of categorization and introductions).

(11) *Ano ne?*
   ano-- mazu
   ano--.. otok otoko no hito desu ka?
   Noofusan ga,
   ano-- ano-- ki no tokoro de,
   yoonashi o totte iru wake nan desu.

   uh you know?
   uh-- first
   uh--.. a man?
   A farmer,
   uh-- uh-- in a tree,
   was picking pears.

(12) *Hito ga tootte tte,*
   sannin,
   ... un--otoko no ko sannin ka na?
   ... tootte kite,

   People went past,
   three,
   ... uh-- three boys?
   ... came along,

Taxonomic switches can also be found in English as in the following cases:

(13) ... And .. on his way ... riding,
   he comes across another ... bicyclist ... bicyclist
   it's a young woman,

(14) and he sees another ... person coming ... toward him,
   ... and it's another little white girl.
   ... with long .. braids, ... brown hair.

As the latter example reveals, in English it is possible syntactically to add descriptive information to a head noun merely by continuing the sentence with relative clauses or modifying "with" phrases. In Japanese, however, speakers apparently prefer to include such information in relative clauses which must precede the head noun. Therefore speakers must pre-plan both their initial categorization of a new character and any qualifying modifiers they wish to use. A common strategy for reducing the amount of pre-planning is to produce the nominal categorization, and then backtrack adding modifiers and repeating or changing the initial categorization before producing the rest of the sentence. The following examples are typical:

(15) *Soide.. sorede moo shuukaku no jiki de,*
  otoko no hito ga,
  ..futotta otoko no hito ga,
  hitori de ne?
  ..sono... seiyoo nashi no... ko mi o totteru no ne.

  Then... then it's already the harvest season,
  and a man,
  .. a fat man,
  by himself, you know?
  .. is picking the fruit... uh of those... western pears.

(16) *De,*
  soko no tokoro.. ni
  ano-- kodomo ga,
  chiisai shoogakkoo.. gurai no ko ga,
  jitensha de kite,

  And,
  to.. that place,
  uh-- a child,
  a little child of about grammar school age,
  came on a bicycle,

In general, it was very common in the Japanese narratives to treat the subject of a sentence as an intonationally separate unit, often followed by the particle *ne,* (translated as "you know") as if wishing to secure the listener's comprehension of the subject before continuing. Therefore, the common strategy of repeating the subject with additional modifiers is not really that different syntactically from many other introductions, and does not seem to cause any real disruption of the sentence structure, as a comparison of the following examples with (11-12) and (15-16) will show.

(17) ... *Sono ki ga atte ne,*
  ... *futotta ojisan ga ne,*
  ... *hige hayashite saa,*

  ... That tree is there,
  ... and a fat man,
  ... with a beard, see,

Sometimes even when there seemed to be no question of wanting to correct or modify the noun initially used, speakers would use more than one nominal reference during the first clauses of introduction, as in the following cases:

(18) ... *tsugi ne,*
     ... *unto* ... *otoko no ko ga,*
     ... *jitensha ni notte ne,*
     otoko no ko ga toorisugiyoo to suru no ne?

     ... after that,
     ... uh ... a boy,
     ... riding on a bicycle,
     a boy is about to pass, you know?

(19) *Sore kara ato,*
     ... *otoko no ko ga* ... *tootte,*
     ... *sono ko wa,*
     jitensha ni notte imashita ne?

     Then afterwards,
     ... a boy ... passed,
     ... and the boy,
     was riding on a bicycle, you know?

In view of such cases, it seems safe to conclude that the "extra" nominal references which occur during Japanese introductions of new characters into narratives are not merely the result of planning problems arising from Japanese syntax, but rather represent a more general tendency to use more than a single noun phrase reference when introducing a new character. It is almost as if ellipsis, which preserves no information about a newly introduced referent, is too radical a form to use after presenting the listener with only a single noun phrase to establish a new character in his mind.[7] Therefore, in contrast with an English narrator, the Japanese speaker will often give his addressee more opportunities to anchor the new referent in mind before continuing the story line using ellipsis.

The other major reason for nominal references in Japanese after the introduction of a new character, when no other characters intervene, was to

---

[7] A remarkable parallel to this finding has been discovered by Maibaum (1978) in her examination of Jirel narratives. Jirel is a Tibeto-Burman language spoken in eastern Nepal; it offers three referential options to speakers: nominal, pronominal, and elliptical reference. Immediately following the introduction of a new character, however, ellipsis may not be used in referring to that character; only nominal or pronominal reference is permissible.

mark the subtle transition from "introduction" to "action" in the story line. New characters were usually first mentioned in terms of their appearance or arrival on the scene, along with some descriptive information.[8] This introduction usually involved the verbs *tooru* ("pass"), *kuru* ("come") and in the case of the threesome *tatsu* ("stand"). Then when the character begins to perform a series of activities, a noun phrase is once again used, as in the following examples:

(20) ... *soshitara,*
        ano ... sannin no ... otoko no ko ga sa,
        ... *ano soko ni ... tatte ta wake.*
        ... *Tatte ta tte yuu ka,*
    5 ... *soko ni ita no ne.*
        Soshitara sono booya tachi ga,
        .. *ano-- ... nashi o irete yattari,*

        ... then,
        uh ... three ... boys,
        ... uh were standing ... there.
        ... Should (I) say standing,
    5 ... (they) were there.
        Then those boys,
        ... uh-- ... put in the pears (for him),

(21) ... *sono ato,*
        jitensha ni notta
        otoko no ko ga,
        hantai gawa kara yatte kite,
        ... *sono ko ga nashi o mite,*

        ... after that,
        a boy
        riding on a bicycle,
        came from the opposite direction,
        ... and that boy looked at the pears,

---

[8]Again, this distinction does not coincide with DuBois's differentiation of narrative and descriptive modes (see Chapter 5). A shift to descriptive mode may occur within what I am considering an introduction, but this is not necessarily the case. In example (20) the shift from descriptive back to narrative mode in line 6 does coincide with the introduction-action shift. In example (21) however, the descriptive mode is limited to the relative clause on line 2 of the Japanese (translated as "riding a bicycle" on line 3 of the English), and in this case the introduction-action shift has no relation to differences between narration and description.

In the English narratives, the switch from introduction to action in cases without interference was never marked by use of nominal reference, although perhaps this boundary was marked by other devices, such as sentence-final intonation or a switch from ellipsis to pronominal reference. In all the English narratives there was only a single case of more than one noun phrase being used after the initial introduction. This was a case in which a comparison was being made between the pear man and the goat man, and the noun phrase in line 7 was probably used either to emphasize the contrast or simply for extra clarity after the initial confusion.

(22) ... Then you see another, ... younger, more
.. this man is ... the first man I described is rather .. portly.
... / this / ... You see a younger Chicano man
... coming acrosst ... um-- ... from the back of th ... of the ...
5   picture frame,
... and-- um-- ... he's .. leading a ... brown and white goat.
... And this man-- .. is--- ... um-- dressed in a sort of a faded, navy
blue, ... denim top, and jeans.

It appears that in English repeated nominal reference is generally felt to be unnecessary in establishing a new character as "old information" eligible for pronominalization, whereas in Japanese a single nominal mention is often insufficient to establish a new character as elligible for ellipsis. In fact, the use of nominal reference at the shift from introduction to action in Japanese is perhaps best regarded as a strategy which not only marks this subtle discourse boundary but which also serves as another opportunity for the speaker to establish a new character firmly in the mind of his listener before becoming involved in the plot line and mentions of other characters.[9]

In English, such minor transitions were frequently marked by a sentence boundary rather than a shift in form of reference. Examining the Japanese data, it seems that of the various devices available for indicating such minor shifts, Japanese speakers do not use sentence boundaries as often as English speakers, but do make use of shifts in reference more frequently. Perhaps in any given language a particular device will carry a certain weight, that is, will tend to suggest a larger or smaller type of dicourse boundary. In English, the

---

[9]Hinds (1979) has found that the typical way of introducing topics in Japanese conversational interviews follows a similar course: initial nominal mention with *ga* as the subject particle, followed by "spotlighting" of the item with *wa* and repeated nominal mention, and finally, ellipsis of the item. Hinds and Hinds (forthcoming) found the same pattern of reference in traditional Japanese folktales. Given the striking absence of any "spotlighting" with *wa* in the great majority of Japanese pear movie narratives, it appears that this is an area of Japanese reference which requires further investigation.

rare referential switches tend to occur at larger episode boundaries, with the more common sentence boundaries marking minor transitions. In Japanese, where the available inexplicit form of reference is less informative, a referential switch is apparently less striking, and therefore marks subtler boundaries, than is the case in English. In contrast, since in Japanese a greater variety of different conjunctions are used quite extensively, sentence-final intonational breaks are less common than in English and, along with sentence-final forms such as *no, wake,* and certain verb inflections, are apaprently used to mark the larger discourse boundaries. In Japanese, where the verb form of each clause is necessarily either sentence-final or not sentence-final in its morphological shape, the use of sentence-final forms is perhaps a rather obvious, unsubtle device, and therefore use more sparingly, at least by some speakers. It is easy to see why there might be rather extensive individual differences in such a nebulous area as the "weights" assigned to different markers of discourse units and therefore in the frequency of their use. In Japanese some speakers used sentence breaks more frequently at minor boundaries than others; however, all Japanese speakers made more frequent use of nominal reference than the English speakers.

In the English narratives, the introduction of new characters has been found to be strongly correlated with the beginning of one discourse unit, the episode. Here I shall examine the relationship between a smaller unit, the sentence, and the introduction of new characters in both languages. In English 44 percent of all introductions occurred in the first clause of a new sentence, 29 percent in the second clause, 18 percent somewhere in the middle of a long sentence and 9 percent as the "finale" or last clause of a sentence. Since sentences in the Japanese narratives tended to be much longer than the English sentences, the corresponding figures reflect the greater number of mid-sentence introductions in the Japanese narratives: 39 percent of introductions occurred in the first clause of new sentences, 14 percent in the second clause, 38 percent in mid-sentence and, as in English, 9 percent in a sentence-final clause.

The position within the sentence in which a certain character is introduced seems to be largely a reflection of the role which that character fills in the story line. Thus the pear man, the first character to be introduced, was introduced more frequently than any other character in the first clause of a new sentence, usually the first sentence of the narrative, and never in the last clause of a sentence. At this point there was as yet no action in the plot line, and since the pear man was never introduced in a sentence-final clause, this position seems to be reserved for characters whose appearance on the scene can be viewed as an event, and in particular the culmination of a series of events (cf. Chafe, Chapter 1). When any information preceded the introduction of the pear man in these narratives, it was primarily descriptive in nature. Apparently it is not felt to be appropriate in either English or Japanese for the introduction of an important character to be treated as the culmination of a scenery description. Therefore, when the speaker gave an initial description of the setting, the pear man was introduced either in the first clause of a new sentence, or the second clause of a longer sentence, with the setting information serving as a background introductory clause. The following example illustrates the typical new-sentence introduction of the pear man:

(23) Well, first thing you see,
   is--..uh--..the landscape is--..um...sort of an agricultural area,
   it's quite green,
   ...and a lot of trees around.
   ...And-- you see a middle-aged..um--..Chicano man,

In contrast, in both languages the bicycle boy, and in Japanese also the girl, tended to be introduced in sentence-final clauses more frequently than the other characters. The boy's arrival may be regarded as the culmination of the initial pear-picking and/or irrelevant passerby series of events, and the girl's appearance as the final event in the boy's flight after his theft.

(24) And..um...in the course of him picking,
   ...a man goes by with a...goat,
   ...and that's the last you see of him,
   ...and then...this...little boy...is riding by on his bicycle.

(25) ...Soshitara,
   choodo...A!...mazu,
   ..saisho ni,
   ...yagi o tsureta otoko no hito toorikakatte,
   sono hito wa,
   ...yagi...o tsureta mama
   tada tootta dake de,
   ...tsugi ni,
   otoko no ko ga,
   hitori--...jitensha ni notte kita no ne?
   ...Then,
   ...just then...Oh!...first,
   ...in the beginning,
   ...a man leading a goat passed by,
   and that man,
   ...just walked by
   leading the goat,
   ...next,
   a boy,
   one boy---...came riding on a bicycle, you know?

In English the bicycle boy was also often introduced in second clause position. In these cases, however, the first clause was often merely a repetition of information already presented in the prior sentence, used again only to serve as a background for the introduction of the new character. The following cases were typical:

> (26) ...and-- he--..ended up..um--...swiping..one of his baskets of pears
> and putting it on his...on his bicycle, on the front of his bicycle and..and riding off.
> ...And-- then-- um as he's riding
> ..there's uh--..a girl...coming on a bicycle in the opposite direction

> (27) ...And-- um...he goes up the ladder
> and picks some more pears.
> ...And he's up there picking,
> ...and a little boy comes by on his bicycle.

> (28) ...*ookii ano nashi no ki ga aru no,*
> *seiyoo nashi ga aru deshoo?*
> ...*Sono ki ga atte ne,*
> ...*futotta ojisan ga ne,*
> ...*hige hayashite saa,*
>
> ...There is a big uh pear tree,
> you know, western pears?
> ...That tree is there,
> ...and a fat man,
> ...with a beard, see,

Introduction in the second clause of a sentence was rare in Japanese compared to English. In English this position was used both for important characters like the bicycle boy, with the first clause acting as a background for the introduction, or for less important characters like the paddleball boy, in which case the first clause was often an event in a series of actions from which the introduction was not really separated. In Japanese, no clear trends were apparent.

Despite such differences, it was generally the case that position in a sentence in which a new character was introduced depended upon similar discourse factors in both languages. The main characters tended to be introduced in the first clause of a new sentence, this apparently being a prominent position for an introduction, and sometimes also in the final clause of a sentence, if the character's arrival could be treated appropriately as the culmination of a series of events. Introduction in the middle of a long sentence tended to imply lesser importance as an autonomous personality in the story line and was very frequently used for introductions of the paddleball boy and the girl. Sometimes the differences between English and Japanese could be attributed to differences in the prominence given to a certain character in the story by speakers of the two languages. For example, the goat man in English was very frequently introduced in an initial, and twice in a final clause, whereas in Japanese this character was never introduced in sentence-final clauses and was introduced in mid-sentence more often than in an initial clause. Probably this occurred because the English narratives were longer and therefore had more space to devote to this rather irrelevant character, who was more frequently omitted in the Japanese than in the English narratives.

Another reason for the discrepancies may be that the Japanese discourse equivalent of English sentence-size units have not yet been correctly identified. In fact, for many Japanese speakers the units which seem to correspond most closely in size and content with English sentences are marked by the occurrence of certain adverbials. For example, in the following passage, it seems that the adverb *sorede* in line 7 begins what would probably be a new sentence in English.

(29) ... *Dakara,*
    mae tsunde atta
    sono ookii basuketto
    un-- yoonashi ga zembu,
  5 *futa ga nai kara,*
    ba--tto zembu koborete shimatte ne,
    sorede,
    ... *isshookenmei hirooo to shite ta tokoro ni,*
    ... *sannin gumi no otoko no ko ga yatte kite,*

    ... So,
    that big basket
    that had already been placed (on the bicycle),
    uh ... the pears all,
  5 because there was no cover,
    boom all spilled out,
    and then,
    ... when (he) was busily picking (them) up,
    ... a group of three boys came along,

Perhaps if equivalent discourse units could be identified more accurately, if necessary using different criteria in the different languages or even in the same language for different speakers, the positions of introductions in these units would coincide even more closely in English and Japanese.

REFERENTIAL CHOICE, SWITCH REFERENCE, AND SENTENCES

Once a new referent has been introduced into discourse and established as "old information" subject to inexplicit forms of reference, what causes speakers to return to the use of nominal reference for that character? As Figures 1–2 (c) have shown, when other characters are mentioned between two occurrences of a particular referent, the result is often a return to nominal reference. In these narratives most nominal references occurred when the referent in question was mentioned again in subject position following a clause having a different subject referent, that is, in cases of switch reference (cf. Jacobsen, 1967). In Japanese 71 percent of all coreferential noun phrases occurred at points of switch reference; the corresponding figure for the English narratives was as high as 92 percent. Thus in both languages this type of interference was a strong force in eliciting explicit forms of reference. Since the basic motivation for the use of noun phrases for switch reference seems to be avoiding ambiguity, we can conclude that once speakers have established a particular character as "old information," the decision to switch to more explicit reference is based to a large extent on monitoring the discourse from the standpoint of the listener's need for clarity.

Another reason for the use of nominal reference following the introduction of a character was apparently to mark the presence of various discourse units, as was the case with the nominal references appearing at the introduction-action shift in the Japanese narratives. Chafe (1979) has suggested that sentences are especially crucial ways of organizing cognitive material. Since switch references seem to represent at least minor breaks in the continuity of discourse, it appears appropriate to investigate the relationship between referential choice, switch reference, and sentential units. Perhaps the organization of information into sentences has something to do with the process of selecting referents for subject position.

The data for this section are based on a count of the subjects of all clauses in the English and Japanese narratives, main, subordinate, and embedded, except for relative clauses used by the speaker to identify more fully a referent appearing in the main clause. The rationale for this procedure was that such "identifying relative clauses" were the only ones never used to effect a lasting subject switch. For example, in the following typical case the relative clause "that he (the bicycle boy) tripped on" is used merely to identify which rock is being referred to in line 1, and the bicycle boy is not preserved as the subject of the following clause. The "he" in line 3 refers again to "one kid," that is, the rock boy.

> (30)　and one kid takes the rock
> 　　　that he tripped on
> 　　　and he throws it off to the side of the road,

In contrast, relative clauses presenting information that continues the story line were used to introduce a switch in the subject referent for succeeding clauses, as in the following example:

(31) ... And-- ... the boy with the ping-pong paddle brings the hat to the
        bicycle boy,
        ... who gives him ... three pears.
        ... tsk .. for .. bringing back his hat.
        Puts the hat on,
        ... and that's the last you see of the bicycle thief,

Figure 4(a–d) presents the percentages of different referential forms used for maintaining and changing subject referents in English and Japanese, and shows how these choices relate to sentence boundaries. It is clear that in both languages there is a relationship between referential choice, the status of a referent as a new or old subject, and the phenomenon of segmenting material into sentences. (See Appendix I for the data on which these figures are based.)

Examining Figure 4(a), we find that, in English, when the subject referent was being preserved, speakers chose different referential forms within sentences and at the beginning of new sentences. Ellipsis was much more common within a sentence than across sentence boundaries, and both pronouns and noun phrases were more common at the beginning of a new sentence than within the same sentence. Thus speakers tend to use pronouns or noun phrases for preserved subjects when they feel that there is a sufficient break in the content being verbalized to warrant beginning a new sentence.

In English both pronouns and ellipsis were used for preserved subjects; this raises the question of why speakers would select one option rather than the other. In general, there were many more constraints on the use of ellipsis than of pronouns; that only 4 out of 224 cases of ellipsis were used for switch reference indicates the major "same subject" constraint on the use of this form. Furthermore, in the great majority of cases ellipsis occurred in immediately consecutive clauses. In only a few cases did one or more clauses having a different subject intervene, as in the following examples:

(32) ... And-- ... he went on walking,
        and one of them stopped him,
        ... cause he had forgotten his hat.
        ... And took him his hat,

(33) ... They start brushing him off,
        and .. picking up the pears for him,
        and ... hold the basket,
        while he gets on .. onto the bicycle,
        and ... are generally very helpful.

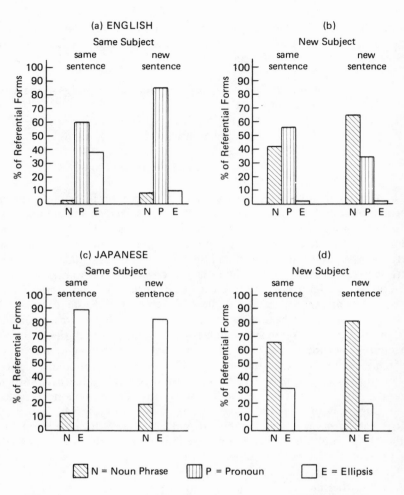

FIG. 4(a-c).   Percentages of Referential Forms Chosen for Maintaining and Switching Subject Reference within Sentences and across Sentence Boundaries

Apparently in these cases the temporal and causal connectives, the semantically subordinate nature of the intervening clause, as well as the shift from ellipsis to "he" to ellipsis, combine to clarify the identity of the referents for the listener. Ellipsis also occasionally operated across one or more embedded relative clauses:

(34) ... A young boy on a bicycle,
     . ... that was much too big for him,
       ... rode ... the ... from the direction in which the goat person had
         come,

...towards the man picking the...the pearpicker,
...tsk...and--...stops.

In such cases the embedding syntax prevents any confusion.

In very rare cases, subject ellipsis occurred across sentence boundaries. Although clauses united by subject ellipsis usually represent semantic units intermediate in size between the clause and the sentence, they sometimes represent units intermediate in size between the sentence and the episode. The following examples illustrate the latter possibility:

(35) ...And they pick it up,
      ...and one boy goes back,
      ...and gives...the boy who fell, his hat.
      ...And..in exchange,
      takes...three pears.

(36) And then he bumps into a rock
      ...And--..um--...falls down,
      and..the..pears all spray all over the place,

At times this may represent a minor failure in planning, with the speaker first intending to end the sentence and then deciding to add more material. But since several speakers did this with no overt hesitations, apologies, and other obvious indications of a change of mind, this seems to be an acceptable discourse strategy (cf. Chafe, Chapter 1), if not as common as the postposed subjects and other "afterthoughts" permissible at the ends of Japanese sentences.

An examination of the semantic context in cases where ellipsis was used reveals that the referent of an elliptical subject must be performing a sequence of at least two actions which can be appropriately regarded as parts in a series of closely related actions. Thus ellipsis was found at the following points in the narratives: describing the pear man's actions as he picked the pears, the bicycle boy's actions as he stole the pears or when he fell from his bicycle, the actions of the threesome as they helped the bicycle boy following his accident, etc. A comparison of these points in the narratives of different speakers shows that speakers have considerable freedom in deciding which actions to unite with ellipsis or separate by the use of pronouns or noun phrases. Sometimes arrivals and departures of characters were included in these series of events; sometimes they were treated separately.

(37) ...They uh--...they sort of come over..to the boy
      and brush him off,
      ...and-- walk away,

(38) but instead they helped him,
...tsk they set his basket up,
and got him going,
and they kept going,

Certain speakers tended to use ellipsis much more frequently than others. In the following example, the speaker used pronouns for all but the final action in a series of events which was a prime target for ellipsis in other speakers' narratives:

(39) ...And uh--...and then he gets down out of the tree,
and he...dumps all his pears into the basket,
and the basket's full,
and one of the pears drops down to the floor,
and he...picks it up,
and he takes his kerchief off,
and he...wipes it off,
and...places it in the basket
which is...very full.

As example (38) shows with the departure of the three, the shift from ellipsis to pronominal reference for the same subject in English sometimes indicates the kind of minor transition in a course of actions which in Japanese tends to be marked by nominal reference. In the following case, for example, the speaker marks the boundary between the helping and exchange episodes by a switch from ellipsis to "they" in line 3:

(40) ...And they..get him all set up on his bike,
and then..start walking away,
and then..they find his hat...on the road,

Thus speakers of English can manipulate the choice between pronominal and elliptical reference to achieve subtle effects.

In Japanese, speakers have only one inexplicit referential form available, and ellipsis is not subject to the strong semantic and syntactic constraints which hold in English. As in English, when a subject referent is being maintained from the prior clause, nominal reference will only rarely be chosen in Japanese. However, a comparison of Figure 4(a) and 4(c) shows that the referential choices made within the same sentence and at the start of new sentences are much more similar in Japanese than they are in English. In part, this may occur because Japanese does not have two inexplicit referential options. In both languages, speakers are reluctant to use nominal reference when maintaining the same subject. In English, however, speakers can use ellipsis within sentences to create a further sense of cohesion and use pronouns at sentence boundaries to suggest a slight break in the discourse. This is similar to the finding of Li and Thompson (1979) that in cases where the same subject was being maintained in Mandarin texts, speakers tended to choose pronominal reference rather than ellipsis following temporal or contrastive elements which "signal the beginning of a new sentence." Japanese speakers do not have this possibility available to them.

The weaker relationship between referential choice and sentence boundaries in Japanese may also reflect the differing role which sentences play in discourse structure in English and Japanese. In the first place, Japanese speakers used sentence boundaries less frequently, and therefore had fewer sentence beginnings to mark with nominal reference. Moreover, since sentences were so long in the Japanese narratives, speakers had more sentence-internal units to mark with noun phrases. Thus there was less opportunity for contrast between the forms chosen at sentence boundaries and those selected within sentences. But in view of the many cases of new sentences which Japanese speakers began with elliptical subject references, it also seems to be true that when the same subject is maintained, Japanese speakers simply do not choose to exploit the available noun phrase/ellipsis contrast to emphasize the boundary at the start of new sentences.

A comparison of Figure 4(a, c) with 4 (b,d) reveals that the referential choices made in both English and Japanese were quite different when the subject referent was changed rather than preserved from the prior clause. Both languages used much higher frequencies of noun phrases and lower frequencies of inexplicit forms in cases of switch reference. Furthermore, referential choice at points of switch reference was clearly sensitive to the presence of sentence boundaries in both English and Japanese.

Figure 4(b) illustrates the relationship between switch reference and sentence boundaries in English. Pronominal reference was preferred within sentences and nominal reference at the start of new sentences. Just as with the pronoun/ellipsis contrast in cases of preserved subjects, narrators used pronouns to convey a greater sense of cohesion within sentences, and noun phrases to imply a greater boundary at the start of new sentences when changing the subject referent.

An interesting type of switch reference in the English narratives involved a shift from ellipsis to pronominal reference. Although this shift usually was used to indicate a subtle break in the course of actions performed by the same character, it was occasionally also used for switching reference. In such cases the discourse context is actually the only source of clarification of the referent of the pronoun. However, perhaps the ellipsis-pronoun shift also functions as a kind of minimal clue to the referential switch:

(41) ... and another guy picks up the rock
     and throws it out of the road,
     and ... he gets ... all situated again,

The "he" in line 3 refers to the bicycle boy, and the presence of the pronoun is apparently the only overt clue that line 3 is not merely the next in a series of events in which the rock boy is the actor. Such cases were rare, however, and in English the most economical strategy would clearly be for the listener to assume whenever semantically possible that subject pronouns have the same referent as the prior subject, including ellipted prior subjects.

In cases of switch reference in Japanese—see Figure 4(d)—there was a clear relationship between referential choice and whether the speaker was beginning a new sentence, although the difference between the choices made within vs. across sentence boundaries was not as great as in English. When the subject referent was changed, Japanese speakers were less likely to use an elliptical reference at the start of a new sentence than within the same sentence. As will be discussed in more detail later, in scenes involving event sequences with several different actors, ellipsis was often used in Japanese despite changes in the subject referents. At boundaries important enough to cause the Japanese speakers to begin a new sentence, however, they were not likely to do so with an unclarified switch reference, which could not be easily disambiguated by virtue of its location in a coherent event sequence.

Since the use of nominal reference when switching subjects seems to be primarily a device for avoiding ambiguity, the use of inexplicit reference at such points should provide some indication of the frequency of ambiguity in each language. In English, since pronouns were often sufficient to identify particular referents unambiguously, both noun phrases and pronouns were used for switch reference. In Japanese, the use of ellipsis at points of switch reference necessarily results in potential ambiguity, however momentary. To avoid this ambiguity, speakers would have to use nominal reference at every changed subject; instead ellipsis was used for switch reference almost 28 percent of the time.

This 28 percent rate of elliptical switch references in Japanese suggests a rather high tolerance for potential ambiguity. In contrast, counting the four cases in English in which ellipsis was used to switch subjects and the subset of 35 pronominal switch references which are potentially ambiguous, we get a rate of 8.5 percent ambiguity at points of switch reference in English. In English potentially ambiguous pronouns were defined as those whose referent was not apparent at the moment they were uttered, assuming a basic strategy of same subject interpretation for all pronominal subjects. In fact, true ambiguity was extremely rare in either language, since the narrative context usually clarified the identity of subject referents. However, assuming that it is at least slightly more difficult for a listener to interpret inexplicit references on the basis of context than to understand references which are unambiguous at the moment of utterance, it would appear that switch reference is one point in discourse at which the Japanese listener must work harder than the English one in order to understand what is being said.

Since subject position in cases of switch reference can be identified as a potential trouble spot for the listener, it is not surprising to find a variety of linguistic devices in Japanese narratives which suggest that speakers are attempting to compensate for this problem by providing extra clarity at these transitions. One such device, already noted in connection with introducing new characters into the narrative, is the immediate repetition, usually with some elaboration, of the subject of a clause which does not have the same referent as the immediately preceding one. As in introductions, this repeated noun phrase is often accompanied by the particle *ne*. Use of this particle suggests that the speaker is concerned that the listener has followed the switch reference and is giving the listener a chance to clarify matters if he has any doubts or, as usually happens, to indicate verbally by a form such as 'un" ("uh-huh") that he has understood. The following example illustrates the use of these devices, with the listener's responses appearing in slashes.

(42) ... *Soshitara,*
    sono otoko no ko ga,
    ... *doroboo shita otoko no ko ga ne?*
    / Un./
    ringo o mittsu o ne,
    ... *ageta wake.*
    / Un./

    ... Then,
    that boy,
    ... the boy who stole (the pears), you know/
    / Uh-huh./
    gave (him)
    apples three apples.
    / Uh-huh./

Japanese speakers use such reassuring "un"'s very frequently, usually upon hearing a clause-final intonation contour, but also often at the separate intonation contours which may be used for subjects and other arguments of the verb, particularly when the speaker has repeated the subject and used *ne* in order to elicit a response.

Another device, which appears to function at least partly to clarify cases of elliptical switch reference, is the use of a postposed subject, as in the last line of the following example:

(43) *aso ... sono toki ojisan ga sa--,*
    shita ni orite kite ne?
    kago mittsu atta no ni ne,

. . . a-- to
. . . o . . okashii to omo . . omotte ru no ne.
Soshitara,
. . sono mae o sa,
to,
kajiri nagara ne,
. . . so tootte iku no,
sono sannin no ko ga.

uh . . . at that time the man,
came down to the ground, you know?
and although there had been three baskets,
. . . huh!
. . . (that's) s strange (he)'s thi thinking.
Then,
. . in front of (him),
uh,
nibbling (on the pears),
. . . (they) go past,
those three children.

These cases support Hinds' claim (1976) that "the function of postposing is to put into a sentence something that the speaker did not originally think was necessary; it is put in either for emphasis or to avoid ambiguity."

Occasionally at such switch references speakers use not only an ordinary preverbal subject but also repeat the subject in sentence-final position, as in the following example:

(44) *. . . ashi o bikko bikko hikinagara*
. . . koni . . . ano aruite itta wake.
jitensha o motte ne?
Soshitara,
5 *. . . A soshite,*
. . booya tachi wa,
. . . koo yuu . . . maa surechi itchatta wake ne?
. . . sono sannin no booya tachi wa.

. . . limping
. . . like . . . uh (he) went walking off.
taking the bicycle, you know?
Then,
5 . . . Oh then,
. . the boys,
. . . like this . . . let's see pass went away, you know?
. . . those three boys.

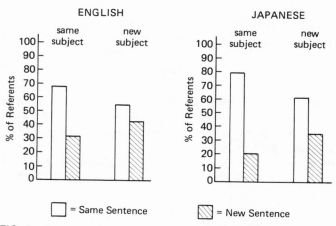

FIG. 5. Percentage of Maintained and Switched Subject Referents within Sentences and across Sentence Boundaries

This "copy-postposing," Hinds claims (1976), "has the sole effect of emphasizing the noun phrase which is copy-postposed." The present data suggest at least one reason for this emphasis: apparently it is felt to be necessary primarily at the potentially difficult points of switch reference. Thus although Japanese speakers have a higher frequency of potential ambiguity in their narratives, since they do make use of elliptical subject switch references, one source of the "extra" noun phrases in their narratives is precisely the various attempts made to compensate for potential ambiguity and to be certain that the listener has understood switch references.

Although speakers of both Japanese and English often modified their choice of referential form in order to avoid ambiguity or to emphasize a sentence boundary, it was also true that regardless of the referential choices made, speakers tended to begin new sentences at points of switch reference. This aspect of the data is focused in Figure 5, which depicts the percentages of maintained and switch reference subjects which occurred within sentences and at the beginning of new sentences. In both English and Japanese speakers tended to begin new sentences when changing to a new subject referent. This suggests that in both languages one of the principles underlying the formation of sentences during the verbalization of these narratives was a change of focus from one character to another.

EPISODE BOUNDARIES

In the two preceding sections we have observed the relationship between two major discourse phenomena and speakers' choices of referential form: the introduction of new referents into discourse and switching subject reference in the course of narration. Since explicit reference at these points in discourse would seem to be a minimal requirement for the listener's comprehension, it may be that these will be among the most important reasons for the use of explicit referential forms in any language. However, these were not the only sources of nominal reference in English and Japanese. As Figures 1–2(a–c) revealed, in both languages there is in fact a range of options used by speakers in the same objective context, as defined quantitatively in terms of intervening clauses, sentences, and referents. For each such configuration of time and interference, the use of nominal reference will either be extremely likely, optional, or unusual. If general cognitive constraints apply to yield the most common referential choices, we might then wonder what is responsible for the selection of the unusual forms, and whether the same factors are at work in influencing the less preferred referential choices in both English and Japanese.

In order to investigate this problem, I have examined individually those cases of nominal and inexplicit reference in both languages which were the least common choices on Figures 1–4. As these data indicate, in English nominal reference was unusual when referring to a character mentioned within the same sentence, when no mention of other characters had intervened since the last mention of the referent in question, and when the subject nominal had the same referent as the subject of the immediately preceding main clause. In the latter two situations, nominal reference was also unusual in Japanese; since Japanese sentences were longer than English ones, however, only nominal reference in the same clause or the clause immediately following the last mention of the referent has been examined as unusual. For inexplicit forms of reference, the following cases were defined as unusual in English: use of a pronoun when three or more sentences has passed since the last mention of the referent in question, when two or more other characters had been mentioned, and when a potentially ambiguous pronoun was used in switching subject reference. In Japanese, I treated as unusual use of ellipsis after three or more clauses had passed since the last mention of the referent in question and when two or more other characters had been mentioned in the interval. Since subject ellipsis in cases of switch reference necessarily results in potential ambiguity, all elliptical switch references were also examined.

In both English and Japanese, the most important reason for the use of nomimal references within unusually short intervals of time was to switch subject reference, and this will not be discussed any further. It is, however, important to note that in many cases, a number of different possible reasons for the use of a particular referential form coincided. For example, a case of switch reference at an episode boundary when the subject of the prior clause could take the same pronoun would result in use of a noun phrase in English, and it would be impossible to claim that either ambiguity avoidance or the episode boundary was solely responsible for the choice. In order to present clear examples I have attempted to select those cases in which a single factor appears to be responsible for the speaker's choice of referential form, and I will assume that discourse factors strong enough to operate as the sole reason for referential choice will act as contributing factors when occurring along with other forces that tend to elicit a particular referential choice.

A major reason accounting for cases of both unusual nominal and inexplicit forms of reference was the occurrence of episode boundaries. Frequently, episode boundaries were marked by a shift from inexplicit to explicit forms of reference. The clearest demonstrations of the effects of episode boundaries on referential choice are provided by the unusual cases in which noun phrases were used within very short intervals when there was no question of interference, as in the following example:

(45) ...And--..they see what's happened to the 1..little boy,
    and they come over sort of very calmly
    ...and--..help him get on his feet,
    pick up his pears for him,
5 ...and-- put them back in the basket
    ...and..brush him off,
    ..and everything,
    ...and-- um--...tsk then they..um--...put him...tsk
    um..back on his bike,
10 and he goes off.
    ...The little boy...that was on the bike, had been wearing a hat.
    ...And--...in the f...in passing the little girl,
    it had..fallen off.

In this example it seems clear that there is an episode boundary at line 11 (with "anticipatory" hesitations at lines 8–9). The speaker had been describing the events in the helping episode, and at line 11 stops to fill in the necessary background before proceeding to the events of the exchange episode, in which the bicycle boy will be given his hat by the threesome and will give them three pears in return.

In Japanese there were numerous examples in which episode boundaries were marked by a switch from ellipsis to nominal reference for the same character. In the following case the speaker shifts from the theft episode to a sweeping summary of the remaining events in the story, and this radical shift at line 4 is marked by a change from ellipsis to a noun phrase in referring to the bicycle boy.

(46) ...De,
    ...sore o nanka ano...e--to...sore o..A! motte itchatta n da
    keredomo,

... *sono* ... *motte itchatta sore kara,*
4 *soko no tokoro de sono s shoonen wa iroiro* ... *ano jiken to yuu*
ka,
... *ano* ... *korondari,*
... And,
... it let's see uh ... well ... it .. Oh! (he) carried it off,
... but ... (he) carried it off and then,
4 at that point that b boy various ... uh should (I) say events,
... uh ... like (he) fell,

Less radical shifts included the following, in which there is a change from the helping episode to the finding of the hat which initiates the exchange episode.

(47) *Sannin otoko no ko ga kite,*
irete kurete,
soide,
sono mama ... *itta n da kedo,*
kondo booshi o otoshite ita no o
otoko no ko ga moo ichido motte kite kureta kara,

Three boys came,
and put (them) in (for him),
and then,
(they) just ... went off,
but the boys brought back again (for him) (his) hat,
(his) hat, the one that had fallen, so,

Similar examples, in which nominal reference is used at an episode boundary even though attention remains on the same character, have been found in other languages; Maibaum (1978) reports that in Jirel narratives the final summarizing paragraph will use nominal reference, even if there has only been a single character in the entire story.

Why should speakers shift from inexplicit to explicit forms of reference at episode boundaries? It may be that this is a listener-oriented strategy, and the speaker has learned that such shifts can be used as narrative devices to indicate these structural boundaries to the addressee. Another possibility, however, is that referential choice, like hesitating, is a speaker-based phenomenon. That is, perhaps the cognitive task of retrieving a new episode from memory causes the speaker to feel that the referents retrieved along with the new episode, even if they are the same as those in the prior episode, are nevertheless also in some sense "new." It may even be the case that to some extent the task of retrieval dims the speaker's sense of continuity with the referential choices he had just made in the prior episode, almost as if in searching his mind for the new material he had deactivated and now must reactivate the referent in question. Since both speaker-based and listener-oriented strategies lead to the same effect, it seems likely that the two factors reinforce one another during the course of learning how to tell an effective narrative.

Since a single episode boundary was often sufficient to cause a switch to explicit forms of reference, it is not surprising that the passage of more than one episode boundary, which almost always involved mention of other characters, invariably resulted in the use of an explicit form of reference, both in English and Japanese. In the following Japanese example, the goat man is mentioned again during the description of the bicycle boy's arrival.

(48) *De sono tsugi ni kondo,*
jitensha--..ni notta, booya.
e u--nto shoogakkoo--,...san yonen gurai no booya ka na?
...ga,
tootta wake.
kotchi kara ne?
... Yagi no ojisan kotchi kara tootte kotchi kara tootte kita no.

And after that next,
a boy, riding on a bicycle,
uh uh a boy in third or fourth grade of grammar school I guess,
...(subject particle),
passed.
from here, you know?
... The goat man came past from here came past from here.

In English the best examples of this occur with respect to the girl. Since there was only one female character in the movie, the pronoun "she" could have been unambiguous at any point in a speaker's narrative. When a number of episode boundaries had intervened, however, this character was always mentioned with a noun phrase, as in the following examples:

(49) ...So--...and then he splits.
... With his hat, with his pears, everything.
...And-- um .. I just remembered another detail.
... Before he meets the girl?
... one of the pears,
... it's a bumpy road little dirt road,
one of the pears ... flies out.

(50) They see that this .. other boy has fallen down,
... also .. before he fell over,
... his hat blew off.
... While he was still looking at the girl.

Since such mentions of characters after the passage of more than one episode boundary were rather rare, it is impossible to estimate at what point nominal reference becomes "obligatory." Given the content of this movie, such mentions necessarily followed considerable interference from mentions of other characters as well as "world" shifts and digressions. The one character who in the movie itself actually reappears after being absent from the story line is the pear man, who figures in both the beginning and end of the plot. Therefore, the number of episode boundaries and amount of interference were maximal. In both English and Japanese all mentions of the pear man at the point when the plot line returns to him at the end of the story were nominal references. Although the data are actually insufficient to be certain, it seems likely that two episode boundaries would be enough to elicit "obligatory" nominal reference.

A digression from the main plot line seems to function as an extreme or strong form of episode boundary. Chafe (1979) has found that such boundaries elicited strong judgments of paragraph boundaries from readers and tended to be accompanied by rather extreme episode markers, such as long hesitations on the part of the speakers. Therefore, it is not surprising to find that shifts to commentary and other types of digressions also resulted in the use of nominal reference when the speaker resumed the story line. Apparently speakers feel that a digression can interpose enough material between two mentions of a referent that it is necessary to reactivate that referent in the mind of the listener at the end of the digression. The following example shows the effects of a long digression.

> (51) um--...g a kid comes by on a bicycle,
> ...he stops,
> ...he gets off his bike,
> ...um−...the movie was in color.
> ...And the movie had a sound track.
> ...It's important.
> And then the mo the whole movie started with a a cock crowing.
> ...And then you see —.
> Anyway.
> I just remembered that.
> ...Anyway,
> so um--...the kid on the bicycle,
> ..gets off the bicycle,

Even when the two mentions of a referent were very close together, such "world" shifts were sometimes punctuated by a shift from pronominal to nominal reference, as though mention in one world were not sufficient to establish a referent as old information in another world. This was very common throughout the English narratives, not only during introductions.

(52) ...tsk...And--...these three boys...go walking by,
     and they each have a pear in their hand,
     so he's..kind of looking at them,
     trying to make a connection
     wondering...how they got the pears,
     ..and..if they were his pears,
     ../you see/ how this is just all what...what you're projecting on
       the man.

Another kind of world shift which occurred in the English narratives was a "send-off" to a particular character at the point when he disappears from the plot line. The following example is typical:

(53) ...And--...the boy with the ping-pong paddle brings the hat to
       the bicycle boy,
     ...who gives him...three pears.
     ...tsk..for..bringing back his hat.
     Puts the hat on,
     ...and that's the last you see of the bicycle thief.

Although world shifts were rarer in the Japanese narratives than in the English ones, similar examples can be found in which the shift from narration to commentary is marked by a switch from ellipsis to nominal reference, as in the following case:

(54) ...Sono kago no,
     ...nashi o ko jitto miru wake ne?
     hoshi hoshikutte sa.
     ...De,
     ..tabun sono ko wa
     zenzen sono...nashi o to totteru otoko no hito to kankei nai to
       omou no ne?
     watashi ga omou ni.

     ...(he) stares at the pears,
     ...in that basket, you know?
     want wanting (them).
     ...And,
     ..(I) think maybe that child had no relation at all to the man pi
       picking those...pears.
     in my opinion.

Perhaps the most subtle type of world shifts were the cases in which the narrator presents the events he is recounting from the viewpoints of different characters within the story. This happened through the use of verbs of perception and knowing, which in a sense establish the mind of the perceiver or knower as the world within which reference is to be defined. Since a referent who is old information to the narrator and listener is not necessarily old information to all the characters being mentioned at any particular point, shifting the point of view to such a character will often result in the use of nominal reference. The following examples illustrate this tendency.

(55) ...then he.. takes a pear,
... after... carefully watching the man in the tree.
... who's still picking.
... doesn't see the boy.

(56) ...The man is in the tree,
and the boy... parked his bicycle here,
... and--... got off the bicycle,.. got off the bicycle,
and.../purposely/ went
5 and felt a pear.
... to s while... watching the man
to see whether he was seeing
whether the boy was stealing the pears,

In example (56) the passage of several clauses and presence of two male characters, as well as the change in point of view, lead to the use of "the man" in line 6. The second reference to the pear man within the bicycle boy's perceptual world is pronominal, as would be expected. In line 8, however, we have shifted to the perceptual world of the pear man, and the bicycle boy is suddenly referred to with a noun phrase, although he had just been the ellipted subject referent of several clauses. Thus the different mental worlds of the narrator and those of the characters in the story may all be treated as separate when it comes to the status of referents as new or old information.

As noted before, however, it is important to emphasize that such referential switches are entirely optional in both English and Japanese, and speakers are free to enter and leave different worlds of experience with no such marking.[10] Compare the following example in Japanese with example (54).

(57) ... *itazura boozu mitai na otoko no ko sannin ga ite ... kita wake.*
Soshite,

---

[10]Hinds and Hinds (forthcoming) found that in traditional Japanese folktales "ellipsis is blocked across episode boundaries." In unplanned oral narratives, this is only a tendency rather than a rule; perhaps a greater attempt is made to mark episode boundaries explicitly in written narratives.

... dakara hajime,
A! ano ringo mottechau n da na to omotta n da kedo ne,
motte iku--
... koo ... naoshite agete ne?

> ... three boys who seemed like mischievous kids were the ... came
> along.

Then,
... so at first,
Oh! (they'll) take away those apples (I) thought,
but (they) brought (them),
... UH ... and (they) fixed (things) up, you know?

In the English narratives, where world shifts were frequent, it was, in fact, more common for speakers to ignore such digressions in selecting referential forms. The tendency was to resume the story line with the pronoun being used for a particular character before the digression, sometimes even when this might result in ambiguity, as in the following case:

(58) ... Three boys came out,
    ... helped him pick himself up,
    ... pick up his bike,
    pick up the pears,
5 ... one of them had ... a toy
    which was like a clapper.
    ... And-- ... I don't know what you call it except a paddle with a
       ball suspended on a string.
    ... So you could hear him playing with that.
10 ... And ... then he rode off

In these cases it is almost as if the narrator were speaking to herself in the digression; clearly the intervening mentions of the paddleball boy in lines 5-9 are treated as if they do not matter. To some extent, this is probably true, since listeners may often recognize digressions as such and quickly realize what the speaker has done. Nevertheless, this seems to be a good example of a "speaker-centered" referential strategy, since it does require at least a moment of greater mental effort on the part of the listener to figure out who "he" is at such a point.

In conclusion, it is clear that one source of unusual referential choices, such as the use of inexplicit forms despite potential ambiguity or use of a noun phrase when the identity of a referent is entirely obvious, is the presence of various types of discourse boundaries. Such referential marking usually occurs at larger, episode boundaries, but can also be found even at extremely brief changes in point of view, as when the narrator makes a single-clause comment about the story he is recounting. The freedom of the speaker in making referential choices at discourse boundaries obviously makes it impossible to formulate any strict linguistic "rules" to describe the phenomena. It is, however, apparent that in addition to the factors of time and interference, which may represent fundamental cognitive limitations, referential choices are sensitive to various "optional" discourse factors, such as episode boundaries, world shifts, and digressions. Since these factors were often the sole reason for unusual referential choices, it seems likely that the marking of discourse boundaries is one of the important factors operating in conjunction with the forces of time and interference to guide speakers' choices in the ordinary cases as well.

NARRATIVE STRATEGIES

In addition to the marking of episode boundaries, what other discourse factors might be responsible for the unusual referential choices which can be observed? Examining the unusual cases, such as the frequent, seemingly unnecessary repetition of nominal reference for a certain character or persistent use of inexplicit reference despite potential ambiguity, we find that there are a number of identifiable, fairly consistent referential strategies which speakers are following in many of these cases. The key to understanding these stratgies lies in Chafe's suggestion (1976) that the role of a particular character within a discourse may influence the speaker's way of referring to that character; thus, for example, the main character may have a stronger hold on the status of old information than other characters.

By using an inexplicit form of reference, such as a pronoun or ellipsis, the speaker is, in effect, telling the listener that he should be able to identify the referent in question without further information. If the speaker is sufficiently skilled in taking the listener's needs into account, use of inexplicit reference forms represents a shared agreement as to the correct interpretation, that is, which character's identity can be taken for granted at this point in the narration. It seems clear that of all the possible characters in the story line at a given moment, the "hero" is the most likely candidate for this status. Having established a particular character as the hero, continued use of inexplicit reference forms is one way in which the speaker can signal that this character is still functioning as the hero of the story.

This type of referential strategy is called "thematic" by Grimes (1978), and researchers on various African languages have also found that the status of a participant as main or subordinate character within a narrative often governs speakers' choice of referential forms. For example, Perrin (1978) has documented the use of this strategy in the folk tales of the Mambila language, spoken in Nigeria and Cameroun. Elliptical reference was consistently used for the main character, whereas secondary characters were referred to with noun phrases. This also tended to be true in Fali, an Adamawa language spoken in northern Cameroun; main characters tended to be referred to with pronouns, secondary ones by proper names or kinship terms (Ennulat, 1978). Gleson (1968) cites an Adamawa Fulani tale showing the same tendency; the main character is realized 14 times by a pronoun and only twice by a noun, whereas the secondary character in the story is realized eleven times by a noun and twice by ellipsis. The tendency in these "thematic" strategies is always toward the use of inexplicit referential forms for the most important character.

In those cases in which speakers seem to be basing referential options upon characters' roles in the plot line, the use of inexplicit reference apparently serves to make the listener identify most closely with, and to some extent to take the point of view of, that character. This claim is reminiscent of the concept of "empathy" which Kuno and Kaburaki (1977) have set forth. In describing a particular event or state, they claim, a speaker may make certain lexical and syntactic choices which indicate that he is identifying with one of the characters being referred to. For example, they state, of the following three descriptions of an event,

John hit Mary.
John hit his wife.
Mary's husband hit her.

the first is objective, whereas in the second the speaker takes the standpoint of John by describing Mary in terms of her relationship to him, and in the third sentence empathizes with Mary by describing John in terms of his relationship to her. Although Kuno and Kaburaki's analysis of empathy phenomena has not been specifically extended to a consideration of the speaker's choice of pronominal and elliptical forms of reference rather than noun phrases, it generally seems true that the character being empathized with tends to be pronominalized or ellipted, whereas nominal reference is used for characters receiving less of the speaker's empathy. Although the intuitions involved are rather subtle, I hope that the examples which follow will be sufficient to support the suggestion that the narrator tends to take the viewpoint of the character he most frequently pronominalizes or ellipts and to take a more objective or neutral stance toward those referred to with noun phrases.

Certain of the "empathy hierarchies" which Kuno and Kaburaki postulate are relevant to the present narratives. For example, the "topic empathy hierarchy" states that it is easier for the speaker to empathize with a referent whom he has been talking about than one he has just introduced into discourse for the first time. According to the "speech-act participant empathy hierarchy," it is easiest for the speaker to empathize with himself, harder to empathize with the hearer, and most difficult to empathize with third persons at the exclusion of speaker or hearer. As we have seen, the speakers in these narratives often chose to distinguish between the world of speaker and hearer and the world of third persons, in this case the characters in the story. Furthermore, the empathy accorded a particular character in the story world is sometimes not automatically transferred to the world of speaker and hearer. In this task of narration, however, primary focus was necessarily on the "story world," with speakers usually taking an "objective-observer" stance. In general, they identified their own point of view with that of particular characters, apparently most strongly influenced by which character was most central to the events currently being described, with point of view changing as the role of the chosen hero in the action increased and decreased. The "surface structure empathy hierarchy" states that it is easiest to empathize with the referent of the subject, next with that of the object, and almost impossible to empathize with the referent of by-passive agentives. This principle seems applicable to these narratives insofar as in English the least explicit form of reference, ellipsis, is permissible only for surface subjects, and in both languages empathy seems to lie on ellipted or pronominalized main-clause subjects of verbs of knowing and perceiving at the expense of the embedded subject, which tends to be a noun phrase.

There seems to be a clear difference between the phenomena discussed by Kuno and Kaburaki and the present data with respect to the "ban on conflicting empathy foci." According to this principle, a single sentence cannot have more than one focus of the speaker's empathy; this accounts for the unacceptability of sentences such as "Mary's husband hit his wife." Obviously, it is possible in English and Japanese for more than one referent to be ellipted or pronominalized and, at least when using the nonrelational terms found in these narratives, for more than one referent to be described with a noun phrase without creating any conflicts. In contrast to the phenomena discussed by Kuno and Kaburaki, it appears that the choice between explicit and inexplicit reference, so far as it is determined by empathy factors, is best conceptualized as a continuum rather than a dichotomy.

This is perfectly natural, since at any point in the course of events being narrated there may be more than one main character and the different characters may have varying degrees of centrality. As characters enter and leave the story line, there will necessarily be shifts of empathy focus, sometimes with momentary equality or balance between two characters resulting. In cases where the speaker pronominalizes or ellipts two different characters, he would seem to be treating both as "equal" on the dimensions of new/old information, plot centrality, and empathy. When two referents are described with noun phrases, the speaker apparently takes an equally objective or neutral stance toward each. Thus at any point in the narrative it seems best to characterize each referent as occupying a certain position along this scale, determined partly by the objective course of events being recounted and partly by the particular way in which the speaker chooses to present those events. Therefore, it is probably true that there may be a number of different foci at any point, although with different degrees of empathy being accorded to them.[11]

Thus the implications of referential choice are by no means easy to decipher, and are further complicated because, as already illustrated, a number of factors other than empathy are influencing the selection of referential forms. For example, if the narrator describes a course of events in such a way that switch reference occurs, he will tend to use a noun phrase even if the referent in question is the hero of the story. Thus potential ambiguity will further cloud the picture, and the resulting "listener-oriented" referential choices will obscure the "speaker-based" empathy phenomena which the narrator may be incorporating in his story. Still, it is often possible to sort out to some extent the different forces in operation. For example, in an episode requiring numerous switch references, speakers will generally choose to clarify certain references and let others remain potentially ambiguous, often motivated by their sense of which character is most easily identifiable. In the following analysis, I attempt to illustrate how the structure of the plot line, in particular, the centrality of different characters in particular episodes, influences speakers' referential choices.

In the first scene, in which the pear man is picking pears, he is the only character "on stage" and the use of pronouns in English and ellipsis in Japanese was very common. When the goat man comes by, a variety of options is available to the speaker. He may treat the scene with the goat man, who is totally irrelevant to the story, as a kind of digression and continue to treat the pear man as the main character, "he." Or, since the actions of the pear man do not change and since the goat man may be regarded as a foreshadowing of the arrival of the bicycle boy, the speaker may choose to focus on the goat man as "he" and to treat the pear man as if he were now the

---

[11]Apparently in some languages it is possible to make a formal distinction between empathy and plot centrality. For example, Levinsohn (1978) states that in Inga narratives the narrator uses the third person pronoun *pay* rather than nominal reference to indicate his "association" with a particular character when more than one character is on stage. On the other hand, status as "major vs. minor participants" determines whether switch reference is accomplished by use of noun phrases in subject position or switch reference morphemes on verbs or "connectors." In the English pear movie narratives there were no obvious indications suggesting that a distinction should be made between these two notions, which could perhaps be characterized as emotional vs. attentional focus. In the Japanese narratives a careful examination of empathy-indicating verbs, such as *ageru* and *kureru,* which were frequently used in the exchange scene but did not seem to correlate in an obvious way with which characters were receiving elliptical vs. nominal reference, would perhaps reveal a distinction between the two concepts.

subordinate character. Finally, the narrator may give similar treatment to both characters, with this scene functioning as a transitional episode in which focus begins to shift away from the pear man.

In both English and Japanese there were examples of these different strategies. The pear man was sometimes kept as the main focus of attention and referred to with pronouns or ellipsis even despite possible ambiguity, as in the following Japanese example:

(59) *Sono tochuu ni,*
      . . . eto--. . . yagi ga,
      hito ni hikarete tootte ta toki mo atta shi,
      . . . sore kara to,
      nobotte tte kara,

      In the middle of that,
      . . . well. . . there was a time when a goat pulled by a person came by,
      . . . after that,
      after (he—the pear man) climbed up,

Since elliptical switch references in Japanese and pronominal ones in English were both potentially ambiguous, it is not surprising that half the Japanese mentions of the pear man and more than half of the English ones were noun phrases. This is a typical case in which it would be difficult to differentiate the effects of ambiguity avoidance from referential strategies based on plot centrality. It does seem, however, that some speakers used noun phrases for both characters because they were assigning them equal importance, leading to a sense of transition from the prior scene in which the pear man was the "hero" to the following scene in which the bicycle boy will take over this role:

(60) . . . And a man comes along with a goat,
      . . . and the goat obviously is interested in the pears,
      . . . but the man just. . . walks by with the goat,
      and the man up in the tree doesn't even notice.

None of the Japanese speakers focused on the goat man long enough to suggest that he had become the center of attention in this scene. But about a third of the English descriptions of this scene did so, as in the following example:

(61) . . . um--. . . Anyway a guy comes by
      leading a goat.
      . . . And the goat's aaarrr
      but. . and they don't talk to each other,
    5 they don't e. . . I don't think they even look at each other,

and .. the guy .. walks by.
And you watch the goat,
disappearing all the way,
and then . . . then you're back to the man in the tree.

Clearly, after the many clauses focusing on the goat man's passing the tree, this speaker could not have referred to the pear man as "him" in the last line, whereas ellipsis was still possible for the Japanese speaker in example (59) after only a two-clause description of this event. In other languages as well, a shift of focus from one character to another will necessitate use of nominal reference when shifting attention back to the first character. This has been documented both in the Tibeto-Burman language Khaling (Toba, 1978) and the Niger-Congo language Fali (Ennulat, 1978).

In the following episode, the theft, the bicycle boy enters the narrative and becomes the main character; the pear man is not seen again until the end of the movie. By the end of this scene, therefore, the bicycle boy is established as "he" in the English narratives and as the character most likely to be ellipted in subject position in the Japanese narratives. The transition from the pear man to the bicycle boy in the following example provides a good illustration of the shift in assignment of the pronoun "he" following a brief period in which both characters are referred to with noun phrases.

(62) and there's a .. basket he puts them in.
. . . And-- you see-- . . . passerbyers on bicycles and stuff go by.
. . . And-- . . . then a boy comes by . . . on a bicycle
the man is in the tree,
. . . and the boy gets off the bicycle,
and .. looks at the man,
and then . . . uh looks at the bushels,
and he . . . starts to just take a few,

In English a common way of accomplishing this transition was through shifts in point of view or "world" at this stage in the story, as in the following example:

(63) . . . And uh . . . then,
. . . he's up in the tree,
and y you see that . . . that within his . . . view you know from his
viewpoint,
. . . he c he could possibly see this little boy coming on a bicycle.
. . . At least .. it seems to me that . . . you know he would notice this
boy
if he was really . . . interested,
but he's not thinking about
his . . . vision is very much you know . . . kind of . . .

he's very bored.
... And-- this little boy--
... this scene ... focuses on this little boy .. coming along,
... obviously,
... well.
... You know he ... because of the goat,
... your idea is on the pears.
And you think "wow,"
this little boy's probably going to come
and see the pears,
and ... he's going to take a pear or two,
and then ... go on his way.
... um-- but the little boy comes,
... and-- uh--... he doesn't want just a pear,
he wants a whole basket.

By introducing and reintroducing the bicycle boy in the different worlds, this narrator was able to effect a gradual transition of attention from the pear man to the bicycle boy.

As suggested at the beginning of this section, one way of estimating the narrator's focus of attention is observing which referent she chooses to clarify and which to leave ambiguous in making subject switches. Thus perhaps the clearest evidence that the speaker's choice of referential forms is being dictated by plot centrality is the use of pronouns or ellipsis for the hero even at the risk of momentary ambiguity. In Japanese, of the eight cases of ellipsis at points of switch reference during this episode, five involved the bicycle boy and three the pear man.[12] The balance of ambiguity was even more lopsided in the English narratives, where there were seven ambiguous pronouns switches referring to the bicycle boy and only one subject switch reference to the pear man that was ambiguous. The following example illustrates this kind of ambiguity imbalance.

(64) ... Well if ... the boy comes by
... and the man is still up in the tree,
... and UH ... he picks up ... one of the ... the con .. the full
baskets,
and puts it on the front of his bicycle,
... and heads down the road.
... All sort of on the sly.
... The man doesn't know that any of this has been done.
... So he heads down this dirt road,

---

[12]Hinds and Hinds (forthcoming) apparently did not find such cases of elliptical switch reference in folktales; noun phrases were used at all points of potential ambiguity, probably because of the more formal and planned style of those narratives.

In the next episode of the narrative, this imbalance was even more obvious in both languages. The bicycle boy, who has been established as the main character during the theft episode and will continue in this role through the next few scenes, has an accident and falls from his bicycle after passing a girl. The girl is never seen again after this episode, and her only function in the movie is to serve as the cause for the accident. This is the clearest case in which one of the two characters "on stage" is significantly more important to the plot than the other.

In Japanese the imbalance of focus in this scene was strikingly clear from the forms of reference used; there were 10 cases in which the bicycle boy was ellipted as a switch reference subject, and no such cases with the girl. The contrast with the prior scenes between the pear man and the bicycle boy is remarkable. In Japanese the potential for ambiguity is, at least from a syntactic point of view, equal, yet in the latter scenes each of the two characters was at least occasionally ellipted despite a switch in subject reference.

Furthermore, Japanese speakers often clarified the elliptical references to the bicycle boy at these points of switch reference by using full noun phrases to refer to the girl even after she had been introduced into the discourse. In Japanese, this strategy apparently serves not only to avoid ambiguity at these points but also to indicate the peripheral status of the girl as compared to the boy.[13] The following examples illustrate this strategy:

(65) *Hashitte*
koo itte wa,
ano-- onna no ko ga kotchi kara kita wake.
Chotto ki ano--- kami no nagai ne?
Onna no ko ga kite,
...soshite,
sono hito ni mitorechatta wake.
Itta n dakedomo,

(he) rode along
(he) went like this,
uh-- a girl came from here.
a rather pre- uh--...with long hair, you know?
A girl came,
...and then,

---

[13]Perrin (1978) cites a similar case in Mambila where the narrator clarifies the identity of a main character who is resuming subject status by using nominal reference for the secondary character who had been subject for several clauses and now appears in an oblique case and using elliptical reference for the main character.

Levinsohn (1978) has also found a tendency to refer to minor participants with repeated nominal reference following their introduction in Inga (a Quechuan language) narratives.

(he) was fascinated by that person.
(He) went along,

(66) ... *Sono tochuu de,*
ano--... onna no ko ga tootta no ne?
sono.. onna no ko o.. mite,

... On the way,
uh--... a girl passed, you know?
(He) looked.. at that.. girl,

In English this was the only scene in which there was absolutely no possibility of ambiguity in using pronouns, since the girl is the only character in the movie who could be referred to as *she*. It is interesting to observe the results of this fact, in conjunction with the peripheral status of the girl, on speakers' referential choices. In the great majority of narratives, the girl was pronominalized throughout this scene despite her peripheral role in the story, as in the following example:

(67) ... And um ... then you see this little girl.
... Coming on a bicycle in the opposite direction,
... and-- uh--... you wonder how she's going to figure in on this.
... And-- uh--... they come,
you see the scene's like this
and you see them both coming coming coming
and you think "u."
You know. "Are they going to collide,
what's going to happen,"
... and uh it turns out
she ... from what I could understand she grabbed his hat.

Thus it appears that in English the dominant referential strategy is to pronominalize referents following their introduction and to continue pronominalizing until episode boundaries or other characters creating potential ambiguity intervene.

This episode also provides some of the clearest evidence for the manipulation of referential options to signal a character's role within the story line. For although the use of more than one noun phrase in introducing a character into the plot line was very rare in English, and the impossibility of ambiguity would seem to eliminate the need for additional nominal references to the girl, 20 percent of the English narrators referred to the girl with noun phrases following her introduction, as in the following cases:

(68) ...So he's going down the road
     he approached a girl on a bicycle.
     And looked up at the girl
     and his bike got caught on the rock.

(69) ...He-- um...a girl...with long pigtails,
     ...happens by going the other way...on a bicycle.
     And there's a long shot,
     ...you see both of them..converging
     and you see him.
     ...He's more interested in
     ...the girl going by
     ...than...taking care of..making sure the basket doesn't do
         anything weird.
     ...And he sees the girl going by,
     ..he doesn't see the rock

Thus in both English and Japanese the use of consistently contrasting referential choices keeps one referent backgrounded as old information and the center of attention, and the other referent highlighted as new information but nevertheless a referent who will not become a focus of the speaker or listener's empathy.

From the standpoint of reference, the most complex and interesting episode is the exchange, in which the paddleball boy gives the bicycle boy his hat and receives three pears in return. In this scene there are four different characters interacting and since all are boys, both explicit and inexplicit forms of reference are potentially ambiguous. Furthermore, it is extremely difficult to describe this episode in either English or Japanese without using a rather large number of subject switches within a brief amount of narration. And since the bicycle boy leaves the story line permanently immediately after this scene whereas the threesome continue to appear until the end of the movie, the plot allows speakers the option of maintaining the bicycle boy as the main character in this scene or of switching the focus of attention to the threesome. In both English and Japanese this episode was responsible for the largest number of ambiguous inexplicit references, as well as the largest amount of "extra" noun phrases which did not seem to be the result of switch reference, intervening mentions of other characters, or large spans of elapsed time.

In the English narratives there were 17 potentially ambiguous references to the bicycle boy and 12 to the paddleball boy in this episode. Two speakers even got through the entire scene using only pronouns, as in the following example:

(70) and then . . they find his hat,
    . . . on the road,
    and then w . . one of them comes back,
    . . . and this one's . . playing with one of those . . . those wooden
        things that you hit with a ball.
    . . . And he . . . he comes back,
    and gives him his hat,
    and so he gives him . . . some . . . pears,
    . . . and . . . so they walk off,
    . . eating these pears.

It was, however, more common to make some concession to the listener's needs and to use a noun phrase at the point of the subject switch from the paddleball boy to the bicycle boy, as in the following case:

(71) . . . And-- . . . then he rode off
    but he forgot his hat.
    . . . So . . . one of the boys whistled to him,
    . . . and then . . . he went
    and gave him the hat,
    . . . and in return . . . the boy that lost the hat . . . gave his
        friend . . . the boy . . . the pears,

The most common strategy in English for this episode, used by 7 of the 20 speakers, was to pronominalize referents immediately following their introduction into the story, using noun phrases only at this point of switch reference. But there were also English speakers who dealt with the complexities of this scene by assigning either the bicycle boy or the paddleball boy to the pronoun "he" and using nominal references for the other character. These cases provided many clear examples of the "empathy" use of pronouns. In the following example, the bicycle boy is "he."

(72) . . . As-- . . . then he-- 's . . about to forg . . . forget his . . . uh-- . . . hat,
    and . . boy walks back,
    gives him his hat,
    . . . he gives the boy some pears,

The high frequency of subject switches in this episode makes it difficult to be entirely consistent in assigning a single character to the pronoun "he," since speakers tend to clarify potentially ambiguous switch reference subjects. For those speakers who did attempt to be consistent, it was often true that the assignment of characters to pronominal vs. nominal reference was maintained within sentences, but then changed at sentence boundaries. As noted earlier, there is a strong tendency for switch references to coincide with sentence boundaries in English. The following example provides a good illustration of the treatment of the sentence as the discourse unit in which referential options are to be defined and maintained.

(73) ...And the one kid,
        I think it was the kid who was playing with the uh...with..the
            whatever it was,
        ...stops,
    5 and picks it up
        and whistles.
        ...And the kid turns around,
        and he goes
        and takes the hat to the kid,
    10 and-- um...the kid gives him three pears.
        ...And-- so the...the other kid comes back to his friends
        and /he/ gives them each a pear.

The long sentence from line 7 to 10 shows that maintaining referential forms for particular characters is one way of achieving unity and clarity across several subject switches. This strategy is not preserved across to the new sentence in line 11, which suggests that the sentence may usually be the largest unit within which speakers of English are willing to presume the listener's cooperation in this attempt to let referential forms be determined by a character's narrative role instead of the usual strategy of maximum pronominalization with ambiguity avoidance at switch references.

Thus in scenes with several subject switches, these two basic strategies that English speakers have available come into conflict. Therefore, it is not surprising that there was considerable variation across speakers, as well as use of inconsistent strategies and changing strategies in midstream. In the following example, the speaker begins with nominal reference for both characters, then has a sentence in which both are pronominalized, and then switches back to nominal reference again.

(74) ...uh...then they..they come across his hat on the road.
        ...And one of the guys picks it up,
        ..and...whistles..to the..g..boy on the bicycle to catch his
            attention.
        ...And he turns around,
        and he runs up..to him,
        ...and gives him back his hat.
        ...And-- the boy who's stolen the pears...gives..three pears to
            the boy who gave him his hat.
        ...And--...the boy...walks back to his two companions
        and he hands a pear to each of them.

Apparently in some languages this kind of alternating action sequence is handled simply by using nominal reference at each subject switch; this strategy has been reported for Jirel (Maibaum, 1978). Speakers' referential choices in the exchange episode were complicated because in English too many pronouns and too many noun phrases are both apparently felt to be undesirable. Speakers are caught in a conflict between naturalness, using pronouns for all old information characters, and clarity, the need to avoid ambiguity in describing a complicated course of events. If too many pronouns are used, the listener will be lost, yet if too many noun phrases are used, a feeling of stilted "super-clarity" results, as in the following example:

(75) ... So-- the little boy that has the hat comes
and meets the boy on the bicycle.
... And-- ... um-- ... tsk ... then ... they exch . . he gives. . . the little boy that picked up the hat . . gave it to the boy on the bicycle,
... and the boy that was on the bicycle . . gives . . . him three pears.
... And-- . . the little boy . . . who . . fetched his hat, . . . took the pears,
... and goes back . . to his friends,
and they each . . gives them each a pear.
... And then the other boy rides off,

This example provides a nice demonstration of the subtle empathy effects usually achieved by the use of pronouns. Since pronouns are almost never used, one gets the feeling that the speaker is struggling, unable to decide upon a consistent point of view for this episode. The result is an extremely objective and neutral-sounding description. Moreover, the high frequency of hesitations of all kinds made by speakers who used a large number of noun phrases in this scene seems to indicate that this was not a natural or easy strategy for them to use.

In Japanese it would seem to be even more difficult to give a successful description of this scene, since even inexplicit references to the threesome will result in potential ambiguity, whereas English speakers could freely use *they*. As in the English narratives, it was extremely rare for speakers to attempt to get through this entire episode without using any noun phrases. However, there was one Japanese speaker who did:

(76) ... *Sorede,* ... *mata,*
... *booshi ga ochite iru no o,*
sono sannin no naka no shoonen ga hitori mitsukete,
... *modotte kite,*
ageta tokoro
... *moo yooi shite ita mitai desu ne?*

...sanko gurai.
Agenakya to yuu koto de.
...Sorede watashite,
...sono mama...modotte itte,

...Then,...again,
one among those three boys found
...the hat that had fallen,
...and came back,
and when (he) gave (it) (to him)
......(he) already seemed prepared, you know?
...with at least three pears.
As if (he) had to give (them).
...So (he) handed (them) over,
...and (he) just...went back,

By far the most common strategy in the Japanese narratives was to use nominal reference at each subject switch, allowing the oblique case referents to remain unspecified. This, of course, is not possible in English, since it would be ungrammatical, for example, to delete the indirect object of the verb *give*. Therefore, the English speakers are forced to use several different case frames involving more than one human referent, causing either a confusing proliferation of pronouns and/or an unnatural number of noun phrases. In contrast, in Japanese a higher frequency of noun phrases is being used throughout the narratives, and the specification of each switch reference subject does not necessarily lead to a sense of "super-clarity," since the oblique cases are usually elipted. The following example is typical:

(77) *De,*
    otoko no...ano..jitensha no otoko no ko wa,
    tobasareta koto o shiranakatta no ne.
    ...De,
 5 *..sono sannin gumi no hitori ga,*
    ...sono booshi o motte,
    otoko no ko no tokoro e,
    motte tte ageta no.
    ...Soshitara otoko no ko ga,
10 *...orei ni tte yuu n de,*
    ...sono nusunda nashi o mittsu hodo agete,
    ..de,
    sono ko wa motte kaette,
    sannin de,
15 *...tabenagara*
    aruite itta no.

And,
the boy...uh..the bicycle boy,
didn't know that (it) had blown away.
...And,
5 ..one of that threesome,
...carrying that hat,
brought (it) back
to where the boy was.
...Then the boy,
10 ...in thanks,
...gave him three of those stolen pears,
..and,
that child brought (them) back,
and the three (literally "being three"),
15 ...eating (them),
(they) went walking off.

In lines 14–15 we can observe a common strategy which allows Japanese speakers to omit subjects while avoiding any doubt as to the identity of the subject referent, namely, the use of phrases with *de,* as in *sannin de* (literally, "being three"). Example (78) again shows the specification of subjects and ellipsis of oblique cases, as well as the repetition of subjects and use of *ne.* In contrast to what English speakers did when trying to be especially clear, that is, specifying both subjects and objects, it is interesting that the Japanese speaker chooses to repeat the subject while still omitting the object.

(78) *A...ato de,*
...ki ga tsuite,
/sode/ hitori no otoko no ko ga ne?
sano sannin no otoko no ko no hitori ga,
...motte tte ageta wake.
Sono otoko no ko ga,
...doroboo shita otoko no ko ga ne?
ringo o mittsu o ne,
...ageta wake.

A...afterwards,
...(he) noticed,
/then/ one of the boys, you know?
one of the three boys,
...brought (it) back (to him).
That boy,
...the boy who stole (them), you know?
gave (him) three apples.

It was quite rare for Japanese speakers to mention more than a single human referent in one case frame; usually either subject or object was omitted. Yet there were Japanese speakers who seemed to be using an unusual number of nominal references in this episode, leading to the sense of awkwardness found in the English example (75).

(79) ... *De,*
 ...sono uchi no hitori ga,
 sono...koronda otoko no ko o..okoshite,
 ...de,
 eto...sono otoko no ko no booshi ga okkotte ite,
 ...de sono...sannin gumi no hitori ga mata,
 ...otoko no ko no booshi o..motte,
 ...sono otoko no ko no ato o oikakete,
 soshitara sono...eto koronda otoko no ko wa,
 ...unto--...mango o mittsu ka na?
 mittsu o sono...otoko no ko...orei...toshite ne?
 ...watashite,

 ... And,
 ... one of them,
 1..lifted up the... boy who fell,
 ... and,
 uh...that boy's hat had been dropped,
 ... and one of those three again
 ... carried..the boy's hat,
 ... and followed after that boy,
 then that... uh the boy who fell,
 ... uh--... three mangos I guess,
 that... boy... in thanks you know?
 ... handed over three,

This impression is probably due to the number of explicit genitives and other oblique case referents which are specified in addition to the subjects.

Despite the general tendency to specify subjects in Japanese, there was also frequent subject ellipsis in this episode. Again, speakers' choice of which referent could be ellipted in subject position gives a clue to their sense of who was the main character at this point. In the Japanese narratives the bicycle boy was ellipted in subject position 10 times, and the paddleball boy only once. Although this occurs, in part, because the paddleball boy did not appear as the agent of as many clauses as the bicycle boy, it probably also partly reflects the tendency to use subject ellipsis in Japanese at points of switch reference only when the character in question is the central figure, the "oldest" information. In contrast, ellipsis of nonsubject referents seems to be applied with greater freedom, and the paddleball boy was often ellipted as the indirect object of the pear-giving frame.

In the Japanese narratives, it was impossible to identify with certainty any case in which a speaker seemed to have chosen a single character to be always ellipted and another to be always referred to with a noun phrase, as happened in the English narratives. The consistency which did occur tended to be syntactic consistency. Two speakers actually ellipted all oblique case referents and no subjects in this scene; nominal subjects and ellipsis of oblique referents seem to be the most common strategy. But the reverse also occurred; sometimes speakers used noun phrases for the oblique referents, allowing the subject to be specified by default, as in the following example:

(80) ... *Dete i* ... *ikoo to shita toki,*
    booshi mo ochita n de,
    ... *kuchibue o fuite,*
    booshi ga ochite iru yo tte yuu yoo na koto de,
5   ... *sorede sono ko ni kabusete ageru n desu ne?*
    ... *Hoide,*
    ... *kaeri ni sono* ... *atama ni booshi o* ... *ano* .. *nosete--* .. *ageta*
        kawari ni,
    yoonashi o sono ko tachi ni,
    sannin ni hitotsu zutsu ageru wake desu ne?

    ... When (he) was about to 1 ... leave,
    since the hat fell too,
    ... (they) whistled,
    "(your) hat has fallen" sort of thing,
5   ... then they put (his) hat on that child, you know?
    ... Then,
    ... on (their) way back in return for (their) having put ... uh ... the
        hat on (his) head.
    (he) gave pears to those children,
    to the three one to each, you know?

The switch reference is not marked by a nominal subject at line 7, but is clarified in the next clause by *sono ko tachi ni* ("to those children"). In contrast, English speakers never seemed to use a syntactically based strategy in dealing with this difficult scene.

Although it does seem to be true that Japanese offers clearer syntactic guidelines for clarifying reference across several subject changes, not all speakers followed consistent strategies. Like the English speakers, they sometimes seemed to be struggling between different approaches, patching up mistakes as they went along. Japanese does, however, offer one syntactic device which is extremely useful to speakers encountering referential problems: the postposed argument. Referential choices in episodes calling for frequent subject switches give some insight into the discourse determinants of postposed arguments, particularly subjects, in Japanese. As the following example illustrates, the use of postposed subjects allows the speaker to clarify reference with a noun phrase at the conclusion of his sentence, and he does not have to repeat or change his original utterance, as an English speaker who decided to use a noun phrase after uttering a subject pronoun would have to.

(81)   ... *De otoko no ko wa orei ni ne?*
       sono nashi o sanko ageru no,
       ... *otoko no ko hitori hitori ni ne?*
       Hitori no ko booshi o--.. motte tte,
       sorede,
       ... *sono .. hitori no ko ni,*
       ... *mittsu agete,*
       .. *de minna ni wakete ageru wake ne?*
       ... *sono moratta ko ga.*

       ... And the boy in thanks, you know?
       gave three of those pears,
       ... (one) to each boy, you know?
       One of the children brought .. the hat,
       and then,
       ... (he) gave three
       ... to that .. one child
       ... and (he) divided (them) up for everyone, you know?
       ... that boy who received (them).

Thus this speaker was free to add the indirect object in line 3 and to clarify the second elliptical subject switch reference with the postposed subject in the last line. Such cases seem to support the notion that postposed subjects in Japanese function rather as afterthoughts in some situations (cf. Chafe, 1976 on "anti-topics").

In summary, the status of a referent as the main character or merely a secondary figure in the narration has some effect upon speakers' referential choices for that character in both English and Japanese. Inexplicit forms of reference are used for the current hero, at times even despite ambiguity, creating the impression that the story is being told from this character's point of view. Explicit forms of reference are used for peripheral figures and to maintain clarity. Perhaps the need to have a point of view causes speakers of both languages to avoid the overly objective feeling of frequent nominal reference and to risk ambiguity by taking for granted the identity of the central character. Of course, as the preceding examples have demonstrated, use of the referential strategies which convey this kind of subtle information is a rather individual matter, and speakers vary considerably in their choice of strategies and ability to use strategies consistently.

CONCLUSIONS

The referential choices which speakers of English and Japanese made in these narratives were influenced by a wide variety of factors, ranging from presumably universal cognitive constraints to apparently individual preferences. That at least 97 percent of all inexplicit references in each language occurred with no more than one intervening referent seems likely to have a cognitive basis. Similarly, the occurrence of over 80 percent of all inexplicit references after intervals of two or fewer clauses probably also has some foundation in the capacity of human short-term memory. If similar findings can be established for other languages, we may be on the way to discovering how human cognition limits possible referential systems in languages.

An examination of several languages may suggest certain universal constraints, but it will also surely reveal a variety of language-specific factors dictating referential choice. For example, in these narratives the total lack of information available in ellipsis is probably responsible for certain of the differences between the Japanese and English referential systems. Given a choice between explicit nominal reference and total ellipsis, Japanese speakers take longer to establish characters as old information after their introductions and allow minor discourse boundaries to trigger a return to nominal reference, even when there is no question of ambiguity. The Japanese narratives have also pointed out the relationship which may exist between syntactic phenomena and the referential system of a language, and how the two may work together in discourse. Thus although potential ambiguity arises more frequently in Japanese, Japanese speakers can use a variety of clarifying devices, such as repeated and postposed subjects, which are not available to English speakers. An interesting problem for future research would be to attempt to sort out the range of linguistic phenomena interacting with the referential system of a language and to establish objective criteria for evaluating the difficulty of the referential task any language imposes on its speakers and hearers.

Yet despite the various language-specific factors, the relationship between certain discourse factors and referential choice in these narratives has proved to be the same in languages as different as English and Japanese. These narratives have pointed out discourse phenomena which may be valuable targets of cross-linguistic research: the tendency to mark discourse boundaries, including world shifts, point of view changes, and episode changes, by nominal reference; to avoid ambiguity at points of switch reference by use of explicit forms, clarifying syntactic conventions, or both; to create a particular point of view by using inexplicit reference to background the main character. Interestingly, examples of these phenomena have already been found in other languages unrelated to English or Japanese, as reported by the contributors to *Papers on Discourse* (Grimes, 1978) and *Anaphora in Discourse* (Hinds, 1978b).

In the area of individual differences, a careful examination of spoken discourse supports the notion that there are few, if any, hard-and-fast "rules" of discourse; rather there are tendencies with greater and smaller numbers of exceptions. Each language apparently offers a wide enough range of options for handling any particular referential problem within discourse to leave plenty of room for individual variation. One speaker may mark each episode or sentence boundary with a switch to nominal reference; another may pay little attention to discourse units in making his choices. Similarly, one speaker may base his choices on a sense of the listener's needs, selecting forms predictable from the factors of time and interference; another may feel free to make the listener work harder, basing his choices on a chosen point of view and ignoring fairly extensive ambiguity. Therefore, the analyses presented here do not give a picture of any individual speaker's choices, but rather a survey of the range of possibilities available to all speakers of English or of Japanese. A more precise characterization of individuals, for example, which kinds of referential choices usually go together to form a profile of a particular type of narrator, would require longer narratives from each speaker.

The relationship between discourse structure and referential systems is a topic which deserves further research. From a psychological point of view, perhaps the most basic tasks include investigations of what in human cognition places the constraints that apparently exist on referential choices, and of how these constraints will interact with language-specific factors to produce the "rules" of a referential system. A more extensive examination of referential choices in a wider variety of different languages is necessary to determine the range of discourse factors which can influence referential choice, and to learn how universal are those that have been discovered by looking at English and Japanese. In these two languages much remains to be done, including a detailed study of the effects of such syntactic factors as subject vs. nonsubject status of a referent, or occurrence in main, subordinate, or embedded clauses. On the other hand, for those interested in analyzing discourse, it appears that referential choice is an important indicator of discourse units, "world" shifts, point of view, speakers' sensitivity to listeners' needs, and will no doubt prove to be a valuable tool for discovering and analyzing many other interesting discourse phenomena.

198 CLANCY

REFERENCES

Bernardo, R. The cognitive relevance of the sentence. Unpublished M. A. thesis, University of California, Berkeley, 1976.

Chafe, W. Givenness, contrastiveness, definiteness, subjects, topics and point of view. In C. Li (Ed.), *Subject and topic.* New York: Academic Press, 1976.

Chafe, W. The flow of thought and the flow of language. In T. Givon (Ed.), *Discourse and syntax.* New York: Academic Press, 1979.

Chafe, W. Chapter 1. The deployment of consciousness in the production of a narrative.

Downing, P. Chapter 3. Factors influencing lexical choice in narrative.

DuBois, J. Chapter 5. Beyond definiteness: the trace of identity in discourse.

Ennulat, J. H. Participant categories in Fali stories. In J. Grimes (Ed.), *Papers on discourse.* Dallas: Summer Institute of Linguistics, Inc., 1978.

Fodor, J. A., Bever, T. G., & Garrett, M. F. *The Psychology of language.* New York: McGraw-Hill, 1974.

Gleason, H. A., Jr. Contrastive analysis in discourse structure. In J. E. Alatis (Ed.), *Georgetown University Monograph Series on Languages and Linguistics,* 1968, *21.*

Grimes, J. E. (Ed.) *Papers on discourse.* Dallas: Summer Institute of Linguistics, Inc., 1978.

Hinds, J. Postposing in Japanese, *EONEO: The Linguistic Journal of Korea,* 1976, *1,* 113–125.

Hinds, J. Paragraph structure and pronominalization, *Papers in Linguistics,* 1977, *10,* 1–2; 77–99.

Hinds, J. The ellipsis of possessor noun phrases in Japanese. Unpublished manuscript, University of Hawaii, 1978. (a)

Hinds, J. Anaphora in Japanese conversation. In J. Hinds (Ed.), *Anaphora in discourse.* Alberta: Linguistic Research, Inc., 1978. (b)

Hinds, J. Ellipsis and prior mention in Japanese conversation. In Makkai, A., & Makkai, V. (Eds.). *The fifth LACUS forum 1978,* Columbia, S. C.: Hornbeam Press, Inc., 1979.

Hinds, J., & Hinds, W. Participant identification in Japanese narrative discourse. In *Festschrift to honor the 60th birthday of Dr. Kazuko Inoue,* forthcoming.

Jacobsen, W. Switch reference in Hokan-Coahuiltecan. In D. Hymes, & W. E. Bittle, (Eds.), *Studies in Southwestern Ethnolinguistics.* The Hague: Mouton & Co., 1967.

Jarvella, R. Syntactic processing of connected speech. *Journal of Verbal Learning and Verbal Behavior,* 1971, *10,* 409–416.

Kuno, S., & Kaburaki, E. Empathy and syntax, *Linguistic Inquiry,* 1977, *8*(4); 627–672.

Levinsohn, S. Participant reference in Inga narrative discourse. In Hinds, J. (Ed.), *Anaphora in discourse.* Alberta: Linguistic Research, Inc., 1978.

Li, C., & Thompson, S. Pronouns and zero-anaphora in Chinese discourse. In T. Givon, (Ed.), *Discourse and syntax,* New York: Academic Press, 1979.

Maibaum, A. Participants in Jirel narrative. In J. E. Grimes (Ed.), *Papers on discourse.* Dallas: Summer Institute of Linguistics, Inc., 1978.

Norman, D. A. *Memory and attention.* New York: Wiley, 1969.

Perrin, M. Who's who in Mambila folk stories. In J. E. Grimes (Ed.), *Papers on discourse,* Dallas: Summer Institute of Linguistics, Inc., 1978.

Piaget, J. *The language and thought of the child.* New York: World, 1955.

Tannen, D. Chapter 2. A comparative analysis of oral narrative strategies: Athenian Greek and American English.

Toba, S. Participant focus in Kahling narratives. In J. E. Grimes (Ed.), *Papers on discourse,* Dallas: Summer Institute of Linguistics, Inc., 1978.

Vygotsky, L. S. [Thought and language.] (E. Hanfmann & G. Vakar, Eds. and trans.). Cambridge, Mass.: MIT Press, 1962. (Originally published, 1934.)

APPENDIX 1
Data for Figure 1(a-c): Distribution of Coreferential Forms in English with Respect to Time and Interference

1uses	*Noun Phrases*		*Pronouns*		*Ellipsis*	
	0	(0)	.01	(13)	0	(0)
	.24	61	.70	737	.96	325
4	.33	85	.24	238	.04	14
10	.25	66	.06	60		
-20	.09	24	.008	8		
+	.09	24				
		260		1056		339
ntences						
	.21	(55)	.64	(677)	.94	(317)
	.39	102	.29	310	.06	22
4	.27	70	.06	68		
10	.07	18	.0009	1		
+	.06	15				
		260		1056		339
tervening *ferents*						
	.23	(59)	.69	(724)	.93	(314)
	.54	139	.29	305	.07	24
4	.18	46	.03	27	.003	1
	.06	16				
		260		1056		339

Data for Figure 2(a-c): Distribution of Coreferential Forms in Japanese with Respect to Time and Interference

Clauses	Noun Phrases		Ellipsis	
0	.08	(19)	0	(0)
1	.35	86	.72	486
2–4	.31	77	.25	168
5–10	.15	38	.03	22
11–20	.05	12	.001	1
21+	.06	16		
		248		677
Sentences				
0	.49	(121)	.76	(511)
1	.29	71	.21	144
2–4	.17	42	.03	22
5–10	.04	9		
11+	.02	5		
		248		677
Intervening Referents				
0	.37	(92)	.64	(432)
1	.45	112	.34	230
2–4	.16	40	.02	15
5+	.02	4		
		248		677

Data for Figure 3(a-c): The Frequency of Nominal Reference in English and Japanese

	English		Japanese	
Clauses	% NP	Total Refs.	% NP	Total Refs.
0	.0	(13)	1.00	(19)
1	.05	1123	.15	572
2	.20	188	.29	134
3	.29	92	.28	67
4	.35	57	.43	44
5–10	.53	126	.63	60
11–20	.74	32	.92	13
21+	1.00	24	1.00	16
Int. Refs.				
0	.05	(1097)	.18	(524)
1	.30	468	.33	342
2	.58	60	.68	37
3	.71	7	.78	9
4	.86	7	.89	9
5+	1.00	16	1.00	4

	English		Japanese	
Sentences	% NP	Total Refs.	% NP	Total Refs.
0	.05	(1049)	.19	(632)
1	.24	434	.33	215
2	.49	85	.65	40
3	.51	35	.57	14
4	.56	18	.80	10
5–10	.95	19	1.00	9
11+	1.00	15	1.00	5

Data for Figure 4(a–d)*: Percentages of Referential Forms Chosen for Maintaining and Switching Subject Reference within Sentences and across Sentence Boundaries

English	Same Subject				New Subject			
	Same sentence		New sentence		Same sentence		New sentence	
	%	No.	%	No.	%	No.	%	No.
Noun phrase	2.1	11	7.6	19	42.1	107	65.4	134
Pronoun	60.5	323	84.4	211	53.1	135	34.1	70
Ellipsis	37.5	200	8.0	20	1.2	3	.5	1
		534		250		254		205
		(68.1%)		(31.9%)		(55.3%)		(44.7%)
Japanese								
Noun phrase	12.0	49	17.0	19	66.6	104	81.8	72
Ellipsis	88.0	358	83.0	93	33.3	52	18.2	16
		407		112		156		88
		(78.4%)		(21.6%)		(63.9%)		(36.1%)

*The column totals, expressed in terms of the percentages of each category of subject referent which occurred in the same vs. a new sentence, were the data used for Figure. 5.

5 Beyond Definiteness: The Trace of Identity in Discourse

John W. Du Bois
University of California, Santa Barbara, Berkeley

The study of narrative discourse, as exemplified in the essays in this book, treats the unfolding of narrative and the expression of this unfolding narrative in words.[1] The opening scene is set, characters and objects introduced, and events described, as the narrative shifts from scene to scene. In approaching this phenomenon, one may choose to examine the portioning of narrative content into discourse units (Chafe, Chapter 1), the selection of a prominent referent to take on the role of subject in a clause (Bernardo, Chapter 6), or the influence of the larger cultural context on the expression of events and evaluations (Tannen, Chapter 2). Or, one may focus on a phenomenon of narrower scope: the verbalization of characters and objects within the discourse. This is the domain of the essays that Downing and Clancy contributed to this book and of the present chapter.

Though apparently narrow, the topic has two distinct aspects. On the one hand, one may consider the static aspect of nominal verbalization. The speaker is confronted by an object whose semantic substance requires expression. He must draw on his cultural knowledge and his understanding of his addressee in order to decide what is salient and hence worthy of verbalization, and he employs his semantic knowledge in the expression of the appropriate categorization. Downing deals with this facet of the problem. But

---

[1]This study was partially supported by NIMH Grant MH25592. I wish to thank the Director of the "pear film project," Wallace Chafe, and my co-workers Robert Bernardo, Patricia Clancy, Pamela Downing, Nancy Ickler, and Deborah Tannen for their comments, general and specific, and especially for contributing to the exceptionally stimulating environment of the project which taught me so much. I also am much indebted to Johanna Nichols and Graham Thurgood for valuable comments on earlier versions of this paper.

the task of verbalization is not yet over when a place has been found in the semantic grid for an object. The object must be first introduced into the discourse as a discrete entity, and then traced through the evolving narrative. The continuity of the object's identity must be established. This continuity of the real object with itself runs as a continuous thread in the real world, but in discourse the continuity can be expressed only intermittently, through phrases which appear at intervals in the narration. This chapter focuses on the linguistic means by which such intermittent phrases may be used to trace continuous identity. The chapter thus includes what has usually been studied as "definiteness," but goes beyond the usual boundaries set for the topic.

Tracing objects through a narrative is not carried out in isolation from other discourse tasks. It interacts in significant fashion with the choice of semantic categorization discussed by Downing. And an integral aspect of the problem is the competition between distinct reference item types, such as full noun phrases, pronouns, and ellipsis. This topic, only touched upon in this chapter, is taken up in detail by Clancy. Further, the present study has repercussions for higher-level phenomena, since reference to an object may, under certain conditions, control the form of the following sentence.

One may state the outlook of this study from two distinct viewpoints: the functional and the formal. Functionally, we may ask how objects are introduced into and traced through a discourse. Formally, we seek to state the distribution of the English articles. This latter approach, though apparently restricted, leads ultimately to the examination of a wide variety of contrasting linguistic forms and, further, to the examination of the functional conditions which govern their distribution. In stating the distribution of the definite article, one must specify not only where it occurs but where it does not occur. The definite singular reference item *the bicycle* contrasts with the indefinite *a bicycle*, and further with the articleless *bicycle*, the possessed *his bicycle*, the plural *bicycles*, the pronominal *it*, and, in the case of subject deletion, a zero realization. The choice among these reference items is in turn governed by the choice between narrative and descriptive "discourse modes," and the choice of semantic/pragmatic features: referential or nonreferential, identifiable or nonidentifiable, generic or individual. It is further influenced by the speaker's exploitation of frames as an economical means of presenting information.

A thorough study of definiteness must give full attention to these secondary, related problems, which in fact form inseparable parts of a single theory of language in use. The literature on definiteness has often dealt only with the definite article and, for contrast, the indefinite article; at the same time it has isolated definiteness from larger considerations of discourse structure as a whole. But the range of contrasting reference items is much greater than the two article forms, and many crucial phenomena related to definiteness are either not found or not easily recognized within the domain of the one-sentence or two-sentence examples which are typically used. The limitation is remedied through the study of whole, naturally produced narratives.

The literature on definiteness in English is quite extensive; only a few studies can be mentioned here. The most substantial work remains that of Christophersen (1939), who collected and classified a large body of important definiteness phenomena and provided numerous insightful observations, although the analysis is often diffuse. More unified but less exhaustive analyses are presented by Jespersen (1924, 1933) and, more recently, Kartunnen (1968) and Chafe (1972). Chafe (1976) defines the crucial and sometimes unrecognized distinction between the statuses of "definite" and "given," and generally provides an effective placement of definiteness in the larger context of packaging. Halliday and Hasan (1976) present a valuable discussion of "phoricity" which will be drawn on in this work. Givón (1978) offers a discussion of definiteness in several languages whch recognizes interaction with other discourse phenomena. In the philosophical literature, a useful examination of the nature of identification may be found in Searle (1969). In psychology, the work of Haviland and Clark on "bridging" (1974) is of interest, although bridging is misleadingly presented as an artifact of givenness rather than definiteness (see Chafe, 1976:41–42). Extensive bibliography may be found in Christophersen (1939) for early sources and in Krámský (1972) for more recent literature. Hawkins (1978), Hewson (1972), and Robbins (1968) illustrate some recent approaches to definiteness.

Though much has been written on definiteness, there is no analysis available which will encompass all the observations made here on the tracing of objects through discourse. Thus, before turning to the detailed analysis of the pear film narratives presented in the latter portion of this chapter, it will first be necessary for me to outline my own typology and analytical methodology. This system is sketched in the Analysis section. I will not present full arguments for each point in the system; this would be beyond the scope of the present article. Nor will I point out all innovations and restructuring of previous systems. A summary of the more important new contributions appears in the concluding pages of the chapter.

In recognition of the importance of examining whole texts, the present study has been based primarily on narrations of the plot of a brief film (the pear film) which was shown to 20 speakers of English. The preface describes the gathering of these data and their transcription and preliminary analysis. (The "repeat narratives" which were collected from several speakers on a second occasion have not been included in the data base for this chapter.)

From the collected narratives, all mentions of characters and objects in the film were isolated for analysis. By *character* is meant simply a person in the film. References by the speaker to herself (*I*) or to the interviewer (*you*) are not included under this term. *Objects* include the nonhuman animates and the objects in the film, as well as sounds, and in a few cases, events that are bounded off and referred to nominally (*a little accident*). Basically the term *object* includes all noun phrases except idioms (*the first place* in *in the first place*), syntactically motivated noun phrases (*whether the boy was stealing pears*), and noun phrases which refer to artifacts of the experimental situation (*the movie*), or to portions of the narrative itself (*that* in *has anybody told you that before?*)

The term *mention*, as applied in this study to a particular character or object, indicates all noun phrases, whether referential or nonreferential, which may be in some way related to the object in question. It is a pretheoretical construct which is not intended to have any psychological or linguistic significance, but merely serves to gather all the data into approachable groups for explanation. I will speak of the *first mention* (*second mention*, etc.) of an object to mean its first (second, etc.) appearance, under whatever label or description, in the narrative text.

The reader will find that some familiarity with the plot of the pear film will be useful in understanding many of the examples presented in this chapter: a synopsis may be found in the Preface.

In addition to the primary source of data just described, some data will be drawn from a second experiment in which three brief isolated film segments were extracted form the original pear film and shown to 98 subjects, after which they were asked to give written descriptions of what happened in each of the three film clips.

ANALYSIS

The most basic function of the English articles is to contrast identifiable and nonidentifiable referents. In one common pattern, a person or object is introduced into discourse with the indefinite article and subsequent mentions receive the definite article:

(1) then a boy [1st mention][2] comes by, . . . on a bicycle; the man is in the tree, . . . and the boy [2nd] gets off the bicycle, (Speaker 8)

---

[2]Mentions of a particular referent are marked "1st", "2nd", and so on, in square brackets following the mention. Only the noun phrases relevant to the discussion at hand are so marked. Following each example an indication of the speaker number is given (Speaker 1, Speaker 2, etc.). Subjects in the second (brief film clip) experiment are indicated as Subject II-1, Subject II-2, and so on. Pauses are indicated by three dots (long pause) or two dots (short pause) rather than with the actual measurement of pause duration, since this is less significant for the present topic. Note that these three dots do not signify omission of material. Examples in this chapter are usually cited beginning from the first word of the clause rather than from the *um*'s, *uh*'s, and so on which may precede it. In order to distinguish the various characters in the film, a set of descriptive names will be used:

The use of *a* in *a boy* shows that the speaker does not expect the hearer to identify which boy is meant; *the* in *the boy* indicates that this identification is expected.

Although the pattern of an indefinite initial mention followed by subsequent definite mentions is quite common, there is a very large body of exceptions. Of the 613 noun phrases that occurred as the initial mention of a particular character or object in the pear film data, fully 34 percent were definite. Perhaps more significantly, a substantial number of noninitial mentions are formally indefinite (4.1 percent for characters). These exceptions to the general pattern are not random and follow several broad principles to be presented later. But in spite of the numerous deviations, it is useful to take the pattern of indefinite first mention and definite subsequent mention as a starting point.

One reason for departures from the basic pattern is that the the basic function of the articles, to mark a contrast in identifiability, is restricted to cases where the contrast is semantically possible. It is not applicable to noun phrases which do not refer and is generally restricted to mentions which are referential and specific. Historically both articles were first used in these circumstances,[3] and this continues to be their characteristic domain of use. Since the articles at an earlier stage of English appeared primarily in referential-specific mentions, many noun phrases bore no article. In Modern English, however, the article has come to be an almost constant accessory to nouns which bear no other determiner. In expanding to noun phrase uses where the identifiability contrast was no longer applicable, the articles either lost their function, becoming neutralized through predictability or interchangeability, or took on new, secondary functions. The result is that the so-called definite article in many cases no longer marks definiteness, even if one equates definiteness with identifiability. This raises the problem of what formal or functional meaning is to be attached to the term *definite*.

The *Pear Man* picks the pears and puts them in baskets.
The *Goat Man* leads the goat past the pear tree.
The *Bike Boy* rides up on a bike and steals some pears.
The *Girl* rides past the Bike Boy on a bicycle.
The *Threesome* help the Bike Boy after his fall.
The *Paddleball Boy* (a member of the Threesome) plays with a paddleball and later returns the Bike Boy's hat.
The *Rock Boy* (a member of the Threesome) removes the rock from the road.
The *Third Boy* (a member of the Threesome) doesn't do much at all.

[3]Christophersen states that the use of the Old English definite article "was at first restricted to cases in which a proper name might have been used" (1939:83, fn 1). Later the indefinite article arose in "cases requiring an individualized sense" (1939:98), that is, where reference was to an individual object rather than, say, a categorizing predicative. At this early period, the function of both articles was primarily referential.

There has been much confusion in the use of the term *definite* in the literature. Different writers have equated definiteness with the features of uniqueness or specificity, or with the "packaging" status of old information. So far as these uses of the word *definite* have been intended as theories of the function of the English definite article, they have been incorrect: the best succinct statement of the function of the word *the* is that it marks identifiable referents. This statement, however, applies fully only within the domain of referential-specific mentions. In other areas, such as generic mentions, it does not adequately contrast the functions of *the* and *a*. Because of the great confusion which has existed in the past over what definiteness is, and because it is not in fact possible to specify a single function of the definite article which will apply in all areas of English grammar, it is perhaps best to divorce the question of semantic/pragmatic function from the question of formal marking. The word *definite* may serve a useful purpose in referring to a formal class of reference items which includes not only noun phrases preceded by the definite article (*the boy, the pears*), but also definite pronouns (*I, you, he, she, it*), proper names (*John, London*), and possessed noun phrases (*his bicycle, the man's pears*). Formally indefinite noun phrases include not only those preceded by the indefinite article (*a boy*), but articleless mass nouns (*water*) and plural count nouns (*pears*), plurals preceded by a numeral (*three boys*), and indefinite pronouns (*someone, something*). Use of the cited formally definite reference items marks a referent as identifiable, as long as the mention is referential-specific. Similarly, a referential-specific use of the foregoing formally indefinite reference items marks the referent as nonidentifiable. Thus a legitimate use of the terms *definite* and *indefinite* is to specify the formal classes as delineated. To state the semantic/pragmatic status of a mention, however, one is less prone to misunderstanding if the actual semantic/pragmatic features, such as identifiable, specific, or unique, are directly stated.

I will in general use *definite* and *indefinite* to refer to the formal classes just described. But in discussing referential-specific mentions, where the formal classes coincide with functional classes, the terms may be used with functional meaning where ambiguity is unlikely.

Having used the term *referential* on several occasions, it will be well to specify the particular meaning I attach to it.

> (2) A noun phrase is *referential* when it is used to speak about an object
> as an object, with continuous identity over time.

The *object* here may be a physical object or an objectified concept; it may be specifically known or it may be unknown; it may exist in the real world or in some hypothetical world; there may be one or more than one object. As long as a noun phrase is used to speak about such objects and the objects are conceived of as having continuity of identity, the noun phrase is referential. In the following passage, all the noun phrases (*a boy, a bicycle, he, the pears*) are referential:

> (3) and a boy comes by riding a bicycle. ... And he sees the pears, ... and he stops. (Speaker 19)

These referential noun phrases may be thought of in cognitive terms as either activating a mental "file" for some object (*a boy, a bicycle*) or referring back to a previously opened file (*he, the pears*). The referential concept is bounded, and may serve as a focus for future references. This is what is meant by *continuity of identity*. Any referential use of a noun phrase may be followed by further noun phrases referring to the same referent. Of course, this opportunity is not always taken.

A noun or noun phrase which is not used to speak about an object as an object is nonreferential. Typically it is the quality defined by the noun rather than the potential of the noun for concrete meaning which is exploited. In the following example, the noun phrase *a uh.. Chicano American,* which is the third mention of the Pear Man, is nonreferential:

> (4) he looks like a uh.. Chicano American, (Speaker 9)

The speaker is talking about the Pear Man. There is no intent here to speak about a Chicano-American, not even an unspecified one. Nor is the subject speaking about generic Chicano-Americans as a whole. Rather, the attributes characteristic of being a Chicano-American are abstracted off from the potential concrete meaning, and certain of these attributes (the visual ones) are assigned to the Pear Man through the predication *look like. A Chicano American,* even though it follows a definite mention of the Pear Man, does not bear the definite article, showing that there is no continuity of identity with the Pear Man, which would exist if the noun phrase referred to the Pear Man. Nor does the noun phrase refer to some Chicano-American: one would not go on to speak about *the Chicano American.*[4]

I now present an outline of the major categories of nonreferential mentions, followed by a discussion of referential uses, broken down by the features which characterize them.

Nonreferential uses of nouns occur in compounds, within negative scope in a sentence, in certain speech acts, in predicating expressions, and in conflated objects.

In compounds such as *pear tree,* the first noun is nonreferential:

---

[4]Kuno (1970) discusses grammaticality aspects of some types of nonreferential noun phrases, primarily categorizing predicate nominals.

(5) there's a--..man...picking pears, in a pear tree, (Speaker 8)

The noun phrase *a pear tree* as a whole is referential, but the word *pear* serves only to subcategorize *tree,* not to speak about a pear or pears. Other nonreferential examples include the first nominal elements in *a fruit picker* (Speaker 18), *the farm laborer* (Speaker 5), *the goatman, the goat..person, the bicycle boy, the bicycle thief,* and *the pearpicker* (Speaker 12), and *a paddle ball* (Speaker 15).

Negative pronouns and formally indefinite noun phrases occurring within the scope of negative quantifiers are typically nonreferential. In the following examples, *conversation, anything,* and *nobody* are nonreferential:

(6) there's no conversation in this movie. [...] the human beings in it don't say anything. (Speaker 6)

(7) and..nobody ever smiles in the movie; (Speaker 14)

A nonreferential mention like *nobody* establishes no mental "file" that can be referred to later, so that a humorous effect may arise when a speaker treats it as though it could be referred to, as Lewis Carroll shows:

(8) "I see nobody on the road," said Alice. "I only wish I had such eyes," the King remarked, "To be able to see nobody—and at that distance too!" (quoted in Halliday and Hasan, 1976:79)

The nonreferential uses of nouns discussed so far are readily distinguished from referential uses by their special syntactic status (in compounds, within scope of negatives) or by their membership in distinct form classes (*nobody*). But nonreferential noun phrases are formally indistinguishable from referential noun phrases in many cases. The noun phrase *a Chicano American,* used nonreferentially in (4), could in other circumstances be used referentially (e.g., *Then a Chicano American came along*). But when the text as a whole is examined, there emerge two overt means of recognizing non-referentiality:

(9) The form of a nonreferential mention is not responsive to the presence or absence of a prior mention.

(10) The form of a nonreferential mention is not responsive to the semantic distinction between singular and plural.

We have already seen an example of the first principle: *a Chicano American,* though it followed a definite reference to the Pear Man, was formally not definite. This nonresponsiveness to prior mention occurs even where the noun phrase is identical:

> (11) Mary's a forester. She's been a forester for three years now.

> (12) Can you swim a mile? When you can swim a mile you'll be ready for the trip.

A forester and *a mile* are nonreferential mentions (of different types). *The forester* and *the mile,* which would ordinarily be expected after prior mentions, are not appropriate in these examples. Thus, overt evidence can be adduced to show that the "indefinite" article does not mark nonidentifiability in such cases: the identifiability contrast is simply not applicable to nonreferential uses.[5]

Also not applicable to nonreferential mentions is the semantic contrast between singular and plural. Nonreferential noun phrases represent a qualitative abstract of the noun. Since this abstract expresses no objective reality, a determination of quantity is not relevant. Nevertheless, the English language typically demands that one of the two available numbers be chosen. But this choice does not always accord with the actual facts of the situation. For example, a newly wealthy musician was discussing his interest in fine cars:

> (13) I finally found out what the best is. I have a Mercedes—three of them in fact.
>
> —(*Downbeat* 4/6/78)

Here "having a Mercedes" is seen as a unitary predicate concept (see p. 214), so that *a Mercedes* does not respond to semantic number (except as an afterthought). The reverse situation may also occur, where a singular referent may be associated with a formally plural nonreferential mention. Thus Lily Q.,[6] who is in the habit of wearing a contact lens in only one eye (her left eye), said

> (14) I only wear one in my left when I'm wearing my lenses.

---

[5]The same principle applies where the nonreferential mention is preceded by a referential mention, as with the nonreferential *a text* preceded by referential *a text* in the following example:

> (i) The intention is . . . to offer an insight into what it is that makes a text a text. (Halliday and Hasan, 1976:328)

[6]In each example where the source citation consists of a first name and last initial, the actual speaker's name has been replaced by a pseudonym, and the example represents an observed natural speech event, which I have recorded over the last several years. Examples for which no citation is given are constructed examples.

In this case, the culturally relevant state of "wearing one's lenses" is seen as a unitary concept. The plural form *lenses* does not refer to some (plural) objects, but rather expresses a general condition at the higher level of the verb phrase. Of course, the formal number of a nonreferential mention frequently coincides with the semantic number of the object with which it is associated, as in (11), but this does not establish that the mention is referential. One sometimes finds variation between one form which coincides with plural number and another which remains uninflected:

> (15) a. He's six feet tall.
> b. He's six foot tall.

Both forms are nevertheless nonreferential.

Though most nonreferential mentions must be recognized through indirect means, one form of noun phrase is in general restricted to nonreferential mentions, and thus may serve to identify them:

> (16) Nonreferential mentions of certain types are typically realized as zero-form[7] noun phrases.

Many performative uses of noun phrases are nonreferential, and these are often realized as singular zero-form mentions:

> (17) I pronounce you man and wife.

More productively, vocatives usually occur in the zero-form, since their primary function is not to refer to the addressee but to attract his attention or index his social position.

> (18) Buddy, could you spare a quarter?

> (19) Hey, man, can't you read the sign?

A wife or *the wife, a buddy* or *the buddy* would be unacceptable in these examples.[8]

---

[7]This term is adopted from Christophersen (1939). An *a*-form noun phrase is marked by *a* (*a pear*), a *the*-form noun phrase is marked by *the* (*the pear, the pears*), and a zero-form noun phrase has no article (*pear, pears*).

[8]There may be a useful sense of the word *referential* that is applicable to vocatives, but vocatives do not satisfy the requirement that they be "used to speak about an object as an object" (2).

The following types of nonreferential mention, though usually not distinctively marked in the noun phrase itself, may in general be shown to be nonreferential by one or another of the means just discussed.

Several types of attribution are nonreferential. Categorizing predicate nominals do not refer:

> (20) he comes across another... bicyclist... bicyclist [1st]; it's a young woman [2nd], (Speaker 5)

> (21) I used to play with/it/when I was a kid, (Speaker 10)

In both examples a prior mention (*another bicyclist, I*) precedes the predicate nominal mention (*a young woman, a kid*) which would thus be definite if it were referential. But their nonreferential status results in formally indefinite marking.[9]

Significantly, speakers may paraphrase a predication containing a nonreferential mention of a character with one which contains no mention at all, as in the following description of the threesome:

> (22) they're   [3d] little boys.... They're... from nine to twelve years old. (Speaker 5)

It is the quality of being a little boy which is expressed in the predication of *little boys,* and this quality can be alternatively expressed in a predication which does not mention the boys at all, but merely states their ages. The same paraphraseablity of nonreferential mentions with expressions that are not nominal at all is seen in the following example:

> (23) They [the pears] were green, [...] they were green pears, (Speaker 15)

Secondary predicates (Nichols, 1978) are also nonreferential, and often occur in zero-form (*muleteer, neighbors*):

> (24) the gardener of the convent, being chosen muleteer, led out the two mules. (Sterne, 1960:408)

---

[9]Not all noun phrases occurring in predicate nominal position are nonreferential. Even definite, referential proper names may occur, though the reverse has often been asserted. For example:

(i) The guy with the mustache is Salvador Dali.

(25) where they lived neighbors. (Sandburg 1922:162)

Comparatives with *like* are nonreferential, and are formally indefinite even following a definite prior mention, as in example (4) and the following examples (*a Mexican-American, bullies*):

(26) Then they walk by--... the man who was picking the pears.... who looks like a Mexican-American if that's important? (Speaker 1)
(26b) they looked like bullies, (Speaker 20)

There remains one major type of nonreferential mention, which may be termed *predicate conflation.* Two examples of predicate conflation[10] have been seen in (13) and (14). The noun phrases in these examples were used in conjunction with a verb to express a unitary predicate concept rather than to refer to an actual object. *Having a Mercedes* or *wearing one's lenses* were expressed as monolithic concepts which did not allow their subsidiary components (e.g., *a Mercedes, one's lenses*) to reflect independently a sensitivity to the actual situation.

The pear film narrations abound in such verb-plus-object conflations, though they are usually recognizable through insensitivity to prior mention rather than the rarer insensitivity to number. In one case, a subject introduced both the Pear Man and the pears he is picking into the discourse with the initial mention *a guy who's picking pears,* and then went on:

(27) ...And..um...the guy who is picking pears, um...um..picks the pears and puts them in a..in um...these baskets that he has...(Speaker 3)

The second mention of the pears is the formally indefinite *pears* just as it was in the first mention, while the Pear Man has shifted from indefinite (*a guy*) to definite (*the guy*). The insensitivity of *pears* to prior mention reflects its nonreferentiality, just as the sensitivity of *the guy* to prior mention reflects its referentiality. The pears are not important in themselves but are conflated into a unitary predicate concept of "pear-picking." The only purpose in mentioning this activity in the noun phrase *the guy who is picking pears* is to characterize the Pear Man, so that recognition of the pears as an objective reality independent of the pear-picking activity is not relevant. Later, when the speaker wishes to refer to the actual pears, she uses a referential and hence definite mention:

(28) [He] picks the pears and puts them in a..in um...these baskets that the has...

---

[10]*Conflation* is used here in a somewhat different sense than in the work of Leonard Talmy.

This particular subject seems reluctant to pronominalize on the basis of a nonreferential mention, preferring to use a full referential noun phrase first, but this is not the general rule. Speakers often make a pronominal mention based on a referential concept which has been introduced nonreferentially. More important in example (28) is that, although the first two mentions of the pears are nonreferential object conflations, the third mention is referential and definite. This might seem problematic: How can a definite, specific reference to a real object be based on a nonreferential introduction? The answer becomes clear if we look ahead to the matter of definite initial mentions which are dependent on frames. It has been pointed out that the use of the verb *sell* may make possible a subsequent definite reference to *the money* (Chafe, 1972:61). But one would hardly say that *sell refers* to money. It simply evokes a "frame" which includes, among various elements, the notion of money. Similarly, the sentence

(29) They went out pear-picking yesterday

does not refer to pears, but it nevertheless evokes a frame which includes a slot for pears. This allows a subsequent definite reference to the frame-evoked pears:

(30) But the pears were green and didn't sell.

Halliday and Hasan, pointing out that a plural noun phrase may be used to refer back to several items presented singly in the discourse, observe that this use follows from "the general nature of anaphoric reference items, that they refer to the meanings and not to the forms that have gone before" (1976:62). It can be further said that anaphoric reference items need not refer to meanings introduced through a direct reference, but may refer to meanings introduced indirectly through frames. We may state this in the form of a principle:

(31) To make a definite reference to an object, it is not necessary for there to be in previous discourse a reference to the object; it is only necessary for the idea of the object to have been evoked in some way.

This evocation commonly arises through the use of frames. And as a general rule, a verb-plus-object conflation evokes a frame which includes the object, allowing subsequent definite reference. This in fact falls under the general principle that definite reference is due to identifiability—with the added observation that the hearer has a variety of identificatory resources at hand.

In this light it is possible to resolve a puzzle posed by Christophersen, who claimed that in

(32) I knocked him on the head

"there can be no doubt that it is a purely individual term; 'the head' of course means 'his head'." He went on to say

> The strange thing is, however, that the singular form is kept even in: we knocked them on the head/they knocked everybody on the head. (1939:132)

But given an understanding of object conflation, this is not at all strange. "Knocking on the head" expresses a unitary concept, and verb and object are conflated into a single unit which does not respond to number. This unitary predicate expression evokes a frame which defines the particular head involved. True, we understand from (32) that it is "his head" that got knocked, but this does not mean that *the head* refers to his head, any more than *sold* in *he sold the cow* refers to money.[11]

Conflated objects may take almost any form. The nonreferentiality of conflated objects is sometimes marked by use of the zero-form singular (e.g., *hunting coon*[12]), but more commonly the *a*-form singular (*a Mercedes*) or zero-form plural (*pears*) are found. These uses are frequently confused with generics. Christophersen suggested that in

(33) Somebody in Dullingham Junction was playing the banjo

the banjo represents "the generic form" (1939:132). It is mistaken to label such uses *generic,* to be lumped with, for example, *the lion* in *the lion is found in Africa.* Conflated objects and generics share the property of nonspecificity and the neutralization of the identifiability contrast, but that does not make them the same thing.

Verb-plus-object conflations have a certain similarity to idioms and collocations in that their component parts do not vary with the usual degree of freedom. But the formation of verb-plus-object conflations is quite productive, and unlike idioms, their meaning is predictable from their component parts. To the extent that the choice of formal options (*a*-form vs. zero-form, for example) is not rule-governed, they may be considered collocational, but their similarity to idoms is not great.

Object conflation is not the only type of predicate conflation. There exist also instrumental conflation and indirect object conflation, among others. But object conflation is by far the most common type, and the other types are similar enough that they need not be discussed here.

---

[11]Object conflation bears some affinity to noun incorporation as found in many American Indian and Asian languages; a comparison would be worthwhile.

[12]For a valuable discussion of "collectivized nouns," to which the notion of object conflation may profitably be applied, see Allan (1973).

The form of nonreferential mentions varies considerably: in the singular, the *a*-form, *the*-form, and zero-form all occur; in the plural the zero-form occurs. The conditions governing the choice are complex and range from general considerations of prototypical expressive realizations, as in *wear one's lenses*, to particular considerations of historical change. For example, either article is possible in nonreferential mentions of *day* where the meaning is paraphraseable as *per day:*

(34) a. To be popt at like pigeons for sixpence a day (in OED *A*)
b. Bricklayers ... have xv d. apeece the day (in OED *The*)

This use of *a* arose from an originally distinct preposition meaning roughly *per*. *The* in this usage arose several hundred years later, suggesting that it arose by analogy with *a* (by now reanalyzed as the indefinite article); influence from French is also possible. This is all to show that, in the domain of nonreferential mentions, quite idiosyncratic historical conditions may govern the choice of article (or, as in this case, allow the choice of either article). The reason for this flexibility is that in nonreferential mentions, *the* and *a* have no direct function. The identifiability contrast which they mark is not applicable to nonreferential mentions. Hence, there is no pressure to keep them distinct in these contexts.

Although the form of nonreferential mentions is often governed by very particular conditions, there are some general rules which apply to broad classes of cases. But a treatment of this problem must be reserved for another context.

Having looked in some detail at nonreferential mentions, we turn now to the domain of referential mentions. As has been pointed out earlier, this is the domain in which the English articles exhibit their most basic function, and in which the correlation of overt marking with function is the closest.

The features described in this section combine to characterize any particular referential mention. A referential mention may be identifiable or nonidentifiable, specific or nonspecific, generic or particular, and it may exhibit various phoricity features. Most of these feature contrasts are applicable only to referential mentions, not to nonreferential mentions. This has already been discussed with regard to the identifiability contrast. Within the domain of referential mentions there also exist certain neutralizations. For example, the contrast of identifiable vs. nonidentifiable is not applicable to generic or nonspecific mentions, and the contrast of endophoric vs. exophoric is also not applicable to nonspecific mentions.

The contrast between identifiable and nonidentifiable is commonly marked by *the* and *a*. The speaker judges identifiability with respect to the hearer: he uses *the* if he expects that the hearer can identify the referent he means, and *a* if he expects that the hearer cannot, as in example (1).

The-forms are not the only forms which presuppose identifiability. Proper names and definite pronouns also presuppose identifiability:

(35) [the pears] were green, ... so I suspect they were going to sell them to Safeway. (Speaker 15)

In this example, *Safeway, I,* and *they* all presuppose identifiability. Possessive noun phrases also presuppose identifiability, and one sometimes finds variation between a possessed form and a *the*-form noun phrase, as in the following example with *his bike* and *the bicycle:*

(36) he gets off his bike, [...] ... Anyway, so um-- ... the kid on the bicycle, .. gets off the bicycle, (Speaker 1)

The choice between *the*-form and possessed form is to some extent rule-governed, and some of the rules will be discussed below in relation to frames.

Identifiability is a property of the relation between reference and referent and cannot apply to either a reference or a referent alone. If a noun phrase is said to be *identifiable,* this means simply that the hearer can establish a link between the noun phrase and the concept it refers to. It is not possible for the concept itself to be identifiable, although proper nouns have sometimes been said to represent "definite concepts" (Chafe, 1972:57). True, proper nouns are distinct from common nouns in that they presuppose identifiability without having to be marked by *the.* But even if the name of a specific individual is known to a speaker this name may mean nothing to the addressee, and in such cases we often find the proper name modified by the indefinite article, marking nonidentifiability:

(37) A Mr. Palermo [1st], who had lived up here helping his uncles in the old days and had a cabin at the foot of the trail, came by at least twice a month. (Vonnegut, 1975:55)

In the following example there is a contrast in the treatment of a familiar name (*W. C. Handy*) and an unfamiliar one (*Cora Fisher*), although both are initial mentions:

(38) ... Bessie Smith, throughout her career, shamefully neglected to acknowledge any indebtedness to her tutor, citing instead W. C. Handy and a Cora Fisher as her early inspiration (Albertson, n.d.)

Some concepts are so particular and so commonly referred to that it is useful to provide them with particular labels such as proper names. But the act of identifying always consists in relating this label to the concept. It is true for most packaging statuses that "It is the constant idea of the individual rather than the shifting words" that may occupy a particular status (Chafe, 1976:29), but this is not true of definiteness, which involves a tracing of the constant idea (referent) through links with the shifting words (references) used to refer to the idea.

Even where the name of a person is known to both speaker and addressee, the speaker is not obliged to use the available definite reference. I once said to a friend *I made squid with someone's help once.* The person who had helped me was known by name to my addressee, so I could have named her, but since the import of the discussion was simply whether I would be able to bring off a squid dish, I did not deem the name of my fellow cook relevant. This demonstrates that speakers have facultative control over definiteness. Even where the concept is potentially identifiable through a proper name, the speaker is free to choose a noun phrase which does not identify the referent.

Nonidentifiable mentions are marked by *a* in the singular (*a kid, a bicycle*) and *some* (*some boys*) in the plural, as well as by various other reference item types including number-modfied nouns (*three boys*) and genitive phrases (*one of the boys*), and indefinite pronouns (*somebody*):

(39) ... a kid [1st] comes by on a bicycle [1st]. (Speaker 1)

(40) and--... some boys-- [1st] come out, (Speaker 8)

(41) ... Three boys [1st] came out, (Speaker 4)

(42) So one of the boys [1st] whistles to him, (Speaker 3)

(43) --uh... somebody [1st] comes by with a ... walks by with a goat or something. (Speaker 10)

Noun phrases marked by unstressed *this* or *these* (*this little boy, these three little boys*) are specific but are unmarked for identifiability, and may occur on both initial and noninitial mentions, at least for some speakers:

(44) he c- he could possibly see this little boy [1st] coming on a bicycle.... At least.. it seems to me that... you know he would notice this boy [2nd] if he was really... interested, (Speaker 2)

(45) He falls over and then these three other little kids about his same age [1st] come walking by. (Speaker 6)

The speaker in (44), Speaker 2, made a total of six noninitial mentions of the Bike Boy with the determiner *this*, showing that for her *this* does not mark nonidentifiable noun phrases. But most speakers tend to restrict unstressed *this* and *these* to initial mentions.

The absence of the zero-form plural (*kids*), which is typically considered indefinite, from the preceding list of nonidentifiable mention types is not an oversight. In all the first mentions of characters in the pear film data (excluding generics) there is not a single zero-form plural. All twenty speakers introduced the Threesome with a nondefinite mention, either one marked for nonidentifiability such as *some kids, some other little kids, three little boys* (17 speakers) or one marked with *these* (*these three little boys*), which may be considered unmarked with respect to identifiability (3 speakers). But not one of the 20 speakers chose to use the available zero-form plural (*boys* or *kids*). The same is true for the plural introductions of nongeneric characters in general: Of the 24 nondefinite initial mentions, which are those that might be considered candidates for an "indefinite" zero-form plural, not one was realized as a zero-form plural. There was a single zero-form plural initial mention, but this was generic (*kids*):

(46) That look could be interpreted as a menacing grin, or a ... [ɨ] or a friendly grin, or just the way kids are, (Speaker 18)

I would suggest that, at least for humans, the zero-form plural is not used to mark nonidentifiable referents, and when it does occur it is either generic or part of a predicate conflation. In contrast with characters, initial mentions of objects as zero-form plurals are not uncommon. Of the 20 speakers who made an initial mention of pears (which in each case were the pears that the Pear Man was picking), 17 used a zero-form plural, *pears*. I suggest that the correlation of zero-from plurals with inanimates as opposed to humans occurs because inanimates commonly become part of predicate conflations, whereas humans rarely do. Humans are generally too independently salient to be conflated with a verb, and tend to take the more active case roles expressed by subject status.

Before going on to discuss the feature of specificity, it will be useful to treat an important function of nonidentifiable mentions, that of introducing new files.

ESTABLISHING NEW FILES

Although in negative terms an indefinite mention may function to mark a nonidentifiable referent, it has a further, positive, function: to establish a new "file" in the hearer's consciousness. In a sentence like

(39) ... a kid [1st] comes by on a bicycle [1st].

the indefinite articles serve both to assure the hearer that he need not look elsewhere to identify the referents (since they are nonidentifiable) and to encourage him to establish new cognitive files, one for a particular kid and one for a particular bicycle.

The opening of a new file with an *a*-form mention tends to raise the expectation that the file will continue to be used, as more information is added to it. Given this expectation, it would be useful to signal cases where little or no further use will be made of the file. There appears to be a slight tendency to use an indefinite pronoun (*someone, somebody*) rather than an *a*-form to mark the introduction of an unimportant character who will not be spoken about much. In the four cases where an indefinite pronoun was used to introduce a character, as in example (43) above, a mean of 6.3 subsequent mentions of the character were made; the 54 *a*-form initial mentions of characters were followed by a mean of 11.9 mentions. Nevertheless, the use of an *a*-form introduction for an unimportant character who is not subsequently referred to is not uncommon. More data would be needed to confirm this trend.

When a new file is opened, the hearer expects to be provided with an adequate understanding of the nature of the file that he is expected to establish. This understanding is usually provided by the noun itself: *kid* in *a kid* makes a good starting point for opening a new file. But in some cases the noun is too vague to allow the hearer to adequately conceive the file, and special measures must be taken to provide the missing information. This is especially true where the new file is opened with a definite mention, as often happens. In the following example, the noun *thing* in *his thing* is too vague to introduce its referent satisfactorily, and so must be explained:

(47) he'd drop them into his...thing[1st], but I don't..he's wearing like
an apron [2nd] with huge pockets. (Speaker 1)

In the example above, we find the curious situation that the first mention is definite and the second mention is indefinite. As it turns out, this pattern of recovery is quite common. For various reasons, the mention which is intended to establish a new file is deemed inadequate; this triggers a recovery process, which will be discussed further in dealing with descriptive modes.

In rare cases a hesitation by the speaker may serve the same file-establishing function as an initial indefinite mention, allowing subsequent definite mentions, and leading the hearer to expect more information in the ensuing discourse. This phenomenon tends to occur when hard-to-code objects are introduced, such as the paddleball:

(48) one of them is..playing like with...I don't remember, I used to
play with /it/ [paddleball - 1st] when I was a kid, but...it's like

> a ... wooden paddle ... that .. there's an elastic string attached to and there's a ball, (Speaker 10)

The definite pronoun *it* refers back, not to a file created by an indefinite mention, but to one created by the hearer's expectation of a file-establishing mention. This expectation derives not only from the pause (*playing like with...*), of course, but also from the syntactic frame (a noun phrase is expected following the preposition *with*) and the semantic expectation that playing typically involves some sort of toy. Somewhat more common is the establishing of a file through the use of a noun phrase which is begun with an indefinite article or determiner but left unfinished. Again, examples are found in attempts to introduce the low-codable paddleball:

> (49) one had a uh ... [1st] I don't know what you call them [2nd], but it's a paddle, and a ball-- .. is attached to the paddle, and you know you bounce it? (Speaker 9)

The definite *them* refers back to the file established by *a uh*.... This, like the file-establishing pause, would of course be an unsatisfactory introduction and unsuitable for subsequent pronominalization if a speaker were to attempt to continue in the narrative mode. However, in each of the three paddleball cases where a pause, or a lone indefinite article or determiner followed by a pause has been made the basis for pronominalization, the speaker switches into a descriptive mode in order to provide a more satisfactory introduction. This is a good example of the importance of the descriptive modes to be described.

New files may be opened by definites as well as indefinites. One important type of such definite initial mentions consists of a definite noun phrase followed by a relative clause:

> (50) and she knocks the hat that he's wearing [1st] off on the ground, (Speaker 7)

The hat alone would be an inadequate first mention here, since it presupposes identifiability. But the information needed for identification is supplied in the accompanying relative clause, making a definite initial mention possible. Hawkins (1978) analyzes such relative clauses as deriving from an underlying pair of sentences, the first of which contains an indefinite which is eventually deleted transformationally. Noting the possibility of *the woman Bill went out with last night* as an initial mention, he suggests that

> (51) What's wrong with Bill? Oh, the woman he went out with last night was nasty to him

is derivable from something like the "pragmatically equivalent" sentences

(52) What's wrong with Bill? Oh, he went out with a woman last night, and she/the woman was nasty to him.

This analysis is faulty in two respects. It suggests that the sentence

(53) Bill passed a woman on the street last night, and the woman was nasty to him

should be transformable into

(54) The woman Bill passed on the street last night was nasty to him.

But in fact the latter sentence is not acceptable as an initial mention of the woman. One may pass many women on the street, so this relative clause is not sufficient to specify one particular referent. The relative clause in (51) does specify one particular referent, because in our culture one may presuppose that a man will typically date only one woman in a night. The second problem is that (51) is not pragmatically equivalent to (52). What is asserted in the latter example (that Bill went out with a woman) is simply presupposed in the former. This has significant consequences with respect to the possible content of such relative clauses. New information may be presented in the presupposed format of a restrictive relative clause, as long as it is relatively unremarkable information (for example, that a man dated a woman). But if the information is remarkable, the speaker is expected to assert it rather than presuppose it. One cannot introduce an unknown woman into a conversation with the sentence

(55) The woman Bill married last night was nasty to him

in part because the new information contained in the relative clause is too noteworthy to be presupposed. This condition may be formulated as the *principle of new information presupposition:*

(56) New information may be presented in a presupposed format (such as a restrictive relative clause) only if it is not particularly noteworthy.

This principle (essentially a conversational postulate) forms part of a general condition on the use of file-establishing relative clauses:

(57) A file-establishing relative clause may be used to allow a definite initial mention only if (1) the relative clause gives enough information to specify a particular referent or referents, and (2) the information in the relative clause, if new, does not violate the principle of new information presupposition.

Both of these requirements are met in *the hat that he's wearing* (50) because in our culture (1) only one hat is usually worn if a hat is worn at all, and (2) wearing a hat, though it cannot be assumed, is unremarkable.

It will be seen that these same principles govern the use of possessive noun phrases (*his hat*) as definite initial mentions.

A formally indefinite referential mention may be specific or nonspecific. In (39), *a kid* and *a bicycle* were both *specific,* meaning that although the hearer is not able to identify the intended referent, the speaker at least has a specific object in mind. If the speaker has no particular object in mind the mention is nonspecific, as with *a pear or two* in the following example:

(58) and you think "wow," this little boy's probably going to come and see the pears, and . . . he's going to take a pear or two, (Speaker 2)

The specificity distinction is usually not overtly marked, and *a*-forms may be either specific or nonspecific. However, unstressed *this* and *these* as in (44) and (45) have only the specific meaning. In many cases nonspecific *a*-forms occur in the scope of verbs of cognition, such as *think* in the preceding example and *want* in the traditional example

(59) Susan wants to marry a Norwegian.

Because of their occurrence in such contexts it may be possible to treat so-called nonspecific mentions as being specific in a hypothetical world established by the verb of cognition. Where it is not possible to treat an *a*-form in this way, it may be that one is dealing with a case of predicate conflation rather than nonspecificity, since conflated objects are often misanalyzed as nonspecific indefinites. For example, in the most common reading of

(60) Everytime I saw him, he was wearing a hat,

a hat is best considered a conflated object rather than a nonspecific indefinite.

Generic mentions may take almost any form (see Jespersen, 1924:203–204), the most common of which are the singular *a*-form (*a fox*) and *the*-form (*the lion*) and the plural zero-form (*kids*):

(61) A fox will chew off its own leg to escape a trap.

(62) The lion is the king of beasts.

(46′) That look could be interpreted as [...] just the way kids are, (Speaker 18)

The three forms are not interchangeable, but express slightly different nuances. The difference which does exist between the *a*-form and *the*-form generics, however, is not a matter of identifiability. As with nonreferential mentions, the contrast of identifiable and nonidentifiable is not applicable. Much could be said about the different functions of the various generic forms, but only one matter immediately concerns us here. A plural generic mention provides access to a concept in the interlocutor's mind which is representative of the whole class, and since there is only one such concept, any mention which is understood as generic will be "identified" with this concept. Generics are like uniques in this respect. Reference to the moon, of which there is one unique instance in the ordinary consciousness of most people, is typically accomplished through the definite noun phrase *the moon*. But if a writer chooses to speak of *A Moon for the Misbegotten,* we do not take the indefinite to mean that some other, nonidentifiable astrological body is meant, but simply think of another aspect of the one moon—perhaps a full moon, a waning moon, a yellow moon.
    In the following example,

(63) A hand rules pity as a hand rules heaven;
       Hands have no tears to flow.

(Thomas, 1972:941)

a hand and *hands* both identify a single generic concept of hand. Since this concept is unique, any recognizeably generic mention provides access to it. It should be noted that generic mentions, like nonreferential mentions, do not shift to a *the*-form following a prior mention.[13] The generic initial mention *a hand* is followed by a second generic mention, also *a hand,* rather than *the hand.* The same phenomenon arises in the pear film data:

---

[13]Although generic *a*-form mentions do not shift to *the*-form, they may be represented by (formally) definite pronouns: *a hand rules pity as it rules heaven.* This suggests that there is a crucial difference in the function of definite pronouns and definite *the*-form noun phrases, but the matter cannot be explored here.

(64) the goat was bahying or whatever goats [generic - 1st] do
/laugh/ ... What do goats [2nd] do? (Speaker 4)

The second mention remains the same as the first rather than shifting to *the goats*. Generic concepts are directly available in the speech situation, and noninitial generic mentions are not processed via the mediation of some prior mention, but rather, directly. In this respect they may be classed with homophoric mentions (along with proper nouns and uniques).

In addition to neutralizing the identifiability contrast, generic mentions also neutralize the semantic contrast of plurality. Both singular and plural forms are used to refer to generic concepts, but the difference in meaning is not that of one vs. many.

Though generic *a*-forms and zero-form plurals may not be morphologically distinguished from nonspecific, nonidentifiable, and nonreferential mentions, they tend to be distinguished by syntactic complementarity. Generic mentions often occur in subject position; the other types usually occur in nonsubject position.

Phoricity, as used by Halliday and Hasan (1976), refers to the need to look elsewhere to interpret a reference item. Referential mentions may have various statuses with respect to phoricity. They may be endophoric or exophoric, homophoric or nonhomophoric, anaphoric or cataphoric, or simply nonphoric.

Endophoric reference points to something in the linguistic context; *exophoric* reference points to something in the situational context. A special case of exophoric reference is *homophoric* reference, in which "The referent is identifiable on extralinguistic grounds no matter what the situation" (Halliday and Hasan, 1976:71). This includes uniques (*the moon*) and generics (*kids*). The homophoricity of generics renders the identifiability contrast inapplicable, which allows the formal apparatus of identifiability to be exploited for other purposes, as noted earlier.

Endophoric references may be anaphoric, pointing backward in the text, or cataphoric, pointing forward in the text. The absence of the latter type of reference in the pear film suggests that it is rare in informal speech.

Nonidentifiable mentions are not phoric, since they do not require the hearer to look elsewhere to interpret them. Rather, they indicate that identification with some known referent is not possible, and a new file must be established. They are, however, referential in my usage of the term, which departs from that of Halliday and Hasan. Halliday and Hasan use the term *referential* only for a noun phrase that directs the hearer to look elsewhere— what in my terms would be a *phoric* noun phrase. Thus in their usage nonidentifiable mentions are classed as nonreferential, whereas I consider them referential and nonphoric.

DISCOURSE MODES

In narrative discourse, different clauses serve to advance the story line to different degrees. In the following example, the first and last clauses advance the story line, but the second clause does not:

(65) he comes across another...bicyclist...bicyclist; it's a young woman,...and...for some reason she catches his attention, (Speaker 5)

The clauses which advance the story line are in what I term the *narrative mode*. The second clause, *it's a young woman,* does not advance the story line, and may be said to be in the *descriptive mode*. Actually, *descriptive mode* is simply a cover term that includes categorizations, descriptions of clothing, statements of relation to other discourse participants, and so on.

Descriptive mode clauses are ordinarily marked by the choice of verb, of which the prime examples are *be* (often in conjunction with *there*) and *have:*

(66) he's white. (Speaker 17)

(67) they're little boys. (Speaker 5)

(68) ...tsk There's like three baskets sitting there (Speaker 11)

(69) and he had three baskets beneath the tree, (Speaker 12)

Other verbs and prepositions that figure commonly in descriptive mode clauses include *look like, wear, have on, be dressed in,* and *with* (in the sense of "having an attribute"):

(4) he looks like a uh..Chicano American, (Speaker 9)

(70) A--nd he's wearing a hat, (Speaker 17)

(71) he also had an apron on (Speaker 15)

(72) And this ma--n..is--...u--m dressed in sort of a faded,...navy blue,...denim top, and jeans. (Speaker 17)

(73) And there was this man with a mustache, and a hat, picking...unripe pears, (Speaker 14)

Narrative mode verbs may include not only concrete verbs like *pick, fall,* and *scatter* but more abstract verbs like *fulfill, grow, ponder.* The narrative and the descriptive modes together constitute the discourse modes, though it is likely that further discourse modes will ultimately have to be distinguished.

Discourse modes have considerable influence on definiteness. Mentions which occur in a narrative mode clause tend to be referential; mentions which occur in nonsubject position in a descriptive mode clause are often nonreferential, and as a result may be realized as *a*-forms or zero-forms. In example (65), *a young woman* is formally indefinite, even though it is not an initial mention. A prediction of definiteness based solely on the presence or absence of prior mentions would not be adequate in this case. But given the information that the mention occurs in a descriptive mode as a categorizing predicate nominal, the prediction is readily made.

Thus, if one knows when a particular discourse mode will be used, one can frequently predict the form of the mention. The use of discourse modes is in fact governed by discernible rules. For example, a speaker often shifts from narrative mode to descriptive mode immediatley after the introduction of a new character. This is true in example (65), where *a bicyclist* is the first mention of the Girl. In this case the choice within the descriptive mode of a categorizing predicate nominal is determined by a further factor, that of salience. The sex and age of a human referent are salient, and given that the word *bicyclist* specifies neither, the speaker feels a lack of needed information. This lack then conditions the use of a predicate nominal to remedy the situation. Discourse modes tend to be governed by such informational need triggers. Given that there is much that is salient about humans—sex, age, occupation, and so on—the informational need is high following introduction of a human character, and tends to trigger a descriptive mode. This informational need is so concrete that a speaker who cannot satisfy it may feel that he does not really know "who" the referent is. This was apparently the case in the following example. The Goat Man, a character peripheral to the film's plot, was introduced with the initial mention *someone:*

> (74) A man was picking pears in ... what seemed to be his orchard, ... and— ... came along first, .. / someone/ came along first. ... ... Someone came along before the kid on the bicycle but I don't remember who it was. (Speaker 16)

One might think that the subject, rather than saying she didn't know who the person was, could simply have said *a person came along first before the kid on the bicycle,* without further elaboration. But the lack of a concrete picture of the individual, providing such salient information as age, sex, and perhaps race and occupation, leads the speaker to feel her knowledge of the referent is insufficient (*I don't remember who it was*). The indefinite pronoun *someone* is chosen over an indefinite noun phrase because the former suggests that the speaker (as well as the hearer) is unable to fully identify the referent. This is consonant with Christophersen's observation on the contrast between *some* and *a:* "if [a man] says 'I have read it in a book', he may still remember which book it was; if he says 'I have read it in some book,' he probably cannot recall the title" (1939:188). In such cases the contrast between *some* and *a* marks identifiability by the *speaker*, which is quite distinct from the hearer identifiability contrast marked by *the* and *a*. Identification by a hearer may consist in relating a definite reference to a rather vague previous mention such as *some book*, which may in fact not be "identifiable" by the speaker himself, in the more demanding sense of, for example, knowing the book's title.

For objects, we do not have the same long list of ready-made questions as for humans, and the questions that do exist are often of a different nature. When the introduction of an object triggers a descriptive mode, the descriptive mode may provide a different class of information, often specifying location in an established scene, or ownership by a character. For example, *an apron* is introduced in a descriptive mode which serves to describe its owner rather than the apron itself, in example (71):

> (71) he also had an apron [1st] on (Speaker 15)

The descriptive mode clause, once triggered, may occur in several positions with respect to the object being introduced. It may serve as the first mention of the object, as with *three baskets* in the following example:

> (75) he has three baskets [1st] ... filled with ... and he's filling them with pears. (Speaker 5)

Once the baskets have been introduced with the descriptive mode verb *have*, they are available for reference in the following narrative mode clause. But speakers do not always take care to introduce an object in the descriptive mode first. Often the flow of narrative mode clauses is interrupted only *after* the object has been mentioned, as in the following example, where a string of narrative mode clauses is followed by a descriptive mode clause referring to the baskets:

> (76) [The Pear Man] picks pears, ... puts them in .. his apron, ... climbs down the ladder, ... and empties the pears .. into ... big .. baskets [1st]. ... tsk There's like three baskets sitting there (Speaker 11)

Apparently a momentum has built up in the narrative mode by the time the baskets are to be mentioned. Rather than break off the verbalization of what is essentially a continuous process of pear-picking, the speaker chooses to defer a "formal introduction" until after the baskets have taken their place in the story line. As in this example, when a deferred descriptive mode introduction is made it tends to come shortly after the initial mention, typically in the immediately following clause. Such deferred descriptive mode clauses are a primary source of indefinite noninitial mentions.

When a deferred descriptive mode is triggered by a narrative mode initial mention of an object, the result is not always a separate introducing sentence as in the example (76). Frequently the introductory information is appended to the narrative mode noun in a relative clause. Once again, the examples given are of the first mentions of the baskets:

(77) he--...was going up and down the ladder,...tsk..picking the pears...and...depositing them in...three baskets,...that were down below. (Speaker 7)

(78) the guy who is picking pears, um...um..picks the pears and puts them in a..in um...these baskets that he has (Speaker 3)

These examples of deferred descriptive mode (*that were down below, that he has*) have in each case been triggered by indefinite initial mentions in the narrative mode. Of course, if the speaker shifts to the descriptive mode before making the initial mention, there is no need for a deferred descriptive mode, as is seen in the following introduction of the Pear Man's apron:

(79) He's picking pears,...um--...he has an apron that he puts them in, (Speaker 10)

Following this descriptive mode introduction, the speaker continues on in the narrative mode in the next clause:

(80) and then he'll...he'll stuff them in that, (Speaker 10)

In such cases the pattern of an indefinite initial mention followed by subsequent definite mentions is maintained. But in a case like (76), the descriptive mode gives rise to another pattern, of an indefinite first mention followed by an indefinite second mention (with subsequent mentions usually definite). Deferred descriptive modes give rise to still a third pattern, of a definite first mention (in the narrative mode) followed by an indefinite second mention (in the descriptive mode). In the following example the initial mention of the Pear Man is definite, and triggers an indefinite descriptive mode introduction:

(81) the first...thing I noticed..was..the sound of the man [1st] picking...pears. ...And of course there was a...a man [2nd] there standing on a ladder in a pear tree, (Speaker 4)

A general understanding of discourse modes and the forces which trigger them sheds light not only on the way narratives are constructed but, secondarily, on the occurrence of indefinite mentions in places where they would otherwise not be expected. The distribution of the articles is most fruitfully examined in the larger context of narrative structure. It is pointless to catalog the myriad uses of the definite article for initial mentions if one disregards the measures which a speaker must subsequently take in order to render such mentions acceptable. If a speaker is obliged to immediately follow his definite initial mention with an indefinite mention, or to shift into a descriptive mode in order to explain that mention, this is hardly to be classed with those cases where a definite initial mention paves the way for the easy continuation of further definite mentions in the narrative mode. The concept of discourse mode, in conjunction with frame analysis, makes it possible to distinguish these two situations and leads to an advance beyond a narrow one-sentence perspective on definiteness.

There is one discourse mode which serves a very specialized function, and may profitably be examined at this point. It may be termed the *defining mode.* Defining the meaning of a word is usually thought of as something that occurs in a dictionary, or as an isolated act in a classroom situation. But actually definitions are found dispersed through ordinary discourse, where they play an important, if occasional, role. When a cooperative speaker uses a word that he thinks his addressee will not understand, he usually defines it. This definition may precede a meaningful use, and be set off in its own sentence, as in the following example:

(82) When the moon has a green rim with red meat inside and black seeds on the red meat, then in the Rootabaga Country they call it a Watermelon Moon and look for anything to happen.
It was a night when a Watermelon Moon was shining (Sandburg, 1922:53)

But frequently the definition is given only after a narrative mode use of the word, and is not set off in a separate sentence. In the following example both a proper noun (*Kutchin*) and a common noun (*phoneme*) are defined in appositional phrases:

(83) Kutchin, an Athabaskan language of Alaska, possesses no less than 55 consonantal "phonemes," distinct consonantal elements of the total phonetic pattern (Sapir, 1929:140).

In both cases the apposition is an indefinite noninitial mention, due to predicate nominal status. Without this indefinite definition, the hearer would not be able to identify the referent of the definite reference *Kutchin.*

The pear film speakers had little occasion to use the defining mode except in mentions of the low-codable paddleball, where a definition of an exotic initial mention, such as *pongo,* was sometimes deemed necessary:

(84) one's playing with this . . pongo, . . . a little . . . paddle, . . . and a ball with it on /the/ end of the elastic? (Speaker 14)

A mid-sentence definition may be given for a verb as well as a noun, as in the following example where a rare use of the verb *salute* triggered a paraphrase:

(85) I can't remember whether they saluted him or not, . . . you know . . . gave him a any kind of a salutation, (Speaker 15)

The indefinite *a salutation* would ordinarily be definite due to the frame evoked by the verb *salute,* but since it is understood as part of a paraphrase definition of *salute* it remains indefinite.

The defining mode is a clear case of a discourse mode that is triggered under well-defined circumstances, and whose implementation governs the occurrence of indefinite mentions in noninitial position. It is remarkable in that it allows an addressee's linguistic competence to be expanded in the middle of a sentence.

CURIOSITY AND IDENTIFICATION

The definite article is said to mark identifiability, but what is meant by identification? This is a complex question, of which only a few aspects will be considered here.

Identification ordinarily involves singling out the particular referent intended by the speaker, as when a reference to *the boy* is associated with a particular boy in the environment, or with a particular boy who has been introduced verbally. But this precise identification is not always demanded for an object. In the sentence

(86) The boy scribbled on the living-room wall

the definite noun phrase *the boy* presupposes that the addressee can identify one particular boy. But *the living-room wall* may be used whether or not the addressee is able to identify precisely which wall is meant. It is expected that the addressee be able to identify the particular living room in question, and thus to narrow down the range of possible referents to one of four walls, but beyond this he need not identify the particular wall. Identification of the precise wall is not considered salient under such circumstances. If the hearer is able to identify the referent as some unspecified wall in a specified room, that is considered sufficient to justify marking the noun phrase as identifiable. If the speaker were to specify exactly which wall, as in

(87) He scribbled on the north living-room wall

he would be violating the Gricean maxim of relevance by giving more information than people care to know. On the other hand, since a speaker ordinarily would choose not to identify the particular wall, it might seem that the logical step would be to mark the wall as nonidentifiable:

(88) He scribbled on a living-room wall.

But, curiously, this sentence still gives the impression of being unnaturally precise. To indicate, by the use of the indefinite article, that the wall will not be exactly identifiable seems to violate the admonishment to be relevant from the other direction. It presupposes an excessive curiosity about walls on the part of the hearer. This suggests the formulation of what may be called the *curiosity principle:*

(89) A reference is counted as identifiable if it identifies an object close enough to satisfy the curiosity of the hearer.

The identification need not be one to satisfy a philosopher or a Sherlock Holmes, who may of course be led to demand "Which wall?" In special circumstances even an ordinary speaker might desire more precise identification. But in everyday speech such partial identification is quite common.

Referents that are treated in this manner are often those which come in small symmetrical sets as part of a well-defined frame. Walls come in sets of four and are part of the "room" frame. Corners, sides, and edges also come in sets and usually receive a definite initial mention due to association with an evoked frame. In each case the reference (*the wall, the corner, the side, the edge*) is partly identifiable due to association with a specific object, while complete identifiability is considered superfluous due to the lack of salient distinctions within the small set of possible referents. This analysis explains a usage that puzzled Christophersen:

Still more strange is the sentence: *towards evening we came to the bank of a river.* Every river on earth inevitably has two banks. Here, however, only *the* is possible... (1939:140)

Christophersen's tentative explanation is that if one knows the direction of travel toward the river one can identify which bank is meant. But this explanation is not possible in

(90) We floated downstream awhile, and then paddled over to the bank.

The key lies in Christophersen's own observation that "Every river on earth inevitably has two banks." River banks come in small symmetrical sets as part of a well-defined frame (the "river" frame), and under ordinary circumstances the difference between the two set members is nonsalient. Hence the curiosity principle allows definite treatment with only partial identifiability.

The curiosity principle figures prominently in the pear film data because of its application to a major class of referents that come in well-defined frame-related sets: paired body parts. Hands, ears, legs, and so on, are parallel to river banks in that definite reference is allowed with only partial identifiability once a specific frame has been evoked (that is, once a specific person has been mentioned).[14] In the following example the definite initial mentions *my hand* and *the arm* both presuppose identifiability:

(91) I offered her my hand
       She took me by the arm   (Dylan, n.d.)

The identification is made possible only because of the relaxed standard of the curiosity principle. Identification of a hand as belonging to a particular person is ordinarily sufficient to satisfy curiosity. Of course the precise body part is sometimes relevant, as in the case of the jeweler referred to in the following example:

(92) she tumbled down a flight of stairs and broke her right (working) wrist (San Francisco *Chronicle, 6/2/78).*

But more commonly the precise body part is left unspecified, and a definite mention is used anyway. In the pear film data five speakers made an initial mention of a single paired body part (*his leg, his knee*) but not one specified whether the right or left member was intended, although all mentions presupposed identifiability. The definite initial mention *his leg* in

(93) he falls over, . . . spills his pears, . . hurts his leg. (Speaker 19)

---

[14]A distinction between frame type and frame token is implicit here. The *frame type* for "human," available in *langue,* includes slots for two arms, a head, and so on; mention of John Smith evokes a *frame token* with slots filled by John's two arms, head, and so on. This distinction allows the observation that a mention of two people evokes two frame tokens, both founded on a single frame type.

is possible only because the curiosity principle allows a relaxed standard of identification.

Human beings, although they occasionally come in small well-defined sets related to a frame, are not subject to the curiosity principle. The differences between two humans are considered too salient to neglect in this way. After speaking of a double violin concerto, one cannot go on to initiate a reference to one of the two soloists as *the violinist*. In general, curiosity about human referents leads to an expectation of full identification. There is, however, a similar phenomenon whereby humans who are members of a crowd may be marked as partially identifiable; this will be dealt with later (p. 265ff).

Having provided a framework with which to view the introduction of objects into discourse and their subsequent tracing through it, it is now possible to take a broader look at the 20 pear film narratives. In the remainder of this chapter, an understanding will be sought of how the speaker's communicative needs and expressive strategies underlie departures from the prevailing pattern of article use.

FRAMES AND THE CRITICAL INTRODUCTION PERIOD

The identifiability-marking function of the articles produces the typical pattern, noted earlier, of an indefinite initial mention followed by definite mentions in noninitial position. Deviations are of two types. Definite mentions may occur in initial position and indefinite mentions may occur in noninitial position; the following discussion tries to show why.

Most definite initial mentions are based on identifiability due to situational context or to frames, as has long been recognized. The result is a rather large proportion of definite initial mentions. In the pear film data 34 percent of the 613 initial mentions of characters and objects are formally definite. When objects alone are considered the proportion is even higher (41 percent of the 467 initial mentions). Since the speakers in question had never met the addressee (the interviewer) and thought she had not seen the film of which they spoke, these definite initial mentions are not due to any special shared knowledge peculiar to the interlocutors. Also, references to discourse participants (*I, you*), which are almost always definite on first mention, are not included in the foregoing figures. In everyday speech, the occurrence of discourse participant references, proper names (almost entirely absent from the pear film data), and other situation-based definites may raise the actual proportion of initial definites to a substantially higher level (though it becomes difficult to decide which mentions are initial in the conversation of long acquaintances).

A striking fact about the pear film narratives is that the tendency to definiteness is not distributed evenly across the various semantic classes.

Rather, certain semantic types have a consistently greater likelihood of being definite on initial mention. Body parts have the highest proportion of definite initial mentions (75 percent), whereas humans are lowest, with 12 percent definite (Figure 1). In general, things which are part of something else (body parts, 75 percent; parts of inanimate objects, 70 percent) or geographically fixed (locations, 73 percent; terrain, 71 percent) have the highest proportion of definite initial mentions; things which can move or be moved independently—the things which are the least predictable—have the lowest proportions (human beings, 12 percent; nonhuman animates, 12 percent; movable objects, not part of something else, 27 percent). In sum, the more independent an object, the less likely it is to be definite on initial mention.

We see that knowing the semantic class of a referent can give an approximate idea of whether it will be definite on first mention. But this crude prediction can be sharpened considerably by asking some more sophisticated questions. The most important are, whether a relevant frame has been evoked by something in previous discourse, and whether the initial mention is made in the narrative mode or the descriptive mode.

Frames may be classed as object-based or event-based. The first were well described by Christophersen; the latter he touched on in passing, under the rubric of "implicit contextual basis" (1939:34). This type of frame has recently begun to receive much attention, in the work of Fillmore (1976) and Chafe among others.

Speaking of the object-based frame *bicycle*, Chafe observed that, "once *bicycle* has been mentioned, *frame, seat*, and the like are as eligible to be treated as *definite* as is *bicycle* itself" (1972:62). As an illustration of this, the following speaker makes a mention of the Bike Boy's bicycle (*a bicycle*) which is followed by a definite initial mention of the front fender:

(94) he picks up a . . . the whole basket of pears, . . . and puts it on the handle . . no on the . . . front . . fender of his bike [1st]. (Speaker 6)

Of the 14 such initial mentions of bicycle parts, 79 percent were definite, with indefinites occurring mostly in mentions of optional bike parts.[15]

---

[15]There was a single case of an obligatory bike frame element which was referred to with a formally indefinite mention(*wheels*):

(i) You could hear the bicycle, . . . wheels going round. (Speaker 4)

Such mentions tend to apply to frame-dependent objects occupying adverbial phrases:

(ii) He walked slowly up the stairs, head held high.

Possibly these should be considered some sort of "adverbial conflation," akin to predicate conflation.

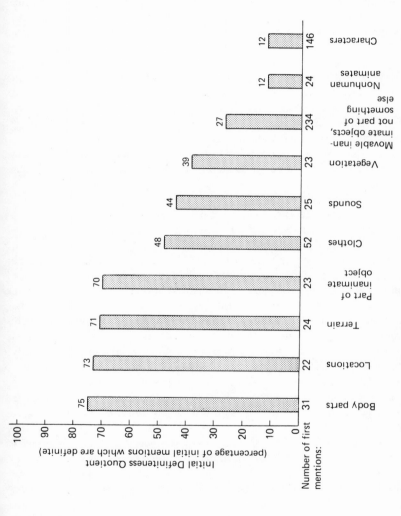

FIG. 1. Definiteness of Initial Mentions, by Semantic Class (for classes receiving at least 20 mentions)

237

It should be clear that the crude percentages cited here and in Figure 1 neglect one crucial consideration—whether the appropriate frame has been evoked in previous discourse. As it happens, all initial mentions of bicycle parts (definite or indefinite) were preceded by a mention of the bicycle. Indeed, the high definiteness proportion for parts in the pear film data depends on the fact that wholes are almost always mentioned before their parts.

A full understanding of the phenomenon of initial definiteness is possible only when the influence of the discourse modes is considered. With this in mind, I examine in some detail two semantic classes which are closely linked to the "human" frame—body parts and clothes. There are 27 initial mentions of human body parts in the pear film data, of which 82 percent are definite.[16] Since every body part mention is preceded by a mention of the part's owner, the numerous definite initial mentions are easy to explain. Once a mention has been made of, for example, the Bike Boy, a definite reference to his head is understandable:

(95) and he's [Bike Boy - 7th]...turning his head [1st].. behind him looking at her (Speaker 5)

We have seen that in other cases a definite initial mention may force the speaker to shift to the descriptive mode, as in example (81) where a definite initial mention (*the man*) triggered a descriptive mode clause containing an indefinite second mention (*a man*). But this never occurred with body parts. These mentions are not anomalous, and as a result not one of the 22 definite initial mentions of body parts triggered a subsequent indefinite mention.[17]

But we are left with the question: Why are not *all* initial mentions of body parts definite? Must we simply say that the human frame sometimes triggers definite body part mentions and sometimes does not, in accordance with some variable rule? In fact the triggering is not simply variable, but is governed by the choice of discourse mode. Mentions of body parts were divided into descriptive mode occurences—objects of the verbs *have, have on, wear,* or objects of the prepositions *in* (in the sense "wearing") or *with* ("having attribute X")—and narrative mode occurrences—subjects, objects of verbs other than *have, have on,* and *wear,* indirect objects, objects of prepositions (except *in* and *with* in their descriptive senses). The following examples illustrate the prevailing pattern that emerges. Initial mentions are indefinite in the descriptive mode (*a moustache* as object of *with*) and definite in the narrative mode (*his knee* as object of *skin*):

---

[16]The percentage cited in Figure 1 differs because it includes four initial mentions of body parts of nonhumans (to wit, the Goat), of which three are indefinite.

[17]Nor were there any indefinite noninitial mentions following the five indefinite initial mentions.

(96) And there was this man with a moustache [1st], (Speaker 14)

(96b) and he falls down and he skins his knee [1st] or something. (Speaker 7)

All other body part mentions follow this pattern. The 22 narrative mode initial mentions have an *initial definiteness quotient* (defined as the percentage of initial mentions which are definite) of 100; the 5 descriptive mode initial mentions have a quotient of 0. Thus, once the discourse modes are considered, predictability of definiteness is no longer variable but absolute (for this small corpus).

It is worth considering whether discourse modes themselves can be predicted. It appears that they can be (at least for body parts), as Table 1 shows. The first column lists human body parts which appear in the descriptive mode; the second, those which appear in the narrative mode. All five mentions for which the speakers felt obliged to use the descriptive mode are optional parts of the human frame: a moustache, which men may have or may not have, and pigtails, which women may or may not have. The body parts which are dropped into the stream of the narrative without special comment are those which can be presupposed, the obligatory elements of the human frame—head, neck, hands, and so on. There is a clear split along the lines of obligatory and optional frame elements, as distinguished by Chafe (1972:62).

Of course, it is possible for someone to make a descriptive mode mention of an obligatory body part, or a narrative mode mention of an optional body part, but the fact that this never occurs in the pear film data suggests that it is rare in spoken language. (In literary English liberties are often taken with this rule, it seems.) But where a leg, say, does receive a descriptive mode mention, this is most likely because it has some remarkable characteristic:

TABLE 1.
Frequency of Occurrence of Initial Body Part Mentions,
by Discourse Mode

Descriptive	Narrative
moustache (2)	—
pigtails (3)	—
—	head (10)
—	face (2)
—	neck (2)
—	hands (1)
—	fingers (1)
—	leg (3)
—	knee (2)
—	feet (1)

If there is something unusual about the body part or about its condition we may...have perfectly natural sentences of the following sort: *Tom has a wooden leg, Tom has a broken leg, Tom has a long head.* (Longacre, 1976:247)

Each of the descriptive mode mentions contains an adjective, and indeed the pear film data on body parts suggest this pattern is general: three of the five descriptive mode initial mentions contain adjectives. For example:

(97) and it's another little white girl. ...with long.. braids,... brown hair [1st]. (Speaker 17)

(98) this other little girl in pigtails,... black pigtails [1st],... rode by, (Speaker 14)

The correlation in the other direction is even stronger. No adjectives occur with any of the 22 narrative mode initial mentions. Although the narratives contain many sentences like *And he sort of...* / *visually* / *...counts them with his fingers* (Speaker 6), sentences of the type *he counts them with his stubby fingers,* so common in the literary language, never occur in the spoken English of the pear film data. Apparently, if a speaker wishes to attribute a special quality to a referent, he tends to shift his full attention to the matter by using the descriptive mode—rather than overloading the limited resources of consciousness (Chafe, Chapter 1) by trying to subcategorize an object adjectivally while advancing the story line. It has long been recognized that attributive adjectives are less frequent in speaking than in writing—Drieman (1962) and O'Donnell (1974)—but it is now possible to be more precise about the restrictions on adjectives in speaking: they are used, but usually only in the descriptive mode (which, it should be noted, may contain attributive as well as predicate adjectives). In writing, the possibility for longer reflection allows adjectives to be used in the narrative mode as well, thus producing a greater overall frequency.

The restriction of adjectives to the descriptive mode seems clear at least for body parts and for clothes, but a full correlation of adjective use with discourse mode has not yet been tabulated for all semantic classes. It is clear, however, that the restriction is not an absolute, but a tendency. In addition, post-nominal modifying phrases are not restricted in the same way as prenominal modifiers. Such phrases do in fact occur with narrative mode initial mentions:

(99) and /he/ sort of... [breath] holds onto his leg [1st],.. which is hurt, (Speaker 11)[18]

---

[18]Restrictive as well as nonrestrictive relative clauses may occur in this context, at least for clothes: *the hat that he's wearing* (50).

It is possible to go beyond the observation that narrative mode initial mentions of body parts are always formally definite to specify which form from among the various definite types will be chosen. In the pear film data, in every case it is the possessed form (*his head, his fingers, their hands*) and never the *the*-form which is chosen; in other words, *the head* is not attested. (Descriptive mode mentions of body parts, in contrast, never appear as possessed noun phrases.)

There is a notable clustering of correllated properties in the case of initial body part mentions—definiteness, possessive adjective, lack of (other) adjectives, and narrative mode on the one hand—and indefiniteness, adjective, lack of possessive adjective, and descriptive mode—on the other. We shall see that time also enters into this clustering, in the form of the "critical introduction period."

The mentions of body parts discussed so far have in every case followed the mention of their owner. This in itself is of interest: apparently it is extremely uncommon to mention a part before its whole. But it is worth considering cases where this does happen, if only to confirm that the high initial definiteness quotient for body parts indeed depends on the prior evocation of the human frame.

A second experiment was conducted in which a brief film clip extracted from the main film was shown to subjects. The clip began with a close-up of the Pear Man's hands picking pears (rather than a long-distance shot of the Pear Man in the pear tree, which is what first appeared in the full pear film). The subjects were then asked to write what they saw. Nine of the subjects[19] mentioned the hands—seven before mentioning the Pear Man, and two after. The latter two fit the pattern we have already seen: one, in the narrative mode, was definite (*his hands* Subject II-8); the other was indefinite due to the descriptive mode verb *have* (*He* [. . .] *had soft looking hands* Subject II-210). But of the seven subjects who mentioned the body part before the whole man, six used indefinite noun phrases: *a hand* (3), *hands* (2), and *a pair of hands* (1) (all in the narrative mode).[20] The low initial definiteness quotient contrasts markedly with the very high quotient for body parts which are mentioned after their owners.[21] The data confirm the common-sense observation that definite mentions of body parts are dependent on a prior mention of the person they belong to. If body parts are so frequently introduced with definite noun phrases, this is, unsurprisingly, because their owners are almost always mentioned before them. In the rare case where the

---

[19]Out of the 98 qualified subjects responding. (A number of further subjects had to be excluded because they were not native speakers of English.)

[20]The seventh subject wrote with telegraphic speech (without most articles), thus neutralizing the definite/indefinite contrast and rendering the result uninterpretable.

[21]Of course other variables are involved here—spoken vs. written response, length of film— making the results simply suggestive.

frame part is mentioned before evocation of the frame whole, it will typically be indefinite.

But this experiment, while confirming a common-sense observation about frames, also reveals a curious asymmetry in their functioning. Mention of a human evokes a frame which allows (indeed, demands) a definite initial narrative mode mention of the person's body parts, but the reverse does not hold. When a body part is mentioned first, no doubt a hearer immediately thinks of the human being who comes with it; nevertheless, this does not always lead to a definite initial mention. Three of the six subjects under discussion followed their mention of the hand with an indefinite initial mention of the man (two of them in the narrative mode). For example:

(100) a hand [1st] came out through some green leaves, and was carefully picking fruit. Then a man with a straw hat [1st] came to view; he was picking the fruit ... (Subject II-33)

The three subjects who did use a definite article (all in the narrative mode) all gave a relative clause specifying ownership of the hands:

(101) We see hands [1st] picking pears, then the man whose hands they are [1st] (Subject II-23)

It seems that all is not equal in a frame like the human frame. In the stereotypical, normal circumstances that frames are supposed to represent, a hand implies a person, just as the reverse holds true. But the whole is more than the part—even if a part is introduced first, the whole may not be introduced with a definite noun phrase, unless an explanatory relative clause is included.[22]

Clothes show a pattern similar to, but less extreme than, that shown by body parts. The 52 initial mentions of clothes have a somewhat lower initial definiteness quotient of 48. The correlation of definiteness with discourse mode, though strong, is not perfect. The 22 descriptive mode initial mentions have an initial definiteness quotient of 0; the 30 narrative mode mentions have a quotient of 83. Illustrations are seen in examples (102) (descriptive mode), (103) (narrative mode, definite), and 104 (narrative mode, indefinite):

---

[22]But contrast the following example from literary English, in which prior mention of *a daughter* triggers a definite mention of her family:

(i) ... if a daughter [1st] asks
    (8) Can I have the car?
    homophoric reference is entailed if the family [1st] has only one car. (Rochester and Martin, 1977:264)

(102) A--nd you see a middle-aged..u--m..Chicano man,...who's wearing..a--..navy blue shirt [1st],...and a bright red..kerchief [1st] around his neck,...and a white apron [1st]. (Speaker 17)

(103) and-- his hat [1st] falls off (Speaker 8)

(104) and he put them in an apron /that he had/ [1st] (Speaker 12)

The definite initial mentions are not anomalous; in only one case (4 percent) was a subsequent indefinite mention triggered, probably for independent reasons—see example (47).

Figure 2 demonstrates graphically the value of distinguishing between the discourse modes. When descriptive and narrative mentions are not distinguished (shaded columns) the predictability of definiteness is not nearly so great as when they are distinguished (white columns).

Definite narrative mode mentions of clothes, as in example (103), exhibit a propensity, reminiscent of body parts, for possessed forms: all but one (96 percent) bear the preposed possessive adjective *his*. The one departure from the prevailing pattern (*the hat that he's wearing*) is seen in example (50), where it illustrates the conditions on definite initial mentions due to file-establishing relative clauses. These same conditions, it seems, govern the use of possessive adjectives for definite initial mentions. The definite *his hat* in

(105) when he turns around his hat [1st] flies off. (Speaker 1)

is possible because *his* makes a contribution to identification in the same way that the relative clause *that he's wearing* does. *His* is similar to *the* in that it demands (presupposes) identifiability, but different in that it supplies some extra information that may help make the identification possible (see Haliday and Hasan, 1976:70–71). This semantic contribution is what allows it to be used so frequently in initial mentions. Once this file-establishing function of *his* has been exploited, the speaker may choose to use *the* subsequently—as in the case of one speaker who followed a definite initial narrative mode mention (*so that his... his hat* [1st] *flies off* Speaker 18) with four subsequent mentions, three with *the* and one with *his*.

Since *his* presupposes identifiability and possession as well, it is presumably subject to the principles of new information presupposition (56). In spoken English, new information on possession tends not to be presented via a preposed possessive adjective unless the possession involved is not particularly noteworthy. Among body parts, those introduced by *his* include the Pear Man's head, face, neck, and fingers, but not his moustache. Clothing items introduced with *his* include the Bike Boy's pants and hat. The Pear

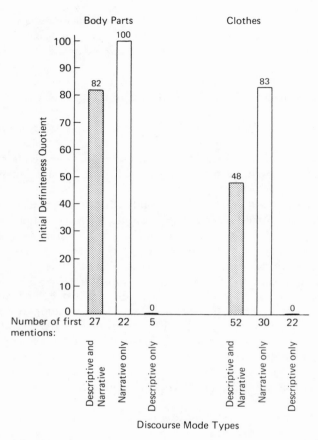

FIG. 2. Influence of Discourse Mode on Initial Definiteness Quotient: Body Parts and Clothes

Man's apron (which is at the fringes of what one might consider clothing) was introduced by eight subjects with the indefinite article—but by five subjects with *his*. Perhaps this occurs because *his* is only weakly governed by the principle of new information presupposition, or perhaps possession (wearing) of an apron is not particularly noteworthy. The goat, which appeared as an undoubtedly noteworthy (for Americans, at least) possession of the Goat Man, was introduced by all 17 speakers who mentioned it with the indefinite article, and never with *his*. In any case, one would wish to examine more instances of noteworthy possession, without added variables such as animacy.

For clothes as for body parts, no descriptive mode initial mentions bear possessive adjectives—that is, *a shirt of his* does not occur—or otherwise indicate possession in the noun phrase. In virtually all cases possession is already expressed (*have*) or implied (*have on,* etc.) in the verb or preposition. In other words, when a "human" frame element (a body part or item of clothing) is mentioned, possession will ordinarily be expressed in one way or another. If the descriptive mode is selected, the verb serves to express possession, but if the narrative mode is selected, possession must be expressed in the noun phrase.

Clothes part company from body parts in one respect: there is no clear correlation between the optionality of the frame element and the choice of discourse mode, like that seen in Table 1.

As with body parts, adjectives that modify initial mentions of clothes are almost entirely restricted to indefinite descriptive mode mentions. Of the 16 initial mentions of clothes which contain prenominal modifiers, 100 percent were indefinite mentions, and 81 percent were descriptive mode mentions. Distinct discourse mode treatments of *a white apron* are illustrated in example (106) (descriptive mode) and the less common (107) (narrative mode):

(106) he looks . . . like your uh . . typical . . farmer or . . whatever, kind of plump and . . . moustache and he wears a white apron [1st], (Speaker 8)

(107) you see him taking . . . picking the pears out of the leaves and putting them in a . . . white apron [1st], (Speaker 6)

The strong tendency for adjectives to be restricted to the descriptive mode supports the notion that in English, speakers (as opposed to writers) usually avoid mixing prenominal modification with the business of advancing the story line.

Whereas object-based frames are relatively tangible, being made up of a whole with a set of more or less unvarying parts, event-based frames (or one might say, "scene-based" frames) are less straightforward. They are composed of a network of related actions, along with the people and objects involved in those actions. But as we shall see, it is often difficult to decide on the limits of a particular event-based frame, and questions arise concerning the status ("dummy" vs. substantive) of frame-related identifications.

When linguists have investigated frames, they have often used definiteness to decide what elements make up a particular frame. For example, the definiteness of *the money* following the verbs *sell* or *buy* is evidence that they are all part of a larger "commercial act" frame, which becomes activated when some portion of it is mentioned. In the pear film data, definite initial mentions of the ladder used in picking the pears support a similar analysis. Fifteen speakers mention the ladder; seven of them do so with the expected indefinite initial mention (*a ladder*, example 108), and eight use a definite initial mention (*the ladder*, example 109). The relevant portion of previous discourse is provided for these examples:

(108) the basic action, . . . i--s that there's--. . a man . . . uh . . on a ladder [1st], . . . uh picking pears from a pear tree. (Speaker 18)

(109) It opens with um--. . . I guess a farm worker, . . . picking pears, . . . in a tree. . . . And--um--. . . you see him taking . . . picking the pears out of the leaves and putting them in a . . . white apron, . . . and he walks down the . . . ladder [1st], and dumps the pears into a basket. (Speaker 6)

None of the definite initial mentions triggered a subsequent indefinite mention; however, three were followed (after a pause) by modifying phrases—two of which were explanatory relative clauses apparently added as an afterthought:

(110) [The Pear Man] climbs up the ladder [1st], . . . uh⌐ that's leaning against a tree, (Speaker 11)

There remain five "uneventful" definite initial mentions like that in (109). Is there something in previous discourse that allows (or requires) these definite mentions? If so, does its absence automatically result in an indefinite mention? There are several candidates, exemplified in (109), that might trigger a frame which includes the ladder: the pear tree (*a tree*) or the Pear Man (*a farm worker*) among objects, and pear-picking (*picking the pears*) or going up or down the tree (*walks down the ladder*) among events. Only one of the definite initial mentions was preceded by mention of the pear tree, so this is apparently not a strong frame trigger. And although all the initial definites were preceded by a prior mention of the Pear Man, so were six of the seven indefinites. Mention of the Pear Man, apparently, does not necessarily cause speakers to activate a frame allowing *the ladder*. A better candidate is the verbal mention of pear-picking, which precedes (in a separate earlier clause) all of the definite initial mentions of the ladder, but only three of the seven indefinites. The frame analysis would suggest that once the speaker mentions pear-picking, a frame token is activated which includes a ladder. When the speaker first comes to speak about the ladder, he usually takes advantage of the hearer's awareness of the frame token and treats the ladder as already identifiable (and hence definite).

One might think that a stronger trigger of definiteness for the ladder is "going up or down (the ladder)," since all definite initial mentions are preceded by this, while only one indefinite initial mention is. But mentions of "going up or down" and mentions of the ladder always appear in the same clause (when both occur) and can hardly be considered independent. By the time a speaker says *he walks down... the ladder* [1st] (Speaker 6), he has already shifted to the narrative mode and is thus most likely to make a definite initial mention, rather than shift to the descriptive mode for a "proper" indefinite introduction. Use of the narrative mode is an important factor in this problem. Eight of the nine narrative mode initial mentions were definite, while all six of the descriptive mode mentions were indefinite. Thus the crucial choice of discourse mode is once again the "proximate cause" of initial definiteness. The ladder's membership in the pear-picking frame may, however, still be necessary for a speaker to feel justified in skipping the descriptive mode introduction.

Figure 3 compares the initial definiteness quotient for the ladder with that for the other "movable inanimate objects" for which no relevant frame was evoked. Most objects have a much lower incidence of initial definites, including some like the baskets (25 percent definite) for which the pear-picking frame may be relevant. The girl's bicycle, with an initial definiteness quotient of 0, does not seem to have benefited from the activation of any frame. The choice of indefinite mentions is not due to the descriptive mode (all mentions were in the narrative mode) but to the fact that the bicycle was in every case introduced on its first appearance in the film, during its critical introduction period (see next paragraph):

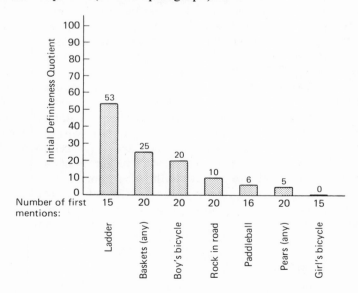

FIG. 3.   Initial Definiteness Quotients: Movable Inanimate Objects, Not Part of Something Else (objects receiving 10 or more mentions)

(111) and-- he looks at .. a girl, that was coming the other way, riding a bicycle [1st], (Speaker 3)

Thus the narrative mode may be used for a proper indefinite introduction, as long as the appropriate time has not passed.

Time is clearly a crucial factor. If a speaker mentions the ladder soon after it comes into view in the film, as in (108), she usually makes a descriptive mode introduction, which is indefinite. But if, as in (109), the speaker has let a lot of time go by without introducing the ladder, she usually uses a (definite) narrative mode initial mention. The mean number of words which elapsed between the beginning of the pear-picking scene and the first mention of the ladder was 27 for indefinites and 83 for definites. Thus, it appears that three main factors are involved in making a definite initial mention of the ladder: the prior occurrence of a frame trigger (or triggers); the choice of discourse mode; and the amount of time elapsed since the ladder first comes into view. The way these three factors bear on the problem is, I suggest, as follows. When a speaker focusses his attention on the pear-picking scene in order to tell what happens, he sees a variety of objects before him—the Pear Man, the tree, the pears, the ladder, and so on. During this period he directs his attention to "getting the scene across" to the hearer, taking care to introduce the salient objects in the descriptive mode. As long as the speaker is in this period—which we may label the *criticial introduction period*—he is well aware of what objects he has or has not introduced to his addressee. Then, having conveyed the salient elements of the scene, he shifts his attention to advancing the story line, for which he adopts the narrative mode. Once he is in the narrative mode, he usually fails to make indefinite introductions for objects whose critical introduction period has passed.

This failure may occur for several reasons. After leaving the critical introduction period he may not attempt to maintain a memory of which objects he has or has not introduced. He may simply assume that he has already taken care of introducing all the salient objects he will need to refer to, forgetting that a particular object has not actually received a proper introduction. In the narrative mode, the full resources of consciousness (Chafe, Chapter 1) would be deployed for the advancement of the story line. Alternatively, he may simply chose not to shift his attention back to the descriptive mode, or he may wish to keep up the momentum of a rapidly advancing story line. Of course, these possibilities are not mutually exclusive.

To this picture we must add a distinction between intrinsic salience and plot salience. The goat had great intrinsic salience, and was mentioned by 18 subjects even though it did not fit well into the plot of the movie. All but one speaker introduced it during its critical introduction period (all with indefinite mentions).[23] On the other hand, the Bike Boy's hat apparently had low intrinsic salience. During its critical introduction period, when the Bike Boy first appeared, only one of the speakers (Speaker 17) mentioned it (with an indefinite descriptive mode mention, as one would expect). Later in the plot, however, the hat began to figure prominently. It fell off his head during his fall and was found and returned by the Paddleball Boy, who received some pears in exchange. All 20 speakers mentioned the hat at some point during this sequence. Of the 19 who had not mentioned it before, 89 percent made a definite initial mention in the narrative mode. The significance of the two types of salience for definiteness should be clear. If an object has high intrinsic salience, it is likely to be mentioned when it first appears, during its critical introduction period. If it has high plot salience but low intrinsic salience it is likely to be first mentioned wherever it fits into the plot. If this happens to come early, during its critical introduction period, it will be indefinite; if not, it will usually be definite.

The importance of the critical introduction period in influencing the use of the discourse modes can be clearly seen in initial mentions of body parts and clothes. Figure 4 tabulates the points at which narrative mode mentions of body parts occur, and contrasts these with when descriptive mode mentions occur. As a measure of "when" a mention of a body part occurred, it was decided to count how many times its owner had been mentioned in prior discourse.[24] For example, Speaker 10 mentioned the Bike Boy's leg only after he had fallen from his bicycle:

(112) and he...checks his leg [1st] to make sure...to see if he's got any...bruises or anything. (Speaker 10)

This is after she had been speaking about the Bike Boy for some time, having mentioned him 16 times previously. This mention of the leg, being in the narrative mode, is tabulated in Figure 4(a); descriptive mode mentions are tabulated in Figure 4(b). The difference in distribution is apparent at a glance. Narrative mode mentions of body parts may occur at any point in the narrative after their owner is mentioned. But descriptive mode mentions are limited to the period shortly following the owner's introduction. The same

---

[23]The one speaker (Speaker 14) may not be a genuine exception, perhaps having misremembered the actual moment of the goat's appearance.

[24]The decision to use the number of previous mentions of the frame trigger as a measure for calibrating the critical introduction period is somewhat arbitrary. Alternatively one might investigate words (as in the earlier discussion of *the ladder*), seconds in real time, idea units (Chafe, Chapter 1), or clauses elapsed. Probably more sophisticated issues are also involved, such as crossing the boundary from descriptive mode to narrative mode.

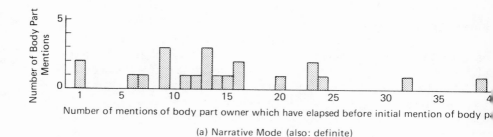

(a) Narrative Mode (also: definite)

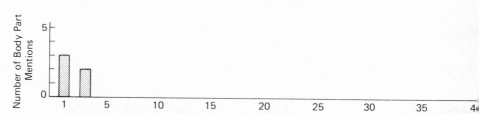

(b) Descriptive Mode (also: indefinite)

FIG. 4. Comparison of When Narrative and Descriptive Mode Initial
Mentions Occur: Body Parts

pattern holds for clothes, though it is less extreme (Figure 5). Here too,
narrative mode mentions are more or less evenly distributed through the
narrative, while descriptive mode mentions tend to occur soon after the
introduction of the clothing item's owner.

If we look at the effect on definiteness of the critical introduction period,
instead of the discourse modes, the picture, as we would expect, is virtually
the same. Figure 6 contrasts definites with indefinites for initial mentions of
clothes. Definite mentions are distributed throughout the narrative;
indefinite mentions tend to occur shortly after mention of their owner. The
similarity to Figure 5 is of course due to the high correlation between
discourse mode and definiteness. For body parts, a chart contrasting definite
with indefinite would look exactly like Figure 4, since there is a perfect
correlation (for this small corpus) between definiteness and discourse mode.

As noted earlier, adjectives tend to occur in the descriptive mode but not
the narrative mode. Figure 7 illustrates the effect of this: adjectives applied to
clothing are usually used shortly after the owner of the clothing item has been
introduced. The picture for body parts seems the same—the three preposed
adjectives all occur within the first three mentions of their owner.

It is interesting to speculate whether any link could be established between
the two stages of eye movements discussed by Chafe (p. 15) and the two
stages I have been discussing (the critical introduction period and the

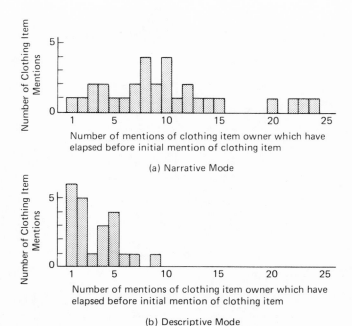

(a) Narrative Mode

(b) Descriptive Mode

FIG. 5. Comparison of When Narrative and Descriptive Mode Initial Mentions Occur: Clothes

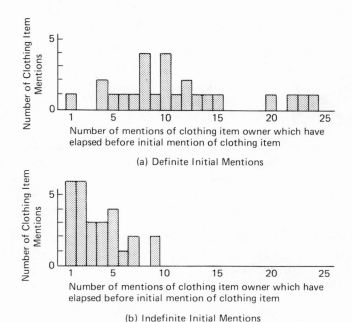

(a) Definite Initial Mentions

(b) Indefinite Initial Mentions

FIG. 6. Comparison of When Definite and Indefinite Initial Mentions Occur: Clothes

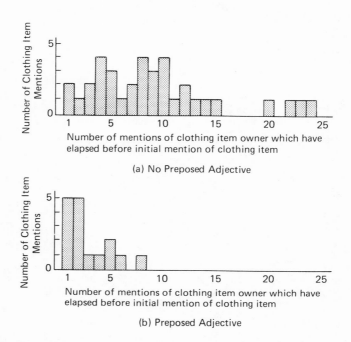

(a) No Preposed Adjective

(b) Preposed Adjective

FIG. 7. Comparison of When Adjective-Modified and Non-Adjective-Modified Initial Mentions Occur: Clothes

narrative mode period following it). In the verbalization Chafe cites in his example (4), idea units corresponding to the first period of eye fixations (a–e) are primarily in the descriptive mode; those corresponding to the second period (f–i) are largely (but not entirely) in the narrative mode. Further investigation would, of course, be required in order to establish whether a connection exists.

I have spoken only about the effects of the critical introduction period on elements in frames—the ladder in the pear-picking frame, body parts and clothes in the human frame. Things which are not part of a frame may not be so often affected by the "accidental" passing of the critical introduction period. Since they are independent of other objects, they are likely to be mentioned on first appearance in consciousness or, if nonsalient, not at all. Frames, though they structure the world and allow the speaker to convey information economically, may make it harder to keep track of what one has overtly introduced. In addition, of course, they make it less important to keep track, since the hearer is aided in making an identification by his knowledge of frames.

The percentage of definite initial mentions of persons which was cited in Figure 1 is 12 percent, but this rather mechanically includes initial mentions of, for example, the Bike Boy and Girl as *they*. Excluding such group mentions, identifiable on the basis of earlier individual mentions, we find that of the 139 remaining initial mentions, 8 (or 5.8 percent) are definite. That even these few definite initial mentions are problematic for speakers is shown by the fact that all but one (88 percent) triggered a subsequent indefinite mention.[25] This contrasts sharply with the recovery-triggering figures of 12 percent for clothes and 0 percent for body parts and for the ladder, and shows that when a human is introduced with a definite mention, a patch-up strategy of some sort will almost always be implemented. There are two questions to be answered: Why do the definite initial mentions occur, and what do speakers do about them?

Theoretical discussions of frames so frequently feature examples like *the buyer* as a definite initial mention (made possible by a previous mention of, e.g., *sell*) that one might expect that some of the definite mentions of humans would be of this type. But in the standard example, *the buyer* does not trigger a subsequent indefinite, unlike most of the mentions being discussed. As it turns out there are no examples of the *buyer* type in the pear film narratives (although a similar type does occur and will be discussed).

Some of the definite character mentions were cases where characters were apparently verbalized before their time had come. In the following example, the speaker is trying to remember more about the Goat Man. While concentrating on her recollection of the Goat Man, she inadvertently (it seems) mentions the Bike Boy and his bicycle:

(113) Someone [Goat Man] came along before the kid on the bicycle [1st] but I don't remember who it was. ... Then a kid [2nd] came along on a bicycle [2nd], (Speaker 16)

This is an example of what I characterize as *premature introduction*. The plot line supplies a natural place for the Bike Boy to be introduced—the critical introduction period. If the speaker reaches this natural place for introduction, and does not let is pass by, the initial mention will be carried out normally, with an indefinite noun phrase. But if the speaker happens to utter a mention of the Bike Boy before reaching this point, while she still has her attention directed to expressing other matters, she may fail to mark the noun phrase as nonidentifiable. On doing so she ordinarily becomes aware of her mistake, which she then rectifies.

Two other instances of premature introduction are found in the narratives, both in initial mentions of the Pear Man. In the first case the speaker seems to be focusing on the film sounds, in the second, on the setting:

---

[25] I have no explanation for the single exception. Perhaps it was simply an unnoticed mistake.

(114) And--... the first... thing I noticed.. was.. the sound of the man [1st] picking... pears. ... And of course there was a... a man [2nd] there standing on a ladder in a pear tree, (Speaker 4)

(115) the setting looks like it's a place... maybe--... in California, the Santa Barbara area,... or something like that. ... uh-- there was ... this orchard's around him [1st]. ... I guess what he's [2nd] picking is pears. ... There's a.. uh... farm laborer, [3rd] a Mexican farm laborer [4th] picking pears (Speaker 5)

In both cases the speakers were apparently directing their attention to other matters; but after the definite initial mention they became aware that a proper introduction was called for, which was then supplied via *there is*. We saw earlier that an object may be mentioned after its critical introduction period has passed. It is remarkable that it is also possible to mention an object before its own critical introduction period has begun.

In either such case (premature introduction or late introduction), the initial mention receives the definite article instead of the expected indefinite article. This suggests that the definite article is the unmarked member of the pair. When consciousness is not focussed on the task of introducing characters, it is the unmarked *the* which is uttered, whether or not the initial mention is in fact identifiable. There are other reasons to consider *the* unmarked, among them sheer frequency. In a corpus of one million words of written English, the definite article was by far the most common word, with 69,971 occurrences; whereas the indefinite article (*a* ~ *an*) had only 26,984 occurrences (Kučera and Francis, 1967:5).

It is noteworthy that in all three cases of premature introduction, the character is first mentioned in a prepositional phrase (as the object of *before, of, around*), rather than in the far more common subject slot. Of 139 initial mentions of characters, 57 percent are introduced as subjects, 18 percent as *there*-introductions (*there's a--.. man... picking pears* Speaker 8), 16 percent as objects, 6 percent as *obliques* (here defined negatively—neither subject, object, *there*-introduction, nor the others), 2 percent as predicate nominals, and 1 percent (one instance) as a topic. As long as a speaker uses one of the three most common introductory syntactic slots (subject, object, or *there*-introduction) for his initial mention, she is likely to make an uneventful indefinite introduction. This can be seen in Figure 8, where these three syntactic slots have low initial definiteness quotients.[26] But if her first mention of a character occurs in an oblique noun phrase, the likelihood that she will fail to use an indefinite is considerably higher. Perhaps the peripheral

---

[26]Predicate nominals (three, all indefinite) and the topic (one, definite) were excluded from Figure 8 as having too few mentions.

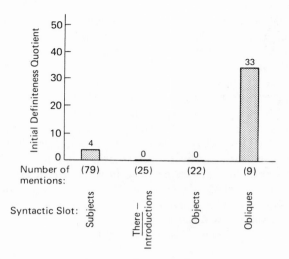

FIG. 8. Initial Definiteness Quotient by Syntactic Slot: Characters

syntactic (and semantic) status of the noun phrase is accompanied by a peripheral degree of attention.

When subjects corrected their faulty introduction of a character with a subsequent indefinite, they usually chose a *there*-introduction, as in (114) above (four of seven cases).

It is worth pointing out that when speakers introduce a character in the object slot, the verb is usually (68 percent of 11) a "verb of perception or cognition"—*see* (13), *look at* (1), *associate* (1). A typical example is the following introduction of the Goat Man as the object of *you see:*

(116) and .. you see a guy [1st] leading a goat .. past the tree where he's picking the pears. (Speaker 6)

Characters may, however, be introduced as objects of other verbs as well, as with the Girl in the following example:

(117) and he passes a girl on a bicycle [1st], (Speaker 19)

Before looking at the second major type of definite character introduction it will be useful to recall an apparent failure of frames to allow definite mentions, in the earlier discussion of *the ladder.* How is it that prior mention of the Pear Man does not trigger the pear-picking frame in the way that mention of the pear-picking action itself does? Although the pear-picker seems as much a part of such a frame (if one exists) as pear-picking is, we find that in the pear film narratives he is almost always introduced in ways that do not convey his role in this frame. The most common initial mention is simply *a man* (nine speakers), which does not indicate a role in any particular event-based frame. In the one case where the initial mention did specify his role in the pear-picking via a relative clause (*a guy who's picking pears* Speaker 3) the subsequent initial mention of the ladder was indeed definite. But ordinarily speakers do not express a character's frame role through noun phrases, they express it through verb phrases (*he picks the pears*). Thus the examples which constantly turn up in discussions of frames—*the buyer,* and so on—are rather rare and special cases. It is no accident that the nouns are so often derived from verbs. It should be clear by now that mention of a human member of a frame in no way activates that frame—except when the speaker specifies his frame role in the course of mentioning him. This leads to the matter of *dummy identification*—identifying a functional slot in a frame rather than an actual person—which I shall now discuss.

In premature introductions the speaker does not deliberately use a definite initial mention, he falls into it. But there is a type of definite initial mention in the pear film narratives which is deliberate. This type is based on the availability of an appropriate frame, but unlike the *buyer* case just described, it does not usually allow one to go on with subsequent definite mentions. Rather, a pattern of definite initial mention followed by indefinite second mention arises. This is due to the speaker's use of what may be called the *slot-and-fill* strategy. First a "dummy" definite is given which sets the stage for the upcoming indefinite mention. Often this dummy serves only to define as the topic a particular slot in an available (activated) frame token. The frame slot is then filled with contentful material in an indefinite second mention. In the following example, *the landscape* is used in this way:

> (118) Well, first thing you see, is--..uh--..the landscape [1st] is--..
> u--m...?..sort of an agricultural..area [2nd], (Speaker 17)

The definite phrase *the landscape* serves to pinpoint a particular portion of the available "outdoor event" frame, and the particular quality to be attributed to this frame element is then specified by the indefinite predicate nominal *sort of an agricultural area.*

This raises the issue of what varieties of identification may be distinguished. Christophersen has observed that

> Talking of a certain book, it is perfectly correct to say "The author is unknown"; this is not a contradiction in terms. ... As it is a common experience that every book has one (and usually only one) author, the knowledge of the book automatically entails the knowledge that there is an author. (1939:73)

What has been identified is a slot in the "book" frame, rather than an actual individual; but this is sufficient to justify use of the definite article. In the following example, a definite *the winner* is allowed on the basis of prior activation of a "raffle" frame token:

> (119)   the caul was put up in a raffle to fifty members at half-a-crown a head, the winner to spend five shillings (Dickens, quoted in Jespersen 1924:120)

Since no actual person has yet been chosen winner, it is clear that *the winner* identifies only a role in a frame and not an individual. Similarly, activation of the "commercial act" frame may allow a definite mention of *the buyer* based on identification of the slot rather than of an actual individual:

> (120)   If the buyer wants to know the condition of the property, he has to have another survey carried out on his own behalf (*The Legal Side of Buying a House,* Consumer's Association, quoted in Halliday and Hasan, 1976:47)

This use of *the buyer* is quite different from the often cited example where mention of *the buyer* follows a mention of an actual sale as in *I just sold my house.* Bertrand Russell's discussion of descriptions illustrates the difference between the two varieties of identification:

> It is possible to have much knowledge concerning a term described, *i.e.* to know many propositions concerning "the so-and-so," without actually knowing what the so-and-so is, *i.e.* without knowing any proposition of the form "x is the so-and-so," where "*x*" is a name. In a detective story propositions about "the man who did the deed" are accumulated, in the hope that ultimately they will suffice to demonstrate that it was A who did the deed (Russell, 1971:174)

Once again, the distinction that must be made in discourse analysis is between identification of a slot in a frame and identification of an individual. These identifications may behave the same in their use of the definite article, but they differ in how they are employed in discourse.

Returning to mentions of characters in the pear film narratives, we find further examples of the slot-and-fill strategy in which a definite initial mention identifies a slot, but then triggers a subsequent indefinite which fills the slot with contentful material. This strategy is not always limited to well-defined frame slots. One speaker introduced the Bike Boy into her narrative according to his order of appearance in the plot:

> (121)   Then the third person that comes in the scene [1st] is a little boy about ... ten years old [2nd]. (Speaker 17)

The reference to *the third person that comes in the scene* is definite simply because it specifies a unique slot, whose referent is identifiable only in the limited sense that one knows there is some person (the "dummy") that came into the scene. The quality of this dummy must be specified in an immediately following mention, often a predicate nominal (which is formally indefinite). This use of a definite dummy is quite distinct from the other, *ladder* type of frame-dependent definites. The *ladder* types, which are "substantive" identifications, are usually followed by definite mentions; the dummy type are often (sometimes obligatorily) followed by explanatory indefinite mentions.

Having discussed the various reasons why speakers sometimes make their first mention of an object definite, the issue arises of why they sometimes make later mentions indefinite. A suggestion of one answer has already appeared in the discussion about various types of initial definites which trigger subsequent indefinites. Further sources of noninitial indefinites will now be discussed.

REASONS FOR LATE INDEFINITES

Though definite initial mentions have occasioned a great deal of discussion in the literature, almost no attention has been directed to the other side of the coin—indefinites which occur after the first mention. This situation has apparently arisen because past investigators have thought of the definite article as the one which required explanation (since the task was, after all, to explain "definiteness"), with the indefinite article often being treated as though it were unmarked. Also, past investigators have not examined texts as wholes but have considered only the phenomena, admittedly more striking, which occur when an object is first introduced into discourse. As a result they missed a great deal.

The one issue that has been raised with regard to noninitial indefinites is how long definiteness can last—whether through the simple passing of time a referent may lose its definite status and become once again indefinite. Chafe pointed out that in an Arthur Koestler novel definiteness was preserved over 105 pages (1976:40). He concludes that

> ...it would appear... that definiteness can be preserved indefinitely if the eventual context in which the referent is reintroduced is narrow enough to make the referent identifiable. (1976:41)

Indeed, it seems that the simple passing of time is very unlikely to cause a referent to return to indefinite status (see p. 266). But Chafe raises an apparent exception:

> Nevertheless, there are also cases where something established earlier as definite is later reintroduced in an indefinite way: *I bought a car yesterday. It's the one I*

told you about. Presumably the car was treated as definite during my earlier conversation with you, but in this later reference its reintroduction was again treated as indefinite. (1976:41)

But this usage is readily understood in the light of the analysis of example (13):

(13') I have a Mercedes—three of them in fact.

As with "having a Mercedes," a speaker may treat "buying a car" as a unitary predicate concept—an object conflation. Thus the indefinite article in the *I bought a car* example is not being used to mark nonidentifiability, but nonreferentiality. Object conflation is one of the main sources of indefinite noninitial mentions for objects, as discussed for example (27), but humans are not often made part of object conflations. They are, however, subject to a variety of other influences, which results in a small but significant portion of indefinite noninitial mentions. Of the 1229 noninitial mentions of characters, 53, or 4.1 percent, are indefinite. The different types are listed in Table 2, with the number of occurrences of each. Although it would be of considerable interest to compare the figures for characters with those for objects, a full tabulation for objects is not yet available. In the following pages I try to show how each type influences definiteness.

Often an indefinite will occur on second mention because of recovery from some sort of false start, as when a speaker breaks off and then simply starts over:

TABLE 2.
Types of Indefinite Noninitial Mentions: Characters

		Number of Occurrences
Repetitions and mistakes		13
Correction	5	
Semi-correction	3	
Digression and repeat	2	
Premature introduction	3	
Nonreferential		15
Predicate nominal	9	
Comparative	4	
Appositive	2	
Other		25
Miscellaneous	3	
Unexplained	2	
Point of view	3	
Member-of-crowd phenomenon	17	

(122) and--.. someone [1st] ... let's see ... someone [2nd] came by on a
bicycle. (Speaker 4)

In such cases it is usually easy for the hearer to recognize that the second
indefinite is a replacement for the first. In other cases, to which I have given
the somewhat loose label *semicorrection,* the speaker does not simply
correct or repeat, but makes a slight amplification in meaning:

(123) there's some kids [1st], there are three other boys [2nd], .. who are
there. (Speaker 3)

In other cases, the speaker may make a proper introduction, but then go off
on a digression of some length before returning to make the introduction over
again. A *digression-and-repeat,* as I have labeled this phenomenon,
ordinarily involves "postponement of the expression of a center of interest"
(Chafe, Chapter 1). In the following example, the Bike Boy and his bicycle are
introduced uneventfully with indefinite mentions (*a kid, a bicycle*) which are
even followed by definite mentions as expected. But then the speaker goes off
on a long digression, and when she comes back to the story line she takes up
where she left off—she repeats her introductory clause exactly, down to the
indefinite articles:

(124) ... a kid [1st] comes by on a bicycle [1st]. ... from the direction
where the goat man left, okay? ... And--... uh--... the bicycle's
[2nd] way too big for the kid [2nd]. ... I'm giving you all these
details. I don't know if you want them. ... um--... the .. the
reason I'm giving you the details is cause I don't know what the
point of the movie was. ... Okay? So maybe you can see
something that I didn't. ... Okay? um--... g-a kid [3rd] comes by
on a bicycle [3rd], ... he [4th] stops, (Speaker 1)

From this example it might seem that the speaker retains an exact memory of
her words which she later repeats. The indefinite article would then simply be
due to a verbatim repetition of a linguistic memory. But this does not always
hold true. In another case, the sentence

(125) ... A man with a goat [1st] ... was in the distance and walked by.
(Speaker 12)

was followed, after definite mentions of the Goat Man and the goat, by a
digression about how the characters looked. The return to the story line was
marked by a slightly different verbalization:

(126) ... so a man with a goat [3rd] ... went by,

Apparently a new verbalization (including a new character introduction) is involved rather than a mere repetition of words.

The next unintentional source of noninitial indefinites is one already examined from the point of view of initial definiteness: premature introductions. As in example (113), the inadvertent utterance of a definite mention prompts a belated indefinite introduction.

All these indefinites due to correction and repetition occur during the first few mentions of the character—never after he has already been talked about for a long time. Figure 9 shows the effect of time on the various types of indefinite noninitial mentions. Each indefinite mention of a character which occurs later than the first mention is tabulated according to whether it occurs on the second mention, third mention, or whatever. All "repetition and mistake" indefinites fall within three mentions after the first. Apparently the pressure to rectify an error is immediate.

A look at the rest of Figure 9 shows that other types also show a tendency to occur within a few mentions of the first—though most other types may occasionally occur later as well. This is made clearer in Figure 10, which shows the total number of indefinites at each mention after the first. On second mentions alone, speakers made 27 indefinite mentions, but by the time they reached the fifth and later mentions they rarely made indefinite mentions. Actually, this may be in part due to not reaching the fifth mention at all, since characters are often mentioned only two or three times. To offset this, Figure 11 tabulates noninitial indefinites for only those characters which speakers mentioned many times.[27] Though less extreme, the tendency for noninitial indefinites to occur soon after the first mention is still clear. The time for indefiniteness is when the character first appears upon the scene—on the first mention or soon after. Thus indefiniteness, rather than being limited to a single precise point, spills over a little into later mentions.

Returning to Figure 9, several types of initial mentions use formal indefiniteness to mark not nonidentifiability—they do not direct the hearer to establish a new file—but nonreferentiality. Predicate nominals often occur shortly after the first initial mention, as with *a young woman* in (20):

(20) he comes across another ... bicyclist ... bicyclist [1st]; it's a young woman [2nd], (Speaker 5)

This occurs because the introduction of a new character has triggered the descriptive mode. Another source of predicate nominals on second mention is the slot-and-fill strategy seen in example (121). Although speakers ordinarily

---

[27]Tabulations are for the Bike Boy, Pear Man, and Threesome. The percentage of subjects who gave the character 10 or more mentions is: Bike Boy, 100 percent; Pear Man, 90 percent; Threesome, 75 percent. The mean mentions per subject for each character is: Bike Boy, 23.2; Pear man, 19.2; Threesome, 14.1.

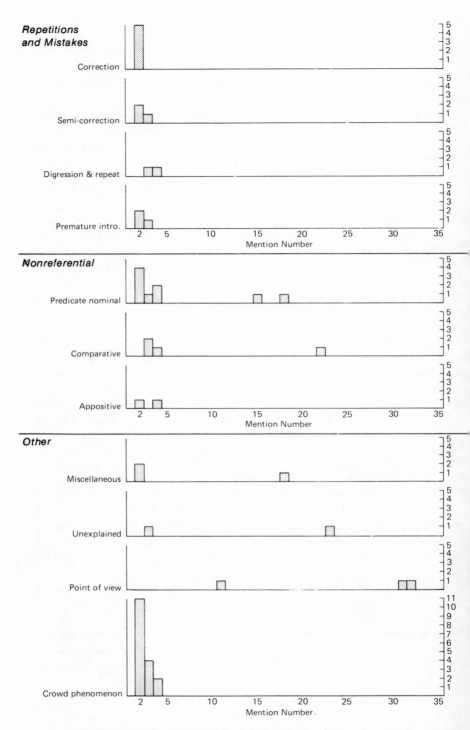

FIG. 9. When Do Indefinite Noninitial Mentions of Characters Occur? Distribution of Sub-Types by Mention Number

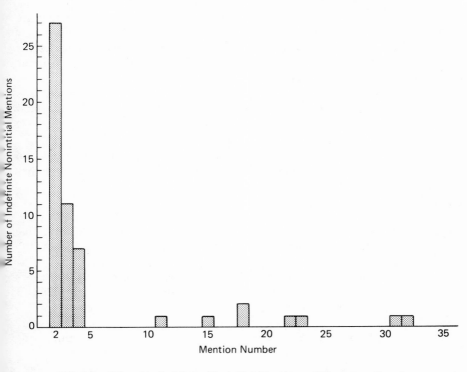

FIG. 10. When Do Indefinite Noninitial Mentions of Characters Occur?
Overall Frequency by Mention Number

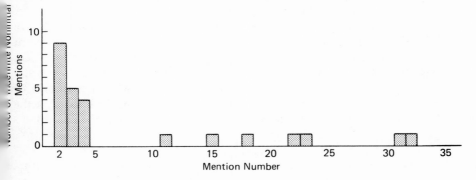

FIG. 11. When Do Indefinite Noninitial Mentions of Characters Occur?
Frequently Mentioned Characters Only

use predicate nominals shortly after a character has been introduced, they are free to do so later, especially if new plot conditions raise the need for a new predication. In the following example, the Threesome have long since left the descriptive mode when the Pear Man's suspicion occasions their return, in the indefinite predicate nominal *like.. Good Samaritans:*

(127) and I thought [...] he's going to accuse the little boys [13th] who'd [14th] actually been like.. Good Samaritans [15th], (Speaker 17)

Comparatives (e.g., *look like*) are essentially like predicate nominals and tend to occur when a character's appearance is still recent (4 and 128), though they may occur later (129):

(128) there's a--.. man [1st] ... picking pears, in a pear tree, out.. somewhere in the country, ... uh--he [2nd] looks ... like your uh.. typical.. farmer or ... whatever [3rd], (Speaker 8)

(129) Then they walk by--... the man who was picking the pears [20th]. ... who [21st] looks like a Mexican-American [22nd] if that's important? (Speaker 1)

Example (130) shows an appositive, which in this case has an amplifying function similar to that of example (123):

(130) There's a.. uh ... farm laborer [3rd], a Mexican farm laborer [4th] picking pears (Speaker 5)

It is somewhat arbitrary to consider this as two mentions rather than one, but the choice does not greatly affect the overall picture.

Besides some miscellaneous and unexplained occurrences of late indefinites, there remain two types of some interest. In the first type the point of view is shifted from the speaker to one of the characters in the story. Then, this character's knowledge rather than that of the speaker becomes what determines whether the other characters are identifiable or not, specific or not. In the following example, the speaker knows that the Bike Boy stole the Pear Man's pears, but the noun phrase *somebody* expresses the Pear Man's knowledge rather than her own:

(131) Anyway, ... then finally he [Pear Man] figured out.. something ... you know somebody's [Bike Boy—21st] stolen the pears. (Speaker 2)

The verb of cognition (*figure out*) is, of course, what marks the shift in point of view. Point-of-view indefinites, unlike all other noninitial indefinites, show no tendency to occur soon after the introduction of a character.

The final type of noninitial indefinite which is attested for characters is the most common, with 17 occurrences. Of these, 14 apply to a single character, the Paddleball Boy—who by himself accounts for 28 percent of all noninitial indefinites. This is due to his particular position in the plot, as one member of the Threesome. It was pointed out earlier (p. 235) that persons, unlike walls, river banks, and so on, are too individually salient to become definite on first mention through application of the curiosity principle. But it is possible for a lack of salient distinctions within a group of humans to cause a partial identification—which is marked as such—even though a full identification would be possible. One speaker began with an unremarkable indefinite introduction of the Paddleball Boy (*one*):

(132) one thing that struck me about the--.. three little boys that were there is that one [1st] had a uh ... I don't know what you call them, but it's a paddle, (Speaker 9)

But the second mention, which should ordinarily be definite, is not. After several intervening events in which the Paddleball Boy is not mentioned (the Threesome pick up the pears; then they and the Bike Boy depart), he is again referred to—with another indefinite noun phrase:

(133) ... one of them [Paddleball Boy—2nd] ... whistles back to the guy on the bicycle, "Here's your hat."

Speaker 9 could have made the reference to the Paddleball Boy fully definite by referring to his paddleball, as Speaker 12 did:

(134) ... The o--ne boy with a ping-pong paddle [3rd], notices .. a hat,

But Speaker 9, like most speakers, apparently thought it was not relevant that "the boy who returned the hat" and "the boy with the paddleball" were the same. What was relevant was that the Paddleball Boy was a member of a salient group, the Threesome. All noninitial indefinite mentions of the Paddleball Boy (and all but two of the initial indefinite mentions, for that matter) specify his membership in the Threesome, using the indefinite replacive *one: one, one of the boys, one of them*, and so on. No speaker used an *a*-form noun phrase (*a boy*), which would have indicated he was not identifiable at all. His status as a member of the Threesome was considered salient, but his precise identity within it was not. This may be termed the *member-of-the-crowd* phenomenon.

It might be thought that "evaporation" of definiteness through the passing of time (p. 258) is responsible for the Paddleball Boy's indefiniteness, rather than the member-of-the-crowd phenomenon. But a comparison with mentions of the Pear Man shows this is not so. As one example, Speaker 1 made 66 references to 6 different characters between the time of her last mention of the Pear Man in the opening scenes of the film and her first mention of him on his reappearance in the closing scenes. Despite the long lapse, the mention was definite:

> (135) Then they walk by--... the man who was picking the pears.

The same pattern of a long lapse followed by a definite mention holds for all 20 speakers: a mean of 39.2 mentions of the various other characters were made between the two Pear Man mentions, but in every case the latter mention was definite. If the passing of time or the distraction of other events was never responsible for an indefinite mention of the Pear Man, it can hardly be the cause of the indefinite Paddleball Boy mentions. There were a mean of only 7.2 mentions of other characters between each such mention and the preceding Paddleball Boy mention.

On the other hand, it might still appear that this phenomenon is due to overloaded memory or perception rather than lack of salience—that the difficulty in keeping track of the actions of three characters at the same time has caused speakers to resort to partial identification. True, some speakers may have been unsure of their memory (*I think it was...*):

> (136) And the one kid, I think it was the kid who was playing with the uh...with..the whatever it was,...stops and picks it up and whistles. (Speaker 10)

Although memory may to some extent be involved in the member-of-the-crowd phenomenon, evidence from a related phenomenon suggests that speakers often know more than they bother to say. In the relevant cases from the pear film narratives, actions that were in reality performed by one group member (the Paddleball Boy) were attributed to the group as a whole (the Threesome). In the actual film it is the Paddleball Boy alone who picks up the Bike Boy's hat, whistles to him, then brings him the hat, receiving pears in exchange. Of the 20 speakers who mentioned the return of the Bike Boy's hat, 17 correctly attributed this action to a single individual (136 and 137).

> (137) So one of the boys whistles to him, and ... stops him, and ... gives him his hat back. (Speaker 3)

But 3 speakers attributed the action to the group of which the Paddleball Boy is a member:

(138) and they [Threesome] gave him his hat, (Speaker 14)

It might be thought that Speaker 14, due to faulty perception or faulty memory, actually believes this. But in another case it becomes clear, thanks to evidence from a partial repetition, that the speaker is willing to attribute the hat return to the Threesome even though she knows it was the Paddleball Boy:

(139) The three boys find the hat down the road, ... and he [Paddleball Boy] gives him [Bike Boy] the hat, ... and .. th- .. they whistle for /him/. There's no dialogue in the whole movie. ... They whistle for him. ... And he comes back. .. And he /w-/ ... and he stops. .. And the guys walk up and give him the hat. (Speaker 15)

At first the speaker attributes the hat return to the Paddleball boy (*he gives him the hat*). After the digression on the lack of dialogue in the movie, she redescribes the same event, this time attributing the return to the Threesome (*the guys walk up and give him the hat*). The speaker apparently chooses to do this because she views the Paddleball Boy's actions as representative of the Threesome as a whole. The difference between an action performed by the Paddleball Boy and one performed by the Threesome is not very salient. This may be expressed as the *principle of group attribution:*

(140) If the actions of a character are seen as representative tokens of the actions of a group to which the character belongs, speakers may attribute his individual actions to the group.

This tendency seems especially strong where the speaker has built up a "topic-chain" of several references to group actions. In the following case, the speaker related a whole series of actions performed by the Threesome (which indeed were performed by the group): walking by the Pear Man, ignoring him, eating their pears. But the final action in the series, playing with the paddleball, is attributable to the group only by virtue of the "poetic license" provided by the group attribution principle:

(141) and I thought maybe that [...] he's going to accuse the little boys who'd actually been like .. Good Samaritans, of stealing his pears. ... But he just sort of watches them, .. as they walk by and they don't pay any attention to them ... to him, he's .. they're just

eating their pears, and .. you know playing with their ... paddle
and everything. ... And that's how it ends. (Speaker 17)

The speaker has built up a long chain of clauses referring to group actions.
Rather than break out of it at the very end of her narrative, she simply
continues the chain one link further—expressing as a group action the
playing, which in any case seems characteristic of the group. She knows that
only one person and not the whole group is playing the paddleball, as can be
seen from her having earlier taken care to state that there was one player:

> (142) ... One boy [Paddleball Boy—1st] .. is .. um ... hitting one of
> those bounce-back things, [...] He's playing with that. (Speaker
> 17)

In addition, even though she later attributes the playing action to the three
boys, she leaves the paddleball singular (*they're ... playing with
their ... paddle and everything*).

The tendency to make a series of attributions internally consistent is
apparently general. Table 3 shows how a chain of three linked actions
performed by the Paddleball Boy was expressed by speakers. As noted earlier,
the Paddleball Boy whistles, returns the hat, and receives pears in exchange.

TABLE 3.
Consistency of Attribution of Paddleball Boy's Actions

Subject No.	Paddleball Boy whistles	Paddleball Boy returns hat	Paddleball Boy is given pears
1	1	1	3 → 1
2	—	3	3
3	1	1	1
4	1	1	1
5	—	1	1
6	1	1	1
7	1	1	1
8	—	1	1
9	1	1	1
10	1	1	1
11	3 → 1	1	1
12	1	1	1
13	1	1	1
14	3	3	1 → 3
15	3	1 → 3	3
16	—	1	3
17	1	1	1
18	—	1	3
19	—	1	1
20	3	1	1

A "1" in the table indicates that the action was attributed to one individual; a "3" indicates that the action was attributed to the group of three boys. An arrow indicates a change in attribution; for example, "3→1" indicates that the speaker first attributed the action to the group but then switched the attribution to one individual. It can be seen that most speakers are consistent with themselves, and self-corrections are in the direction of greater consistency, not less. It is perhaps not surprising that Speaker 1 changed a group attribution to an individual attribution, since this is what appeared in the film. More noteworthy, Speaker 15 changed an individual attribution to a group attribution (139)—apparently for the sake of making the series of attributions consistent, whether or not this corresponded to actual events.

In the light of attribution of individual actions to a group, it is easy to see how the member-of-the-crowd phenomenon arises. Although it is salient that a certain action is representative of a group, the precise identity of the individual is often not salient. It is not important to establish the continuity of identity of the group member who returned the hat with the group member who was playing with the paddleball—*one of the boys* is sufficient.

The nonsalience of identity continuity may result in partial (but referential) identification of a human, but it often results in a nonreferential mention of an object. Predicate conflations (which are indefinite and nonreferential) do not establish continuity of identity. We may use the term *prop* to refer to an object whose continuity of identity is ignored, as opposed to a *participant*—a human, animal, or object whose continuity of identity is salient enough to be maintained.[28] An object may be treated now as a prop and now as a participant, depending on whether attention is being focused on it at the moment. In the following example both the Bike Boy and his bicycle are introduced with indefinite mentions, but in the next sentence only the Bike Boy becomes definite (*he*):

(143) ...a boy probably about...I don't know,..eight or nine [1st]...comes up on a bicycle [1st]. ... He's [2nd] going by on a bicycle [2nd] on this dirt road, (Speaker 10)

The bicycle, which has none of the properties of animacy, agency, or subjecthood which contribute to the Bike Boy's prominence, is conflated into a unitary concept of "going on a bicycle" in a nonreferential mention—see example (27).

Props are often found in phrases which modify participants. In such cases they are mentioned not for their intrinsic interest but for their contribution to identifying or characterizing a participant, usually a human. In the following

---

[28]The terms *prop* and *participant* have been used in a somewhat different sense by Grimes (1975:43).

example the speaker mentions both the Paddleball Boy and his paddleball with indefinite mentions:

> (144) and one has a ping-pong p- paddle. .. those bouncy ball things with a great big... [29] (Speaker 12)

But in the next mention the paddleball remains indefinite (*a ping-pong paddle*), while the Paddleball Boy becomes definite (*the one boy with a ping-pong paddle*):

> (145) ... The o--ne boy with a ping-pong paddle, notices .. a hat,

Probably the only reason the paddleball is mentioned here at all is because it serves as a useful prop with which to identify a participant. But its continuity of identity with the earlier mention is deemed nonsalient, so that the indefinite article (marking nonreferentiality, which entails nonphoricity) is used rather than the definite article.[30]

I have said that the positive function of an initial indefinite is to open a cognitive file for its referent (p.220). But if a speaker recognizes that a particular initial mention is only a prop, he may not bother to open a file for it as he would for a participant. If a writer suddenly treats such a file-less prop as a participant, a startling effect may be produced. In the following example, Lawrence Sterne, ever one to toy with his readers, has us blithely tossing away a whole string of props without bothering to keep track of them, since it seems so obvious that they have been dragged in by the heels only for their dazzle. We expect we shall never see them again, so why open a file?

> (146) "for what hindrance, hurt, or harm doth the laudable desire for knowledge bring to any man, if even from a sot, a pot, a fool, a stool, a winter mittain, a track for a pulley, the lid of a goldsmith's crucible, an oil bottle, an old slipper, or a cane chair?"—I am this moment sitting upon one (Sterne, 1960:161).

A speaker has some choice in whether he treats an object as a prop or a participant. When the pears that the Pear Man was picking were mentioned in a relative clause modifying the Pear Man, some speakers chose to make the pears definite (147); others, describing the same scene, made them indefinite (148):

---

[29]Here the speaker goes off on a digression about gestures in the film, and fails to return to her paddleball description.

[30]The mention of the Paddleball Boy in (144) is actually the second mention; its indefiniteness is due to the member-of-the-crowd phenomenon. This confirms that continuity of identity may be deemed salient at one time but not salient at another.

TABLE 4.
Object Conflation and Tense/Aspect: Noninitial
Mentions of Pears Occurring Within Mentions of Pear
Man

	Indefinite (pears)	Definite (the/his pears)
is ___-ing	4	—
was ___-ing	2	3
has been ___-ing	—	2

(147) So that eventually they would go pas--t the... the man,.. who's been picking... the pears, (Speaker 18)

(148) And on the way back they pass... the guy who's up in the tree,... collecting pears, (Speaker 11)

Of the 11 such noninitial mentions of pears occurring in relative clauses that modify the Pear Man, 5 are definite and 6 indefinite. It is noteworthy that there appears to be a connection between the choice of article and the choice of tense/aspect in the verb. Table 4 illustrates the correlation between definiteness and verb form for the pear mentions under discussion.[31] Whenever the perfect progressive is used, as in (147), the pear mention is definite (and referential). Whenever the present progressive is used, as in (148), the pear mention is indefinite (and nonreferential). When the past progressive is used, as in (149) and (150), either definite or indefinite may occur:

(149) Then they walk by--... the man who was picking the pears. (Speaker 1)

(150) They were walking back in the direction,... uh... toward the man... who was picking pears in the pear tree, (Speaker 16)

It seems that the present progressive is associated with conflated object mentions—which have often been mislabeled *generic* mentions—and that the verb-plus-object combination expresses a general concept of the activity rather than a concrete action. It may be that such a predicate phrase indexes

[31]The 11 noninitial mentions were distributed across 9 different speakers. There was one case, not included in Table 4, of a Pear-Man-modifying pear mention which was an initial mention. (Speaker 3)

neither a concrete time nor concrete objects. The perfect progressive phrase, on the other hand, indexes both a concrete time and concrete objects.

Although indefinite mentions are probably not caused by "evaporation" of definite status over a long span of time, they may arise for other reasons of cognitive and linguistic import, and within a comparatively brief time. In some cases formal indefiniteness is due to the speaker's reverbalization of an introduction (with or without a digression between the two verbalizations); in other cases it simply represents a nonreferential use, such as a predicate nominal. Such predicate nominals may be part of a deliberate slot-and-fill strategy, in which the speaker defines a frame slot using a definite "dummy" as an initial mention and then gives the dummy substance through a predication. Other intentional uses of indefinites occur when the speaker decides to project his verbalization from the point of view of someone other than himself, or when he decides that the continuity of an object's identity with earlier mentions is not salient. The reason for mentioning an object in spite of its intrinsic nonsalience may be that it serves as a prop in characterizing a full participant, or that it is needed in combination with a verb to fully express a particular activity. In either case it is the quality abstracted from the noun which is employed, without regard for the noun's capacity to refer back to an available, identified, individual.

SUMMARY

This chapter has attempted to go beyond a simple investigation of the English articles to consider how speakers introduce objects into a discourse, and how they trace them through the discourse. An analytical framework was first built up which reflects the fact that the articles are governed by other parameters beyond the primary one of identifiability. In particular, noun phrases frequently fail to receive definite marking, not because they do not refer to an identifiable object, but because they simply do not refer. Nonreferential mentions are frequently employed because the speaker decides that an object is not important in its own right, but serves only as a prop to specify an individual or subcategorize a general activity.

One conclusion that emerges clearly from this study is that a speaker's use of definiteness is not a merely automatic reaction to prior mention or to presence of a referent in the discourse situation. Speakers exert a considerable degree of control over their choice of alternatives. With the curiosity of the addressee in mind, the speaker makes judgments as to the salience of tracing an object's identity. He may decide that continuity of identification with an earlier mention is not salient, in which case one or another type of indefinite mention may be used—either a nonreferential mention as in object conflation or a partially identifiable mention as in the member-of-the-crowd phenomenon. Or he may decide to mark a first mention as identifiable even though in a strict sense it is not, if the referent is part of a small frame-defined set of objects between which distinctions are not salient.

The influence of frames on the way objects are introduced is of course considerable. Since parts are typically mentioned after wholes, objects like bicycle parts and body parts (and clothes as well) can be treated as identifiable on first mention—unless the mention is simply nonreferential, as if often true when the descriptive mode is employed. Possessive adjectives not only presuppose identifiabiity but contribute to identification, usually by indexing the frame with which a reference is to be associated. Because of their contribution to identification, both possessive adjectives and relative clauses may allow an object to be marked as identifiable on first mention. However, this is constrained by the conversational postulate which, for nonliterary English, limits the information presented in such presupposed formats to old information, or to new information which is not particularly noteworthy.

The distinct tasks of introducing an object into a discourse and tracing it through the discourse are performed separately, and there is an appropriate time for each task. When an important object first appears in the story line, the speaker often shifts into the descriptive mode to introduce it and provide background information, subsequently returning to advance the story line in the narrative mode. If this critical introduction period has elapsed—or if it has not yet begun—the speaker will usually fail to indicate that the referent is being newly introduced. This, plus evidence from the distribution of adjectives and of narrative or descriptive verbs, suggests that speakers direct their attention either to the task of introducing or to the task of advancing the story line, but not to both at once.

The overall intent has been to describe how a speaker uses his cognitive capacities in conjunction with a variety of available grammatical resources in order to fulfill the expressive need of conveying his thoughts to an addressee. The study may be viewed as a chapter in the ecology of grammar.

REFERENCES

Allan, K. Huntin', shootin,' 'n' fishin' and the overt plural morpheme: or the collectivising of hunted animals and other things. *Works in Progress 2: Department of English, Ahmadu Bello University, Zaria, Nigeria,* pp. 46–74, 1973.

Chafe, W. L. Discourse structure and human knowledge. In R. O. Freedle & J. B. Carrol(Eds.), *Language comprehension and the acquisition of knowledge.* New York: Halsted Press, 1972.

Chafe, W. L. Givenness, contrastiveness, definiteness, subjects, topics, and point of view. In C. Li & S. Thompson (Eds.), *Subject and topic,* New York: Academic Press, 1976.

Christophersen, P. The articles: a study of their theory and use in English. Copenhagen: Einar Munksgaard, 1939.

Drieman, G. H. J. Differences between written and spoken languages: an exploratory study. *Acta Psychologica,* 1962, *20,* 36–57, 78–100.

Fillmore, C. J. The need for a frame semantics within linguistics. *Statistical Methods in Linguistics* 1976, pp. 5–29.

Givón, T. Definiteness and referentiality. In H. Greenberg (Ed.), *Universals of human language.* (Vol. 4, *Syntax*).

Grimes, J. E. *The thread of discourse.* The Hague: Mouton, 1975.

Halliday, M. A. K., & Hasan, R. *Cohesion in English.* London: Longman, 1976.

Haviland, S. E., & Clark, H. H. What's new? Acquiring new information as a process in comprehension. *Journal of Verbal Learning and Behavior* 1974, *13*:512–521.

Hawkins, J. A. The pragmatics of definiteness, Parts I and II. *Linguistiche Berichte,* 1977, *47:* 1–27; *48:*1–27.

Hawkins, J. A. *Definiteness and indefiniteness: a study in reference and grammaticality prediction.* London: Croom Helm, 1978.

Hewson, J. 1972. Article and noun in English. *Janua Linguarum, series practica,* 104. The Hague: Mouton, 1972.

Jespersen, O. *The philosophy of grammar.* New York: W. W. Norton and Company, 1965. (Originally published, 1924.)

Jespersen, O. *Essentials of English grammar.* University, Alabama: University of Alabama Press, 1964. (Originally published, 1933.)

Karttunen, L. What makes noun phrases definite? *Report* p-3871, The Rand Corporation. Santa Monica, 1968.

Krámský, J. The article and the concept of definiteness in language. *Janua Linguarum, series minor,* no. 125. The Hague: Mouton, 1972.

Kučera, H., & Francis, W. N. *Computational analysis of present-day American English.* Providence, R.I.: Brown University Press, 1967.

Kuno, S. Some properties of nonreferential noun phrases. In R. Jakobson & S. Kawamoto (Eds.), *Studies in general and oriental linguistics presented to Shirô Hattori.* Tokyo: TEC, 1970.

Longacre, R. E. *An anatomy of speech notions.* Ghent: Peter de Ridder Press, 1976.

Nichols, J. Secondary predicates. *Proceedings of the Fourth Annual Meeting of the Berkeley Linguistics Society.* Berkeley Calif.: Berkeley Linguistics Society, 1978.

O'Donnell, R. C. Syntactic differences between speech and writing. *American Speech,* 1974, *49:*102–110.

Robbins, B. L. *The definite article in English transformations.* The Hague: Mouton, 1968.

Rochester, S. R., & Martin, J. R. 1977. The art of referring: the speaker's use of noun phrases to instruct the listener. In R. O. Freedle (Ed.), *Discourse production and comprehension: Advances in discourse processes* (Vol. 1). Norwood, N.J.: Ablex, 1977.

Russell, B. Descriptions. In J. F. Rosenberg & C. Travis (Eds.), *Readings in the philosophy of language.* Englewood Cliffs, N.J.: Prentice-Hall, 1971.

Searle, J. *Speech acts: an essay in the philosophy of language.* Cambridge: Cambridge University Press, 1969.

Literary Citations

Albertson, C. Liner notes, *Bessie Smith: the world's greatest blues singer.* Columbia Records CG 33. New York: Columbia, n.d.

Dylan, B. "As I went out one morning," in *John Wesley Harding.* Columbia Records. CS9604, n.d.

Sandburg, C. *Rootabaga stories.* New York: Harcourt, Brace and World, 1922.

Sapir, E. 1929. Central and North American languages. *Encyclopedia Brittanica* (14th ed.), 5: 138–141.

Sterne, L. *The life and opinions of Tristram Shandy, gentleman.* New York: Signet, 1960.

Thomas, D. The hand that signed the paper. In Helen Gardner (Ed.), *The new Oxford book of English verse.* Oxford: Oxford University Press, 1972.

Vonnegut, *The Eden Express.* New York: Bantam Books, 1975.

6 Subjecthood and Consciousness

Robert Bernardo
University of California, Berkeley

This chapter examines the phenomenon of subjecthood in English from the standpoint of discourse production. My goal in developing a discourse production model is to account for discourse form—why a particular discourse, or discourse in general, is the way it is. I assume that discourse form is ultimately dictated by two things: As a purposeful behavior, discourse acts are the result of speaker's intentions; e.g., the intention to enter into a conversation, the intention to be polite or informal, the intention to express a certain piece of information, etc. (Bernardo, 1979). As cognitive behavior, discourse processes are dependent upon the apparatus of the mind.

Subjecthood, as I will show, is a phenomenon dependent upon the apparatus of consciousness. The issue here is the following: when the speaker intends to express a state or event with a clause, what determines which entity gets expressed as the subject of the clause?

COGNITION AND DISCOURSE

Memory and Consciousness[1]

Discourse largely involves the expression of what I call *conceptual material.* By conceptual material, I mean such things as memories of past experiences, knowledge one has, new thoughts one is having, ongoing perceptions, etc. In

---

[1]The cognitive model briefly sketched in this subsection has largely evolved from that developed by Chafe. I direct the reader to Chafe (1977) and Chafe (Chapter 1) for a more elaborate discussion of his version of this model.

other words, conceptual material is essentially the content of what has been called *mental representation*.

We may speak of conceptual material being *in consciousness*. *Consciousness* is the state conceptual material is in when it is being attended to. So, current perceptions, new thoughts, knowledge and memories while recalled, etc., are examples of conceptual material in consciousness. When conceptual material is not in consciousness, we may speak of it as being *stored in memory*. So then, for example, when somebody recalls a past experience, expressing it as a narrative, we say that a memory has been brought from memory into consciousness and then narrated. But instead of using this everyday spatial metaphor of conceptual material being "located" in consciousness or in memory, let us speak of conceptual material being activated, or not being activated, respectively. We can then also speak of conceptual material being highly activated, not so activated, not at all activated, etc. The *in consciousness vs. in memory* terminology provides only a binary distinction, while we want to allow for the possibility of degrees of activation.

When conceptual material is activated, it seems to be activated in unified pieces or *chunks*. Thus, pieces of knowledge and memory often have names, e.g., "Denis," "the Holocaust," "Berkeley," or can be referred to with *ad hoc* names, e.g., "my trip to Yosemite," "the gasoline shortage," "the tune-up my car got last month."

Actually conceptual material seems to be composed of two sorts of elements, (1) *individuals,* that is, particular people, particular things, etc., and (2) *states* and *events,* that is, relations and interactions among individuals. (For simplicity's sake, hereafter I use *event* to mean *state or event*.) This dichotomy between individuals and events is supported by the ability to refer to a chunk with a name or a noun phrase description, e.g., "Denis," "a tune-up," "the gasoline shortage," "a dog"; or with a clause, e.g., "The country is running out of gas."[2]

When I speak of individuals, states, events, and experiences, I am not referring to things in the real world, but rather to a person's mental representation of them.

Two Processes of Extraction— Subchunking and Clausalization

When a person wants to express a memory of a past experience, the memory is first activated before it is expressed. In other words, you must think about a memory before you talk about it. So, for example, I might think about (activate my memory of) my weekend in Yosemite, and then say to you:

---

[2]Note that the noun phrase "the gasoline shortage" and the clause "the country is running out of gas" essentially refer to the same chunk of conceptual material. This shows that some chunks that can be conceived of as events can also be reified.

(1) I spent last weekend in Yosemite.

The entire memory is represented here as a single event, and so it has been expressed as a single clause. However, you might say "Oh?" letting me know you want to know more. I would then say:

(2) Well, I drove up to Yosemite on Friday with some friends, and we rented a tent-cabin in Curry Village. We climbed up Tenaya Canyon and had a pretty good time.

In this case I have conceived of this memory not as a single event, but as a set of component events, before narrating it. This illustrates the process of *subchunking,* the extraction of component event chunks from a larger chunk (Chafe, 1977).

It is important to note that a given chunk may be subchunked in different ways on different occasions. For example, in the pear movie experiment, Speaker 13 narrated part of the movie as two events:

(3) (a) [.8] A--nd s .. and so the bike .. falls over,
    (b) and the pears all go / khp̃ /.

But six weeks later, the same speaker narrated this part of the movie as three events:

(4) (a) And then he falls over with all the pears,
    (b) and and the bicycle,
    (c) and and [.5] the he's all over the ground,

This speaker seems to have divided up the same information into different parts on these two occasions. The fact that the same chunk can be subchunked in different ways shows that a chunk is not like a jigsaw puzzle with precut pieces that simply fall out. Rather it is like a picture that still needs to be cut up; consequently it can get cut up in different ways on different occasions. The speaker seems to have some choice as to which portions of the larger chunk will be extracted as individual chunks and expressed.

Let us use the term *minichunk* to refer to a chunk that on a particular occasion is conceived of as a single event and is not further subchunked. I will use the terms *minichunk* and (mental representation of an) *event* interchangeably in this chapter; cf. Chafe's term *focus of consciousness* (Chapter 1). Now, as a person is narrating a past experience, s/he is aware of both the larger chunk (the memory of the whole experience), and the particular minichunk that s/he is focuing on at the moment. The former seems to be in the back of her/his consciousness; the latter is in the focus of her/his consciousness. We would say then that the minichunk is more highly activated than the larger chunk.

A minichunk usually gets expressed as a clause or a clauselike expression; that is, as a construction containing a verbal phrase and one or more associated noun phrases. The noun phrases refer to the various individuals involved in the event, and the verbal phrase refers to the relationship between them.

Now, just as subchunking is the extraction of minichunks from a larger chunk, *clausalization* is the extraction of individuals, and a relationship between them, from a minichunk. And just as a larger chunk may be subchunked in different ways on different occasions, a minichunk may be clausalized in different ways on different occasions. For one, a speaker may extract out different individuals from the same minichunk. For example, pear movie Speaker 10 narrated the fall of a boy off his bike as 5 (d):

(5) (a) so he sort of turns around,
     (b) [.2] to look at it [his fallen hat],
     (c) [.45] and runs into a rock,
     (d) .. and [.6] crashes over.

Six weeks later, the same speaker narrated this event as:

(6) [.4] And I think the bicycle [.85] keel well the bicycle does fall over.

In 5(d), the event of falling was conceived of as involving a single individual, the boy. In example (6), it was conceived of as involving a different single individual, the bicycle. Such examples show that a minichunk, too, is not like a jigsaw puzzle with precut parts. Rather the speaker must extract out individuals and a relationship among them, and the speaker seems to have some choice about how to do this.

Even if the same individuals are extracted out of the same minichunk on different occasions, the clausalizations may still differ in at least one other way; they may differ with regard to which individual is expressed with the subject noun phrase, which individual is expressed with the direct object noun phrase, etc. For example, of the 20 pear movie narrators 15 explicitly mentioned the event of a girl and a boy passing by each other on bicycles. Two mentioned only one individual, the girl, in expressing this event; e.g., Speaker 14 said:

(7) (a) [1.0] U--m [1.3] this other little girl in pigtails,
     (b) .. black pigtails,
     (c) [.35] rode by,

Of the remaining thirteen (who all mentioned exactly two individuals, the boy and the girl), eight used a plural subject, e.g., Speaker 1 said:

(8) (a) and they [.3] cro you know.
    (b) [.35] cross paths.

Three expressed the boy as the subject and the girl as the object, e.g., Speaker 8 said:

(9) (a) [.95] a--nd [.2] he passes um . . a girl,
    (b) [1.25] like this on the road,

One, Speaker 17, did the opposite:

(10) as she-- [.35] passes him,

These examples show that in clausalizing a minichunk, a speaker has choices to make which result in determining which individuals are extracted and which noun phrase positions express them. *These choices affect which individual becomes the noun phrase subject of the clause.*

The Goal of This Chapter

To repeat what was said earlier, the main goal of my discourse production model is the explanation of discourse form in terms of speaker's intentions and cognitive apparatus. I have just shown that there are many ways of clausalizing the same event, which may differ with respect to which individual gets expressed as clause subject. In accounting for how an event is clausalized, a discourse production model must specify the factors that determine which individual is thus expressed.

EXTRACTION AS ACTIVATION

Suppose you ask me "What did you do four weekends ago?" I think back and realize that that was the weekend I spent in Yosemite. Now, for that split second of this realization, my memory of that weekend is in my consciousness as a single, fairly highly activated chunk. However, during this split second, before I start to think about exactly what happened that weekend in greater detail, such details as my hike up Tenaya Canyon, the food I had that Saturday night, the good weather we had, are not very strong in my consciousness; they are not highly activated. I assume that this is also true for minichunks: when an unclausalized minichunk is activated in one's consciousness, its potential component individuals are not necessarily as highly activated. I will not be able to prove this assumption in this chapter, but in conjunction with the data to be presented, it will provide a convincing explanation of the phenomenon of subjecthood in English.

A corollary of this assumption is that the extraction of a part of a chunk involves activating that part more fully. That is, the extraction of a minichunk from a larger chunk involves a greater activation of that minichunk; the extraction of an individual from a minichunk involves a greater activation of that individual. Now, when a speaker wants to express a minichunk with a clause, s/he has to extract out individuals, and a relationship between them, from the minichunk. As just shown, the individuals and the relationship do not simply fall out of the minichunk like pieces of a jigsaw puzzle. The speaker must do work in extracting these parts.

This chapter hypothesizes that one individual, the one that is the first to be extracted, the one that is the easiest to activate sufficiently for extraction, is the one that gets expressed as the clause subject. I will not be able to prove this claim, but in conjunction with supportive data, the reader will, I hope, see this as a reasonable explanation of subjecthood in English.

In the rest of this section I argue that two types of factors determine which individual in a minichunk is the first to be sufficiently activated for extraction. First, the more an individual is already activated the more likely it is to be expressed as clause subject. Second, certain more permanent properties individuals may have lend them greater salience. Consequently, individuals with such properties are more quickly activated and are more likely to get extracted as subject. Such properties include the semantic role that the individual plays in the event.

Prior Activation

Suppose that a given minichunk is conceived of as an event involving two individuals that play the same role in the event. Then only the difference in their prior activation should determine which one will be the first to be extracted. This I call the *prior activation hypothesis*. There is a class of events that I call *symmetrical events* precisely because they involve two (or more) individuals playing the same role. For example:

(11) Claire is getting married to David in June.

expresses a symmetrical event. Consequently, the same event can be referred to if we switch the subject and object of the clause. For example:

(12) David is getting married to Claire in June.

(13) Claire and David are getting married (to each other) in June.

can both be used to refer to the same event as 11. Kuno and Kaburaki (1977) recognized this in their discussion of "subject-centered verbs," but it should be noted that this is not a property of the lexical verb used, but rather of the conceptualization of the event that such verbs refer to. This is evidenced by the fact that replacing the verbal phrase with a synonym in such a case does not alter the symmetricality of the event. For example:

(14) Claire is getting hitched to David in June.

can be used to refer to the same event as clauses 11 through 13.
Other examples of clauses referring to symmetrical events are:

(15) Denis went to the movies with Jason.

(16) Jason went to the movies with Denis.

(17) Denis and Jason went to the movies (together/with each other).

(18) Donna ran into Joan at the bank today.

(19) Joan ran into Donna at the bank today.

(20) Donna and Joan ran into each other at the bank today.

The prior activation hypothesis says that when a minichunk is conceived of as a symmetrical event, the individual that is already more activated is the one that gets expressed as the subject. That is, of the two (or more) individuals that will get referred to in the clause, the one that has just been more in the focus of the speaker's attention/awareness/thoughts is the one that will become the clause subject. As a consequence, everything else being equal, a discourse participant is more activated than a third person, and when a symmetrical event involves both, the former is expressed as the subject. Hence,

(21) I hear you are getting married to David in June.

sounds better than

(22) I hear David is getting married to you in June.

Similarly, everything else being equal, a discourse-mentioned individual is more activated than a discourse-unmentioned individual, and when a symmetrical event involves both, the former is expressed as the subject. Hence,

(23) David is getting married to a thirty-three-year-old woman.

sounds better than

(24) A thirty-three-year-old woman is getting married to David.

For convenience, we may speak of these as *situational* and *textual* activation, respectively.

Experimental Evidence

The prior activation hypothesis was tested using the shared armchair introspections of four colleagues and me.[3] Each gave her/his judgment on which of three ways of expressing a given symmetrical event sounded best in various linguistic contexts. Each test unit consisted of a paragraph mentioning two human characters, X and Y. The paragraph ended with three possible ways of expressing their accidental meeting, "X bumped into Y," "Y bumped into X," and "X and Y bumped into each other." Each judge indicated which way fit best in the paragraph. For example, one of the test units looked like this:

Despite all her efforts, Pam is having a hard time avoiding Nick ever since their fight.

(1) Today alone she bumped into him on campus three times.
(2) Today alone they bumped into each other on campus three times.
(3) Today alone he bumped into her on campus three times.

The various test units differed in two ways in order to manipulate the degree of activation that the judges would consider X and Y to have in the imaginary speaker's mind. First is the *referential factor*, the way in which X and Y were referred to in the test unit. There were four ways in which X and Y were referred to:

---

[3] I thank Robin Lakoff, Denis Lahey, Margaret Rader, and Deborah Tannen for their assistance in this task.

1. One of X and Y was referred to with a first person pronoun, and the other with a first name (and then third person pronoun), e.g., "Bill"/"he"/"him." Everything else being equal, the former should be preferred as subject on the basis of situational activation.
2. One with a first name (and then third person pronoun), and the other with an indefinite description, e.g., "a Russian linguist." Everything else being equal, the former should be preferred as subject, on the basis of textual activation.
3. Both with a first name (and then third person pronoun). Everything else being equal, neither should be particularly preferred as subject over the other.
4. Both with an indefinite description. Everything else being equal, neither should be particularly preferred as subject over the other.

The second way in which the test units differed was the *contextual factor,* the nature of X's and Y's occurrence in the text preceding the "bump into" clauses. There were five context types designed to differentially manipulate the imputed activation of X and Y:

1. One of X and Y is discourse-mentioned, and the other is discourse-unmentioned. Everything else being equal, the former should be preferred as subject on the basis of textual activation.
2. Both are discourse-mentioned. Everything else being equal, neither should be particularly preferred as subject over the other.
3. Both are discourse-unmentioned. Everything else being equal, neither should be particularly preferred as subject over the other.
4. One is a discourse topic, and the other is merely discourse-mentioned. This context tested the possibility that one discourse-mentioned individual might be more activated than another merely because it is more central to the discourse.
5. Both are discourse topics. Everything else being equal, neither should be particularly preferred as subject over the other.

Each test unit was created by plugging one of the referential conditions into one of the contextual conditions. For example, the test unit resulting from plugging referential condition 1 into contextual condition 4 looked like this:

> Mary seemed to be in a rotten mood last week. Thursday she picked a fight with me. In the afternoon she picked a fight with Andy.
> (1) So when I bumped into him on the bus Friday,
> (2) So when he and I bumped into each other on the bus Friday,
> (3) So when he bumped into me on the bus Friday, we discussed it and decided to have a talk with her.

The results of the judgments were as follows:

1. When X and Y were both discourse topics, or both discourse-mentioned, or both discourse-unmentioned (contextual conditions 2, 3, and 5), and one was a first person and the other was a third person (referential condition 1), the former was preferred as subject in 14 of 15 judgments. But when one was referred to with a first name and the other with an indefinite description (referential condition 2), the former was preferred as subject in all five judgments.
2. When X and Y were both referred to with a first name or both with an indefinite description (referential conditions 3 and 4), and one was a discourse topic and the other was merely discourse-mentioned (contextual condition 4), the former was preferred as subject in four of five judgments. But when one was discourse-mentioned and the other was discourse-unmentioned (contextual condition 1), the former was preferred as subject in all of five judgments.
3. Needless to say, when both the contextual and the referential factors favored the same individual as most activated, that individual was almost always preferred as subject.
4. When the two factors favored different individuals, or when neither of the two factors favored either X or Y, there was little pattern in the judgments, except that the compound subject ("X and Y bumped into each other") was often preferred.

The foregoing results nearly totally fit the predictions based on the prior activation hypothesis.

Discourse Evidence

In the preceding subsection I have shown that armchair judges feel that symmetrical events expressed with clauses having the most activated individual as subject sound better than those that do not. In this subsection I introduce actual discourse data, from the pear movie narratives, that show that prior activation is a factor in subject extraction.

One event in the pear movie was conceived of as a symmetrical event by as many as 13 of the 20 narrators, that of a boy and a girl passing by each other on bicycles. This event occurs at a point in the movie when the boy has been the main protagonist for about 2 minutes, during which he has stolen a basket of pears and ridden off with it on the front of his bicycle. The girl first appears only several seconds before she and the boy pass by each other. Consequently, the passing is the first event in which she is mentioned.

Of the 13 narrators who expressed this event as a symmetrical event, 10 had previously introduced the girl and 3 had not. In expressing the symmetrical event, of the 10 who had previously introduced the girl, 9 used the collective subject "they" in reference to the boy and girl; e.g., Speaker 18 said:

(25) and u--m [.7] they [.9] go very close past each other,

and one, Speaker 17, expressed the girl as the subject:

(26) as she-- [.35] passes him,

But all three who had not previously mentioned the girl, expressed the boy as the subject; e.g., Speaker 16 said:

(27) [.75] and he passed a little girl on a bicycle,

The prior activation hypothesis accounts for these data in the following way. In the cases in which both the boy and girl were recently discourse-mentioned, both were probably already activated to roughly the same degree in the speaker's mind. Hence, in all but one such case, they were expressed with the collective subject "they" in the expression of the symmetrical event. In the cases in which only the boy had been discourse-mentioned, the boy had much greater prior activation than the girl. Hence, in all these cases, he was expressed as the subject in the expression of the symmetrical event. The prior activation hypothesis cannot account for the one case (Speaker 17, example 26 above) who expressed the girl as the subject of the symmetrical event. But the untypically long hesitation between the subject and predicate in this case suggests the possibility that Speaker 17 had encoding difficulties possibly related to this counterhypothesis instance of subjecthood.

Salience

Chafe (Chapter 1) has pointed out that consciousness shares three important properties with vision: (1) consciousness has limited capacity, just as one's field of vision is limited; (2) consciousness has a focus and periphery, just as the eye has foveal and peripheral vision; (3) consciousness jumps from focus to focus as do eye fixations. In this subsection, I argue that consciousness shares an additional property with vision and that this property plays a role in subject extraction.

When we first look upon a scene, our attention is attracted to objects with certain properties: brightly colored objects, moving objects, human beings (especially their faces), and unexpected objects. I propose that our consciousness is attracted to parts of an undivided activated chunk in a similar fashion. Specifically, I propose that when a minichunk is activated but not yet clausalized, our attention is directed to individuals playing certain semantic roles in the event. Let us call this the *salience hypothesis*.

The statistical correlation between subjecthood and such properties as animacy and agency has been well recognized by linguistics (e.g., Keenan 1976). Fillmore (1977) has dealt with it in his "saliency hierarchy," which he uses to account for choices a speaker has in assigning individuals to the various noun phrase positions in a clause. He claims that the highest ranking individual is realized as the subject. The salience hierarchy, Fillmore says, will look something like this:

1. An active element outranks an inactive element.
2. A causal element outranks a noncausal element.
3. A human (or animate) experiencer outranks other elements.
4. A changed element outranks a nonchanged element.
5. A complete or individuated element outranks a part of an element.
6. A "figure" outranks a "ground."
7. A "definite" element outranks an "indefinite" element.
   The intention is that this hierarchy is to be consulted in the order in which these statements are listed. Thus, an active element outranks everything else; a causal element outranks everything but an active element; and so on (1977:102).

This saliency hierarchy is interesting, but for two reason, it cannot be directly adapted as a hypothesis about what gives an individual salience in an unclausalized minichunk. First, the property of definiteness is not a property of an individual, but rather of a linguistic description of an individual. Presumably, a speaker does not have a linguistic description of an individual in mind before the individual is extracted from a minichunk. So, although there may be a correlation between definite noun phrases and clause subjects, one cannot claim that definiteness is a causal factor in subjecthood.

The prior activation hypothesis can account for this correlation. Since definite noun phrases often refer to discourse-mentioned individuals, and indefinite noun phrases do not, referents of definite noun phrases often have more prior activation than referents of indefinite noun phrases.

Second, saying that an individual that is "figure" is more salient than an individual that is "ground" is nearly tautological without a precise definition of "figure" and "ground."

My hunch is that causal roles, e.g., those traditionally called *agent* and *instrument,* "human" roles (roles than can be played only by individuals with a psyche), e.g., those traditionally called *intentional agent* and *experiencer,* lend great salience to individuals. By mere perusal of the pear movie narratives (given in the Appendix), the reader can verify the high correlation between individuals playing human and causal roles and individuals expressed as clause subjects.

"Why" Questions and Humanness of Role

Evidence that human and causal roles lend salience to individuals comes from the interpretations given to "why" questions. The analysis of "why" questions presented here is distilled from the linguistic behavior of 134 students in an introductory linguistics course. Each was given a piece of paper listing six "why" questions. They were instructed to imagine for each question a situation in which the question would make sense, to write down an appropriate answer, and then if there was a better way of asking the same question, to so indicate. The questions varied on three two-valued factors, producing eight formal types. The factors were:

1. whether the voice was active or passive,
2. whether the causal individual was intentional (i.e., an agent) or nonintentional (i.e., an instrument), and
3. whether the action mentioned involved an *experiencer* (a person undergoing a change of psychological state (as denoted by such verbs as *frighten, surprise,* and *interest*), or not (as denoted by such verbs as *hit* and *kill*).

In general, a "why" question asks for the cause of something. I have found it useful to distinguish between three things that "why" questions may ask the cause of. If the "why" question involves an intentional agent, it may ask for the cause of the agent's decision to act, as in

(28) Q: Why did Norman kill Sally?
(29) A: She had scratched up his records.

If the "why" question involves an experiencer, it may ask for the cause of the experiencer's change of state, as in

(30) Q: Why was little Steve frightened by the lightning?
(31) A: It cast scary shadows on his bedroom wall.

If the "why" question involves neither an intentional agent nor an experiencer, it asks for the cause of the action, as in

(32) Q: Why was Cary hit by the lightning?
(33) A: He was standing in an open field.

TABLE 1

"Why" Question Type	Is the Agent Intentional?	Is there an Experiencer?	Voice	Question Asks for the Cause of the
A	no	no	active	action
B	no	no	passive	action
C	no	yes	active	experiencer's state
D	no	yes	passive	experiencer's state
E	yes	no	active	agent's decision
F	yes	no	passive	agent's decision
G	yes	yes	active	agent's decision
H	yes	yes	passive	experiencer's state

Table 1 summarizes the correlation between these three answer types and the eight types of "why" questions under consideration.

A "why" question mentioning an action involving neither an intentional agent or an experiencer (types A and B) can ask only for the cause of the action. Such a question in the active voice, e.g.,

(34) Why did the lightning hit Joseph?

or in the passive voice, e.g.,

(35) Why was Joseph hit by the lightning?

received such answers as

(36) He was standing under a tree.
(37) Because he was the tallest object in the area.
(38) He was swimming in the lake.
(39) Because he was standing in an open field.

But if the action involves an experiencer (types C and D), the question asks for the cause of the experiencer's resultant state, whether the voice is active or passive. Hence,

(40) Why did the lightning surprise Huey?

and

(41) Why was Huey surprised by the lightning?

received such answers as

(42) Because it was awfully close.
(43) Because it split the tree.
(44) He isn't used to lightning.
(45) Because he didn't expect it.

Now, if the action involves an intentional agent, but not an experiencer (types E and F), the question asks for the cause of the agent's decision to act, whether the voice is active or passive. Hence,

(46) Why did Matilda kill Solomon?

and

(47) Why was Solomon killed by his wife?

received such answers as

(48) Because she didn't like him.
(49) He was trying to molest her.
(50) Because he always left the cap off the toothpaste tube.
(51) Because he was fooling around.

Notice that such questions cannot ask for the action causing the patient's resultant state, e.g.,

(52) She shot him with a gun.

Such information is elicited with a "how" question, e.g.,

(53) How did Matilda kill Solomon?
(54) How was Solomon killed by his wife?

Now if the "why" question involves both an intentional agent and an experiencer, and if the voice is active (i.e., the agent is subject) (type G), the question asks for the cause of the agent's decision to act, not the experiencer's resultant state. Hence,

(55) Why did Huey frighten Barbara?

received such answers as

(56) He got a kick out of her reaction.
(57) He liked the idea of being able to "control" someone.

but none such as

(58) Because he would show her insects.
(59) Because he was creepy.

To elicit such answers keeping the voice active, one would have to use a "how" question, e.g.,

(60) How did Huey frighten Barbara?

If, however, the voice is passive (i.e., the experiencer is the subject) (type H), the question asks for the cause of the experiencer's resultant state. Hence,

(61) Why was Barbara frightened by Huey?

received such answers as (58) and (59), but not (56) or (57).

In dealing with the different interpretations given to different "why" questions, we may speak of the *focus* of the question. For example, if a question asks for a cause of an agent's decision to act, we can say that the question focuses on the agent. Or if a question asks for a cause of an experiencer's change of state, we can say that the question focuses on the experiencer. Using this notion of focus, we can note the following generalization about "why" questions: the question focuses on the one individual playing a human role if only one occurs in the question; if more than one occurs, the question focuses on the one that is the clause subject. Therefore, the respondent's interpretation of a "why" question depends not only on its syntax, but also on the semantic roles played by the individuals mentioned. These data suggest that individuals playing human roles in events have special salience, at least in the interpretations respondents give to "why" questions.

Now in English almost every verb that denotes an event involving exactly one human or causal role takes the individual in such a role as the subject in the active voice, e.g., *kill, hit, walk, eat, think, hear,* etc. The passive voice of such verbs has the effect of not expressing the individual in the human/causal role as the clause subject. The passive voice expresses as subject the individual that would be the direct object in the active voice. If human and causal roles do lend salience to individuals and are therefore factors in subject extraction, then the passive voice of such verbs should be used only when the individual in the human/causal role (the "underlying" subject) has much less prior activation than the "underlying" object. Furthermore, the passive voice of such verbs should sound odd when the "underlying" subject has more prior activation than the "underlying" object. More specifically, it should sound odd to use the passive voice when the "underlying" subject is discourse-mentioned and the "underlying" object is not; it should sound odd to use the passive voice when the "underlying" subject is a discourse participant and the "underlying" object is a third person. Such clauses should sound odd because the "underlying" subject would be more salient by its semantic role and also have more prior activation than the "underlying" object (actual subject). This seems to be the case. For example,

(62) He was killed by me.

sounds odder than

(63) I killed him.

(unless, perhaps, the third person has been the discourse topic and the first person has not been recently mentioned in the discourse). Also,

(64) A tree was hit by the car.

sounds odder than

(65) The car hit a tree.

(One should note that a speaker may deliberately use the passive voice in such cases as these for the striking effect it creates.)

These data support the salience hypothesis: that certain properties of individuals, namely, their playing a human or causal role in an event, give them salience that increases their likelihood of being extracted as clause subjects.

SUBCHUNKING

I have argued that prior activation and salience-lending properties are factors in one process of clausalization, namely, subject extraction. In this section I show that prior activation and salience-lending properties play a role in *subchunking*, the extraction of smaller chunks from a larger chunk. I will speak of the *global* aspects of subchunking (the overall organization of the larger chunk), and of the *local* aspects of subchunking (the sequential extraction of minichunks from a larger chunk).

Prior Activation and Subchunking

There is evidence that prior activation plays a role in the subchunking of a larger chunk. More specifically, it seems that when a speaker is narrating a memory, the activation of individuals affects how the next minichunk is extracted from the larger chunk. Let us look at clauses in the pear movie narratives that meet the following conditions:

1. The clause mentions a human individual that was mentioned in the preceding clause. Let us refer to it as the *old individual.*
2. The clause mentions a human individual that was not mentioned in the preceding clause. Let us refer to it as the *new individual.*
3. Either the new or old individual is expressed as the clause subject.

We find that 87 percent of the subjects of such clauses were an old individual and 13 percent were a new individual. This should not surprise us: The old individual would strongly tend to have greater prior activation than the new individual from its more recent occurrence in the discourse. Since we have no reason to suspect that there is a tendency for the new individual to play a human role more often than the old, or vice vesa, we would expect the old individual to turn up as the subject of these clauses more often than the new individual. Hence, the fact that the old individual turned up as subject in 87 percent of these clauses is strong evidence for the prior activation hypothesis.

It is worth noting that in every single case in which the new individual turned up as clause subject, it played the only human role occurring in the event. This, too, is not surprising; a new individual would have less prior activation than the old individual, and so it could turn up as subject only if it played a human role and the old individual did not. So, the fact that whenever the new individual turned up as a clause subject it played the only human role in the event is strong evidence for the salience hypothesis.

But what is surprising is: When there was only one human role in these clauses, it was played by the old individual in 86 percent of the clauses. To express this in a different way, in 99 percent of the cases in which the old individual was clause subject, it played the only human role in the event. This means that there is an unexpected correlation between being an old individual and playing the only human role in an event. When we look more closely at the narratives, we see that this is actually a result of two tendencies, the avoidance of lowly activated individuals as clause subjects, and the promotion of highly activated individuals as clause subjects. I have identified six ways in which this was achieved.

First, speakers often use clauses begun with the dummy subject "there" to introduce a new character, as Speaker 9 did in introducing the girl on the bicycle:

(66) (a) .. you see a scene
     (b) where he's .. coming on his bicycle this way,
     (c) [.5] and there's a girl coming on a bicycle,
     (d) [.2] this way.

Second, speakers may use the passive voice (which was actually quite rare in the twenty narratives). Speaker 12 did this:

(67) (a) [.15] So a man with a goat [.35] went by,
      (b) [1.2...tsk...] and the goat [.25] balked,
      (c) a--nd [.9] was [.35] pulled along by this [.35] w--one fellow
      (d) who just disappeared.

Third, speakers often mention events that are rather unimportant to the story line, as Speaker 17 did in introducing the girl on the bicycle:

(68) (a) [.45] And so,
      (b) .. he's driving along,
      (c) [.45] a--nd
      (d) riding his bike along,
      (e) and he sees another [.45] person coming [.35] toward him,

Instead of 68 (e), Speaker 17 could have just as well said

(69) and another person is coming toward him,

since the fact that the boy on the bike saw the girl approach him goes without saying.

Fourth, speakers often use a dummy event (one outside the content of the movie), using the omnipresent movie viewer as subject, as Speaker 1 did:

(70) (a) and gets up,
      (b) and brushes himself off,
      (c) .. and he goes .. you know (brushing gesture)
      (d) [.6] and then you see three other boys about his age.

For the fifth and sixth devices, let us examine the part of the movie where the action abruptly shifts from the three helpful boys to the man picking pears. This segment was faithfully narrated by Speaker 13:

(71) (a) and the three boys .. start walking down the path,
      (b) [.8] a--nd u--m [1.0] by that time the man who was [.55] taking the pears off,
      (c) [.4] comes down,
      (d) .. he starts to empty out his apron,
      (e) and he notices one of his baskets is gone.
      (f) [.25] He stands up,
      (g) looks back,
      (h) and counts,
      (i) let's see,
      (j) o--ne,

    (k) two--,
    (l) and the third one's gone.
    (m) [.9] And then..he sees these three boys walking around,
    (n) crunching on pears,

(Notice that 71 (m) introduces the three boys with the relatively unimportant event of the pear picker seeing them.) The change of scenes between 71(a) and 71(b) is a difficult one; no character that appears at the end of the first scene appears at the beginning of the second. Several of the narrators handled this difficulty by narrating the events out of their temporal order, namely, by mentioning the three boys' arrival at the pear tree, and then mentioning the pear picker's activities that occurred before their arrival on the scene. That is what Speaker 6 did:

  (72) (a) [.15] And then they walk past the [.35] the tree,
      (b) [1.1] where the picker,
      (c) ..was picking pears,
      (d) [.9] a--nd u--h [.9] he has already come down from the ladder,
      (e) [.65] to deposit his [.4] more of the pears that he picked in the basket

Several other of the narrators actually misrepresented the order in which the events occurred; for example, Speaker 1:

  (73) (a) [.15] and they walked by the p [.8] the pear tree,
      (b) ..the man was picking pears.
      (c) ..And he looked down,
      (d) ..saw that [1.05] he was missing a basket.
      (e) ..And he looked at the boys walking off,

    The first two devices mentioned, use of the passive voice and of the dummy subject "there," show how a speaker can clausalize a given minichunk so that the subject is not a lowly activated individual. More important are the second through sixth devices, which show a strong tendency to maintain a highly activated individual as clause subject from one clause to the next. Use of the passive voice does this by clausalizing a minichunk in an advantageous way. But mentioning dummy and unimportant events and altering and misrepresenting the temporal order of events does this by extracting advantageous minichunks in an advantageous order.

    The latter demonstrates that prior activation is a factor in subchunking. The speaker seems to have a highly activated individual already in mind to express as clause subject before s/he has extracted out a minichunk. It seems that a highly activated individual acts as a nucleus around which a mass of conceptual material congeals into a minichunk, in much the same way as a particle of dust acts as a nucleus for the condensation of water vapor into a raindrop.

Perhaps subjecthood plays a similar role in comprehension. Let us suppose that when a listener hears a clause, s/he first builds up a semantic representation of the clause, and then attaches this newly conveyed information to information already in her/his memory. Since the speaker has a strong tendency to use a just-mentioned individual as clause subject, such a subject would be highly activated for the listener as well as for the speaker. It therefore provides an excellent starting point for the listener to construct her/his semantic representation of the clause, and also an excellent point at which the listener can attach this newly conveyed information to information already in his/her memory.

Salient Individuals and Subchunking

There is evidence that the salience of human characters plays a role in subchunking, namely, in the overall organization of a larger chunk. Chafe (Chapter 1) has pointed out that narratives are organized around human characters.

The backbone of a narrative consists of the introduction of people, their description, and especially their engagement in activities which are worth telling about.

Chafe (1979) has also argued that memories of past experience are often organized into "episodes," that is, chunks of memory unified by a set of characters, location, and time. Evidence for this occurs in the pear movie narratives, where especially long hesitations occur when there is an arrival or departure of a character, a change of location, or a break in the flow of time. Chafe argues that these long hestitations are a result of the work it takes for the speaker to retrieve the next episode from memory.

Clearly, the pear movie narratives are organized around the human characters. All 20 of the narrators organized their memory of the movie by following the actions of the human characters. It is noteworthy that no single main character predominated in all or nearly all parts of the movie, but that in a more objective perspective, the events centered around the pears, which provided a common thread from beginning to end. The following is a narrative that might have occurred, had a narrator organized the events around the pears instead of the human characters:

The movie opened with a shot of a pear tree. The pears were just hanging there, but then got picked off one by one by a Mexican farmer. They were picked from their tree and put into his apron. Then they'd be taken down on the ground and dumped into baskets that the farmer had. One of the baskets was taken away by a boy who came by on his bicycle. When he ran into a rock in the road, the basket fell off the bike, and the pears splattered all over. However, the pears were put back in the basket by the three boys who came by and helped the boy. Three of the pears were a reward he gave them for their help. So three of the pears continued down the road, in the hands and mouths of the three good Samaritans. Since they were walking in the direction in which the boy on the bike had come, the three pears wound up going past the tree on which they had grown. But now they were being eaten.

Memories are organized around human characters, not pears, because human characters are salient and pears are not. I should like to speculate on the source of the salience of human characters.

I have already argued that human roles lend salience to individuals in a minichunk. It is clear from the "why" question data that human individuals in human roles are salient in minichunks by virtue of their human role, not by virtue of their being human. Since human characters often play human roles in an event, human characters tend to be salient in minichunks.

I have also argued that when a large chunk, say, one's memory of the pear movie, is activated but not yet subchunked, its potential extractable events are not necessarily activated. Consequently, when the movie is thought of as a whole, any salience a human character has in a potentially extractable event in which it played a human role, cannot be seen as pertaining to the character in that event, but rather to the character globally in the larger chunk. That is, individuals that would be salient in many would-be parts of a larger chunk are seen as globally salient in the larger chunk. This might explain why memories are globally organized around human characters.

Salient Events and Subchunking

In this section I have argued that the activation of individuals influences subchunking locally and have speculated that the salience of individuals playing human roles influences subchunking globally. I would like now to discuss briefly how the salience of *events* might influence their extraction from a larger chunk much in the same way as the salience of individuals influences their extraction from a minichunk.

It has been well recognized by linguists who deal with narratives that in narrating a past experience, one mentions mainly the unexpected, the unusual, the unpredictable events—Chafe (1977), Polanyi (1979), Schank and Abelson (1977), and Tannen (1979). The explanation has been that the speaker mentions only the unpredictable and unusual events because the predictable ones can be inferred by the listener (Schank and Abelson), and the usual ones will bore her/him (Polanyi). There seems to be an implication that there is a sort of conscious, almost deliberate filtering out of these events.

I offer here an additional explanation. It seems reasonable to assume that certain component events of a past experience are likely to be more salient to the speaker than others. They may be salient because they are not mundane or because they have special emotional significance to the speaker. For example, when I think of my weekend at Yosemite, certain things immediately stand out in mind, e.g., hiking up Tenaya Canyon, the magnificent view of the full moon's light filtering palely through the smoky night air, how well I got along with the people I shared a tent-cabin with. Other things come into my consciousness only after I have thought about the weekend for a while, e. g., wearing a thermal T-shirt when it was cold, nibbling on trail mix, walking to the showers. The former events are much more interesting and important to me than the latter. I think these would be the things I would be more likely to mention in describing my weekend at Yosemite.

This suggests a generalization about the salience of individuals as the cause of their extraction from an event (minichunk) and the salience of minichunks as a cause of their extraction from a larger chunk. When a chunk of conceptual material gets activated, certain potential parts may be more salient than others. They therefore attract one's attention to them, thereby increasing their activation, and they are more likely to be extracted out and mentioned in a narrative.

SUMMARY

In this chapter I have shown that the way in which consciousness processes information is an important factor in linguistic behavior.

First I examined a model of how information or *conceptual material* coming from memory is activated, or structured in consciousness. I contended that conceptual material can be activated to varying degrees, that it is activated in whole chunks, and that an activated chunk's potential parts are not activated as a result of the activation of the larger chunk.

Then I discussed two processes of extracting parts from chunks. These occur when one expresses conceptual material linguistically. One was subchunking, the extraction of minichunks (chunks conceived as single states or events) from a larger chunk. The other was clausalizing, the extraction of individuals (people or objects) and a relationship between them from a minichunk. Using the pear film narratives, I showed that the extraction of parts from a chunk is not like a jigsaw puzzle falling into pieces, since a speaker may break a chunk into parts in different ways on different occasions. When a minichunk is linguistically expressed, it gets expressed as a clause, its component individuals get expressed as noun phrases, and the relationship between the individuals gets expressed as a verbal phrase. I then hypothesized that the first individual to get extracted from a minichunk is the one that gets expressed as the subject of a clause.

Then I argued that two factors determine which individual would get extracted from a minichunk first. One factor was the individuals' degree of activation; an individual that was already somewhat activated in the speaker's mind (because, say, the speaker had been thinking or talking about it) would be quicker to get sufficiently activated for extraction than a less activated individual. The other factor was the salience of individuals within the minichunk. I argued that certain properties of individuals may attract one's attention to them, thus causing them to be activated more quickly. Using the pear movie narratives and other data, I demonstrated that individuals with high prior activation and individuals playing "human" or causal roles are the ones that get expressed as clause subjects.

Then I went on to show how these two factors influence subchunking as well as subject extraction. First, I showed that there was an overwhelming tendency in the pear movie narratives to keep a highly activated individual as clause subject. From this I argued that a highly activated individual seems to act as a nucleus around which the next minichunk to get expressed congeals out of a larger chunk. Second, I speculated on the cause of human characters' salience in chunks larger than minichunks. I suggested that a particular character's salience in a larger chunk is a generalization from its salience in potentially extractable minichunks. Third, I drew a parallel between the salience of individuals as a cause of their extraction from a minichunk and the salience of events as a cause of their extraction from a larger chunk.

The main conclusion to be drawn from this paper is that the way in which consciousness processes information is a very important factor in linguistic behavior. It is clear that linguists need to deal with consciousness in their analyses of discourse processes.

REFERENCES

Bernardo, R. "Some general aspects of a discourse production model." Paper presented at the Ninth Annual California Linguistics Association Conference, California State University at Sacramento, 1979.

Chafe, W. L. Language and consciousness. *Language,* 1974, *50,* 111–133.

Chafe, W. L. Givenness, contrastiveness, definiteness, subjects, topics, and point of view. In C. N. Li (Ed.), *Subject and topic.* New York: Academic Press, 1976.

Chafe, W. L. The recall and verbalization of past experience. In R. W. Cole (Ed.), *Current issues in linguistic theory.* Bloomington, Ind.: Indiana University Press, 1977.

Chafe, W. L. The flow of thought and the flow of language. In T. Givon (Ed.), *Discourse and syntax.* New York: Academic Press, 1979.

Fillmore, C. J. Topics in lexical semantics. In R. W. Cole (Ed.), *Current issues in linguistic theory.* Bloomington, Ind.: Indiana University Press, 1977.

Keenan, E. L. Towards a universal definition of 'subject.' In C. N. Li (Ed.), *Subject and topic.* New York: Academic Press, 1976.

Kuno, S., & Kaburaki, E. Empathy and Syntax. *Linguistic Inquiry,* 1977, *8,* 627–672.

Labov, W. The transformation of experience in narrative syntax. In (W. Labov) *Language in the inner city: Studies in the Black English Vernacular.* Philadelphia: University of Pennsylvania Press, 1972.

Polanyi, L. False starts can be true. *Proceedings of the fourth annual conference of the Berkeley Linguistics Society,* 1978, 628–639.

Schank, R., & Abelson, R. *Scripts, plans, goals and understanding: An inquiry into human knowledge structures.* Hillsdale, N.J.: Lawrence Erlbaum, 1977.

Tannen, D. What's in a frame? Surface evidence for underlying expectations. In R. Freedle (Ed.), *New directions in discourse processing.* Norwood, N.J.: Ablex, 1979.

Appendix

The following are transcripts of the twenty original pear film narratives in English. Certain transcription conventions are used here and in the excerpts quoted in the chapters in this volume:

.   sentence-final falling intonation
?   sentence-final level or rising intonation
,   clause-final but not sentence-final intonation
/X/   X may not be an accurate transcription
/?/   portion unintelligible
ay   indefinite article pronounced to rhyme with "say"
thee   definite article pronounced to rhyme with "see"
--   lengthened segment
..   break in timing too short to be measured as pause
[X]   pause lasting X seconds
[X [Y] a--nd u--m [Z]]
    a sequence lasting a total of X secnds, consisting of a pause of Y seconds, "a--nd u--m,"
    and a pause of Z seconds

Speaker 1

Okay. [2.0 [.75] U--m [.75]] the s the scene opens up [.5] with [.2] um [1.45] you see a tree, k kay? And there's [.1] a ladder coming out .. o of the tree, and there's a man at the top of the ladder, you can't see him yet. [2.4 [.9] A--nd [.95]] then .. it shifts, and you see him, plucking a pear from the tree. [.4] And you watch him pluck a few pears, and he'd drop them into his [.25] thing, but I don't .. he's wearing like an apron with huge pockets. [.5] But I don't think you see the apron at first. I don't know if that's important or not. [3.3 [.85] A--nd u--h [1.5]] and then he gets down out of the tree, and he [.3] dumps all his pears into the basket, and the basket's full, and one of the pears drops down to the floor, and he [.65] picks it up, and he takes his kerchief off, and he [.5] wipes it off, [.45+ and [.45]] places it in in the basket which is [.25] very full. [.74] That's why it fell off in the first place. [1.3 [.95] A--nd u--m] then he climbs back up the ladder, [.35] and he [.3] and he .. starts picking pears again. [.65] And then while he's up in the ladder, [.9] let's see is it while

301

he's up in the ladder? Or.. or before. [2.3 [1.1] U--m [.55]] anyway, a guy comes by leading a goat. [.85] And the goat's aaarrr but.. and they don't talk to each other, they don't e.. I don't think they even look at each other, and.. the guy.. walks by. And you watch the goat, disappearing all the way, [.4? and then [.2]] then you're back to the man in the tree. And he's up there in the tree. [.95 [.4] And then [.25]] definitely when he's up there,.. a kid comes by on a bicycle. [.7] From the direction where the goat man left, okay? [2.45 [.75] A--nd.. u--m [.75]] the bicycle's way too big for the kid. [.45] I'm giving you all these details. I don't know if you want them. [1.2[.6] U--m [.2]]the.. the reason I'm giving you the details is cause I don't know what the point of the movie was. [.5] Okay? So maybe you can see {laugh begins } something that {laugh ends} I didn't. [.7] Okay? [1.65 [.35] U--m [.75]] g a kid comes by on a bicycle,.. he stops, [.5] he gets off his bike, [2.9 [.95] u--m [.65]] the movie was in color. [.6] And the movie had sound track. [.4] It's important. And then the mo the whole movie started with a a cock crowing. [.25] And then you see /?/. Anyway. [.5] I just remembered that. [2.2 [.35] Anyway, so u--m [.6]] the kid on the bicycle,.. gets off the bicycle, [.45] I think he [.85] he picks up the b--asket of pears, and he puts it on his bicycle,.. on the front? [.25] And he rides off. [4.75 [.75] A--nd [3.2]] you see him, [.35] riding off and the next scene you see him, [.4] like [.25] at a at a distance, a pan shot. [.35] And he's riding on a lane, [.35] riding on a bicycle and they [.3] cro you know. [.35] Cross paths. [.5] And he kind of watches her go by. [.6] And.. because he's watching her, [.45] he when he turns around his hat flies off. [.2] Okay? [2.] And then he bumps into a rock. [3.0 [1.6] A--nd.. u--m [.35]] falls down, and.. the.. pears all s--pray all over the place, [3.5? and [.25]] and then.. you see him fall down, and he gets up, and brushes himself off,.. and he goes.. you know {brushing gesture} [.6] and then you see three other boys about his age. He's like maybe.. what, ten or something?.. Twelve? I don't know. [1.85 [.65] A--nd] and you look at them, and and they see him, and they come up, [1.35 [.95] a--nd] without saying anything, there's no speech in the whole movie. [.6] Without saying anything, [.6] they.. u--m.. help him.. put the pears back in the basket. Only they don't wipe them off first. Just pick them up,.. and pour them in. [.35] And they-- help him get his bike u--p, and one kid takes the rock that he tripped on and he throws it off to the side of the roa--d, [1.0? and [.75]] and they set him upright,.. and they.. and then he.. you know they I don't they don't say thank you, he just [.25] splits. [.6] And then.. they walk.. the three boys walk down the road and they see--.. the kid's hat. [.35] And so one of them whistles. [.3] And the kid on the bike turns around, [.35] and then he brings his hat to him, [.5] and the g guy on the bike [.2] gives [.5] the other kids [.5] gives the kid that returns his hat.. three pears to share with his buddies. [1.35 [.75] So-- [.25] and then he splits. [.35] With his hat, with his pears, everything. [4.2[.8] A--nd um [2.4]] I just remembered another detail. [.35] Before he meets the girl? [.1] One of the pears,.. it's a bumpy road little dirt road, one of the pears.. flies out. [.3] Whatever. [3.85 [.2] A--nd u--m [2.8]] then you don't see the kid with the bike with the pears anymore. And the three kids that are walking, one of them has a.. what do you call those little [1.15? um [.85]] paddleball? You know, with a ball on ay uh /??/?.. chong chong chong chong. [.6] So they're walking along, and they brush off their pears, and they start eating it. [.35] Then they walk by-- [.35] the man who was picking the pears. [.55] Who looks like a Mexican-American if that's important? [2.4 [.6] U--m [.25]] and he's ge he's getting down out of the tree, and fucking with the ladder. [1.65 [.7] A--nd [.45]] he sees.. and and there's one [.25] full basket of pears there, and and an empty basket. [.4] And the other full basket is gone. [.65] And he goes.. {counting gesture} [2.7] And he sees the kids walking by and eating their pears. .. And he and he looks after them, and they disappear, [.6] and that's the end of the movie. [.85] And there's no [.55] no language,.. used,.. throughout the whole thing.

Speaker 2

All right, well--, the first scene is about [.9] there's a man up in the tree. It's a pear tree.. and u--h it shows him.. he's [.35] picking the pears. [1.1 [.7] A--nd] he's not really.. doesn't seem to be paying all that much attention [.55? because [.45]] you know the pears fall, and.. he doesn't really notice, [1.6? and [.5]] anyway, he comes down with a load of pears, and he [.25] puts them into the basket, [.6] and then he's . . going back up into the tree, it's like he's . . been doing this all day, and . . it's just a monotonous kind of thing for him. [.75] And a man comes along with a goat, [.7] and the goat obviously is interested in the pears. . . But the man just . . walks by with the goat. And the man up in the tree doesn't even notice. [.25] So he's not really paying attention to . . you know just kind of [.75] picking the pears, and is doing his thing. [2.6 [.6] And uh [.35] then, [.4] he's up in the tree, and y you see [.65? that [.45]] that within his [.75] view you know from his viewpoint, [.55] he c he could possibly see this little boy coming on a bicycle. [.5] At least . . it seems to me that . . you know he would notice this boy if he was really [.3] interested, but he's not thinking about his . . vision is very much you know . . kind of . . {gestures tunnel vision} he's very bored. [1.25 [.85] A--nd] this little boy--, [1.2] the scene [.3] focuses on this little boy, . . going along--, [.4] obviously, [.9] well, [.4] you know he, [.95] because of the goat, [.4] your idea is on the pears. And you think "Wow, this little boy's probably going to come and see the pears, [.4? and [.3]] he's going to take a pear or two, and then . . go on his way." [1.3 [.75] U--m] but the little boy comes, [1.8? . . a--nd u--h [1.0]] he doesn't want just a pear, he wants a whole basket. [.55] So he puts the-- [.2] bicycle down, and he [.25] you wonder how he's going to take it with this. [.4] He just has this [1.0] I don't know, I wonder how the hell he's going carry this basket. [.3] But okay. . . He manages. He takes the pears, [.7] and he . . puts it on the bicycle, and the man up in the tree doesn't even [.5] doesn't notice anything. He didn't hear the little boy, he didn't /right/. [1.05] So then the little boy goes off on his way, . . and you think "Aha. [2.05 [.5] uh [.85]] Are we gonna go back to the man over there" but no. [.3] You never [.85] The man's just still picking his pears, and the little boy's going along, [1.95 [.55] and um [.6]] then you see this little girl. [.55] Coming on a bicycle in the opposite direction, [2.15 [.75 a--nd u--h [.75]] you wonder how she's going to figure in on this. [3.05 [.75] A--nd u--h [1.4]] they come, you see the scene's like this, and you see them both coming coming and you think "ū." You know "Are they going to collide, what's going to happen," [1.05 [.55] and uh] it turns out she [.7] from what I could understand she grabbed his hat. [.5] All right, and then he . . crashes into a rock. [1.4 [.75] And uh . .] pears go out all over the place. [2.1 [.65] And then u--m [.5]] he's [.75] fixing himself up, [.6 and [.6]] then all of a sudden you see these three little boys who're [.4] saw this whole thing. [.7] And they come down, and then [1.15] I don't know, I thought [.15] here was this little boy just stole the pears and these other little boys come and they're helping him, and they're very helpful, [.5] and they [.95] put all the pears in the basket, [2.3 [.55] a--nd u--m [.75]] you know this little . . other little boy just has to go on. . . He's kind of crushed, and I don't know [.55] you know [.4] I think his ego was hurt. {laugh} You know really [.35] bruised all over. [.6] And the other little boys, one boy has a little . . bat, [.35] and a ball, [.3] and they're just [.8] they're kind of just [.75] I guess they're just enjoying the afternoon and they go walking off, . . and they see his hat, [.35] and they [.7] bring the hat back, [.95+ [.25] and u--m [.7]] I find the little boy, . . who had the stole the pears, [2.55 [.65] u--m [1.2] I thought "Why didn't he think of it before." But he finally gives these . . three boys, . . each a pear. [2.95 [1.2] A--nd u--h [.95]] then you know "Aha. It's all beginning to come together now." [.75] You just know that those little boys are going to go back, [.35] to where the pear tree was, and you just know that old man's going to see [.45] these little boys coming and say "Ha. . . You're the ones who stole the pears." [1.9] [.7] But u--h [.35]] still. . . /It/ comes back to the old man, [.3] up in the pear tree, he's still picking the pears. He doesn't . . he doesn't even notice that the pears are stolen yet. [1.25] And then he comes down from the [.4] from the tree, [.35] the little boys start /walk/ [.95] walking down, [2.95 [.75] and u--h [1.3]] suddenly you see [.85] he begins to notice that . . something's not right. [.9] And he's going {gestures counting} /and/ he's counting them, [.15] and he's [.6] really slow you know. [1.35 [.75] Anyway, [.15]] so then finally he figured out . . something [.35] you know somebody's stolen the pears. [.6] And the little boys [.5] come walking down and they're all eating their pears, . . and they just walk by. They both [.65] little boys don't even say anything to the old man or anything. [2.0 [.45] A--nd u--m [.75]] but the old man, [.15] you don't know quite what he's thinking. Either, [.95] first thing I thought was [.75] that they they're the ones that stole the pears. [.45] Or,

[.6] "Hm. Whoever stole the pears is down there. And he's passing the pears around." ẽ? [1.15] So he's standing there kind of scratching his head, and the little boys just walk off. [.3] That's it.

Speaker 3

Okay, [2.05 . . u--h [1.1]] the movie is basically about uh [.2] u--m [.85] a number of [.45] individuals, [.6] uh a guy who's picking pears, [2.1 [1.0] u--m [.6]] and a kid on a bicycle. Basically those are the two . . protagonists in this. [2.8 [1.05] And . . um [.6]] the guy who is picking pears, [3.15 um [2.35] um [.35]] picks the pears and puts them in a [.45] in um [.4] these baskets that he has. [1.6 [.9] U--h . .] and he's picking the pears, [1.0? and [.45] and um . .] along comes a man with a donkey. Uh uh a don uh a goat. [.45] And he comes along . . by . . you know, [.4] passes him. [.4] And then this kid comes along with a bicycle. [.55] And he rips off . . one of the [1.0] baskets of . . of pears that he has. [.8] So the ki the the um . . the boy goes along, and he has [1.4 . . um [.8]] he's riding his bicycle, a--nd he looks at . . a girl, that was coming the other way, riding a bicycle, [.9 [.7] uh] he loses his hat, a--nd . . there's a stone in the way, so his bicycle falls over, . . and the pears get [3.5 [1.65] um [.85] um [.4]] fall down on the ground. [.75 [. . U--m [.5]] there's some kids, there are three other boys, . . who are there. [.35] They help him, . . get straightened out, . . put the pears back, [.55] in the basket, straighten out his bicycle, and so forth. [.85] And he goes on his merry way. [1.25? . . But then . . um [.35]] the boys realize that he's forgotten his hat. [.55] So one of the boys whistles to him, [.45+ and [.45]] stops him, [.2+ and [.2]] gives him his hat back. [3.55 [1.5] And then . . um [1.1]] the boy with the pears . . gives [.55] the boy who just gave him his hat [1.85 [.7] um [.75]] three pears to . . divide among his friends. [1.9? [1.0] And . . then . .] the boys go . . um . . walking along, eating their pears. [2.9 [1.1] And um [1.0]] then the man [.25] uh . . who was picking pears, [.6] comes down from his-- [2.45 [.35] um [1.65]] his . . ladder, [.65] where he's been picking these pears, [.5] and he's goes to empty out the ones that he's just picked. [.6] And he notices that [.35] instead of the three baskets that he had before, [.4] there are only two. [.8] And . . so . . he's puzzled, [.45] and . . just when he realizes that [.45] one basket is . . gone, [.45] the three boys come along, [.8] eating their pears. [.75 And [.65]] you're left with this . . dilemma, [.4] what does this guy {laugh} you know what does this guy really think. I guess he thinks that [.95] "I wonder if those guys ripped off with my pears or what." He just doesn't know. [.35] He was up in the tree when . . the boy on the bicycle ripped off the uh / ?s / . . the pears. Okay?

Speaker 4

Okay. The movie seemed very [.25] sound oriented. [.4] Even though there weren't [.6] there was no dialogue. [3.15 [1.5] A--nd [1.3]] the first [.75] thing I noticed . . was . . the sound of the man picking . . pears. [.8] And of course there was a [.7] a man there standing on a ladder in a pear tree, [.75] and it was very visual. . . . But you k . . you kind of noticed the sounds more . . than [.6] what you're seeing. [.55] And then he dropped a pear, and I heard it drop, [1.4 [.55 {laugh}] . . . a--nd [.35]] he walked down the ladder, and he emptied pears into baskets. And I heard the pears [.35] being emptied into the baskets. [.7] And when he walked back up I heard [1.3] the ladder creak, as he stepped on . . each rung, [1.55 [.65] and [.7]] before the film started, . . see there's a rooster crowing. [1.6 [.55] So [.6]] immediately I felt that it was going to be sort of [2.35] a film oriented towards hearing . . rather than a visually oriented film. [1.05] And later on, [.25] as he was picking pears a man came along with a goat, [1.85 [.9] and [.5]] the goat was bahying or whatever goats do, [2.1? {laugh} . . .] What do goats do. [.4+ {laugh} [.4]] / Baeing hmm / . . Bae. [2.95 {laugh} [.5] A--nd [.65] then . .] I heard the [.5] bell on the goat's neck, [1.35 [.95] a--nd . .] someone [.4] let's see. [.3] Someone came by on a bicycle. [.7] You could hear the bicycle, . . wheels going round. [3.3 [1.25] A--nd [1.45]] someone stopped, and picked up . . a basket of pears that the man had picked and while he wasn't looking, [.7] took the whole basket away on his bicycle. [.75] So he's going down the road, he approached a girl on a bicycle. And looked up at the girl and his bike got caught on the rock. [1.45 [.95] And [.6] he fell over, and all the pears.. spilled.. all over. [.4] Three boys came out, [.75] helped him pick himself up, [.55] pick up his bike, pick up the pears, [.55] one of them had [.6] a toy, which was like a clapper. [2.4 [1.1] A--nd [1.1]] I don't know what you call it except a paddle with a ball suspended on a string. [.25 {breath}] So you could hear him playing with that. [2.25 [.8] A--nd [.95]] then he rode off, but he forgot his hat. [1.7 [.55] So [.75]] one of the boys whistled to him, [1.85 [1.05] and then, [.4]] he went and gave him the hat, [.2] and in return, [.8] the boy that lost the hat, [.4] gave his friend, [.55] the boy,.. three pears,.. to give back to his friends, [.9] and they went off,.. eating the pears, [.15] and they walked by the p [.8] the pear tree,.. the man was picking pears... And he looked down,.. saw that [1.05] he was missing a basket... And he looked at the boys walking off, eating the pears, [1.6 [.6] and [.7]] I think it ends there {laugh}.

Speaker 5

Okay, well, [.3] it starts out [1.2] it's [1.4] the setting looks like it's a place [.4] maybe-- [.4] in California, the Santa Barbara area,.. or something like that. [.65 [.2 U--h]] there was [.35] this orchard surrounding him. [.15] I guess what he's picking is pears. [.15] There's a .. uh [.4] farm laborer, a Mexican farm laborer picking pears and he has three baskets,.. filled with [.8] and he's filling them with pears. [2.65 And [1.15] um [1.0]] in the course of him picking, [.2] a man goes by with a [2.4] tsk goat, [.75] and that's the last you see of him, [2.45 [1.0] and then [.85]] this [.7] little boy [1.5] is riding by on his bicycle. And he sees .. the pears, so he stops to take a pear, [.85] then he decides [.5] since .. the .. farm laborer .. isn't watching, to take the whole bushel. So he takes the bushel, puts it on his bike, and starts to ride away. [1.45 [.75] And [.25]] on his way,.. riding, he comes across another [.3] bicyclist, [.25] bicyclist, it's a young woman, [2.2 [.5] and [1.15]] for some reason she catches his attention, and he's [.4] turning his head,.. behind him, looking at her, [.35? and [.2]] there's a rock in the r road, and he [.25] hits it with his bike,.. and falls. [2.55 [.8] A--nd then [.7]] his um [1.15] pears go all over the road. [1.15] And then there's these three little boys, who are walking, [.45] they're around [.65] they're little boys. [.65] They're [.7] from nine to twelve years old. [.2] /And that [.2] the little boy is like approx about ten years old/. And they see, [.7] him on the ground, with all these [.5] pears strewn out all over the road,.. and so they decide [.8 [.65] /like/ ..] there's no spoken .. communication at all... Going on... Throughout the whole movie, and they just [.6] pick up his basket. [.5+ [.5] A--nd] no word is exchanged. [.35] It's really kind of neat. [1.05 [.6] And then [.15]] they start walking away, [.3] and they .. get him all set up on his bike, [.3+ and then [.3]] start walking away, and the .. they find his hat, [.5] on the road, and then w .. one of them comes back, [1.2] and this one's .. playing with one of those [1.6] those wooden things that you hit with a ball. [1.1] And he [.15] he comes back, and gives him his hat, and so he gives him [.6] s--ome [.9] pears, [.8] and so they walk off,.. eating th/e/se pears. [.65] And then they pass by where the farm laborer is, and .. while this is going on, the farm laborer realizes that a whole basket's missing. [.9] And he's wondering where it is and he sees these three boys approaching, and they're eating pears, [1.2+ [1.2] a--nd] they walk off,.. into the distance, and he's sitting there, [.35] with a puzzled look on his face. [1.8] That's it {laugh}.

Speaker 6

Okay. We--ll, [3.1 [.75] let me see. [1.5]] It opens with [.9? u--m [.4]] I guess a farm worker, [1.2] picking pears, [.75] in a tree. [4.35 [1.0] A--nd u--m [2.6]] you see him taking .. picking the pears off the leaves, and putting them in a .. white apron, [.5] and he walks down the [.75] ladder, and dumps the pears into a basket. [3.2 [1.2] U--m [1.2] tsk] then you see him going back up in the tree. [6.4 [.75] and [.9] u--m [1.2] let me see. [.8]] In the ba .. and .. you see a guy leading a goat,.. past the tree where he's picking the pears. [3.55 [.95] Then u--m [1.5]] a little boy on a bicycle, [1.15] comes riding past the tree, [1.45 [.75] a--nd [.2]] sort of goes past the pears [.3] the

[.2] pears in the baskets and then stops [1.0] and looks up at the guy in the tree, he's still on the ladder, and he's not .. watching him, so he [1.0] st .. puts his bike [.6] down, [.85] he walks over, a--nd he picks up a [.2] the whole basket of pears, [.9] and puts it on the handle [.2] no, on the [.4] front [.15] fender of his bike. [.6] And holds on to it. [1.1? [45] And / ?? / ..] as he's holding on to the handlebars he t takes off with them. [6.35 [1.1] U--m [.7] then [.4] u--h [2.1]] a .. girl on a bicycle, [1.15] comes riding towards him, .. in the opposite direction. [.9] And as they pass, [.45] he sort of turns, and looks at her, [.6] and his hat flies off, [2.1 [.2] a--nd [1.2]] his [.3] bicycle hits a rock... Because he's looking at the girl. [.75] Falls over, [1.5 [1.35] uh] there's no conversation in this movie. [.6] There's sounds, you know, like the birds and stuff, but there .. the humans beings in it don't say anything. [1.0] He falls over, and then these three other little kids about his same age come walking by. [3.05 [.6] And .. um [1.3]] I don't know, I guess they've been playing or something, the guy has a paddle with a ball attached to this [.5] with a string that kind / of you know/. [.7+ [.7] A--nd] they see that he's [.8] fallen off his bike, [.3] and his pears [1.4] have scattered, [2.25 [.45] a--nd uh [1.0]] they walk over to help him, [.6] they g [.25] gather all the pears and put them in the basket, [1.8 [.8] a--nd [.15]] one of the guys, helps him brush off the dust, [.9] and another guy picks up the rock, and he throws it out of the road, [.4+ and [.4]] he gets all situated again, and he .. takes off, [.15] and the [.5] boys [.4] keep walking in their direction, [2.15 [1.1] uh [.35]] then they .. they come across his hat on the road. [.5] And one of the guys picks it up, [1.2 [.15] and [.6]] whistles .. to the .. g .. boy on the bicycle to catch his attention. [.65] And he turns around, and he runs up [.1] to him, [.95] and gives him back his hat. [1.8 [.9] A--nd] the boy who's stolen the pears, [.4] gives .. three pears to the boy who gave him his hat. [3.2 [1.25 A--nd [1.25]] the boy [.15] walks back to his two companions, and he hands a pear to each of them. [1.6 [1.0] Um [.15]] and they start eating them. [.15] And then they walk past the [.35] the tree, [1.1] where the picker, .. was picking the pears, [3.05 [.9] a--nd u--h [.9]] he has already come down from the ladder, [.65] to deposit his [.4] more of the pears that he picked in the basket and then he notices that there are only two baskets instead of three. [.9] And he sort of [.75] / visually/ [.25] counts them with his fingers. [2.95 [.8] A--nd [1.6]] leans back up against the tree, [1.2] I guess, [.55] wondering .. what happened to [1.3] the missing basket. [1.9 [.8] A--nd [.5]] right at that moment the three boys come walking .. by, munching on the pears, [.5] that he had picked, [.9] and go walking, .. past him, and he just sort of looks at them. [2.9 [1.2] A--nd [.95] that's it {laugh}.

Speaker 7

I'll try. [2.15 [.5] U--m [.6] tsk [.2] well, [.25]] there was-- [.25] a man, [.2] who was picking pears, [2.0 [.55] a--nd [.9]] it was in a y uh [2.2 ... tsk ...] large open field, it wasn't a pear orchard, [.2] or anything like that. [4.45 [.9] A--nd [2.5]] I don't know. [.4] Something that I noticed about the / movie/ particularly unique was that the colors .. were [.35] just [.5] very strange. [.6 [.2] Like [.3]] the green was a [2.2] inordinately bright green, [.55] for the pears, [.4 .. and [.25]] these colors just seemed a little [.5] kind of bold, almost to the point of [1.15] being artificial. [2.25 [.6] tsk [.1] A--nd [.75]] he-- [.35] was going up and down the ladder, [1.1 [.9] tsk ..] picking the pears, [.8 [.25] and [.25]] depositing them in [.35] three baskets, [.7] that were down below. [3.85 [1.2 ... tsk ...] A--nd [1.95]] there's .. one .. sequence right there [1.15+ that [1.15]] that I've forgotten. [2.5 ... tsk ...] Oh. [.3] A .. man with a goat [.9] tsk comes by, [1.5 [.75] a--nd [.15]] you can kind of hear the goat mewing in the background, [.15] and they get up, [.2] and approach, [.2] and just kind of walk off. They don't really seem to have too much to do, [.6] with .. what's going .. on. [1.55 [.3] A--nd [.7]] the man goes back up into the tree, [.3] to pick some more pears. [1.9 ... tsk ...] Along comes-- .. a young boy, .. about seven years old, [.2] eight years old, [.6] on a bicycle that's way too big for him, and he's riding it through this great open field. [1.4 [.85] A--nd [.15]] he [.35] sees this three pear [.2] these three baskets of pears, and then sees this man up in the [.5] tree, and decides [.45] that he'd like some pears. And at first looks like he's going to take one or two. [.6] Then decides that he'd [.15] much rather take a whole basket, [.55] puts the basket on the bike, [1.45? [.9] tsk a--nd . .] kind of struggle /??/ cause it's much too big for him. And the bike is much too big for him. [.8+ [.8] A--nd . .] gets on the bike, [.2+ and [.2]] rides off. [2.7 [1.85 . . . tsk . . .] Then-- [.2]] he's riding . . across this . . great [.25] expanse, [1.15+ and [1.15]] a girl comes, [.4] riding a bike in the opposite direction, [1.35 [.55] and [.4]] you can see them riding [.65] towards each other, and you wonder if there's going to be a collision. [.85? [.7] But . .] instead they just . . . kind of . . brush . . by each other and she knocks the hat that he's wearing off on the ground, [3.75 [1.4 . . . tsk . . .] a--nd [1.7]] he's . . um [.35] kind of looking back [.2] at her . . and the hat, [.2] and doesn't see that he's going to run into a rock, . . which he does, [.25] and the pears all [.45] spill on the ground, and he falls down and he skins his knee or something. [1.85 [.4 . . . tsk . . .] A--nd [1.1]] and then you hear this-- [.7] kind of rhythmic . . thud/ding/ [.35] sound, [1.4 [.55] a--nd [.4]] and you look up, [.3] or the boy looks up. [1.95 [1.1] tsk . . A--nd [.45]] there are three [.15] other boys standing there one of them has a paddleball, [.4] type thing which was /???/ sound, [2.1? [1.8] a--nd] they look [.25] kind of ominous at first, . . like they might [.5] steal his pears and run off or something but instead they [.15] help him [.45] pick up all the pears, [.6] one boy goes over and helps him brush-- [.75] his pants off, [1.3? /and then [.5]] then/ another one [.35] /I don't know/ picks up the bicycle I think, [.15] or they just all put the pears back in the basket, [.2] they set the basket back on the bike, [.3+ and [.3]] and /they g/ [1.25] they go on their way walking down the road /and/ he rides . . off. [1.05 [.7] A--nd] they come across his hat, . . that he neglected [.55] to pick up he forgot the hat. [1.2] So one of them whistles . . to him, [.5] he was saying, [.15] "Hey you forgot your hat," [.65? and [.5]] he stops, [.3+ and [.3]] one of the . . three boys brings the hat back, [2.4 [.9 . . . tsk . . .] a--nd [.85]] he gives th [.4] that boy three pears. [1.3 [.65] tsk Fo--r [.2]] you know kind of as a gesture of thanks. [.7 [.35] tsk [.15]] He rides off. [1.15 [.6] A--nd] the boys keep walking back [.3] the way the first boy came. [1.35+ [1.35] Meanwhile . .] the man who's picking pears, [.35] comes down from the tree, [.35] and starts emptying [.5] his . . um [.95] load of pears into [.8] one of the two /remaining/ baskets, [.75] he notices that the third basket is gone. [1.9 [1.1] A--nd [.3]] the [.6] /at/ . . just about this time, he's just kind of looking a little [.55] /um/ [.55] kind of visibly a little upset. [2.15 [1.3 . . . tsk . . .] A--nd [.35]] these three boys [.9] go walking by, and they each have a pear in their hands, so he's . . kind of looking at them, trying to make a connection wondering [.35] how they got the pears, . . and . . if they were his pears, . . /you see/ how this is just all what [.6] what you're projecting on the man. [2.3 [1.1] And [.75]] I think that was it. [.75] /It was neat/.

Speaker 8

Okay, [.3+ u--h [.3]] there's a-- . . man, [.45] picking pears, in a pear tree, out . . somewhere in the country, [1.1+ [1.1] u--h] he looks [.95] like your uh [.2] typical . . farmer, [.3+ or [.3]] whatever, kind of plump, [.95 and [.7]] moustache, and he wears a white apron, [1.55 [1.3] to . .] hold the pears in. [.6 [.1] A--nd] he [1.0] fills his-- . . thing with pears, and comes down, and there's a . . basket he puts them in. [.65 [.2] A--nd] you see-- [1.25] passersbyers on bicycles and stuff go by. [2.2 [1.15] A--nd [.1]] then a boy comes by, [.1] on a bicycle, the man is in the tree, [.9] and the boy gets off the bicycle, and . . looks at the man, [1.5? and then [.9] uh] looks at the bushels, and he . . starts to just take a few, and then he decides to take the whole bushel. [.9] And he puts it on his [.35] b--icycle rack in front, [.4] and /he/ rides off, [1.75 [.95] a--nd [.2]] passes um . . a girl, [1.25] like this on the road, [.7 [.1] a--nd] his hat falls off, and he turns, and he runs into a rock, [1.0 [.5] a--nd] he falls, the bicycle . . and all the [.75] pears fall out, [2.6 [.15] a--nd [1.3]] some boys-- come out, . . and they're s standing around, help him pick it up. [2.5 [1.7] As--] [1.15] then he--'s . . about to forg [.65] forget his [.15] u--h [.5] hat, [1.05 and [.65]] boy walks back, gives him his hat, [.25] he gives the boy some pears, and they go off, [.65] eating the pears, [.3] and they walk by, [.95] the ma--n [1.15 [.8] tsk [.15]] who--'s [1.8 u--h [1.3]] well he's . . befo . . he comes down the tree first, [.3] and /you see he notices that the bushel's missing, and counts them, [.3] can't figure out what's happening, and then he sees the three . . boys, [.75] walking by, eating pears, [.4] and he still can't [1.0] figure it out, and that's where the movie [1.1] ends {laugh}.

Speaker 9

Okay. [4.4 [.8 {sniff} [2.5] {throat clearing} [1.55] tsk [.35] There's [.65] a farmer, [.15] he looks like ay uh . . Chicano American, [.5] he is picking pears. [4.85 [.25] A--nd u--m [3.35]] he's just picking them, he comes off of the ladder, [.35+ [.35] a--nd] he-- u--h [.3] puts his pears into the basket. [1.0 [.5] U--h] a number of people are going by, [.35+ and [.35]] one . . is [1.15 . . um] / you know/ I don't know, I can't remember the first thing that . . the first person that goes by. [.3] Oh. . . a l u--m . . a man with a goat [.2] comes by. [.25] It see it seems to be a busy place. [.1] You know, fairly busy, it's out in the country, [.4] maybe in u--m [.8] u--h the valley or something. [2.95 [.9] A--nd um [.25] {throat clearing} [.35]] he goes up the ladder, and picks some more pears. . . And he's up there picking, [.4] and a little boy comes on his bicycle. [1.35 [.95] A--nd] he sees . . u--m . . that there are baskets of pears there. [1.1] T so he gets an idea that maybe he'll get off his bicycle, and get one. [.4] And he gets off his bicycle, [2.45 [.6] a--nd u--h [.6]] he he takes one, and then he says "well wait a minute." Well, he says it to himself. There's no language in it. [1.15 [.55 U--h [.15]] he says u--h "/ Well/ maybe I'll take the whole basket." So he [.4] picks up the basket, . . and makes sure [.3] that the-- . . farmer isn't looking at him, [4.3? [.6] a--nd u--m [1.3] tsk [.8] u--h] takes it over to his bicycle, and gets on his bicycle and I don't know how he does it, but he puts the . . the big basket of pears on his bicycle, and when he drives off, [.5] / the/ farmer doesn't know anything about it. [.8] So the little boy the [.25] story . . focuses on the little boy now. [.55] And he's driving along the road, [.2+ [.2] {throat clearing} . .] a--nd he comes up [.8 [.1] u--h [.2]] oh. There's another girl, [.35] driving on a bicycle, about his age, [.25] on the road, [1.2 [.7] a--nd u--h] they come across, and they [.25] you know go like that {possible gesture}, and he . . sort of [.2] takes a second look at her, [.5] and he bumps into a rock, [.65] [.4] and . . has a little accident. [3.4 [1.0] tsk A--nd u--m [1.2]] the pears fall all over, okay. [.5 [.2] Meanwhile] , there are three little boys, [.15] up on the road a little bit, and they see this little accident. [1.6 [.55] A--nd u--h] they come over, and they help him, [.4? and [.2]] you know, help him pick up the pears and everything. [2.7 [1.0] A--nd [1.15]] / the/ one thing that struck me about the-- [.3] three little boys that were there, is that one had ay uh [.4] I don't know what you call them, but it's a paddle, and a ball--, [.2] is attached to the paddle, and you know you bounce it? . . And that sound was really prominent. [4.55 Well anyway, [.45] | so-- u--m [.1] {throat clearing} [.45] tsk [1.15]] all the pears are picked up, and . . he's on his way again, but his hat fe . . is u--h [.55] is on the [.2] okay, wait a minute. [1.05] The boy who has the pears', [.3] hat, . . is way back on the road, so when the . . boys are the-- . . three boys . . are walking down the road, [.25] after they've helped him, and . . the other one's on his way, [.7] one of them . . whistles back to the guy on the bicycle, "Here's you hat," [.35] Or he [.4] I don't know, and he goes and takes it, . . and the little boy gives him three pears . . sort of to thank [.7] the three boys for helping him. [2.25 [1.7] A--nd u--h] then he goes off, . . and that's the end of that story, but then . . it goes back to the farmer. [.6] Finally he comes down from his tree, [2.4 [1.2] a--nd u--h [.3]] he looks at the baskets, and there's one missing, and he counts them, [2.15 [.85] a--nd u--h [.4]] he doesn't know what's happened at all. [.8] And the . . three boys who-- . . helped the other one on the bicycle, . . comes up uh . . come up [.3] to near where the farmer is, and they're eating pears. [.6] And the farmer sort of looks at them like "Hmmm, how did they get those pears {laugh during 'pears'}." [.35] And that's the end of the . . story.

Speaker 10

Okay. [2.5 [.8] U--h [.3]] there's no [.25] to begin with, there's no [.65] spoken [.5] speech [.4] in it. The most that you hear like [.45] you hear noises, [.35] in the background. [.2] Somebody will whistle, [1.1 [.5] o--r [.2]] noises of like a bicycle kind of thing, but there's no spoken [1.85] language kind of communication. [.65] And it opens up . . probably about around noon, [.65] sunny day, [1.0] in uh [.15] it would be difficult [.6] to get some idea of the country, I would be hard to say that [.3] it opens up in a country scene. . . In a [.55] setting [.2] outside of the city and all, [.5] dirt roads, [1.3 [.6] u--m [.25]] there's a ma--n . . who appears to be . . you would . . might guess of like . . some sort of [.65] Spanish or Mexican [.35] descent, [.95] who is um [.4] picking pears. [.55] They seemed pretty [.2] green. I don't know what [.45] I wasn't sure at first if they were apples, or if they were pears, [1.3 [.15] but [.7] um . .] he's picking pears, [.95] at a fairly lei--surely pace. [.25] There's nothing [.45] doesn't seem to be very . . hurried. [.45] In the movie. It's fairly [.5] slow, [.65] he's picking the pears, [4.15 [.85] u--m [2.8]] he has an apron that he puts them in, and then he'll . . he'll stuff them in that, and then he'll walk down the ladder, a--nd put them in a couple of [.25] barrels, that he's got down there. [1.45] {creaky onset} As he's doing this-- [.95 uh [.5]] somebody comes by with a [.65] walks by with a goat or something . . . Kind of thing, just meandering by. . . And there doesn't seem there's no communication between the two of them, [.85] or anything, [1.4 [1.0] and the--n] [1.9 um [1.5]] just . . how . . I mean how picky do you want. Like he [.45] he um [1.5] drops . . he does a thing and he comes down to [.9] he drops a pear, when he's picking it, [.65] up in the tree, and he comes back down, [1.1? [.7] a--nd] he's putting the rest of the pears away, and he picks this pear up, and polishes it up, and everything else. [.95] Then he goes back up, and he--'s [1.05] continues to pick . . the pears . . at a very leisurely pace. [1.75 [1.15] The--n uh. .] after the [.6] person . . leading the goat has gone by, [.3] a boy probably about [.8] I don't know, . . eight or nine, [.5] comes up on a bicycle. [.75] He's going by on a bicycle, on this dirt road, [.5] and stops and looks at the pears, and apparently decides "Aha. It would be nice to have [.4] one of the pears." [.6] But he just doesn't [.3] just take . . one of them. He stops, [.35] they he had like wicker baskets, about this tall. [.65] And this is something that I don't know you might notice when you see or not, [.9+ but [.9]] I would have sworn almost that there were two baskets at the foot of the [.65] the tree. [.85] When the kid came by. [.35] And I don't know if thi--s [.6] really is important, that [.75] I'm not sure if I noticed it. [.2] And I'm [.2] not sure that's the way it was, [.75+ but [.75]] it appears that he had been [.2] putting things into two baskets. [2.05 [1.55] Well if [.3]] the boy comes by, [.35] and the man is still up in the tree, [4.2 [.8] and uh [2.8]]] he picks up, [.3] one of th [.65] the con . . the full baskets, and put it on the front of his bicycle, [1.0 [.75] and . .] heads down the road. [1.4] All sort of on the sly. The man doesn't know that any of this has been done. [.3] So he heads down this dirt road, [.35] on the bicycle, [.65] and there's just this scene where he's coming this way, . . on this dirt road, and there's hills in the background, it's like [.7] it might . . almost look [.3] sort of like southern California. [.25] Inland. [.75] Sort of thing. Not [.45] obviously not desert, . . but . . sort of that [.25] kind of a [.2] of an area. [1.45] And he's heading . . you see a scene where he's . . coming on his bicycle this way, [.5] and there's a girl coming on a bicycle, [.2] this way. [.75] And then also, [.5] you see somebody walking on a hillside. [.2] Back behind them. [.5] But he's [.2] coming on a bicycle, and they . . they cro . . they pass, [.5] and apparently he [.9] I think by the breeze, . . his hat sort of gets [.7] blown off his head so he sort of turns around, [.2] to look at it, [.45] and runs into a rock, [.8 . . and [.6]] crashes over. [.95] And all the . . pears a--nd the basket and everything goes [.7] goes uh [.35] flying. [.4] Or all spills all over the ground. [1.55 [1.2] A--nd] so he sort of gets up, and he's [.7] checks his leg to make sure [.6] to see if he's got any [.25] bruises or anything. [1.5 [.5] A--nd uh [.6]] three boys, probably about the same age, [.85] {creaky onset} are walking by, [2.15 [1.35] and uh [.3]] I don't /know/, . . for some reason I remember one had a blue shirt on, one had a red shirt on, /and/ one had a yellow shirt on. [2.8 [1.8] A--nd [.55]] one of . . they were probably [.3] the two /there/ were [.3] see . . two that seemed about . . to /be/ about his age, and one maybe a little bit younger or something. [.55] And they come by, and see what's [.45] what's happened. . . And the /n/ one of them is . . playing like with [.4] I don't remember, I used to play with /it/ when I was a kid, [.9 but [.75]] it's like a . . wooden paddle [.6 [.3] that [.15]] there's an elastic string attached to and there's a ball, [.3] you know that that kind of thing that you [.4] you [.15] I . . don't remember the name of them [.35] but I played /with them/ for hours. [1.0 [.6] U--m . .] and he's . . paddling, [.55] playing around with this. [.55] So they see what's happened, so one of them [.5] one of the . . the people picks the kid up, [.5] and sort of dusts him off, . . and another one picks up the bicycle, and another one [.45] loads the pears, [.7] back on [.15] into three [.45] the wicker basket, [.7] a--nd puts it on the [.35] the bicycle, [.8? and [.25] and . .] no [.3] communication or anything. [.4]

During the time, [.95] and so the kid head [.95] the kid with the bike, . . heads off down this way. [.85] And the thee / oth/ . . the three [.25] kids head back down, [.35] the way they were going. [.55] And the one kid is still hitting . . playing with the [.35] the thing. [.35] And they run across his hat that's been [.4] that was blown off. [.8] And one kid, I think it was the kid who was playing with thee uh [1.7] with . . the whatever it was, [.9] stops and picks it up and whistles. [.5] And the kid turns around, and he goes and takes the hat to the kid, [2.2 [.85] a--nd um [.65]] the kid gives him three pears. [1.6 [1.25] A--nd] so the . . the other kid comes back to his two friends and gives them each a pear, and then they [.4] continue to meander on down the road. [1.75 [.85] And so [.3]] about this time, . . well the next scene you see, it's switched to the man who's been picking [.3] the pears. [.85] And he has come down, [.4] and then this is the thing that I'm not sure if this happened or not [.4] or it's just [1.2] but I thought that he had had two baskets. [1.05] And then that the kid had come and taken one. [.5] I'm not sure. You might want to look when you see the film. [.4] But anyway, when he comes back down the tree, there are two baskets there, [1.45] you know and I don't know-- [.15] /like I say/ I don't know if I [1.6] saw that wrong, [.3+ or [.3] or what. [.6] It doesn't matter, to the story, but it's just one of those things. [1.2] And he comes down and notices that one of them's full and the other one is empty. [1.4] Which also doesn't really make much sense. [2.15] Because the kid took a basket, he didn't just take . . the [1.25] the pears. [1.0] Then when he comes back down and he notices this, and he's standing there scra--tching his head sort of like wondering what [.55] what's gone wrong, or where [.25] obviously he's missing some pears somewhere. [.95] And about this time, the three kids that are munching on the pears, [1.45] sort of meander by--, right in form of him, and he's sort of [.3] jus--t [.55] kind of puzzled, wondering how-- [.25] in the short space of time that the pears that were here, apparently, [.5] they're coming back at him now, [.3] being eaten by . . by three different kids. [.6] And so they just sort of meander in front of him, and he doesn't say anything, or doesn't do anything. [2.9 [1.1] Bu--t um [1.35]] that seems to be about it. [.9] It's ju--st um [.5] like I said, [.9] sort of a scrub . . kind of an area, with trees, and some fruit, [.7] fruit trees, [1.75] difficult to say [.3] what country, or [.5] ascribe some sort of nationality to it. [.95] Because the . . the kid . . a lot of the kids a couple of them were blonds. [1.0] I mean it's just . . it wasn't . . I didn't get a specific feeling like this is [1.8 [.95] u--m [.5]] this is Mexico, or this is [2.3 [1.2] u--m [.6] the southern part of the United States, or anything like that. [1.0] Clear weather, [1.0] nice day, [.95] kind of thing. [1.7] But, . . that's about it.

Speaker 11

[4.75? [4.25] Um [.15?]] it starts out . . there's uh [3.3 tsk . . .] well, [1.45] the– landscape is like u–h a f-- [2.35] sort of peasant landscape but it isn't really farmland, it's like an orchard. [.6] It's like a small orchard, [2.2 [.65] a--nd u--h [.55]] it's green. And there's this sort of [1.75] Latin . . looking . . middle-aged man . . who's [.95] um [.75] climbs up the ladder, [1.4] uh| that's leaning against a tree, . . and picks pears, [.95] puts them in . . his apron, [.4] climbs down the ladder, [.75] and empties the pears . . into [.55] big . . baskets. [1.15] There's like three baskets sitting there and he's already got two baskets full. . . He does this a couple of times. [7.05 [2.55] Um [4.05]] the thing I noticed all the way through is that . . there's [.5] there's no-- . . dialogue in the film, but there . . is [1.0] a lot of sound effects. [1.1] Which are not [.55] totally u--m [1.45] consistent. I mean . . sometimes they'll be really loud, [.35] Has anybody told you that before? Or r you're not supposed to tell me that. [1.2] Sometimes he'll put a pear down, it'll go blã. . . Really loud. Blã. . . And sometimes he'll put a pear down, and there won't be any noise at all. I don't know if [1.7] that's on purpose. [2.0 [1.2] U--m [.4]] and the [.8] the ladder creaks when he goes up and down it. [3.55 [.6] And then u--m [2.1]] you hear the sound of a . . sheep, . . neighing, / and/ you don't know what it is . . and then the camera goes to the side, and this man is pulling . . a goat / h/ . [.3] It's a goat. [.25] Pulling a goat, [1.6] on a rope. . . And he pulls the [.8] tsk goat by the guy who's up in the tree, [.9] and disappears. [4.35 [.9] A--nd [2.9]] the next people . . who come by, [.9] / and there's/ a little boy on a bicycle . . who comes by from the other direction, . . he's riding a bike, . . it's a little too big for him, [2.05 [1.15] a--nd [.4]] he rides by, . . and then he stops, [2.2] tries to . . take a pear, . . a--nd the he [.35] he can't reach it. . . So he puts down his bike, [.9] he sort of takes a pear, and then he decides he wants the whole basket. . . So he takes the whole basket, . . and puts it near his bike, . . lifts up the bike, . . puts the basket on . . the front part of his bicycle, [.5] /n/ rides off. And all this time the guy's up in the [.6] tree, . . and he doesn't notice it. [.9] However the sounds are extremely loud. [1.95 {cough} [1.3]] /So/ . . it's kind of funny. [6.1 . . And then [5.2] tsk so-- . .] then we switch to the boy riding on the bicycle, and he's riding down the gravel . . path. [3.3 [1.4] {clear throat} A--nd [1.0]] we see it, . . the gravel path, from his point of view, [.8] and then we see . . a girl riding a bike, coming the opposite direction. [.9] And then . . the camera's backed up and you see them going like this. . . And then you see it from his point of view again. [.5 . . And [.3]] his hat blows off, [.55] when they cross, [1.2 [.25] and [.65]] his bike hits into a rock, . . and he falls down, the bike falls down, and all the pears scatter. [3.3 [.95] So-- then [1.5]] /I guess/ the girl keeps going on, [.75 . . and [.6]] he-- . . um [.85] he's fallen down, . . and he sits up, . . and he [1.25] he wipes the . . dirt off of him, and /he/ sort of [1.1] {breath} holds onto his leg, . . which is hurt, [.55] and then the [.6] camera goes up, and you see three boys. [3.1 [1.05] A--nd u--h [1.15]] one of them . . is [2.15] tsk has this toy, . . which is like a ping pong paddle with a [.7] ball on an elastic string /?/ go like that, [1.6? [1.1] a--nd u--h . .] it's making [.45] loud noises inconsistently. [3.05 {laugh} [.8] A--nd u--m [1.3]] it wasn't a really funny film, . . it was just . . that . . that sound part/was really neat/. It was funny. [1.55] They u--h [3.35] they sort of come over, . . to the boy, and brush him off, [2.3+ [2.3] a--nd] walk away. He . . holds up his bike, and starts limping, [.75] down the road, . . carrying [.55] pushing his bike, and they find his hat, [1.25? [1.05] {breath}] and whistle to him. [.65] tsk one of the boys. And one of the boys runs back, . . with the hat, and puts it on his head, and the guy give [sic] him [1.45] three pears . . for each of his friends. [2.35] So the guy goes limping off with his bicycle, and the other boy comes back and gives the pears to his friends, . . and they go off. [.55] And on the way back, they pass [.9] the guy who was up in the tree, [.5] collecting pears, and he just comes . . he's just come down, [2.15+ [2.15] and . .] he discovers that there's one basket missing. [.85] And he sort of [.75] counts them, . . and realize [sic] that there's a . . basket missing. [1.75 [.75] A--nd [.45]] then he sees these three boys go by with pears in their hands. [.85] He's a little [.45] bewildered. . . And it ends.

Speaker 12

Certainly. [1.3 [.6] uh [.35]] The opening scene, . . was . . uh . . a--y [1.8] kind of middle-aged round, [1.0] possibly, he looked like he was made up [.25] to be [.2] a Mexican, [.7] or th [.95] that [.45] kind of person, [1.0] picking . . pears from the tree, and he had three baskets beneath the tree, there was w--one was full, one was half-way full, and one was empty, [.6] and he had a ladder up . . to the tree, and it was [.75] the rooster crowed in the beginning, so [.35] it didn't look like morning, [.45] and it looked like [.45] it was filmed in California, those dusty kind of hills that they have out here by Stockton and all, [.9+ [.9] so . .] it's very funny to make this [.35] telling. [3.15 [.9] A--nd u--h [1.25 . . . tsk]] he was picking pears. [1.45] Just rather slowly, and he did it [.55] /so that/ you could hear the sound of the pears being [.45] torn from the [.95] tree, and he put them in an apron /that he had/, [.85] /the whole idea/ he picked pears came down the ladder, [.5] put them [.2] one by one . . into this basket. [.85] He [1.1] y you got [.2] the feeling that he pretty much liked his pears, . . because he was so . . gentle with them /???/. [2.05 [.35] A--nd u--h [.9]] put them in /the/ basket. [1.5] Ay man with a goat, [1.05] was in the distance and walked by. [1.1 He-- [.55] the goat [1.5] just [.2] he was kind of pulling him. [.35] And the people looked very funny, because they [.8] were suppo--sed, [.95] to be-- [.4] far--mer--ish, [1.1] and really just had [.4] clothes like a person with like [.5] store levis, and [.9] a n--ew red bandana around his neck and a [.5] things like [.15] so a man with a goat [.35] went by, [1.2 . . . tsk . . .] and the goat [.25] balked, [.9+ a--nd [.9]] was [.35] pulled along by this [.35] w--one fellow who just disappeared. That was a--ll that you saw of the man with goat. [.85] Went up . . across . . the hill, the setting was ay [1.25] geographically there was a [.35] hill that kind of went down, the tree was [.6] halfway up the hill. [.7] The man with the goat went that way. [1.4 [.8] Then--, . .] a young boy, . . he went back up in the tree, and was [1.65] picking, . . I thought . . that the goat . . would eat the [.3] pears, as they went by. That's [.2] I don't know whether you're supposed to think that or not. [3.1 [.75] A--nd [.45] then [1.15 . . . tsk . . .]] he [.45] the goat [.25] and the goatman . . disappeared. [.55] A young boy on a bicycle, [.45] that was much too big for him, [1.35] rode [.45] thee . . from the [.2] direction in which the goat [.25] person had come, [.8] towards the man picking the [.75] the pearpicker [3.0 [1.45 . . . tsk . . .] a--nd [1.25]] stops. [1.3] Beside the baskets. [.5] While the man was upsta he had gone up the tree. [.35] The man is in the tree, and the boy [.45] parked his bicycle here, [3.55+ [1.25] a--nd [2.3]] got off the bicycle, [2.5] got off the bicycle, [.55 and [.4] furtively went and felt a pear. [2.05] To s while . . watching the man to see whether he was . . seeing [.45] whether the boy was stealing the pears but he wasn't he was just involved in [.55] picking . . more pears, [1.0] and he decided not just to take one, [.9 but [.7]] move the whole, ba full basket [.3] onto the front of th lifted up his bike, and then put the basket on the front of the bike. [.55] And made off with the whole pasket of pears. [1.3+ [1.3] tsk . .] Which the man, [2.5] the pearpicker . . man, did not notice. . . Because he was busy picking pears. [1.4] Came dow . . oh no, that didn't happen yet. [.8] So-- [.55] the sequence is funny . . if you don't really [.7] remember. [1.7 [1.1] U--h [.2]] he rode away, [.25] on his bicycle. [.2] And you see him riding away, . . and then . . into the screen . . comes [.55] just the girl--, [.4] riding [.55] on another bicycle, [.55] in an opposite direction, [.15] where they pass. [3.95 [1.0] A--nd [2.45]] he-- . . looks at her, [1.0 [.4] a--nd [.15]] is involved in looking at her riding his bicycle, [.3] bumps a rock, don't say yes, because you don't you've never seen that /??/. All right. Okay. [2.55 [1.1] Uh [1.0]] he rides /ba/ and looking at her, bumps into a rock. . . a large rock. [2.5] Upsetting his bicycle, upsetting the pears, [1.5] she rides past. [.65] That was all that . . you saw of her in the movie. [1.05] So he's . . the /baw/ the thief [.15] boy has . . taken . . the pears, and . . bumps [.4] up. [.9] So instantly, . . the film . . flashes to [2.0 [1.45] u--h [.1]] there are three little boys. [.95] Also about the same age not really necessarily, one real little, one [.55] medium sized, and one about [.25] my height five two? [.7] Young boys. [.2] Ten, eleven years old. [1.35] And they . . help. They see that this [.25] other boy has fallen down, [.8] also, . . before he fell over, [.2] his hat blew off. [.25] While he was still looking at the girl. [.65] So he's f--a . . the pears/ 've/ fallen off, [7.2 [.45] a-- -nd [3.7] u--h [2.4]] and they help him pick up the pears, and they kind of toss them back into the [.5] basket, where . . he-- has had them, [1.1] a--nd he [.3] gets up, [.7] uprights his bike, they put the basket . . on, and . . send him on his way. [2.05 [.85] A--nd u--h [.25]] they walk this way, and one has a ping-pong p paddle. [.7] Those bouncy ball things . . with a great big . . if this is for gestures, this is a great movie for gestures. [2.2 [.85] Because [.95]] of all the things involved. [3.95 [.9] A--nd [2.45]] they walk this way, [.3] the other boy walks this way. [1.0] The o--ne boy with the ping-pong paddle, notices [.25] a hat, . . his hat, [.25] the thief's hat lying in the . . ground. [.75] The road, [.6 [.15] and [.2]] picks it up, and whistles, [.3] {whistle} [1.0] which is one of about four sounds that you hear in the movie, [1.2] and the . . boy with the bicycle who's now walking the bicycle, not riding it, turns around, [.55] and sees that he's forgotten his hat. [2.5 [1.4] A--nd [.6]] the boy with the ping-pong paddle brings the hat to the bicycle boy, [.95] who gives him [.45] three pears. [1.95 . . . tsk . . .] For . . bringing back his hat. Puts the hat on, [.25] and that's the last you see of the bicycle thief, [1.1] but no--w, [.95] the-- [1.3] three boys, who now are eating /the/ [.2] polished have polished and /are/ eating their pears, [.3] are walking back towards . . the pear picker's [.35] area, [4.45 [.95] a--nd [2.9]] just eating their pears, walking along, [.5] nobody talks during the whole movie there's no dialogue. [1.8] Did you know that? No. [5.15 {laugh} [.45] A-- nd u--h [2.55] he has just clambered down, [.35] from his ladder, [.8] and notices [.4] "Whoa. [.45] My [.3] pear my basket is gone." And goes . . one, [.55] two, [1.35] and the . . third one is missing. [.55] Then he sees the three little boys chewing on pears, . . walking his way [.75] and l--ooks at them, like they're [.55] very suspiciously, and they walk off into the distance, and that's it.

Speaker 13

Okay, well, [.4] there.. is [.2] ay uh [.5] there's a man, [1.2? [.6] who--] looks of Latin descent, [1.55 [.75] a--nd [.25]] he-- is-- on a ladder he's rather large. [1.95 [.7] A--nd.. u--m [.25]] he's [.45] on a ladder,.. picking pears, [.15] from a tree, and putting it in his.. apron, [.25] sort of. [2.2 [.4] A--nd.. u--m [.85]] and you watch him and the sound is just [.55] is [.55] is really intensified /well/ [.3] from what.. it.. usually.. would be, I think. [1.35..| [.65] U--m [.35] it's like they have a microphone right {laugh begins} next to the branch so you could hear him picking off thee [.35] {laugh ends} the--.. pears. [1.75 [.7] A--nd u--h [.15]] so-- that that's really sort of intensified. [1.45 [.45] A--nd u--m] something that you notice right away about the film is [.1] no one is talking. [1.2] It's [.15] and.. and [.15] sort of [.4] which makes the sound even more intense of [.2] of what's [.4] going on, like the picking of the pear--s, or whatever. [.35] And it shows him sort of tumbling them into a.. in a [.4] in a basket, and there's three baskets on the ground. [.9 [.5] A--nd] two are full and one is [.45] is sort of empty. [1.45 [.55] A--nd u--m..] so he's emptying them ou--t, [.45] and then he.. starts going back [.55] up his ladder, [1.55 a--nd u--m [1.2] oh. [.75] The film starts off,.. with just [.4] sort of a scene [.15] of the country,.. and a path. [.7] And you hear.. a rooster crowing. [.25] And then it.. it.. pans into this man. [2.15 [.8] And the--n u-- m [.3]] then you hear, [.15] while he's [.6] putting the pears inside the.. basket, [1.75 [.55] u--m [.7]] a noi.. an animal noise, [.2] which turns out to be /a/ goat. [.35] Cause when he goes back up the ladder you see this ma--n, dragging this goa--t, [1.1? and you know [.5]] past the scene, [.9 [.45] a--nd] then you start hearing this other.. intensified noise, which turns out to be a bicycle,.. some.. a little boy, [.5] on a.. bicycle who's coming by. [3.85 [.55] A--nd.. u--m [1.3] so--.. um [.25]] he starts coming by--, [.25] and he ends up [.45] stopping where the pears are, and looks up at [.4] at the man who's up the ladder and the man doesn't know that the little boy is there. [2.55 [.8] U--m [1.2]] which [1.1] it was sort of funny, in certain parts of the movie it seemed like sounds-- [.6] that [.8] should be intensified just to keep with the [.3] the norm of how the movie was going,.. it went silent sort of. [2.0 [1.35] And like [.25]] so the man didn't hear the little boy, [.7.. you know [.4]] being there, [.2] a--nd he-- [.15] ended up.. u--m [.95] swiping.. one of his baskets of pears, and putting it on his [.35] on his bicycle, on the front of his bicycle, and.. and riding off. [2.15 [.9] A--nd the--n um] as he's riding,.. there's u--h.. a girl, [.4] coming on a bicycle in the opposite direction. [1.0] A--nd they--.. they're going /like/ you know [.95+.. and then [.95... /{creaky: ɨ/ ..]] they come really close /toward ea/ .. each other, and she brushes off this little hat that he has on, [.7] and so his hat.. comes o--ff, [.5] and then he turns his head back looking at it,.. and he's riding along /and/ he hits a rock. [1.35 [.8] A--nd s..] and so the bike.. falls over, and the pears all go /khp̃/. [1.3 [.4... tsk...] And then, [.2 tsk]] all of a sudden,.. three boys come alo--ng, [1.1] tsk and one has one of those.. paddles with a.. a ball on it that goes {gesture?} [.45] you know,.. one of those things? [2.2 [.25] tsk A--nd anywa--y, [.45] u- -m [.15]] the--y [.35] help him up, they.. dust him off,.. and put all the pears back in the ba--sket, and.. put the basket back on the bicycle, and he starts on his merry way again, [.3] and the boys walk in the opposite direction. [1.2 [.5] And the--n, [.2]] one of the boys, [.4] u--h [.4] finds the hat,.. lying on the road. [.5] And then he whistles at the boy at the bicycle, and.. the boy on the bicycle s [.45] stops, [2.15 [.75] u--m [.8] tsk..]] he was walking it at that time,.. he didn't [.55] he didn't ride it. [2.35 [.7] A--nd the--n u--m [.2]] he whistles out at him,.. and takes the hat.. back, [.25] to him, [.2] and in exchange,.. the boy gives him three pears. [.15] One.. for each of the boys. [.7] And then,.. he goes off again, and the three boys.. start walking down the path, [2.65 [.8] a--nd u--m [1.0]] by that time the man who was [.55] taking the pears off, [.4] comes down,.. he starts to empty out his apron, and he notices one of his baskets is gone. [.25] He stands up, looks back, and counts, let's see {voiceless vowels}, o--ne, two--, and the third one's gone. [.7] And then.. he sees these three walking around, crunching on pears {laughter}, {laugh}.. and he can't, . . and he sort of just [.45] what? [4.15 {laugh} [.4] A--nd u--m [1.5] tsk [.2]] let's see--, was that it? . . Yeah, I think s . . I think so, . . I think that was about it.

Speaker 14

The movie opened up on this [.3] nice scene, [.35] it was in the country, . . it was oaks, . . it /was/ seemed like West Coast. . . Maybe it wasn't. [.25] But it was hills and dry grass, [2.7 [1.1] um [1.15]] and scrub. [.95] But there was pear trees in it, . . and that was odd. [.5] And there was this man with a moustache, and a hat, picking [.45] unripe pears, [2.4? [2.0] um] and he was in this [.25] he went up the ladder, [.25] in the tree, [.75] cause the tree was high, it wasn't pruned, [.3+ [.3] like . .] they usually are, [.35] to keep them prostrate, [.45] but it was [.25] it had a large [1.05 [.25] uh [.55]] tall trunk, [1.0] and he's {tense ambiguous} picking unripe [.2] unripe pears. [.15] And what I noticed [.25] first off, . . was that all the noises in the movie, [.5] were u--m [1.8] out of proportion. [1.4] Like you could hear the [.15] the creaking [.35] of the [.4] ladder, [.8] and the picking of the pears, and then from a long way off [.35] they zoomed in on a [.35] /on a/ [.2] a [.2] child on a bicycle, and you could hear the [.4] the gears on the bicycle going round, more than [.25] it was [.15] way out of proportion of everything else. [4.1 [1.9] And u--m [1.35]] this man came by, [.3] walked by, and he's leading a goat, . . that didn't want to go with him, [1.0 [.65] ae [.15]] and this first [.15] okay, [.2] let me see. [3.25] The man climbed down out of the tree, . . and put the pears in the basket, and it looked like he was [.35] giving birth. [.85] It did. . . He was just kind of . . {creaky voice} [.65] rolling them out of his pouch, in his [.35] in his apron, [3.75 [.75] and u--m [2.25]] then this-- he came /back/ down, . . and put the pears in the basket, [.6] and he went back up the ladder, and you could hear the creaking, . . and then you could hear the goat [.15] a long way off, . . and it was braying. [.45] But it was [.2] a very . . like . . a lo--ng drawn out bray, like the movie [.2] the . . sound track had been slowed down, so it was b*** {creaking voice on last word}. [3.05 [1.5] Um [1.05]] and he went [.15] and he went by, [.45] and there was two baskets of . . pears there, and one empty one, [.55] and then this little kid came by, [.55] and you could hear the gears in the [.15] on the bicycle, [.75] and you could hear the crickets, . . and the . . grasshoppers, [.5] and the little kid came by, and he /si/ [.4] and he [.25] hesitated, but then he stole, . . one of the baskets of pears, . . and put it on his [.6] bicycle and rode off. [.9] And as he was [.45] riding down the r [.15] this [.5] this uh . . dirt road, [.6] /it/ was full of rocks, . . you could hear the . . the rocks creak underneath, [2.8 [1.0] u--m [1.3]] this other little girl in pigtails, . . black pigtails, [.35] rode by, [.55] and he tipped his hat to her, [.3] and as he did that, . . lost his hat, . . and ran into a b--ig rock, and the [.15] pears spilled all over. [.65] Out of nowhere, [.65] he looks up, and out of nowhere, [.6] everyone else, . . even the viewers are s [.4] there's [.2] three other little boys, one's playing with this [.15] pongo? [.6] A little [.3] paddle? . . And a ball with it on /the/ end of the elastic? [.6] And you could hear this paddle-ball going, [2.75 [.95] a--nd u--h [1.15]] and they help him pick up the [.75] pears, and put them back on his bicycle, and dust him off, [3.35 [2.4] a--nd u--m [.3]] then he goes off, and . . nobody ever smiles in the movie, there isn't any emotion on any /of/ boy's faces. [2.75 [1.8] A--nd] then they /nowt/ . . they were walking down the road, they notice his bicycle was there, [.4] I mean his hat was there, [.75] so they picked up his hat, and whistled to him, [.35] and they ran back, and you could hear the running. . . And it was just so much out of proportion, it was [.85] . . easy to notice. [2.7 [.9] U--m [1.4]] and they gave him his hat, . . and the [.25] the little . . boy that fell off the bicycle gives him [.45] gives him three-- . . pears, . . and they went back, [1.55 [.95] a--nd [.15]] then you switch back to the ma--n, that's [.4] climbing down out of the tree, again with another . . pouchful of . . of pears. [.75] And he kneels down to put the pears in the . . third empty basket, [.8] and he s [.3] scratches his head, [2.7 and [.55] u--m [1.6]] he goes . . one two three, [.6] and but there isn't a third one there, and he scratches his head some more, and looks, and these little . . three little boys go by, [.9] just walking, not paying any attention, . . no--t paying any attention to the man, [.35+ /and/ [.35]] eating these pears. . . And that's the end of the movie.

Speaker 15

[.6] Okay. [.7 [.1] Uh. .] the movie opened. [1.4] And ay [1.4] man, [1.7 [.65] uh [.7]] I would sus . . I would suspect that he's Latin, [1.9 [1.1] um [.45]] since you associate Latin people with picking fruit, [1.0] was picking pears, [2.6 [1.55] a--nd u--m [.15]] he was dropping some down on the ground, . . on a straw mat. [1.55] And he was filling some up. . . And he [.7 [.25] but [.2]]] I didn't n I didn't notice this at first, [.15] but he was also he also had an apron on and he was filling /those/ up. [2.65 [1.4] A--nd [.8]] he went down the ladder, [.3] and he dumped them in the . . dumped them in the bucket, [1.15] and ay man with ay uh [.4] a goat, . . I couldn't tell whether it was a male or female. [2.65 [1.55] A--h] would you like to know what [1.1] the goat looked like? /Thee uh/? I hate to take away the suspe--nse or anything. [1.65 [.7] U--m [.4]] it was a [1.05] I wou [.35] I had a . . I have a friend who would know what breed it was, [1.6? but uh [1.45]] /it was/ short-haired, [1.35] I don't know, white face, and dark eyes, [.45+ and [.45]] stripe down the mi . . kind of a . . white and . . white and dark stripe down the middle, [1.0] well he walked by, [.9 [.5] a--nd] he didn't uh [1.6] he did't bother with the pears at all. [.25] The man was picking pears. [.1] They were green, [.7] so I suspect they were going to sell them to Safeway. [3.35 [1.05] {laugh} [1.3] Um] they were green pears, [3.15 [.8] a--nd uh [1.65]] then a little kid happened by on a bicycle. [2.1] /Then the for some reason I go/ [.15] "His father probably owns the o . . probably owns the orchard." [2.6? [1.0] Um [.4] mm . .] he pick . . he /wõ/ . . he stops by, [.5] the man is still picking the pears, and he doesn't notice [1.6] the kid there, [1.7 [.6] and [.85 . . {creaky sound}. .]] the kid stops, . . at the three baskets of pears, [.4] /and/ he picks one up, and . . he only wants to steal one, but then he decides he's gonna [.15] he's gonna take the whole basket. [3.5 [1.4] U--m [1.45]] then he drives a [.5] h--e-- rides away on his bicycle. [3.45 [1.1] A--nd [1.9]] oh goodness. [.6] And he's as he's riding through an open field, [1.0] um hills in the background, and . . stuff like that, [.9] he-- [1.8? um [1.45] a girl [.3] with long pigtails, [1.6] happens by, going the other way, [1.1] on a bicycle, and there's a long shot, [.35] you see both of them, . . converging, and you see him. [.4] He's more interested in [.45] the girl going by, [1.55 [.9] than [.3]] taking care of . . making sure the basket doesn't do anything weird. [.8] And he sees the girl going by, . . he doesn't see the rock, . . it's right in front of him, [.65] and the bike stops in the rock, [1.15? and . . u--m [.45]] he piles over, and . . all of the pears come out, [.8] and he checks [.3] and his hat flies off also. [.65] He checks to see that [.25] his knee is okay, [.9] pulls up his pants, [.6] pulls /it/ down, [.7] oh goodness what else. [1.25] And then three boys happen by. [.65] Three boys, three different sizes, three different colored shirts, [1.55] oh goodness. [1.15 U--m /b/ [.15]] and they help him pick up the pears. [.8] One guy's playing [.25] /you/ remember those? I don't know what they're called, they had a little ball? [3.2 . . . Um . .] you know like a paddleball. [.85?] We used to see {Pat responds in this pause} how many we could do. I could u I used to do one or two. [3.6 [.7] A--nd he-- [.7] u--m [.2] and [.25]] he kind of helps, . . but his two fr . . /mĩ/ . . the two guys that are with him. [.6] do most of the major . . end of the work. [.5 /And/ [.4]] they help him up. [1.95 [.8] A--nd [.7]] they help him get the basket up. [.3] And they're . . and he [.1] the little boy drives off, [.4] drives [.2] rides his bicycle off. [1.3 [.8] A--nd . .] they find a uh [2.05] they find his hat. . . The three boys find the hat down the road, [.65] and he gives him the hat, [1.0] and . . th . . they whistle for /him/. There's no dialogue in the whole movie. [1.0] They whistle for him. [.75] And he comes back. . . And he w [.2] and he stops. . . And the guys walk up and give him the hat. [.95 [.65] And [.15]] he looks /in/ . . and the little . . and the boy looks [.4] in the basket . . /for/ [1.0] for three pears to give to the kids. [1.8 [.75] And [.75]] the pears that you saw at the beginning were bi--g. [1.05 . . A--nd . .] they were . . they were almost perfect. [.75 [.15] /m/ [.4]] Whatever you can call a pear to be perfect. [4.9 [1.2] A--nd [2.4] but [.35]] he gives them the three pears, [.15] and as they're walking, [.35] as the guys were walking off up the road, I could see that the pears weren't the best of the bunch. [1.2? [.9] That . .] there wa . . there were . . bruises. You could only see it [.1] like in a side shot from under here. [2.9 [1.05] U--m [1.25]] and they walked by eating the pears, and the guy . . in the meantime [.35] the . . the shot changes to [1.0]| the man coming down the ladder. [.6] And he disco . . and he's dumping the pears that he has in his apron, [.4] into the basket. [.8 [.55] And . .] they discover [1.75] and he discovers that his basket is gone. [.9 [.65] And . .] he just kind of sits there. [.9 . . And [.7]] he doesn't really do anything. [.55] The three boys happen by eating the pears. [1.15] I don't kn . . I can't remember whether they saluted him or not, [.25] you know, [.55] gave him a any kind of a salutation, [.6] but he [.3] the three boys walk off, [1.0] and the man jus-- sits there [.25] sits there on the ladder, [2.15 [1.6 u--m [.15]] kind of like this, and jus--t [.35] watches the three boys go off. [1.75] And that's-- the end of the movie.

Speaker 16

Oh. You want to know what happened in the movie. [.4] Okay, [5.3 . . u--m [4.65 . . .]] a man was picking pears in [.45] what seemed to be his orchard, [2.55 [1.1] a--nd [.8]] came along first, . . /someone/ came along first. [4.7] Someone came along before the kid on the bicycle, but I don't remember who it was. [.45] Then a kid came along on a bicycle, and parked the bicycle, [1.2 [.85] a--nd] checked the tree to make sure the man wasn't looking, and he was about to steal . . a--y pea--r, . . but he /t/ he . . he . . picked up a basket, [.2] instea--d, [1.85 [.9] a--nd [.3]] went riding along [.45] the road, . . on a bicycle. [1.2 [.6] A--nd] he passed [1.3] a . . little girl on a bicycle, [.7? . . and [.35]] turned his head, . . and hit a rock, [.65] and fell over, and spilled the pears all over the [.7] road. In the meantime, . . some other little kids came along, a--nd helped him pick up the pears, . . a--nd brushed him off, [1.5 [.9] a--nd] that sort of thing, [1.6 [.65] a--nd [.45]] he went on walking and one of them stopped him, [.85] cause he had forgotten his hat. [1.6 [.85] A--nd] took him his hat, . . and he gave them [1.5] um [.9] he gave the three kids each a pear. [.45] They were walking back in the direction, [1.5 [.7] uh [.25]] toward the man [.7] who was picking pears in the pear tree, and . . about the time, . . he came down, [.85] the pear tree, . . and discovered [1.2] that a basket of pears was missing, . . he saw the three kids eating pears, as they were [.4] walking up the road. [.7] For some reason he didn't stop them or ask them where they got the pears. [1.95] Was that it? I think that was it. [.3] That's all I remember. You should have caught me [.15] ten minutes ago when I remembered. Who passed the [1.0] the man before the kid on the bicycle, I don't remember. [1.3] Anyway. Okay.

Speaker 17

Well, first thing you see, is-- . . u--h . . the landscape is-- . . u--m [.9 . . . . . .] sort of an agricultural . . area, it's quite green, [.35] and a lot of trees around. [1.05 [.5] A--nd] you see a middle-aged [.2] u--m [.15] Chicano man, [.55] who's wearing . . a--y . . navy blue shirt, [.5] and a bright red [.2] kerchief around his neck, [.4] and a white apron. [1.3 [.6] A--nd [.3] he--climbs a ladder, and is [.15] all right, /ei/ either that or he's on a ladder, already, and he's picking [1.0] pears, off a tree, and they look to be-- [.4] not quite ripe yet. They're still quite gree--n, . . and they look [.35] still hard. [1.95 [.7] A--nd [.65]] he's [.15] it . . the . . camera spends a lot of time watching him [.55] pick these pears, [.45] putting them in his apron, [1.05? [.35] and the--n . . u-- m . .] going . . down off the ladder, and putting them into these /buh/ . . bushel baskets. [2.4 [1.15] tsk U--m [.85]] so that's [.25] part of the activity of the [.25] the first [.5] portion of the film. [.4] Then you see another, . . younger, [.5] more . . this man is [.35] the . . first man I described is rather [.15] portly. [.35] /This/ [.15] you see a younger Chicano man, [.4] coming acrosst [.7] u--m [.3] from the back of the [.2] of the [.3] picture frame, [1.7 [.45] a--nd u--m [.25] he's . . leading a [.5] brown and white goat. [.45] And this ma--n . . is-- [.4] u--m dressed in sort of a faded, [.25] navy blue, [.25] denim top, and jeans. [.4] And he's got a hat on, [.4] so does the first man that I described. [1.45 [.65] A--nd [.25]] he just walks through the picture, not paying much attention to the other man, . . who's [.35] picking pears, [.4] and goes off in the distance, leading his goat. [.7] Then the third person that comes in the scene is a little boy about [.7] ten years old. [.4] And he's white. [1.3 [.6] A--nd] he's wearing a hat, [.5] and he's [.7] dressed in sort of faded . . red clothing. [.5] And he's [.7] riding his bicycle, [.5] and he stops, [.5] at the [.15] bottom of the tree, [.7] tsk looks up at the man who's picking the pears, [.4] and seeing that he's preoccupied, [.35] with [.35] u--m [1.0] you know, his business, he decides [2.2 [.85] to-- [.45] u--h] steal a bushel basket full of pears. [1.35 [.6] So-- [.35]] he-- [.55] picks up the basket, and all the while looking up sort of furtively at the man who's . . you know, . . to make sure he's not going to get caught. [.4] But he's very brazen. I mean there's ō . . they're only about three feet apart. [1.2 [.4] A--nd uh] he puts the b--ushel basket on the front of his [.3] bike, . . and he drives off with it. [3.4 [.75] U--m [.75] no--w [.65] tsk] he's driving along this road that's uh it's not paved, it's just sort of a dirt road, and it's sort of jutty. [.45] And so, . . he's driving along, [.45] a--nd riding his bike along, and he sees another [.45] person coming [.35] toward him, . . and it's another little white girl. [.35] With long [.15] braids. [.4] Brown hair. [1.55 [.6] A--nd [.35]] he's paying attention to her, as she-- [.35] passes him, . . and isn't . . watching too much where he's going, [.35] and hits a rock in the road, . . falls down, [2.6 [.45] a--nd [.3] u--m [.6] tsk] all the pears fall off. [.5] In the [.3] you know the bushel basket falls off, and all the pears fall off, and everything. [.7] Now three little boys are . . a little b--it away from him. [.5] And they see what's happened. [.2] One boy . . is . . um [1.4] hitting one of those bounce-back things, . . you know, the little thing that had elastic, and it has a ball, and / then it's/ a paddle. [.35] He's playing with that. [.25] And they're sort of various sizes, I'd say from . . maybe [.3] six to twelve years old. [1.3 [.65] A--nd] they see what's happened to the l . . little boy, and they come over sort of very calmly, [.5+ [.5] a--nd] . . help him get on his feet, pick up his pears for him, [1.1? [.6] a--nd . .] put them back in the basket, [.15+ [.15] and . .] brush him off, . . and everything, [2.5 [.55] a--nd u--m [.7] tsk] then they [.9] u--m [1.2] put him [1.5] tsk u--m [.15] back on his bike, and he goes off. [.35] The little boy {creaky sound} . . that was on the bike, had been wearing a hat. [1.3 [.55] A--nd [.3]] in the [.55] i--n passing the little girl, it had . . fallen off. [1.55 [.5] And so, . . u--m] he still doesn't have his hat, when he [.15] starts [.35] uh . . bicycling off. [.4] And then he picks up [.4] uh the li . . the three little boys sort of go in the opposite direction, down the road, [.85 [.45] a--nd] one of the little boys, [.55] sees his hat. [.25] And he picks it up. [.25] And he-- whistles to the boy that's on the bicycle. [.6] / A--nd s/ [.45] you know, motions that he has his hat. [.95 [.55] So-- . .] the little boy that has the hat, comes and meets the boy on the bicycle. [5.35 [.9] A--nd [.6] u--m [2.1 . . . tsk . . .] then [.1]] they excha . . he gives . . the little boy that picked up the hat, . . gave it to the boy on the bicycle, [.3] and the boy that was on the bicycle, [.2] gives [.3] him three pears. [1.25 [.55] A--nd [.1]] the little boy, [.4] who . . fetched his hat, [.25] took [.45] the pears, [.2] and goes back, [.2] to his friends, and / they/ each [.25] gives them each a pear. [.4] And then the other boy rides off, and they [.2] continue walking in the [.15] in the-- . . the direction they were walking in. [.4] And they start eating their pears. [1.1 [.45] A--nd [.15]] in the meantime, . . the scene flashes back to-- [.35] the-- [.2] man . . who . . was pick . . the / ori/ [.15] initial man who was picking his pears. And he gets down, [.7] from . . the-- . . u--m [.5] tree, . . off the ladder, [1.3 [.4] a--nd [.5]] i--s about ready to unload his cape, [1.2 [.4] whe--n [.2]] he notices that one of his bushel baskets is gone and he registers [.55] a--y u--h [.9] tsk [.15] an expression . . of dismay, . . you know and anger, and that sort of thing. [1.5 [.5] A--nd [.45]] as he's sitting there, the three little boys, [.45] come by, [.4] eating the pears. [.35] And he looks at them, [.9? u--m [.6]] sort of [.75] impassionately, like [.35] I knew that it was leading up to this, . . and I thought maybe that there was going to be a big dramatic moment, [.55? where [.2]] he's going to accuse the little boys who'd actually been like . . good Samaritans, of stealing his pears. [.35] But he just sort of watches them, . . as they walk by, and they don't pay any attention to them [.3] to him, he's . . they're just eating their pears, and . . you know playing with their [.25] paddle, and everything. [.4] And that's how it ends.

Speaker 18

Okay, [2.2 [.3] U--m [1.0]] let's see. [1.85 [1.1 . . . tsk . . .] U--h] the first part of the . . m [.45] movie, [.4 [.2] uh well], the . . the-- . . the basic action, [.5] i--s that there's-- [.2] a man [.4] uh--on a ladder, [.55] uh picking pears from a pear tree. [1.7 [1.05] A--nd] he's [2.2 [u--h [1.55]] y . . you get this idea that he's [.2] he's sort of chubby--, [1.1? and u--h [.7]] sort of [.6 . . ɨ {creaky} . .] not inclined [.15+ to-- [.15]] to do a lot of work, [1.8? [.8] a--nd u--h] sort of [.5 . . ɨ {creaky}] a little bit slow mentally. [.6 . . . ɨ-- {creaky}. .] He's very deliberately [.55] plucking the . . the um [.45] the pears off the tree, [.55? and [.45]] you know you hear this [.65] s-- sharp little crunch as . . as he pulls each one off, and he's doing it . . very slowly, and putting them in [.7 . . . {breath} . . .] his apron. [1.4 [.9] tsk And then . .] climbing very carefully . . down the [.2] the ladder, and placing them in baskets, and he'd never make it as a fruit picker. [2.1 [.55] {laugh}] He would starve. [2.6 {breath} [.1] A--nd u--h [.25]] different people go past him. [4.0 [1.0] A--nd u--m [1.75 . . . ɨ {creaky} . .]] I don't know, oh. . . Somebody went past him with a goat. . . I don't know why. [.4] You know, but I guess [.95 . . . ɨ {creaky}] an [.7 ɨ {creaky}] sort of . . audience anticipation . . of [.45] well this guy's going to go past with the goat and the goat's going to break off the leash and eat all the apples. But what does happen, is this little boy goes past on the bicycle that's [.7] almost too big for him to handle. [.6] And he picks up . . not . . just one . . or two pears, . . but the whole basket of pears. [1.05?+ [.75] A--nd] drives off down the [.25] the road with the-- u--h [.25] with the . . pears, and . . on the road [.6] he meets-- u--h a-- [.5 . . ɨ ɨ {creaky}] . . girl . . coming on a . . bicycle, in the opposite direction, [1.6? and u--m [.7]] they [.9] go very close past each other, so that his [.6] his hat flies off. [2.0 [1.3] A--nd] he-- looks around for the hat, [.4] doesn't watch where he's going, [1.5? [.45] a--nd [.3] u--m . .] hits a big rock in the road, . . and . . all the pears fall down. [.5] And then there's a shot of u--m [.45] uh three kids, [.3] sort of [.15] u--h standing, [.65] by the roadside, . . a--nd you don't know at first whether they're hostile or not, /and/ you get a shot, [2.05 [.8] /the--n/ u--m [.35]] they're sort of [.5] standing there, grinning, [3.2 and uh [1.1] tsk . . u--h [1.5]] it could . . ɨ {creaky} that look could be interpreted as a menacing grin, or a [.5] ɨ {creaky} or a friendly grin, or just the way kids are, [.4+ and [.4]] u--h they go over to him, and the--y . . the--y u--h help him, [.35] they start brushing him off, and . . picking up the pears for him, [.5+ and [.5]] hold the . . basket, while he gets on . . onto the bicycle, [1.3+ and [1.3]] are generally very helpful. They walk down the r . . he [.2] g--ets back on the bicycle, rides off, . . gets u--m [.85+ [.85] a--nd] they walk down the road, [2.45 [.5] a--nd u--m [.75] tsk] they find his hat, [.55] farther . . m [.7] farther down the road, in the direction they're going, and he's going in the opposite direction. [.7] So one of them goes back with the hat. [.4+ [.4] A--nd] says . . u--h [.6] uh . . doesn't say anything, . . but gives him back the hat. [.4+ [.4] So--] he-- r . . reaches into the basket, takes out three pears, [1.05 and [1.1] u--h [.2]] gives them to the [.3] the-- other kids. [2.75 [.9] A--nd [.55] so-- . .] these kids are walking, . . in the direction from which the boy came. [.15] So that eventually they will go pas--t the [.4] the man, . . who's been picking [.15] the pears, [.75] who-- [.15] in the meantime, has . . come down from the ladder, [.6] and looks, [.3] and sees that he's [.15] u--h [.55] he's missing a basket of pears. [1.0] And these-- . . u--h three kids come past, in the opposite direction, eating pears, [.5] and he's trying to figure out, [3.5 well, [.15]] how . . how did that happen. [.4] It's-- a [.2] there's just this look on his . . his face of bewilderment. [1.9 [1.0] A--nd] at first you . . you sort of think [1.6? . . well-- . . you know u--m [.6]] he's going to accuse them. [.25] Of having taken his pears. [1.5 Bu--t u--h [.65]] the he s [.15] he sees them coming, and watches them going, and he's just totally confused [1.75] {laugh}.

Speaker 19

All right, [.35] it [.8] starts, [.15] it seems to be morning. [.8] In the countryside. In rolling hills, [1.7] it's bright and sunny, [1.2] and you hear roosters [.2] crowing. . . So it's a very pastoral setting. [.35] There's some trees. . . An orchard. [.6] And a ma--n, [.5] is [.75] picking pears. [1.6] In the trees. [.55] On /a/ ladder. And he comes down, . . from the ladder, [1.1] and he's wearing an apron, that holds the pears, in deep pockets. And he dumps them [.45] into some baskets . . that he has. [.35] Sitting . . at the bottom of the tree /s/ . [2.2] And then you hear some sound, [.5] in the distance, [.2] approaching, [.45] and a man comes by leading a goat. [.45] They walk past the pears, . . and the goat looks at them, but . . goes on, with the man. [1.0] And the other man continues picking pears. [2.35 [1.55] Then, [3.5]] another sound is heard, a clanky sound, and a boy comes by riding a bicycle. [1.05] And he sees the pears, [.55] and he stops. [.6] Gets off his bicycle, . . hesitates as to just how to put it down, [.75] then he . . takes a pear, [1.3 [.6] after [.2]] carefully watching the man in the tree. [.35] Who's still picking. . . Doesn't see the boy. [.45] Then the boy decides not to take the pear, but to take the whole basketful. [1.7 {laugh} [.5]] And gets back on his bicycle, has /this/ [.65] some trouble loading the basket. [1.55] Which is large. [1.25] And he rides off, [1.55] with the basket, [.3] in front of his handlebars, [.8] balanced, . . and he hits some bumps, and a few pears spill out. [.85] He goes on down the road, [.75] and he passes a girl on a bicycle, [.35] and in passing her, his hat comes off, [.55] and he turns his head, and looks back, [.5] then his bicycle hits a rock in the road, and he falls over, [.2] spills his pears, . . hurts his leg {laugh}. [1.4] And at that time, [.55] three [.25] boys [.35] appear, [1.8? [1.6] um] one's playing with a paddleball. [1.7? [1.3] A--nd . .] they stop, [.45+ [.45] and . .] two . . the other two boys, . . help him, . . pick up . . himself, . . pick up the pears, [.3] and they throw them into the basket. [1.55] And then they walk on, [1.0] and the boy on the bicycle proceeds . . in the direction he was going. [.8] While the boys that [1.15] helped him, find his hat, further down the road, [.9] and they pick it up, [.25] and one boy goes back, [.9] and gives [.8] the boy who fell, his hat. [1.2] And . . in exchange, takes [.5] three pears. [1.05] And the boys continue walking, [.3] in . . and the one riding in opposite directions. [.65] The boys who've taken the pears, [.4] walk past the tree where the man is still picking {laugh} . . picking pears, but he's comes down, [.25] and has [.25] noticed that one of his baskets . . of pears is missing. . . And he can't find {laugh} . . can't discover {laugh} where it could have gone. [.5] Then these three boys walk past [.4] all of them eating pears, {laugh} and he . . just kind of scratches his head, and wonders /uh/ [.25] end of film {laugh}.

Speaker 20

Sure. There was a ma--n, picking--, [1.3 [.9] u--m [.1]] a Latin looking man, /and/ he was picking pears, [1.0] in an apron--, [.25] that . . he had baskets . . for. [.6] So he didn't have to go down to the ground, [.65] to put the pears in the baskets. [.35] He just kept /trae/. [.7] And a man walked by with a goat, and nothing happened and he kept on going, [.3] and then a little boy, [.35] /about/ [.15] a bic a red bicycle, that was too big for him, [.8] he stopped, . . took a pear, and then on second thought he decided [.6] to take the entire basket. . . So he picked it up, and he put it /up/ on [.65] there was a little platform on top of the front wheel, [.25] he rode away. [2.0 [1.1] A--nd . .] he's riding down the road, . . and he had a hat on. [1.25 [.85] A--nd] he-- . . almost ran into a girl, [.35+ and [.35]] somehow she took his hat. . . Not on purpose but [.8] it came off. [.3] So he goes /nnnd/ looked around, and he . . hit a rock. . . And he fell. And all his pears fell. [.4] And she kept on going. [.6] And there were three [.45] other boys walking down the road. [.3] /And/ that walking towards where he had come from. [.8] And . . they looked sort of mean, one was [.25] had a little [.55] paddle with a ba--ll, and they looked like bullies, I thought they were going to take [.8] away [.3] mmm {This sound was a hesitation and also something to take the place of an unuttered NP.} But instead they helped him, [1.2] tsk they set his basket up, and got him going, and he didn't give them anything. [.65] And he kept going, and they kept going, and then one of them [.35] found his hat, so they whistled back at him, . . and one of them gave him his hat, and he gave [.55] him [.25] three pears back, [.8] which . . he kept one and gave the other two to his friends, [.7] and he and his friends continued walking, and they [.4] and in the meant Okay. Then the man comes down, [.3] from the tree, and he notices the basket's missing, and then the [.2] and then the three boys walk by, each eating a pear, [.6] and he just kind of looks at them [.4+ and [.4]] doesn't do anything. [.1] And they keep on going. [.15] And then it's over.

Author Index

321

Subject Index